Travel
Geography

Travel Geography

Rosemary Burton

Pitman

PITMAN PUBLISHING
128 Long Acre, London, WC2E 9AN

A Division of Longman Group UK Limited

First published in Great Britain 1991

British Library Cataloguing in Publication Data

Burton, Rosemary
 Travel geography.
 1. Tourism. Geographical aspects
 I. Title
 338.4791

 ISBN 0-273-03262-3

Printed and bound in Great Britain

Contents

Acknowledgements

Thanks are due to all those who have played a part in the production of the book: Paul Dyke and the other cartographers, colleagues, friends and family who have both provided help and shown great tolerance while the book was being prepared, and to Margaret, Julie and the ladies of JL who typed the mosaic that has finally come together as this book.

Specific thanks go to Dr V Costello for Fig 4.2 and Miss C Pearce for Fig 4.3.

Acknowledgments

Preface

Tourism is a growing phenomenon in the world today, both in terms of its penetration into new parts of the world, and in terms of the numbers of people participating in travel and holiday-making. The social and ecological problems it may bring in its wake are also increasing; its economic impact is also growing. It is a controversial activity but one that gives pleasure to millions.

This book is concerned specifically with the spatial variations in tourist activity throughout the world; it will give the reader some understanding of the distribution of tourism in the different regions of the world, and it offers geographical explanations of these patterns. The text also outlines the range of factors that lead to changes in travel flows and patterns of tourist development. In order to understand these processes the student must be aware of tourists' motivations, and the other social, political and economic circumstances that both generate tourism and control its spatial expression. This is discussed in Chapter 1.

Students, particularly those wishing to work in the travel trade, must also know the world distribution of geographical resources that function as tourist attractions (described in Chapters 2 to 5), the way in which transport networks evolve to link tourist generating regions with potential destinations (see Chapter 6), and their regional expression (see Chapter 7).

The bulk of the text analyses, in greater detail, the world's regional patterns of tourism that result from the interaction of these factors. Four main regions are identified:

1 Europe – the world's focus of international tourism generation and the world's primary destination region (see Chapters 8–18, plus parts of Chapter 19).

2 North America – an equally significant world tourist region in terms of the volume of tourist movement, whose general patterns of tourist development show striking similarities with those of Europe (see Chapters 21 and 22).

3 The Pacific and Australasia. The world's most rapidly growing tourist region (see Chapters 23 and 24).

4 The peripheral regions of the world (South Asia, Subsaharan Africa, the Middle East and Central and South America). These regions are peripheral in terms of their economic relationships with the developed world and in terms of their tourist linkages with the major Western tourist generating regions (see Chapters 20, 22 and parts of Chapters 19 and 24).

It should be noted that for ease of reference for vocational students, Chapters 9–24 are organised on a continental basis rather than explicitly on the basis of these functional regions, but it is hoped that this does not obscure the functional regions of the world.

The text provides the student with a knowledge of the major tourist attractions and resources of each destination. It outlines the level of tourist development there and the reasons for the development (or lack of it). It analyses the spatial distribution of tourist activity in individual countries, identifying their congested, developing and untouched regions and their potential for different types of tourism, indicating potential points of conflict between domestic and international tourists. The book will, therefore, give geography students an understanding of the geographical processes shaping spatial pattern of tourism, while those preparing to work in the tourist industry will also acquire the basic geographical knowledge that will allow them to provide an informed service to potential travellers.

It does not pretend to be a substitute for an atlas, in fact the student will gain more if the book is read alongside an atlas. The maps provided here will add to the geographical information available and complement the atlas. Nor does the text aim to be a complete catalogue of tourist attractions, that is the role of travel guides and encyclopedias. Rather, the book is designed to give the reader and understanding of the changing patterns of tourism and the vocational student in particular with the knowledge to work effectively within an ever-changing environment. The assignments are specifically designed to help develop the skills that will enable the vocational students to use and apply their geographical knowledge to practical effect in their work environment.

World Tourism Generation

Introduction

The starting point of the study of the geography of world tourism must be to answer the following questions.

1 Where do international tourists come from; i.e. which countries and regions of the world generate international tourism, and is there any clear spatial pattern of tourist generation in the world?

2 Why do these countries and regions generate tourism, i.e. what combination of social, economic and political circumstances lead to the development of international (and also domestic) tourism in a country?

3 Has the level of world tourism generation changed over time; i.e. has the performance of the world economy affected the generation of tourism on a world scale?

Chapter 1 addresses these questions and shows that tourist generation is particularly closely related to economic circumstances, and that tourist generation on a world scale is heavily concentrated in Europe, North America and, to a lesser extent, in the Pacific region.

CHAPTER 1

Tourist generation

LEARNING OBJECTIVES

After reading this chapter you should be able to

- list the factors necessary for tourist generation
- understand the relationship between the socio-economic development of a country and the development of its domestic and international tourism
- identify the economic core and periphery of the world
- locate the major world tourist generating countries
- analyse and interpret economic data and tourism statistics to recognise the stage of economic and tourism development of a country
- understand the nature of the economic and tourism inter-relationships between countries of the world
- understand the factors influencing the growth of world tourism.

Determinants of tourist demand

Travel, whether it is within or between countries takes both time and money. Before anyone can take the decision to travel, first they must have time free of other commitments, available in long enough blocks and distributed at suitable times during the year.

Second, the individual needs money in order to utilise the time for tourism; for example, the unemployed may have plenty of time but be unable to travel widely because they cannot afford to. Their resources are used for items of greater priority (i.e. food, accommodation, clothing etc.) and they have little disposable income available. A country can only generate 'mass' tourism if time and affluence are coincidentally distributed throughout its population.

Third, political factors may constrain the indi-

vidual's choice of destination, or even their freedom to travel at all. For example, governments, if motivated by economic pressures on their balance of payments, may impose limits on their citizens, perhaps curbing the amount of currency that may be spent abroad. This was experienced in Britain in the period between 1967 and 1969. On the other hand, governments may control travel more overtly for purely political reasons by limiting the individual's freedom of movement within or between countries.

These three factors – time, affluence and freedom of movement – are the necessary predisposing circumstances for tourism to take place, but even where they coincide travel will not occur unless the individual chooses to use their resources of time and money in this particular way. There may be different reasons (i.e. motivations) for travel:

1 **Religion** – an individual may wish to make a pilgrimage to a particular holy place, for instance Moslems may want to visit Mecca at least once in their lives, Hindus may desire to bathe in the Ganges, and Christians to visit Jerusalem.

2 **Business tourism** – people may be required to travel as part of their work to develop international trade, attend conferences and trade fairs, etc.

3 **Visiting friends and relatives** – immigration or jobs may lead people to settle in other countries; their friends and relatives may wish to visit them or the immigrants themselves may periodically wish to return to their old home to maintain social contact.

4 **Sport or cultural purposes** – a person may travel in order to take part in, or watch national or international cultural festivals or sporting events, such as the Olympic Games, the World Cup, or the Cannes Film Festival.

5 **Holiday travel** – to take part in leisure pursuits in an 'away from home' environment. The motivation is generally that the leisure pursuit is more enjoyable away from home because, e.g. the **climate** may be better for that particular pursuit (be it sunbathing or skiing), or that travel is necessary to get to the **natural facilities** required for a given pursuit (for example, caves for potholing are located in limestone mountain regions) or the **customs** and **cuisine** are better or at least different from home, or finally, purely because travel to a particular country or resort is fashionable and tourists believe that they gain a certain sort of social acceptance or even social prestige from holiday travel. These motivations are a result of social attitudes, pressures and values of each society and the individual's response to them.

If these factors are important, one would expect to see different patterns of tourist generation in countries with different levels of economic development and affluence, and also in countries of different political religious and social organisation.

Economic development and the growth of tourism

Time and money become more easily available to the individual in increasing quantities as a country's economy develops; the volume, type and distribution of tourism through the population changes in parallel with economic change. This process of social and economic change is best illustrated by outlining the changes that have occurred in the UK.

Social and economic change in the UK

The UK has taken around 250 years to change from an agricultural economy through a relatively well defined process of urbanisation and industrialisation and some would argue it has entered a 'post-industrial' phase of economic change. Other countries (such as those in Africa) may have only just embarked on this process, and others (e.g. Japan) have completed the transition much more quickly and in a very different way.

It is not suggested that the pattern of change shown by the UK is that necessarily followed by other countries but it does clearly illustrate the processes of social and economic change that have led to the growth of mass tourism, processes that can be identified in the current development of many countries of the world.

Medieval times to 1750 – a subsistence economy with leisure travel only for the elite

Before 1750, the UK economy was based on agriculture. Although some regions produced surpluses for export, the economy was essentially a self-sufficient economy, both nationally and regionally, with the majority of the population working very long hours on the land or as craftsmen associated with the agricultural industry.

Leisure for the majority consisted mainly as rest from toil, but life was not all work. Non-work time was devoted to socially structured activities such as religious holidays, festivals, and social occasions to celebrate festivities such as weddings, christenings, birthdays and others associated with the change of the seasons (harvest suppers, rituals to welcome spring, etc.). These activities took place at, or close to home. These occasions were, however, numerous: in the Middle Ages there were over one hundred public holidays.

Leisure in the modern sense was unknown to the general population and due to the physical difficulties of travel and the relative self-sufficiency of regions there was little motivation for the common person to travel. Only the few elite aristocracy and wealthy landed gentry, who derived enough income from their lands to support themselves and led lives of leisure, might have the motivation to travel. Before the days of modern hygiene and medicine in the UK, the wealthy travelled in search of health cures, and for social intercourse. The 'spa towns' grew up where pure, unpolluted springs of mineral water occurred, to provide accommodation for the visitors who travelled to 'take the waters' to improve their health, e.g. Bath.

The 'spas' developed a social life in the local assembly rooms, promenades, libraries and at balls 'designed to provide a concentrated urban emergence of frenetic socialising for a dispersed rural elite', and elite who 'out of season' lived on their country estates. It was not until 1752 that the use of sea water was first advocated on medical grounds.

During this pre-industrial period, culture and education were also the motivation for international travel. The young aristocracy were encouraged to travel across the Continent to Italy on the 'Grand Tour' to the city states where the cultural developments of the Renaissance were centred, e.g. Florence. Thus, domestic and international tourism was limited to a very small number of very wealthy people.

The Industrial Revolution 1750–1830: the 'loss of leisure' by the working population, but travel for the elite

As a response to the influence of Puritanism which made work a virtue and leisure an extravagant luxury, there had been a trend towards longer hours of work and less public holidays for the manual worker. In 1750 the Bank of England was shut on 47 days in the year, but by 1854 this was reduced to four days. These trends were reinforced by the changes of the nature of manual work with increasing industrialisation and factory work. Until the 1840s (not only in the UK but also in France and America) the average manual factory worker worked a 12-hour day (or 70-hour week). The process of industrialisation was paralleled by the rapid growth of insanitary and unhealthy urban areas, which provided very poor living conditions for the workers. The gap between the affluence and living standards of the rich and poor widened further, though some

non-landed individuals who could profit from industrialisation became affluent and these 'noveau riche' attempted to gain social acceptance and prestige by imitating the leisure habits of the aristocracy. Sea bathing (a logical extension of attempts to gain the supposed medical benefits of sea water), once adopted by royalty, became a fashion for everyone and by 1815 steamboat day-trips from London to North Kent coast were on offer.

The growth of domestic tourism 1830–1900

Pressure for the reform of work and urban living conditions came from both the socially motivated educated classes and from agitation by the industrial workers themselves.

In 1850 Parliament established 50-hour week for women in the textile industry. The building industry adopted a 54-hour week in the 1870s and engineering in the 1880s. Shortening the working week created the Saturday half day holiday (while Sunday remained a sober Victorian Sabbath). Lloyds closed on Saturday afternoons in 1854, the Civil Service gained its Saturday half day holiday in the 1860s, followed by the textile operatives in 1874.

In the 19th century the annual summer holiday was also invented. It began informally with many workers taking time off work at their own risk and expense. In the north of England, however, where there was the most conflict over factory discipline, better holiday benefits were achieved. Factory owners began to acknowledge 'works weeks' as regularised weeks of holiday which were, in effect, traded in exchange for regular attendance at work. In certain industries, for example, the pottery industry in Stoke-on-Trent, works weeks are still observed. The 'potters holiday' in June, is a fortnight during which all the potteries shut down together.

However, in 1900 a holiday 'was taken for granted as a luxury which could be enjoyed at a certain level of income but which there was no special hardship in going without'. At the same time affluence began to both increase and spread throughout the population. The real national income quadrupled over the 19th century, and between 1860 and 1913 there was a 91 per cent rise in real wages, with the most rapid rise occurring in the 1870s and 1880s.

The pioneering of the railway age in the 19th

century, made travel much easier and available to the masses, and the country now had a more affluent urban population with both time and the means available to travel. This led to the start of mass domestic day-trip tourism, with the first day excursion offered by railway companies running trips from London to Brighton in 1841.

The week holiday by the sea also grew in popularity during this period of time. Blackpool, for example, developed very rapidly in the period 1840–1860 as the industrial workers holidayed by the sea in their works week.

International tourism was still limited to the affluent elite, though the motivations for travel were beginning to change. The Romantic Movement of 1840s onwards nurtured the appreciation of wild landscapes, and led to summer tourism to the mountains of Switzerland, while the need to explore and pioneer led to the development of Alpine climbing and of many geographical exploratory expeditions to more remote parts of the world as the British Empire widened.

The consolidation of the domestic tourist market and the beginnings of international tourism 1900–1950

The early years of this period saw the consolidation of domestic tourism. By 1911 it is estimated that 55 per cent of the population of England and Wales were taking day-trips to the seaside, and 20 per cent of the population were taking staying holidays on the coast.

The general trend towards greater affluence, more holidays and greater domestic tourism continued but was slowed down and punctuated by two world wars and the economic depression of the 1930s. By 1925 1½ million workers received holidays with pay and in 1938 the Holidays with Pay Act was passed. By 1945, 80 per cent of population took paid holidays. This was reflected in the growth in use of the railway network for mass travel to the seaside for domestic summer

holidays. It was the heyday of the seaside resorts.

International tourism also began to spread through a wider cross-section of the population, and winter sports holidays became fashionable. At home, the level of car ownership which was 109 000 in 1919 rose sharply to one million in 1930, and to two million in 1939, spreading the convenience of personal mobility through the population.

Growth of mass international tourism – 1950 to the present

This period is marked by the spread of affluence and leisure time through the whole population. The decade of 1950 to 1960 was a period of post-war economic austerity and gradual recovery, and saw the transition to a more middle-class society well under way.

Holidays with pay become universal. By the 1960s 97 per cent of population had two weeks' holiday with pay. By 1980 the vast majority had four weeks. There was a transfer of holiday travel from rail to road (car and coach). At the same time, car ownership was becoming much more widespread which quickly changed the nature of domestic tourist travel (*see* Fig 1.1). Access to flexible personal mobility allowed families more choice of holiday activity and destination, and railways and the seaside resorts began to decline in use.

High levels of car ownership also led to the development of new forms of holidays in the 1960s, such as camping and caravaning in new locations outside the traditional holiday resorts. International travel in the 1950s was mainly to France and Switzerland, reflecting the patterns set by the aristocracy in the previous century, but this period saw Spain becoming known first to the elite and then in the 1960s becoming the playground of the holiday masses with the expansion of air transport and holiday packages.

In the 1980s air travel became even more

	1950	1960	1962	1965	1968	1970	1980	1985	1987
Car	27	47	54	60	66	68	71	71	73
Bus/coach	27	21	18	21	16	15	12	14	14
Railway	47	30	26	21	14	13	13	10	8
Other	0	0	0	0	5	4	4	4	4

Fig 1.1 Mode of transport to main holiday destinations in Britain

accessible to the general population, and the travel industry responded by providing package tours to farther flung destinations (e.g. Moscow, Morocco, The Gambia) and developing a widening net of long-haul tourist destinations. The elite responded by retreating to more distant or inaccessible parts of the world.

Patterns of domestic tourism have adjusted to these increasing levels of international tourism. The total number of main holidays in Britain has declined, leading to substantial loss of business by the traditional seaside holiday resorts, while second holidays and short breaks in Britain are on the increase.

Phases in the evolution of international and domestic tourism

As exemplified by the UK experience, the process of economic development and the evolution of domestic and international tourism can be summarised as follows:

Phase 1 – a subsistence economy, society divided into peasants who have no leisure in the modern sense, and a small minority of the wealthy elite whose lives are totally leisure-orientated. This small element of the population participate in international tourism.

Phase 2 – the spread of wealth through the whole population through the processes of industrialisation, urbanisation, and institutionalisation of leisure time (in the form of holiday time from work). The development of mass domestic tourism and the provision of domestic tourist infrastructure to supply the needs of domestic tourists.

Continuation of international tourism by the small, but growing, affluent elite section of the population.

Phase 3 – increasing affluence throughout the whole population, leading to the growth of mass international tourism to nearby countries and a continuation of mass domestic tourism. The elite turn to long-haul destinations.

Phase 4 – high levels of affluence throughout the majority of the population. Diversification of

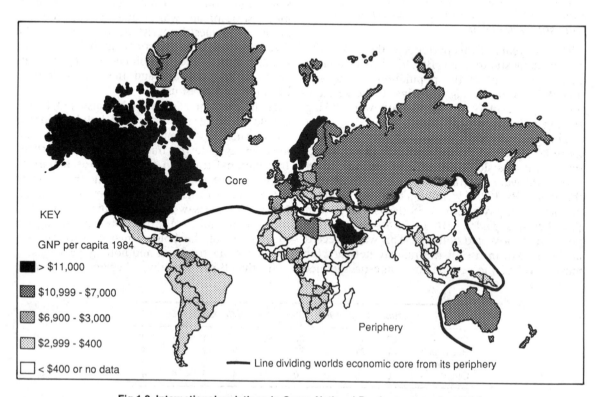

Fig 1.2 International variations in Gross National Product per capita (1984)

mass international tourism to a greater variety of other countries. Increase in long-haul destinations and a corresponding change in domestic tourism in response to the loss of the mass main holidays to overseas competitors.

The two main factors regulating the nature and volume of tourism activity in a population are:

1 the **overall affluence** of a country (measured in terms of the Gross National Product per head of population); and
2 the **social, political and economic structures and organisations** within a country that regulate the distribution of the country's wealth between the members of the population.

It might, therefore, be expected that the main tourist-generating areas of the world are those combining economic systems that generate high levels of wealth with social and political systems that allow the spread of wealth through the population as a whole.

World distribution of affluence

Figure 1.2 shows international variations in the Gross National Product per capita for 1984, one of the most widely used international economic indicators. One interpretation of this world pattern would divide nations into:

1 The **affluent 'North'**, consisting of 'core' countries who play a dominant and active role in world trade – generally market-type economies

which are large importers and exporters of goods, and exporters of capital.
2 The **poor 'South'** consisting of the 'peripheral' countries whose economies are dependent on the core countries. The core countries are the source of their imports and are a destination for the products and exports of the peripheral countries.

Affluence and international tourism generation

The dominance of the 'core' or affluent 'North' in the generation of international tourism is illustrated in Fig 1.3.

	International tourism expenditure (millions US dollars) 1988
The 'core'	
Europe	95 480
North America	38 428
East Asia and Pacific (including Japan and Australia)	25 154
Total	159 062
The 'periphery'	
Africa	3 181
Central and South America	9 207
Middle East	4 707
South Asia	4 824
Total	21 919

Fig 1.3 The generation of international tourism in the core and peripheral economies of the world

Country	International tourist expenditures 1988 (millions US dollars)	GNP 1988 US dollars per head	Total population 1988 (million)
USA	32 112	16 400	246.1
West Germany	25 036	10 940	61.0
Japan	18 682	11 330	122.2
UK	14 650	8 390	56.8
France	9 712	9 550	55.6
Netherlands	6 888	9 180	14.6
Canada	6 316	13 690	26.1
Italy	6 053	6 520	57.4
Switzerland	5 019	16 380	6.6
Austria	4 842	9 150	7.6
Sweden	4 572	11 890	8.4
Belgium	4 428	8 450	9.9
Norway	3 405	13 890	4.2

Fig 1.4 International tourist expenditure by the most affluent 'core' countries

This shows that roughly 88 per cent of world expenditure on international tourism is generated by the economic core. Examples of individual countries from the core show a close relationship between GNP per head and international tourist expenditure (*see* Fig 1.4).

Affluence and domestic tourism generation

Figure 1.5 shows that the economically advanced 'core' countries also have well developed domestic tourist markets, whereas some of the countries of the 'periphery' have hardly reached the stage of having even a significant level of domestic leisure travel.

	1984 GNP per head (US dollars)	1984 % of population as domestic tourists
Countries of the economic periphery		
Zaire	190	0.41
Togo	430	0.41
Senegal	510	0.64
Congo	540	0.65
Philippines	720	2.01
Jamaica	1 095	4.9
Turkey	1 100	4.94
Bolivia	1 250	6.82
Brazil	1 510	5.77
Syria	1 440	12.42
Cuba	1 407	48.61
Countries of the economic core		
Portugal	2 230	23.11
Yugoslavia	3 230	59.24
Poland	3 515	34.41
Hungary	3 665	25.48
Spain	5 100	41.46
Czechoslovakia	5 540	58.77
Netherlands	10 590	54.7
Norway	12 920	72.8

Fig 1.5 Domestic tourist generation on 'core' and 'periphery' countries

Variations in world economic organisation and tourist generation

It may be noted from Fig 1.2 that not all the countries with 'peripheral' economies have very low levels of GNP per head, for example, the average income per person in some of the oil exporting countries may be very high (e.g. Saudi Arabia 14 075 and Qatar as high as 31 840 US dollars per head). The World Bank, therefore, divides the economies of the countries of the world into five types.

1 Industrial market economies – those that are in the main parliamentary democracies (e.g. all the members of OECD except Greece, Portugal and Turkey).

2 East European non-market economies – centrally planned economies which up until 1989 were all under totalitarian forms of government (for example, Albania, Bulgaria, Czechoslovakia, Hungary, Romania, USSR).

3 High income oil exporters – often Sheikdoms where wealth is concentrated in the hands of ruling families (e.g. Bahrain, Brunei, Libya, Oman, Qatar, Saudi Arabia, UAE).

4 Middle income developing countries with a 1984 GNP of over 400 US dollars per head. These have a variety of economic and political systems. These are sub-divided economically into:

(*a*) oil exporters (e.g. Algeria, Angola, Egypt, Indonesia, Iran, Mexico, Nigeria, Peru, Syria, Trinidad and Tobago, Tunisia, Venezuela etc.); and

(*b*) oil importers, such as Argentina, Greece, Israel, Portugal, Hong Kong, Singapore, and

	International tourism expenditure (millions US dollars) 1984	% total world international tourism expenditure 1984
Industrial market economies	68 993	74.99
East European non-market economies	603	0.65
High income oil exporters	5 382	5.85
Middle income economies	16 042	17.43
Upper middle income	10 930	11.88
Low middle income	5 109	5.55
Low income economies	973	1.05
World total	93 144	100

Fig 1.6 Types of world economies and international tourist generation

Yugoslavia which are major exporters of manufacturers, plus countries that do not export manufactured goods.

5 Low income developing countries with GNP of less than 400 US dollars per head (e.g. Bangladesh, Cambodia, Chad, Haiti, Somalia, Sri Lanka, Zaire, etc.).

Region	1980 estimated million domestic tourist arrivals	% of world domestic tourist arrivals
Europe	1 179.0	86.6
Americas	122.5	9.0
East Asia and Pacific	45.0	3.3
South Asia	6.0	0.4
Africa	4.7	0.3
Middle East	4.6	0.3

Fig 1.7 World regional patterns of domestic tourist generation

The patterns of international tourism expenditure reflect the level of economic development and political organisation in these countries (see Fig 1.6). Although statistics concerning the development of domestic tourism are more fragmentary, in 1980 it was estimated that on a regional aggregate, the industrial market economies of Europe and America accounted for the

vast majority of domestic tourist arrivals in the world (see Fig 1.7).

This confirms the fact that the most economically developed market economies of the world have reached the stage of having both a fully developed international and domestic tourist market, whereas the poorest countries of the world have yet to develop even a significant domestic market.

Thus, the characteristics of the tourist markets in the five types of economies classified by the World Bank may be summarised as follows.

1 The industrial market economies. High values of GNP per head, wealth reasonably well spread over the whole population; well developed domestic tourism and substantial proportions taking holidays abroad (phases 3 and 4 of the cycle of tourist market development) – see Fig 1.8.

Figure 1.8 shows that there is a close relationship between GNP and the proportion of the population taking any holiday away from home. As GNP reaches around 9–10 000 (at 1984 values) US dollars per head, 50 per cent or more of the population may be expected to take a holiday away from home, and as affluence increases further, the proportion of these holidaymakers that go abroad increases to the point where it may even overtake the rate of domestic holiday

	(a) Departure Rate (% of population taking at least one holiday of 4 nights +)	(b) Place where holiday taken % Home	Abroad	(c) GNP US dollars per head 1988
Switzerland	75	48	52	16 380
Norway	74	63	37	13 890
Sweden	71	54	46	11 890
Netherlands	65	35	65	9 180
West Germany	65	31	69	10 940
Denmark	64	54	46	11 240
UK	61	65	35	8 390
France	58	85	15	9 550
Austria	52	47	53	9 150
Belgium	41	33	67	8 450
Italy	57	87	13	6 520
Greece	46	93	7	3 550
Spain	44	92	8	4 360
Finland	43	80	20	10 870
Portugal	31	92	8	1 970

Fig 1.8 Tourism in industrial market economies

taking (e.g. as in West Germany, Switzerland, Netherlands).

2 East European non-market economies (up to the 1989 revolutions). Middle-low income earnings measured in terms of GNP per head; wealth evenly spread through the population. Fairly well developed domestic tourism (e.g. 30–50 per cent of population taking holidays) but international travel tightly controlled and mainly between communist countries. Travel outside these countries limited to a political elite (for example, only just over five per cent of the Bulgarian population travelled abroad in 1985). (In Phase 2 of the cycle of development but further progress dependent on the removal of political constraints.)

3 High income oil exporters. These countries include those with the world's highest values of GNP per head, but wealth is generally concentrated in the hands of the few; though in some countries such as Saudi Arabia a new 'middle class' is developing. These countries have as yet no real domestic tourism, but generate small numbers of very high spending international tourists. (In Phase 1 of the cycle of tourist market development.)

4 Middle income developing countries. The more affluent countries of this group have a significant domestic tourist market at the upper level, (e.g. Greece, Portugal, this may mean 30–40 per cent of the population taking a domestic holiday), and are just beginning to generate international tourists (up to eight per cent of the population). The lower income group, e.g. Syria, Brazil, Philippines, have only the beginnings of a domestic market with perhaps 2–12 per cent taking domestic holidays and have yet to generate any international tourists other than members of political or economic elites. (These countries illustrate the beginning of Phase 2 of tourist market development.)

5 Low income developing countries. This group includes the very poorest countries of the world. Virtually no domestic tourism occurs (other than perhaps limited travelling to visit relatives) and such economies generate little international tourism. (These countries illustrate Phase 1 of the cycle of tourist market development.)

The examples shown in Fig 1.5 on page 8 suggest that under one per cent of the total population take any form of domestic holiday.

Inter-relationships between the economies of the world

The world thus consists of 169 countries all at different stages of economic change (or economic 'development') from highly affluent 'core' countries to the poorer peripheral countries; and all at a different phase of the development of tourism. It must be remembered that the countries of the world are closely interlinked and interdependent both in the economic sense and in terms of tourist movement.

Economic interdependence

The division of the world's economies into 'core' and 'peripheral' is based on one level of interdependence – core countries are dependent on peripheral countries for raw materials and to some extent markets for their exports. The peripheral countries are very highly dependent on the core for capital investment and for imports, and peripheral economies will be crucially affected if the core countries change their requirements for raw materials.

A second level of interdependence relates to energy sources; all industralised countries have increasing energy needs, and are dependent on their own or on world supplies of energy sources. The production of one of the world's main sources of energy (oil) is restricted to relatively few world locations and, thus, to relatively few countries (coal is both more widely spread and less easily transported). Therefore, the second level of economic interdependence relates to the role of oil in a country's economy, as to whether it is an oil importer or an oil exporter.

Because of these economic links, the performance of any country's economy (and, therefore, the growth of its affluence and its tourist generation capacity) cannot be considered in isolation and must be viewed in the context of the economic changes that occur throughout the world from time to time.

Interdependence of countries' tourism flows

By definition, a country that generates international tourism is economically linked to the countries which are the destinations of its tourists.

The tourists of the generating country will spend money in the receiving country, and the economy of the destination may rely heavily on tourism for both the foreign income and the employment that international tourism brings. This may be particularly significant for the economically 'peripheral' countries that have few other economic resources. Any sudden changes in tourist flows between countries may, therefore, have significant economic consequences for these countries. Tourism receipts may be relatively less important to the more affluent and highly diversified 'core' economies, and any changes in tourism flows may have a less dramatic impact in these countries.

Tourism is highly sensitive to economic change. On a personal level it is likely to be one of the first items of expenditure to be cut down in times of economic hardship and will expand very rapidly (both in terms of numbers of people travelling and in terms of the amount of money they spend) when economic conditions improve. Changes in the level of economic activity in the world as a whole will inevitably have repercussions for the growth of tourism.

Growth of world tourism since 1950

The total amount of international tourism in the world as a whole has been growing steadily since 1950. The same pattern of growth is shown whether tourism is measured in terms of international arrivals, tourism expenditure or tourism receipts.

When the number of arrivals is considered (see Fig 1.9), it can be seen that the increase in the total volume of tourism is accelerating. The average increase in numbers of arrivals per year ranged from five million a year in the early 1960s, to nine million a year by the early 1970s. This rose to nearly 13 million a year by the late 1970s and in the late 1980s the increase had grown to over 25 million arrivals per year. However, when the rate of increase is expressed in terms of the percentage increase of one year over the previous year, the rate of increase is shown to be much steadier: generally between four and eight per cent a year. Only rarely since 1950 has the rate of increase fallen below this band.

It has been demonstrated earlier in this chapter how tourist generation and the growth of tourism

Year	International tourist arrivals (in millions)	Annual growth rate %
1950	25.3	–
1960	69.3	–
1961	75.3	8.6
1962	81.3	8.0
1963	90.0	10.7
1964	104.5	16.1
1965	112.7	7.8
1966	119.8	6.3
1967	129.5	8.1
1968	130.9	1.1
1969	143.1	9.3
1970	159.7	11.6
1971	172.2	7.8
1972	181.9	5.6
1973	190.6	4.8
1974	197.1	3.4
1975	214.4	8.8
1976	220.7	2.9
1977	239.1	8.3
1978	257.4	7.7
1979	274.0	6.5
1980	284.8	3.9
1981	288.8	1.4
1982	286.8	−0.7
1983	284.1	−0.9
1984	312.4	9.9
1985	326.5	4.5
1986	334.5	2.5
1987	361.1	8.0
1988	393.1	8.8
1989	405.3	3.1

Fig 1.9 World tourism growth 1950–1989

expenditure is related to economic development and how the economies of the countries of the world are interdependent. It is not surprising, therefore, that these temporary slowdowns in the rate of growth of world tourism have been related to major changes in the world economy.

1 The late 1960s. This brief check in world tourism growth coincided with the war in the Middle East and its economic consequences.

2 The mid 1970s. The pause in the growth of world tourism in 1974 and 1976 was triggered off by action taken by the oil producing and exporting countries (OPEC). The Group decided to both limit the production of oil and also raise its prices. This action had many economic implications. As far as world tourism was concerned the immediate effect was a sharp increase in the cost of travel (particularly air travel), to which tourists responded by cutting down on international travel. When the short-term impact of the price increases had been accommodated, the annual growth rate rose to 8.8 per cent in 1975. The short-term economic impact of the 'oil crisis' was a period of extremely rapid inflation in many of the world's economies, and this was reflected in the dramatic increase in total tourism receipts in the period 1977–80, and in a second check in the annual growth rate of international arrivals in 1976.

3 The early 1980s. The virtual standstill in the growth of world tourism in the period 1981–3 can also be attributable to the economic implications of the oil crisis of almost ten years before. The economies of the countries of the world showed two longer term responses to the increase in oil prices:

(*a*) The rapid inflation of the late 1970s led to a loss of purchasing power and a decrease in demand for goods and services; a general economic recession, and a decline in the rate of growth of the GNP.

(*b*) This led to widespread unemployment in many countries of the world and a reduction in disposable income for many individuals; some people responded by cutting out international tourism altogether, others economised by going on shorter holidays and thus spending less money or choosing cheaper holiday locations. It can be noted that as in the two previous occasions, once

the worst of the economic problems were over and both tourists and the travel trade had adjusted, there was once more a sudden sharp increase in the rate of growth world tourist arrivals from −0.9 per cent in 1983 to +9.9 per cent in 1984.

Figure 1.10 summarises the impact of the oil crisis on both the world economy and on world tourist activity. The spatial impact of the recession has been uneven, with some countries and some regions of the world faring better than others. The oil producing countries were the initial beneficiaries of the economic upheavals of the 1970s and early 1980s, and their wealth increased dramatically. By 1981 Kuwait's GNP per head was US$19 200, while in Saudi Arabia it grew to US$14 075 per head. They were among the very few countries of the world whose tourism grew very rapidly during the period 1975–83, in terms of trips made, nights spent and in terms of travel expenditure (*see* Fig 1.11). Of the other countries of the world, the strongest and most affluent of the market economies (i.e. USA, West Germany, Japan, Norway, Switzerland) were least affected, but many of the weaker market economies saw a decline in international tourist activity, and the economically peripheral and the destination countries were hardest hit both from the change in the world economy and by the reduction of their revenues from tourism.

	Average annual growth rates (%)		
	Boom years 1960–73	Oil crisis years 1973–82	Recession and recovery years 1982–87
World economic indicators			
World industrialised nations' real production of goods and services (GNP)	5.0	2.1	3.1
World tourism indicators			
World international Tourist arrivals	7.8	4.3	4.3
World scheduled airline traffic (recorded passenger miles)	13.0	6.9	6.3
World passenger car registrations	7.0	4.2	3.5

Fig 1.10 **The impact of the 1974 oil crisis on world tourism trends**

	Average growth rates % per annum 1975–83		
	Number of trips made	Number of nights spent abroad	Travel expenditure (excluding fares) at constant relative prices
Oil producing countries			
Kuwait	24.2	23.8	19.7
Saudi Arabia	18.9	17.5	11.6
Venezuela	17.5	15.4	14.4
Strongest market economies			
Switzerland	8.0	6.1	7.0
Norway	5.4	5.0	7.6
Japan	4.7	4.0	7.2
Netherlands	3.9	2.4	2.8
USA	2.9	1.7	3.5
West Germany	1.9	1.5	2.9
Weaker market economies			
Belgium/Luxembourg	−0.3	−1.3	+0.1
Canada	−1.5	−2.8	−2.5
France	−0.6	−1.9	−0.7
Italy	−0.3	−1.2	+2.0
Mexico	−1.7	−2.9	+5.2

Fig 1.11 **The impact of the 1974 oil crisis on tourism in specific countries**

Conclusion

This chapter has viewed the generation of tourism at a general level on a world scale, and has illustrated the relationship between the performance of the world's economy and the generation of international tourist travel. This relationship also holds good at the scale of the individual country.

A country's ability to generate tourism is related to its social, political and economic character, and this chapter suggests that each country goes through a clearly defined sequence of phases of tourist generation – from phase 1 when only a tiny elite travel abroad, through phases 2 and 3 when first mass domestic and then mass outbound (international) tourism develops, and through to phase 4 when, finally, the proportion of the population travelling abroad is greater than that holidaying at home). These phases occur in parallel with economic and political change.

Different countries of the world are at different stages of economic development and tourist generation. The countries of the affluent economic core (mainly the continents of the Northern Hemisphere) currently generate the vast majority of the world's international and domestic tourists. Thus, tourist generation on world scale is heavily concentrated in Europe, North America and, to a lesser extent, in the Pacific region. The countries of the economic periphery (essentially the poorer countries of South and Southeast Asia, Africa and Central and South America) play relatively little part in generating world international or domestic tourist travel.

QUESTIONS AND DISCUSSION POINTS

1 List the factors necessary for tourism to take place in a country. Is it possible to rank the factors in order of importance? If yes, on what basis have you assessed their relative importance. If not, why can the factors not be separated?
2 In which types of economy in the world would you expect the most rapid increase in:
(a) domestic tourism; and
(b) international tourism.
to occur in the next few days and why?

3 What were the effects of the 1974 oil crisis on the development of world tourism? Have there been any more recent events that have had a similar effect?

ASSIGNMENTS

1 Research the economic, social and tourism history of a country other than the UK. To what extent does the development of its domestic and international tourism parallel that of the UK? What factors appear to have influenced the development of its tourism.

2 Study the data shown in Fig 1.1 on page 5. Is a bar chart or a graph the most appropriate method of plotting this data? When you have plotted the data, identify the period of time that saw the most rapid change in travel habits amongst British holidaymakers.

World Geographical Resources for Tourism

Introduction

The second part of this book is concerned with tourist destinations and geographical resources that make them attractive for tourists, and seeks to answer the following questions.

1 What geographical features of the world attract travellers to them; i.e. which types of climate are most suitable for different types of tourist activity; what sorts of coast and landscapes do tourists find attractive? Which historical, cultural and wildlife resources have the potential for tourism?
2 Where are these features located in the world, i.e. what is the world distribution of climatic, landscape, coastal, wildlife, historical and cultural resources for tourism?

Each chapter in this section examines the attraction and world distribution of each type of resource. Where appropriate, the chapters include case studies illustrating the relationship between the nature of the resource and the type of tourism that it supports. The cumulative evidence of the chapters together indicate that there are two regions of the world where there are strong concentrations of attractive tourist resources (ideal climates and beaches, with outstanding historic and cultural resources set in attractive landscapes all grouped around the sheltered waters of enclosed seas). These two regions are:

1 the Mediterranean basin, which lies directly to the south of the main European tourist generation region; and
2 the Gulf of Mexico/Caribbean Sea, which is similarly situated to the south of the population concentrations that generate most North American tourists.

The tourist resources of the huge Pacific region (the third major tourist generation region of the world) are more dispersed, but on the whole its most attractive resources are also located between the generating populations and the Equator. Resources with a high tourist potential are more widely scattered throughout the economic periphery, while the world's best wildlife resources are almost entirely now confined to the remoter parts of the world.

CHAPTER 2

Climatic resources for tourism

LEARNING OBJECTIVES

After studying this chapter you should be able to

- explain how the climate affects human bodily comfort
- identify the climatic factors that limit tourist activities
- locate the climatic regions of the world most suited to tourist development
- locate the parts of the world where there are severe climatic limitations to the development of tourism
- understand the effects of relief on temperature and precipitation, and the special character of mountain climates
- be aware of the importance of reliability and length of season for both tourists, tour operators and the providers of tourist infrastructures.

Introduction

In order to enjoy their holiday, tourists must be physically comfortable in the climatic conditions at the holiday destination. They must be comfortable irrespective of their activity, be it passive (sunbathing) or at the other extreme, very active (e.g. surfboarding, horse riding, snow skiing, and so on). Second, the climate of the holiday destination must be attractive. People tend to be more relaxed and cheerful when it is sunny and clear than when skies are overcast and gloomy.

Characteristics of climate associated with human comfort

Temperature and relative humidity

The normal body temperature of a human being is 36.5° C. This will rise with physical exertion or exposure to heat (such as bright sunshine). Body temperature is controlled by evaporation from the skin by sweating. Our body temperature would rise by 2° C per hour if we did not sweat. The ability of the air to take up moisture depends on its relative humidity (RH). If the relative humidity is too high – generally over 70 per cent – the air will not take up enough moisture from the skin to cool it, and the body will begin to overheat and the person will feel uncomfortable. In conditions of high relative humidity, there may be a risk of heat stroke at temperatures of only about 26° C, whereas in dry conditions bodily stress may not occur until the temperature nears 36° C. Figure 2.1 shows the range of temperature and relative humidity conditions within which a human feels comfortable.

The coincidence of high temperatures and high relative humidity thus render climates unsuitable for tourist development, as holiday activities cannot be limited to air-conditioned buildings

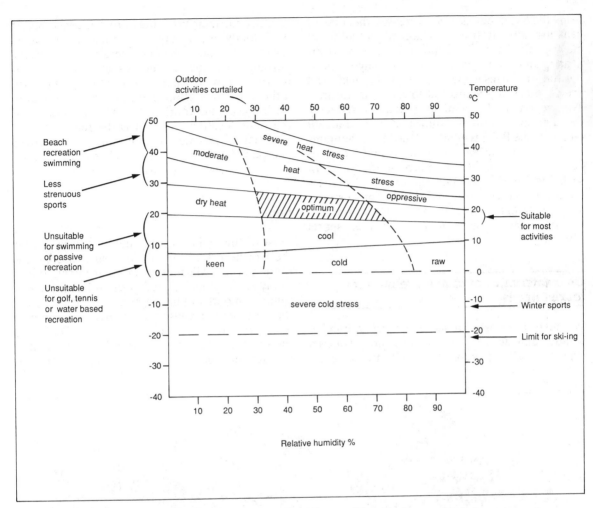

Fig 2.1 Temperature and relative humidity conditions for human comfort

and vehicles alone. The equatorial regions of the world are, therefore, not generally developed for tourism to any great extent.

Dry heat is more tolerable, as long as the body is shielded from direct sunshine, and it takes in sufficient water to replenish the moisture lost by sweating. The discomfort and danger of hot desert climates comes as much from dehydration as from the body overheating. Both adventure holidays and package tours are now extending into the more accessible fringes of the hot deserts and outings to a Saharan oasis is now an option on package tours to the North Africa coasts.

It has been noted that any physical exertion raises the body temperature; land-based activity holidays will thus have a slightly different spatial

distribution needing slightly lower temperatures than water sports and 'sun, sea and sand' holidays. Figure 2.1 shows the range of comfortable climatic conditions for a range of tourist activities.

Wind

The comfort chart (shown in Fig 2.1) indicates that conditions begin to feel uncomfortable for a lightly clothed, sedentary person at temperatures below about 16° C to 18° C. The body begins to feel cold when the temperature drops to 10° C and at this point extra clothing is necessary. Heat loss is accelerated by the wind because this not only increases the speed of moisture evaporating from the skin, but is also increases the rate of heat lost directly from the skin to the adjacent moving air. A breeze may thus reduce over-heating and restore comfort at high temperatures, but the wind causes the body to chill quickly and brings intense discomfort at lower temperatures. This action of the wind in effectively reducing the air temperature is known as the **windchill factor**. In the Polar regions and the high mountains of the world, the air temperature may be at or below freezing point for much of the year. In such conditions, windchill considerably increases the level of discomfort, and the risk of frostbite, as wind strength increases, which in turn reduces the potential of such areas for winter sports activities.

Characteristics of climate related to tourist needs

Whatever a tourist's choice of activity, a holiday is much enhanced if the weather is fine. Tourists want as near as possible to a guarantee of good weather for their visit: they are not concerned if it is cloudy and wet at other times of the year. On the other hand, the tour operator and property developer may be very interested in the seasonal distribution of sunshine and rainfall, particularly if they wish to develop an infrastructure providing for both summer tours and winter sun holidays in the same location. Thus, it is the reliability and seasonal distribution of sunshine, cloud cover and rainfall rather than the total amounts of each that are crucial for tourist development.

Rainfall

Most of the main tourist generating areas are in the Northern Hemisphere. A resort catering for these markets will thus be more attractive if it is sunny and dry during the Northern Hemisphere's summer months (June-September), whereas for the Southern Hemisphere tourist, December-February are the crucial months. Figure 2.2 shows the seasonal distribution of rainfall throughout the world. The subtropical and

Rain at all seasons
- a. Evenly distributed or double maximum
- b. Summer maximum

Periodic rains (marked dry season)
- a. Summer or spring maximum
- b. Winter maximum

Constant drought

Fig 2.2 World seasonal distribution of rainfall

Mediterranean climates are characterised by long, reliable summer drought seasons when virtually no rain falls at all. The quantity and spatial distribution of rainfall is locally variable, even within a given climatic regime because of the influence of topography on precipitation. This may be particularly pronounced in mountain areas. Rainfall induced by high land is known as **orographic rainfall**.

The nature of rainfall may also be significant for tourism. Short, sharp downpours mixed with long, sunny and dry periods (e.g. tropical climates, Mediterranean winter weather) are preferable to the overcast sky and hours of drizzle and light rain that frequently occurs in Western European temperate climates.

Cloud cover

Cloud cover is obviously related to patterns of rainfall, though not invariably. In some locations there may be high amounts of cloud or fog which produce little in the way of precipitation, for example along the Californian coast where cold sea water cools the air passing over it and produces foggy conditions, but little rain when the air reaches the coast. On the other hand, some equatorial climates have good sunny periods each day in spite of very high rainfall totals.

Sunshine

This is perhaps the most difficult climatic characteristic to measure accurately, and some resorts may be guilty of over-optimistic interpretations of their sunshine records. By definition, the total daily hours of sunshine can never exceed the hours of daylight which vary according to latitude and season. Amounts of sunshine must be inversely proportional to rainfall and cloud cover; that is when rainfall and cloud cover increases, the total amount of sunshine must decrease. Air pollution will, however, reduce the clarity of the sunshine, and in extreme cases (e.g. Los Angeles) will even produce smog which dramatically cuts down the penetration of sunlight.

World climates and their suitability for tourism

We have noted that clothing can modify the effect of the climate on bodily comfort by insulation and thus creating more comfortable internal microclimate. This operates in both hot and cold climates. The loose, flowing robes characteristic of the traditional dress of the Bedouins and Nigerians, for example, shield the body from excessive radiation from the sun while still allowing evaporation to cool the skin. On the other hand, clothing can protect the body by reducing heat loss in the cold climates. The climates of the world have been classified according to conditions of human comfort and the amount of clothing needed to maintain comfort. The world's climates fall into six clothing zones which can be further subdivided according to their seasonal pattern of temperature and rainfall. These seasonal variations will finally determine the overall attractiveness of the climate for tourism at different times of the year.

There are five temperature zones in the world, (*see* Fig 2.3), with each zone corresponding to one of the clothing zones (*see* Fig 2.4).

Hot climates: minimum clothing zone

A nude man begins to feel cold below 30° C so some clothing is required, yet any clothing at all may impede evaporation from the skin and increase discomfort. Such climates may not suited to tourism depending on the season.

Hot climates can be subdivided according to their pattern of rainfall.

Equatorial climates

These climates are limited to a zone within about 10° N and 10° S of the Equator forming the central part of the hot climatic zone. They are typically very hot (over 26° C) and humid (over 75 per cent relative humidity) and have heavy rainfall all year round, mainly in violent regular afternoon downpours. Such climates are not attractive to tourists as the heat and humidity make any outdoor activity exhausting. However, particular circumstances may lead to specialised forms of tourism being developed in the equatorial zone.

Fig 2.3 The world's five temperature zones

Latitude	Temperature zone and climatic type	Corresponding clothing zone
Equator	1 Hot (Equatorial, tropical and desert)	Minimum clothing and light protective clothing
	2 Warm temperate (Mediterranean and eastern margin climates)	One layer clothing
	3 Cool temperature (marginal and continental types)	Two layer clothing
	4 Cold climates	Three layer clothing
	5 Arctic and polar climates	Maximum clothing.
Poles		

Fig 2.4 Temperature and clothing zones

Case study: Singapore

Singapore, a tiny city state, lies just 1° north of the Equator. Figure 2.5 shows that it has a typical equatorial climate.

The combination of temperature and humidity make the air feel oppressive, the moist heat feeling like a smothering wall when leaving the shelter of air-conditioning. Nevertheless, Britain recognised Singapore's strategic location and developed the island as a trading base from 1819 to 1942, when it became a major communications and commercial centre for South East Asia, through the development of its port facilities. Later a major international airport was added, which now functions not only as a hub and gateway to SE Asia, but also as a major interchange and stopover location for round the world flights. Apart from business tourism, its main tourist function is for stopovers rather than as a site for long stays. With the help of air-conditioning, short stay visitors can tolerate the climate for a day or so. In spite of the high annual rainfall total, the days can be quite sunny, as the rainfall comes in regular late afternoon deluges.

Outdoor activity is, therefore, possible, but must be taken at a leisurely pace to avoid heat exhaustion. Light loose cotton clothing is most comfortable.

	Average temp. (°C)	Average rainfall (mm)	Average relative humidity (RH) %
Jan	27	253	80
Feb	27	172	74
Mar	28	195	73
Apr	29	189	76
May	29	174	76
Jun	29	174	76
Jul	29	171	76
Aug	29	171	75
Sep	29	179	76
Oct	29	210	75
Nov	28	256	77
Dec	27	259	80

Fig 2.5 Singapore's climate

Tropical climates

These are hot climates (generally over 23° C) with moderate to heavy summer rainfall and a clearly defined slightly cooler dry (or drier) winter season. These climates occur in the zones of latitude roughly at 10–25° N comprising East and South Asia, the West African coast (around the Gambia) the Caribbean and the coast of Mexico, and Hawaii.

A similar zone 10–24° S of the equator, covering northern Australia, Mauritius and Madagascar, parts of the South American coast and many of the South Pacific Islands.

The oceanic islands and the eastern coast locations (i.e. on the eastern margins of the continent) tend to have rain throughout the year but with a clear summer maximum, and are subject to seasonal tropical storms of great intensity (known as hurricanes, cyclones or typhoons). These occur most frequently in summer.

The western margin locations (i.e. on the west coast of the continents) have a much more pronounced completely dry winter period and much heavier summer rainfall. The monsoon climates of South and East Asia are even more extreme with a prolonged winter drought and a torrential summer wet season (the 'monsoon'). Monsoon climates also suffer the risk of severe cyclonic storms.

At the outermost limits of the tropical zone (around 24–26° N and S), the temperatures are a little lower, and the dry season less distinct.

Case study: Jamaica (18° N)

This Caribbean island has an east margin tropical climate. Its capital, Kingston, has 870 mm rainfall a year – on the low side for a subtropical climate. This is mainly due to the fact the Kingston itself lies in the rain shadow of the Blue Mountains which rise to over 2200 metres. In contrast the west-facing coasts of many of the other mountainous Caribbean Islands (such as Montserrat) have 1280 mm to 1660 mm of rain a year. In short, the total amount of rainfall is very dependent on aspect and topography; windward coasts and mountainous islands receive the heaviest rainfall, and the flat islands (e.g. Aruba and the Bahamas) may get very little.

The wettest months in Jamaica are May to October. In spite of this, many visitors come in July and August (the Northern Hemisphere summer) though the rest of the wet season (May/June and Sept/Oct) is the low point of Jamaica's tourist year. Most visitors come in the dry season (January–April) for Northern Hemisphere winter holidays (*see* Fig 2.6).

	Average temp °C	Rainfall mm	RH%	Number of staying visitors to Jamaica 1987 (thousands)
Jan	25	26	61	79.6
Feb	25	16	62	69.9
Mar	25	26	62	87.4
Apr	26	31	66	68.2
May	27	110	68	59.5
Jun	27	105	68	49.5
July	28	43	65	59.5
Aug	28	95	70	79.3
Sept	28	105	70	47.5
Oct	27	192	73	43.5
Nov	26	79	68	50.6
Dec	26	26	62	44.0

Fig 2.6 Jamaica's climate (Kingston)

Tourism levels will have inevitably dropped since 1987 as Jamaica was hit by Hurricane Gilbert in September 1988. The 110 mph winds did much damage – the hurricane caused 500 deaths and billions of dollars worth of damage as it gathered momentum on its passage through the Caribbean and across the Yucatan peninsula. The track of Hurricane Hugo in 1989 followed a more northerly track, well clear of Jamaica, but it devastated Guadeloupe, Montserrat, the Virgin Islands and San Juan in Puerto Rico. Jamaica's tourist resorts have been rebuilt but tour operators and investors in tourist facilities must take account of the risk of hurricane damage. The hurricane season runs from July to October with the greatest incidence in August and September.

Case study: Darwin (12° S)

Darwin is on the north coast of Australia and it has a monsoon type of tropical climate. Tourism in Darwin is more clearly seasonal and is focused on the National Parks inland rather than on coastal resources. The summer rains (November to April) are very intense and make travelling on unsealed roads difficult; many of the adventure safaris and other trips from Darwin operate only between May and October. The climate in these months is dry and hot, and is just on the upper limits of the optimum comfort zone (see Fig 2.1) but the low relative humidity makes it just suitable for all kinds of activity and adventure holidays. Tropical cyclones in this part of the world are a little less frequent than in the Caribbean, but Darwin also suffered devastation in 1974 from Cyclone Tracey, but has since been completely rebuilt.

	Av temp °C	Rainfall mm	RH%
Jan	29	381	75
Feb	28	305	76
Mar	29	254	73
Apr	29	102	62
May	28	25	55
Jun	26	0	54
Jul	25	0	52
Aug	26	0	54
Sep	28	25	57
Oct	30	51	59
Nov	30	127	63
Dec	29	229	69

Fig 2.7 Darwin's climate

Darwin's climate is nearer the monsoonal variation of tropical climate, though it is not quite as extreme as the Northern Hemisphere monsoons of the Indian Subcontinent. Bombay, for example, has a maximum of 610 mm in its peak summer wet month (July) and a total of 1827 mm, but a five-month complete winter drought.

Other variants of tropical climates

Western margin tropical climates

Banjul in the Gambia on the West African coast, and Acapulco on the Pacific coast of Mexico, have many climatic similarities. The summer period of rainfall is pronounced (but not as quite as intense as in a monsoonal climate). Neither region is subject to cyclones, and the winter dry season is ideal for winter sun, sea and sand holidays, though the relative humidity at Acapulco is a little on the high side for more active holidays (between 73 and 79 per cent).

	Av temp °C	Rainfall mm	RH%
Jan	23	0	27
Feb	24	0	26
Mar	25	0	29
Apr	25	0	41
May	26	5	49
Jun	27	74	61
Jul	26	280	72
Aug	26	504	78
Sep	27	257	73
Oct	26	95	65
Nov	24	5	47
Dec	25	3	36

Fig 2.8 Banjul's climate (16.8° N)

Oceanic tropical climates

The Pacific islands, e.g. Hawaii and Cook Islands, have variable amounts of rain, depending on their precise location and topography. In spite of less clearly defined dry seasons with virtually all year round rainfall and high humidity values, the islands may be developed for 'sun sea and sand' tourism, which are relatively less strenuous holidays. Sea breezes also make the climate feel more comfortable. The extent to which the islands are developed for tourism depends on their accessibility, most of the islands being very isolated.

The hot deserts

In these regions, mean temperatures rise above 33° C with daily maxima well over 37° C and there is persistent sunshine. Some clothing is necessary to protect the body from the sun but it must be loose and light to allow cooling by evaporation to continue, e.g. Insalah (Algerian Sahara), see the following table.

| | | | | | Av temp °C | | | | | | |
Jan	Feb	Mar	Apr	May	Jun	Jul	Aug	Sep	Oct	Nov	Dec
12.6	14.8	19.8	24.2	29.7	34.1	37.0	35.8	33.0	26.4	19.8	14.3

	Av temp °C	Rainfall mm	RH%
Honolulu (Hawaii) Latitude 20.8° N.			
Jan	22	105	71
Feb	22	67	71
Mar	22	79	69
Apr	23	29	67
May	24	26	67
Jun	24	18	66
Jul	25	23	67
Aug	25	26	68
Sep	25	36	68
Oct	25	29	70
Nov	24	64	71
Dec	23	105	72
Rarotonga (Cook Is) Latitude 21° S.			
Jan	26	256	78
Feb	26	225	81
Mar	26	276	80
Apr	25	179	79
May	24	174	72
Jun	23	107	77
Jul	22	95	75
Aug	21	125	74
Sep	22	125	73
Oct	23	131	74
Nov	24	143	75
Dec	25	233	76

Fig 2.9 Oceanic tropical climates

The hot deserts have virtually no rain at all. Winters are not quite so hot as the summer months, but at all seasons there is a very wide diurnal range of temperature. The nights may be cold enough for slight frosts in winter, but all year round the daytime temperatures climb rapidly. Maximum of over 45° C in the shade have been recorded in the peak of summer. The relative humidity is very low (about 30 per cent or less), and the discomfort of the dry heat is increased by frequent strong and gusty winds.

Tourism in the hot deserts is limited in two ways; in summer the daytime temperatures are too high and in winter the night-time temperatures may drop too far for comfort. At all times dehydration is a danger, causing discomfort in the eyes and nose, but creating a real danger of illness if enough liquid is not taken at frequent intervals. Tourism is possible in the desert environment, for example, cruises and tours to the ancient Egyptian sites in the Nile valley, if the hottest season is avoided (at Aswan, the June-August average temperatures reach 33° C.)

Arid zones

These are hot regions of the world on the margins of the hot deserts, but which have up to 250 mm of rainfall a year.

Case study: Alice Springs (23° S)

Alice Springs is in the 'red centre' of Australia. The proximity of Ayers Rock and the Olgas National Parks has led to the development of tourism in Alice Springs.

The average monthly temperature does not rise above 28° C but the daily range is, nevertheless, very great.

	Av temp °C	Minimum temp	Maximum temp	Rainfall mm	RH%
Jan	29	13	41	46	27
Feb	28	13	40	43	29
Mar	25	10	38	31	31
Apr	20	4	34	20	34
May	15	1	31	18	40
Jun	12	−2	27	16	45
Jul	11	−3	27	10	40
Aug	15	−1	31	10	32
Sep	19	2	35	10	27
Oct	23	6	38	18	24
Nov	26	10	40	26	24
Dec	28	12	41	41	26

Fig 2.10 Alice Springs' climate

This leads to problems in managing the safety of tourists. The energetic climb to the top of Ayers Rock must be undertaken in the relative cool of the early morning to lessen the risk of heat exhaustion. Twenty-seven people have died climbing Ayers Rock, from heat exhaustion, heart attacks induced by heat stress, and from falls. Except for the more energetic bush walks and safaris (which are offered from April to around September) all the tours and trips from Alice are offered all year round, although, of course, transport is air-conditioned. The rainfall very rarely disrupts tourism, but rainfall in arid zones is notoriously variable. There may be several years with no rain at all followed by a brief period of torrential downpours which may cause extensive flooding and make travel on the unsealed roads hazardous. In 1988 Alice experienced such floods at Easter when many sections of roads were washed away, that many communities were effectively isolated until the floods receded and repairs were carried out.

Warm temperate climates – one layer clothing zone

These climates can provide the optimal conditions of temperature and humidity for human comfort and some are ideal for tourism which may be possible all year round. Mean monthly temperatures are generally within the range of 10° C in winter up to 25° C in the summer, but daily maxima sometimes reaches the 30s. The torso may need the protection of light clothing but not the body's extremities. Relative humidities are generally low enough to make activity holidays possible, though maximum temperatures may be high enough to enforce a midday siesta. The winters are cooler than the summer but are never cold (average winter temperatures do not fall below 6° C). Such climates occur roughly in the zone of latitude 25° N–40° N and 25°–40° S of the Equator (see Fig 2.3 on page 20).

The characteristics of the warm temperate climates vary according to their location. The western margins of the continents enjoy the classic Mediterranean climate, with hot, dry summers and rainfall only in the winter. The eastern margins of the continents are exposed to rainbearing onshore winds all year round and are much more humid and their rainfall is much more evenly distributed throughout the year. (This pattern of variation between east and west coasts is similar to that shown by the tropical climates.)

Mediterranean climates

The world location of these climates coincides with the regions of winter rainfall as shown in Fig 2.2 on page 18. The Mediterranean basin itself is the most extensive area, and the continental influence of the surrounding land masses accentuates the extremes of the climate: in summer the temperatures rise much higher than in this type of climate elsewhere in the world, and in winter (in the northernmost parts of the Mediterranean) night temperatures can occasionally fall low enough for a frost. Similarly, in the heart of the Mediterranean basin, the summer drought may be several months longer than in other parts of the world. These differences make the climate even more suitable for tourism, particularly summer sun holidays.

Case study: Athens (37° N)

Athens is located more or less in the centre of the Mediterranean basin. In July and August the average temperature reaches 27° C but the maximum can go as high as 38° C. Such summers can be graphically described as baking as the summer is very dry, with the period April to September receiving negligible amounts of rainfall. Sunshine totals are high, with 2737 hours of sunshine a year. The sunniest summer month has 362 hours of sunshine (compared with 203 in London). The relative humidity is low, making the heat much more bearable than in comparable temperatures in the more humid tropical climates (see Fig 2.11). Not surprisingly, Greece has developed sun, sea and sand packages for the European market, extending tourism to the less developed areas as some of the Athens beaches have become more polluted. The northern Europeans, from Britain, Scandinavia, Switzerland

	Av temp °C	Rainfall mm	RH%	Av sunshine hours per day
Jan	9	62	70	5
Feb	10	37	66	6
Mar	11	37	63	6
Apr	15	23	57	7
May	19	23	54	7
Jun	24	14	54	10
Jul	27	6	41	12
Aug	27	7	41	11
Sep	23	15	50	9
Oct	19	51	61	7
Nov	14	56	70	4
Dec	11	71	71	3

Fig 2.11 Athens' climate (37.58° N)

and Austria, single out the climate as the main reason for choosing Greece as a holiday location. The reliable heat and sunshine provide a welcome contrast to the greyer climates of the north of Europe.

Although the climate is suitable for this type of holidaymaking all the summer (from May through to October), the demand is heavily concentrated in July and August. Greece has tried to extend the holiday season, both for sun holidays but also for cultural tourism. City breaks

and tours of the historic resources of Athens and its hinterland have been promoted, particularly in the spring, when the maximum temperatures stay below 26° C, making sightseeing much less exhausting than in the August heat. In this way, the season has been spread a little into the spring (*see* Fig 2.12).

It has been noted that Athens is one of the hotter examples of a Mediterranean climate. The other parts of the world that enjoy Mediterranean climates are narrow coastal strips on the western sides of the continents. The proximity to the open ocean moderates the summer temperatures, though in other respects (such as sunshine, rainfall and humidity) they conform to the pattern set by Athens.

Fig 2.13 shows the average temperature of the warmest summer month in the Mediterranean climates in the other continents of the world. The winter conditions of Mediterranean climates make winter sun holidays possible, though the winter provides less reliable and more variable weather than in the summer. Some locations (e.g. some of the Spanish costas) have promoted winter holidays for the retired who can benefit most from the milder winter conditions without needing the high levels of sunshine offered by many competing winter sun destinations.

Eastern margin warm temperate climates

These climates have temperature regimes very similar to the Mediterranean climates (though a few degrees cooler than the central Mediterranean basin), but are more humid and have rainfall all year round, e.g. Sydney, Australia.

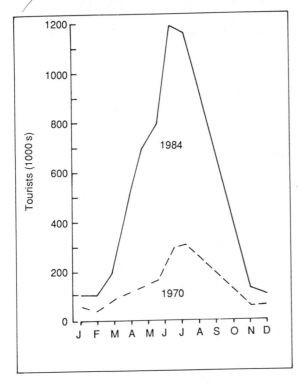

Fig 2.12 Athens' tourist flow

Location	Latitude	Continent	Highest average summer month temperature
Los Angeles	34° N	North America	August 22° C
Valparaiso	33° S	South America	January 19.5° C
Cape Town	34° S	South Africa	January/Feb 21° C
Perth	32° S	Australia	January/Feb 23.5° C

Fig 2.13 World Mediterranean climates

	Temp °C	Rainfall mm	RH%
Jan	22	95	66
Feb	21	110	68
Mar	20	123	69
Apr	18	143	70
May	15	131	70
Jun	13	123	70
Jul	12	123	68
Aug	13	77	64
Sep	15	74	61
Oct	18	82	61
Nov	19	72	63
Dec	21	74	64

Fig 2.14 Sydney's climate (34° S)

Case study: Florida, USA (25° N)

The best known tourist area with a eastern margin temperate climate is the State of Florida, USA: indeed, some claim that it is the leading tourist destination in the world. Florida, lies on the extreme southernmost boundary of the warm temperate climatic zone (extending from about 26° N to roughly 31° N) so the southern tip of the Florida peninsula may occasionally suffer from hurricanes straying north from the tropical Caribbean region. Thus, it shows some transitional features between tropical and warm temperate, but is generally classified with the warm temperate climates.

Miami is located well to the south of Florida, and thus shows maximum temperatures comparable to nearby tropical locations.

Florida has a range of attractions, from the beach for sun, sea and sand holidays, the Everglades National Park for outdoor activities, and a wealth of indoor and entertainment facilities, such as the Epcot centre and Disneyworld, and Miami has diversified into conference and business tourism. Not surprisingly, Florida has all year round tourism. With an average winter temperature of 20.5° C and under 50 mm of rainfall per month from December to February, the winter is the peak season. The majority of winter visitors fly in from the freezing weather of the north east of the USA. In spite of the high summer rainfall totals, there are almost as many visitors in the second and third quarters of the year as in the peak winter season (*see* Fig 2.15).

1985 Air and auto arrivals in Florida (millions)		
Air	Auto	Total arrivals.
Jan-March 4.87	3.70	8.57
April-June 3.28	4.32	7.60
July-Sept 2.85	4.21	7.06
Oct-Dec 3.30	3.55	6.85

Fig 2.16 Seasonal distribution of visitors to Florida

The number of overseas visitors gradually increases from April to August, peaking in the wettest season. The final quarter of the year (Oct-Dec) has only slightly fewer visitors than the other periods of the year. So in spite of the high rainfall and humidity of the summer months, Miami (and Florida as a whole) is virtually a non-seasonal destination.

Cool temperate climates – two layer clothing zone

Cool temperate climates are typified by the Western European climates. Mean monthly temperatures range from about 0° C in mid-winter to 16° C in mid-summer, making only the main summer months really suitable for the more passive tourist pursuits. A large proportion of tourist generating areas lie within this climatic zone and tourists will be seeking a more comfortable and attractive climate than their own e.g. Falmouth in the South of England, where the average temperatures are as follows.

	Minimum temp °C	Maximum temp °C	Rainfall mm	RH%
Jan	6	28	50	72
Feb	7	29	48	70
Mar	8	30	58	69
Apr	12	31	99	68
May	17	33	163	69
Jun	20	34	188	73
Jul	22	34	170	73
Aug	22	34	178	73
Sep	22	33	241	76
Oct	17	23	208	75
Nov	10	30	71	72
Dec	7	28	43	73

Fig 2.15 Miami's climate

	Jan	Feb	Mar	Apr	May	Jun	Jul	Aug	Sep	Oct	Nov	Dec
Temp °C	7.0	6.6	7.7	9.3	11.5	14.8	15.9	16.5	14.8	12.1	8.8	7.0
RH%	85	83	83	79	79	80	80	83	85	87	85	85

These climates have a definitely cold winter season (usually below 6° C) and rain occurs all year round.

In this zone the western coastal margins of the continents have their peak rainfall in the winter, and annual ranges of temperature are quite low. These climates are characterised by very variable weather with many sudden temperature and cloud cover changes. Rainfall levels and cloud cover are greatest on the most westerly margins, and decrease inland. Spells of settled hot weather may occur in the summer, but their timing cannot be predicted in advance with any certainty. Tourists, when planning and booking their holidays, will want some guarantee of the weather they might expect, and are thus likely to opt for the locations with more predictable and reliably hot, sunny climates such as those of the Mediterranean countries. The interiors of the continents in the cool temperate zone have much greater ranges of temperature throughout the year (even up to a range of 30° C). Neither variant of this type of climate is ideally suited for tourism except in the peak summer months of July and August. It has been noted that this zone covers the main tourist generating areas rather than any significant tourist receiving areas. Many of the older coastal tourist resorts in the cool temperate zone are experiencing a significant decline in visitors due to increasing competition from resorts in more attractive climates in other parts of the world.

The cold climates – the three layer clothing zone

The average temperature in this zone for at least six months of the year is below 6° C. In these latitudes the winter days are very short and the summer days are long. Summers are short and cool (June-August) and the season changes rapidly from winter to summer. Such areas may be suitable for scenery and activity holidays but the tourist season is inevitably short too. The continental interiors in this zone have much more extreme climate, with intense winter cold, below minus 30° C (way below freezing) but with summer averages climbing to 19° C.

The Arctic and polar climates – maximum clothing zone

These climates are always cold, with less than three months' average temperature above 6° C. The tundra climates have a short period when the ground is free from snow but in the more northerly areas there is permanent snow cover. It may be possible in the future to develop the Arctic regions for special interest tourism, for example, wildlife cruises to Antarctica, but the potential of such areas is thought to be very limited.

Mountain climates

Mountain regions will generally follow the climatic regime of the region where they are situated: mountains in desert regions will be dry, while those in tropical zones will have rainfall according to the local seasonal pattern. However, their height modifies their climate in three ways.

1 The effect of altitude on temperature. The temperature drops at a regular rate as the land rises above sea level e.g. in the Alps the temperature decreases by 0.75° C per 100 metres on north-facing slopes. So upland areas are cooler than surrounding lowlands. The actual temperature at the summit will depend on two variables: the height of the mountain and the air temperature at the bottom of the mountain (which is determined by latitude). Thus, on the Equator, mountains are cold enough for there to be snow all year round at heights above 5500 metres. Moving away from the Equator into cooler temperature zones (see Fig 2.3 on page 20) the 'snowline' (i.e. the height at which snow lies all year round) drops (see Fig 2.17).

Temperature zone	Latitude	Mountain	Mountain height	Snowline height
Arctic	70° N	–	–	sea level
Cold	62° N	Glitter Fjeld	2598 m	1200 m
Cool temperate	46° N	Mont Blanc	4807 m	2750 m
Warm temperate	28° N	Everest	8834 m	4800 m
Hot	Equator	Chimborazo	6243 m	5500 m

Fig 2.17 Height of snow line in different temperature zones

2 Effect of altitude on air pressure. The air gets thinner with increased altitude, so that at 5500 metres the air pressure is only half that at sea level, and there is less oxygen available in such a rarefied atmosphere. Thus, at about 5000 m humans begin to feel breathless and lethargic (a condition known as 'mountain sickness') which will make any energetic activity difficult.

3 The effect of altitude on rainfall. Mountains generally experience greater rainfall than lowlands similarly placed. This is caused by the air being cooled as it is forced up the slope of the mountain side, and as it cools, the moisture in the air condenses to form rain. The effect is most pronounced where high land forms a barrier to rain-bearing winds.

In summary, mountains are often cooler, wetter and at high altitudes, less comfortable places than the surrounding lowlands. Nevertheless, many mountainous regions are important tourist destinations. First, in hot, humid, equatorial and tropical climates, the very coolness of the mountains may make them attractive hot season resorts (such as Simla in the Himalayas). Second, the scenery of the mountains may attract tourists, even in spite of unfavourable weather conditions. Indeed, in many resorts in the European Alps, summer visitors outnumber winter tourists, although the mountains are at their wettest in the summer. Finally, the mountains may be developed for winter sports. Skiing needs a very particular combination of climatic conditions: good snow quality (dry and powdery) abundant sunshine, little wind, and a long enough winter season (at least 120 days) with snow lying to make the very substantial investment in ski facilities (lifts, tows, hotels etc) economically worthwhile. In addition, the resort must necessarily be well below the height at which people start to feel the effects of mountain sickness.

This specification is most closely met in the European Alps, where snow falls in autumn and early winter but high pressure then builds over the mountain chain bringing very cold, sunny and settled weather for long periods. The clear air, although very cold, allows the sun's rays to penetrate with little loss of intensity. The sunshine warms the skin and will quickly produce a deep tan, so although the air temperatures are very low (e.g. average January temperature is −7° C in Davos, Switzerland) skiers will not feel uncomfortably chilled.

	Av temp °C	Precipitation mm
Jan	−7	46
Feb	−5	56
Mar	−3	56
Apr	2	56
May	5	59
Jun	10	102
Jul	12	125
Aug	11	128
Sep	8	95
Oct	3	69
Nov	−1	56
Dec	−6	64

Fig 2.18 Davos' climate (47° N) – altitude 1564 metres

There may be great local variations in ski conditions within a mountain region: the amount and quality of snow and length of time it persists depends very much on aspect and will vary considerably from slope to slope. Similarly, one part of a valley may be much windier than another, depending on local air circulation. The precise location of ski resorts and ski slopes within a mountain region will be constrained by these local factors.

QUESTIONS AND DISCUSSION POINTS

1 Locate Los Angeles on a world map and study the climatic data for the city.

Los Angeles (Latitude 34° North)

	Av temp °C	Rainfall mm	RH%
Jan	13	79	57
Feb	14	76	64
Mar	15	71	64
Apr	16	25	69
May	17	10	73
Jun	19	3	73
Jul	21	1	71
Aug	22	1	71
Sep	21	5	67
Oct	17	15	62
Nov	16	30	50
Dec	14	66	52

Total rainfall (mm): 382
Total annual hours of sunshine: 3500
Average number of rainy days: 50.

What type of climate does Los Angeles have? Suggest reasons why the relative humidity is so high in July and August, even though there is negligible rainfall. Is this likely to constrain the development of the tourist potential of this location?

2 Identify the world locations of the most ideal climates for tourism. Where are these climatic zones in relation to the main tourist generating regions of the world (*see also* Chapter 7).

3 Which climatic zones of the world are climatically unsuitable for all but certain very specialised forms of tourism? Why are they unsuitable for mass tourism?

ASSIGNMENTS

1 Assessment of Palma's climate for tourist activities. Trace the human comfort chart (from Fig 2.1) onto squared paper. Plot the monthly temperature and relative humidity figures for Palma on the chart. Which months' values fall within the 'optimum' zone? What range of tourist activities (other than beach activities) could take place in a climate such as Palma's?

Palma de Mallorca, Balearic Islands, Latitude 39° N

	Av temp °C	Rainfall mm	RH%
Jan	10.7	43	78
Feb	11.8	39	76
Mar	13.1	39	75
Apr	15.3	36	72
May	18.5	31	72
Jun	22.2	20	68
Jul	25.5	9	68
Aug	25.8	17	70
Sep	23.8	44	74
Oct	19.2	77	77
Nov	14.4	50	78
Dec	11.3	55	77

2 You work for a tour company wishing to expand its winter sun holidays for the British market. You have been asked to identify three possible locations with ideal climates for winter sun holidays.

Select and map three locations, and using the human comfort chart, demonstrate why they are ideal for the promotion of winter sun tours.

CHAPTER 3

Coastal resources and the sea

LEARNING OBJECTIVES

After studying this chapter you should be able to
- list the characteristics of the sea coast that are of significance for tourism
- locate the areas of the world where the best natural conditions exist for sun, sea and sand tourism
- understand the relationships between climate, and the processes of erosion and deposition that fashion the coastline
- be aware of some of the physical factors that constrain or facilitate coastal tourist development.

Introduction

For many people, going on holiday means going to the seaside. In Britain about 70 per cent of domestic holidays have traditionally been to the coast and 'sun, sea and sand' holiday packages are overwhelmingly the most popular overseas trips. After the climate, the coast and the sea are perhaps the most important geographical resources for tourism, the nature and quality of the coast and beaches play a very important part in making a successful and enjoyable holiday.

What the tourist is looking for

The sea

The tourist is first and foremost looking for a clean, sandy beach that is comfortable to sunbathe on and safe for swimming, with gentle waves that allow children to play at the water's edge. There must be no dangerous tidal or offshore currents that might sweep the unwary swimmer, small boats or inflatables out to sea. A shelving beach may also get the non-swimmer into trouble though the sea must still be deep enough inshore (perhaps chest deep) to give the more serious swimmers scope to enjoy themselves.

The beach

A wide and fairly flat beach provides plenty of room for all the holidaymakers and their beach equipment (which may include tables, chairs and parasols). On the other hand, the sea must not be too far away for the swimmer to walk to, so a low tidal range is ideal. Finally, the beach should be only a few yards away from the tourists' accommodation; a long walk or a climb up and down a steep cliff can be tiring and inconvenient.

From the tourist developer or tour operator's point of view, access to the beach is also crucial. Level land suitable for hotel development as close as possible to the beach makes for a more attractive product. For them, the winter climate is another important factor as development close to the high watermark may be vulnerable to wind and wave damage if there are winter storms. The long-term stability of the coast is an additional consideration as investment in such development is pointless if erosion by the sea will eventually undermine the buildings or wash away the sandy beach.

Specialised sea-based sports such as surfing, angling, diving, sailboarding, sailing and other forms of boating may require additional or even perhaps totally contrasting features. For example, the best surfing beaches need very much bigger, regular, slowly breaking waves rolling in to a sandy beach. The sailboarders, however, need a relatively quiet rather sheltered sea where the inexperienced or less fit sailboard enthusiast will be safe.

The experienced yachtsman may relish more of a challenge and in common with other boating people will need launching facilities or deeper water inshore for anchorage. The anglers and divers will be looking for clean, unpolluted waters where marine wildlife abounds. Although the real specialist will be pleased to find these qualities anywhere, the ideal situation would have such coasts alongside the best swimming and sunbathing beaches for the perfect holiday. Thus it is clear that the following physical characteristics of the beach and coast are of crucial importance for tourism:

(*a*) composition of the beach (its lithology) – for comfort.
(*b*) the nature and size of the waves – for safety.
(*c*) the tides and currents in the sea – for convenience and safety.
(*d*) cleanliness and pollution – for health and comfort.
(*e*) the shape of the beach in plan and in profile – for safety and convenience.
(*f*) The shape and character of the land above high water mark – for ease of access and development.
(*g*) The stability of the beach and coast – for long-term investment.

The composition of the beach

This is perhaps the most important characteristic. A sandy beach is an attractive beach, a shingly or muddy beach is of relatively little use for tourism. Of course, the type of rock that makes up the coast is important as this may form the immediate source of the sand or mud that accumulates on the shore. A soft sandstone will easily crumble under the action of the wind and rain to yield sand for the beach but chalk on the other hand will dissolve away leaving a residue of rounded flint nodules which form the shingly beaches which are typically found under the White Cliffs of Dover on the south coast of England. The purer limestone rock of the Dalmatian coast of Yugoslavia produces neither sand nor pebbles, so the coastline consists mainly of bare rock. However, where the characteristics of beaches are examined on a world scale there seems to be a distinct regional pattern of occurrence of sandy, muddy and shingly beaches, and surprisingly enough this pattern seems to be more closely associated with the climate (past and present) than with the present characteristics of the rock that makes up the coast.

Figure 3.1 shows that pebbly beaches are much more common in the high latitudes; these coincide with those parts of the world dominated by icecaps either now or in the glaciations of over ten thousand years ago. The icecaps and glaciers leave a coating of mixed crushed and broken rocks and gravel which are reworked by the sea to form shingly beaches. Figure 3.2 shows the distribution of the types of material of which beaches are made, according to their latitude. This shows that while shingle is dominant in high latitudes, mud is much more common nearer to the Equator (0–20° latitude).

The present equatorial climate, with its hot, wet conditions, allows rapid chemical decomposition of rocks to take place, so that they eventually disintegrate into mud. This zone of intense chemical weathering is shown on Fig 3.1. The great equatorial rivers (e.g. the Amazon and Congo) also add vast quantities of mud to the coast in these parts of the world. Although Chapter 3 suggests the climate of this zone to be far from perfect for tourism, there are some attractive tourist beaches in the hot climate zone, namely, coral beaches. Where the warm waters of the tropics are clear and shallow, coral grows in abundance, and corals may be ground up by the sea to form attractive beaches of coral and shell sand – the white beaches typical of the tropical coral island. The Great Barrier Reef off the Queensland coast of Australia is perhaps the

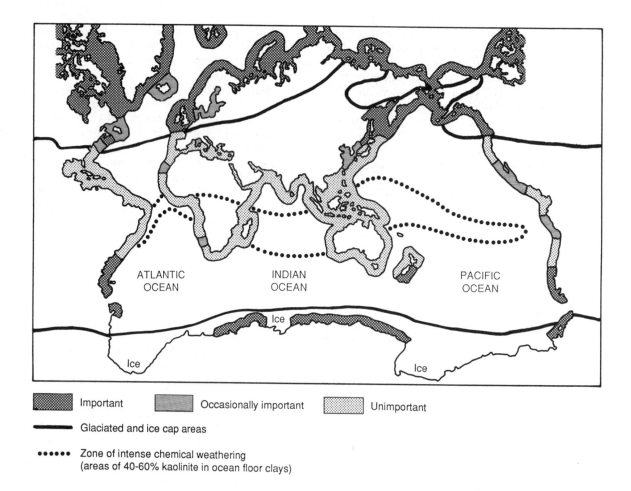

Important   Occasionally important   Unimportant

Glaciated and ice cap areas

•••••• Zone of intense chemical weathering
(areas of 40-60% kaolinite in ocean floor clays)

Fig 3.1 World distribution of pebbly beaches (showing the importance of pebbles as a beach material)

world's most spectacular area of live coral, with a wealth of opportunities for tourists to snorkel and scuba dive to look at the coral, fish and other marine wildlife.

Figure 3.2 shows that sand is most frequently found in latitude 20–40° N and S, coinciding roughly with the world distribution of the types of climate most suitable for tourism (i.e. tropical and warm temperate climates).

It appears that the characteristics of the wave and currents in this zone of the world also tend to encourage the accumulation of sand. However, shingle does occur on some of the coasts of the semi-arid and desert areas where the humidity is too low to allow chemical weathering of rock to take place.

The waves

It has been noted that size and nature of the waves are significant for the safety and enjoyment of the tourist in the summer. The waves, along with tides and currents, are also major factors in determining the processes which erode or build up the beach and coast. However, the climate is once again the underlying factor that controls these proceses, because the waves themselves are created by the action of wind on the surface of the sea.

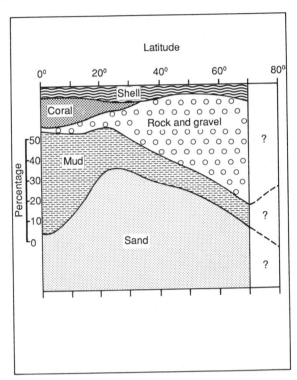

Fig 3.2 Distribution of types of materials that form beaches

Storm waves

Certain types of climate are windier than others, some of the windier being the cool temperate climates that are found in latitudes 40°–60° (*see* Fig 2.3). It is in these latitudes that most storms occur. These frequent storms and winds generate big energetic waves which crash onto the coasts of these zones causing wear and tear and erosion. Figure 3.3 shows the world distribution of these 'storm wave environments'.

These waves carve out dramatic coastal landforms such as cliffs, stacks and caves, in the hard rocks that are abundant in this zone. The erosion also tends to shift and erode away sand to create and reform the beaches. The storm waves tend to be short, steep and rapid, with the next wave breaking before the first has completed its backwash. This may make paddling or swimming in the surf zone uncomfortable and even dangerous in rough weather particularly on a steeply sloping beach. In the winter, waves over 7 metres high have been recorded which are capable of doing great damage to any buildings or constructions near the high watermark. However, the cool temperate climates are characterised by their variability and the storm waves that wash the beaches are as ephemeral and variable as the weather that created them. In summer, of course, the weather is generally calmer, when weather and waves may combine to produce ideal paddling and bathing conditions.

Severe storms (called **cyclones**) do also occur in tropical latitudes (*see* Fig 3.3), for example the hurricanes in the Caribbean. Although these storms cause more damage to buildings than the storms experienced in higher latitudes, they are too infrequent and localised to affect landforms and beaches to any great extent.

In summary, it can be concluded that the storm wave environments of latitudes 40°–60° are areas of high wave energy, though of course there are periods of calm seas in the summer season. The action of such waves creates gently sloping shores often leading up to cliffed coasts. Beaches are limited in development and frequency and are often pebbly. However, where sand does accumulate locally to form beaches they are often backed by sand dunes creating an attractive beach for the tourist. It must be remembered that this is a broad generalisation, and local variations in geology and climate will lead to some variations in coastal characteristics within this general pattern.

Swell waves

The waves created by high winds in mid latitude zones radiate outwards through the oceans like ripples on a pond, penetrating into the parts of the world with much less windy climates. These ripples form the sea swell which makes waves break on shores many thousands of miles away from winds that created them. This swell causes waves to break on the coasts in the low latitudes (0°–40°) even when there are no winds blowing in the vicinity.

In the South Pacific, persistently strong westerly winds blow, which build up huge waves that radiate out from the centre of the south of the Pacific Ocean. It is these big regular swell waves that create the best surfing conditions. The most popular surfing beaches are found where such

Storm wave environments ▦ Protected sea environments ☑ Swell environments ▥ Tropical cyclone influences

Fig 3.3 Wave conditions round the coasts of the world

waves meet the shore head on, such as Bondi Beach on the eastern Australian coast at Sydney and the famous Californian surfing beaches on the other side of the Pacific. On some Pacific beaches, however, the combination of big waves and local currents can create dangerous swimming conditions.

Swell waves in the other oceans are generally smaller and less steep than the Pacific swell. They are also less frequent, so that the backwash is able to return to the sea before the next wave arrives. This creates an environment wherein the tourist is both safer and more comfortable. In addition, this type of wave is far less destructive than storm waves and tends to encourage the accumulation of the sand and mud on the shore.

The coasts of the world in latitudes 20°–40° thus show the coincidence of all the factors favourable for seaside tourism. The best climates, abundant sand, good surfing or gentle reliable and regular waves that tend to accumulate the sand into offshore sandbars, lagoons, splits and some of the best and biggest sandy beaches of

the world. Hard rocks and cliffs are rarely found in these latitudes, though pebbly beaches may be found on the coasts of semi-arid desert areas.

The tides

The tides are caused by the gravitational pull of the moon on the body of water of the seas. The range of the tide (i.e. the difference in height of the water at low and at high tide) varies over the world. The world distribution of tidal range at spring tides (those very high tides occurring when the sun reinforces the gravitational pull of the moon) is shown in Fig 3.4. In the open oceans the range is generally about two metres but this may be considerably greater where the configuration of a coast line may form a funnel. This is particularly the case around Great Britain. The Severn Estuary is a classic example of this; at Avonmouth the tidal range at spring is 16.3 metres. The significance of tidal range for tourism is the fact that the greater the tidal range the

| ■ > 6m | ▤ 2 - 6m | ▥ < 2m |

Fig 3.4 World distribution of tidal range at spring tides

wider the beach tends to be. The erosive power of the sea is spread over a wide area between the tidal limits and the sea tends to cut a wide, very gently sloping beach platform. Although this may at first glance seem an advantage for tourism in that it provides plenty of space on the beach, another consequence of this is that the sea may recede a very long way from the shore at the lowest tides, giving the tourist a very long walk to find the sea! Also, having reached it, the sea is often too shallow for swimming (e.g. as at Weston Super Mare in Avon).

An additional problem in such areas is that the tide may come in unexpectedly rapidly on wide, very gently sloping beaches, which may catch the unsuspecting tourist unawares. A fast incoming or outgoing tide is also often associated with dangerous tidal currents. In the British Isles, some of the fiercest tidal currents are experienced in the shallow, funnel-shaped estuaries, rendering them unsafe for swimming and some even too dangerous for boating and sailing (e.g. on the Severn Estuary).

Dangerous tidal currents may also occur around and between islands, (e.g. the Menai Straits in Wales) and off promontories. There is one advantage of a reasonable high tidal range for tourism: the tide acts as a very effective cleaning and scouring agent, carrying away rubbish and resorting the sand (though rubbish may be deposited and accumulate at the winter high watermark). Beaches in areas such as the Mediterranean which has a very low tidal range may have to be cleaned manually.

The enclosed seas

Figure 3.3 classifies certain of the seas of the world as 'protected seas'. These are bodies of water linked to the main oceans but which are almost cut off by the configuration of the land masses, e.g. the Mediterranean, or by strings of islands (for example, the Gulf of Mexico). Because they are relatively small bodies of water, the effect of the moon on the tides is less. In fact, many of these seas have very small tidal ranges or are virtually tideless.

Because they are effectively enclosed, these seas are not affected by the waves and swell created in the high latitudes of the open oceans, so these seas experience only very small waves, even in winter. This pattern is only disturbed by local weather conditions when bigger waves may be temporarily generated. The waves have little power to cause erosion, so safe, sandy beaches are frequently found: all in all, a perfect tourist environment.

Finally, the enclosed seas although benefitting on the whole from their protected character suffer one disadvantage: because the water in the enclosed sea does not circulate and mix with the water of the open ocean, any pollution entering the sea is not dispersed or diluted, and indeed pollution tends to build up virtually irreversibly in such locations. This is a particular problem in the Mediterranean. Due to the restricted flow of water through the narrow Straits of Gibraltar, it takes 75 years for the whole of the water of the Mediterranean to be replaced by fresh Atlantic water. In the late 1980s the northern Adriatic coastal resorts were badly hit due to the consequences of the build up of pollution.

Sea pollution

There are five main types of pollutants that affect the sea:

1 Solid debris washed up at high tidemark. The debris such as bottles, plastic containers and boxes originates both from coastal towns, rivers washing into the sea and from ships at sea.
2 Oil, in the form of liquid slicks floating on the surface and as coagulated lumps of tar. Oil may come from urban onshore industrial centres, from ships cleaning out their holds or from accidental spillages both at sea and at coastal oil terminals.
3 Other chemical pollution dissolved or suspended in water entering the sea. This originates mainly from fertilisers in the run off from farmland, or from industrial effluent containing industrial waste products.
4 Sewage, either treated or raw. This comes from urban areas onshore.
5 Hot water that has been used for cooling purposes, either in industrial process or in power

stations. This is perhaps the only form of pollution that has no undesirable effects on tourism.

The first four types of pollution make the beaches less desirable for tourism but some forms of chemical pollution and raw sewage effluent may make them totally unusable on health grounds. Oil pollution is perhaps the most obvious and visible form of pollution and has received most attention in the press; consequently, tourist resorts have given more priority to overcome this pollution problem than any of the others.

World pollution

Oil

In 1983 48 per cent of the volume of world marine oil pollution came from land-based sources and 52 per cent from ships. Only about one third of the ship-generated oil pollution was due to accidental spillages, and only a tiny proportion from the oil and gas fields. Thus, industry and routine shipping are the major sources. Surveys completed in 1978 not surprisingly showed the greatest concentration of oil pollution along shipping lanes and in coastal waters, where tourism is concentrated. Virtually the whole of the Mediterranean falls into the highest category of pollution; the fact that it is an enclosed sea prevents the dispersal or dilution of the oil.

Natural biological processes may remove the oil in time, but the solid tar balls may be swept on shore before these processes are complete. Where the tar arrives depends on winds, waves, and currents, but in general terms it will tend to accumulate in the same places and by the same processes as sand and other sediments. The solid tar will tend to be concentrated where sand is accumulated, i.e. on the most extensive sandy beaches.

Detergents are successfully used to clean the beaches, but it must be recognised that these detergents are themselves as much a pollutant as the oil and can damage marine wildlife, although it is a more acceptable form of pollution (at least in visual terms) to tourists.

Other forms of pollution

Sewage and chemical pollution are the other most serious hazards to tourists on health grounds. Chemical pollution can sometimes be very dangerous but perhaps the resident population (i.e. the population that is continually exposed to the chemical) is at greater risk than visitors of a week or so's duration.

On the other hand, untreated sewage is just as dangerous to residents and tourists alike. The technology exists to treat all sewage products to a high standard but tourist resorts may not be willing or able to afford to install the equipment capable of meeting the extra volume produced in the few months of the peak holiday period. The excess sewage produced in July and August may be pumped straight into the sea with partial or no treatment at all. Beaches polluted in this way are not only visually repellent but are also, of course, a great health hazard. Research in the USA has shown that of all the bathers swimming in their areas of sewage polluted waters, 18 out of every 1000 succumb to some form of pollution-related illness (such as gastroenteritis, skin allergies, ear, nose or throat infections).

In Europe, the EC has set standards of cleanliness and water quality that bathing beaches should meet. In Britain, the Government monitors 392 beaches, and by 1988, 75 per cent of these beaches had been brought up to the EC standard. However, 22 beaches in the North West, including Blackpool, and some of the beaches in South East England failed to meet the standard. Most of the beaches of southwest England were adequate.

Tourist development on the coast

However attractive a beach may be, it cannot be developed for tourism unless it is both accessible and has space for development to landward. This depends on the location of the beach in relation to the landforms above high watermark. Very attractive pocket, bayhead and bayside beaches may be found along irregular cliffed upland coasts, the beaches being found in the bays of various sizes interspersed between the headlands which are composed of harder, more resistant rock. The attractive beaches of the Lleyn and Gower peninsulas of Wales are generally of these types.

Bayhead beaches may sometimes be found where valleys are cut into the higher land, with the river valley providing an accessible route to the coast. Or they may occur where the cliffs are lower and less rugged. In either case, some low level land may be available for tourist development and small resorts may develop. However, where such beaches are backed by high or steep cliffs, land that can be developed is scarce, and is both difficult and very expensive to build on. This may lead to very exclusive development of cliff top hotels, having access to their own small private beaches. No long-term development at all is possible where the coastline is unstable. Some geological features such as cliffs made of soft clays, glacial deposits or rock consisting of alternate horizontal layers of soft and harder rocks, are particularly susceptible to erosion. The sea can accelerate the erosion, particularly during winter storms by undercutting the cliff foot and rapidly removing material that falls onto the beach from the cliff face. These circumstances combine to create a highly mobile, unstable cliff, often characterised by slumping, landslides and sometimes even mudflows. The undercliffs at Lyme Regis in Dorset are a classic example of an unstable area generated by repeated landslips on the cliff face which prohibits any development. Access to beaches at the foot of such mobile unstable cliffs is also often difficult, as any steps or stairways built down the cliff face will need repeated replacement every year or so, e.g. as at St Marys Bay, Brixham.

Where erosion is a continuous problem, attempts may be made to reinforce the shore by building sea walls, bulkheads or revetments. These are generally of concrete or stone, and are designed to dissipate the energy of the breaking wave so that less damage is done. These sea defences are typical of many of the coastal resort areas in the high latitude storm wave zone, where the waves generated by winter storms can do great damage to tourist installations. However, it is unusual for the defences to be anything other than temporary expedients, needing eventual repair and replacement.

In mid latitudes, where marine erosion is more common than the accumulation of sand, the beaches themselves may also be very changeable. As the waves and the tides repeatedly flow over them, the sand is shifting, sorted, rearranged and replaced. Where the supply of sand brought by the waves and currents to the beach is less than that renewed by the sea, then the beach is eroded. In general, sand is moved along the beach if the waves break on the beach at an angle. Where beach material is on the move, a tourist resort has great interest in artificially retaining or increasing the amount of sand on its beach.

Groynes may be constructed to trap the sand and help build out the beach. The beach sand accumulates on the updrift side and is removed on the downdrift side leading to differences in height or size of beach on either side of the groyne. This may, however, create a potential danger for paddlers or swimmers stepping over the groyne into deep water.

A more drastic and expensive solution is to replenish the sand at the same rate, or faster than it is being removed. This is possible if there is a suitable source of sand, and the resort can afford the cost of the engineering work. Bournemouth beach has been reinforced by sand dredged up from Poole Harbour. In the storm wave environments at this latitude there is always the risk that winter storms will render such actions ineffective. The violent storms of February 1990 rearranged the sand at Bournemouth, eroding some and depositing the rest on coastal roads.

Elsewhere in the world, other tourist resorts have also tried to improve their beaches. In Magalluf, in Mallorca, for example, the resort was so popular that the beach was just not large enough for all the tourists. The local authority responded by importing sand and widening the beach. In the enclosed sea environment of the Mediterranean this is likely to be a more successful long-term investment. Thus, it is possible for engineers to modify and possibly improve the natural qualities of the beach and coast for tourism. The amount of public money spent to control pollution, stabilise or improve the beach depends on the investment decisions of the local authority (or other agency that is responsible for the infrastructure) and the extent to which they perceive the promotion of tourism to be in the public interest.

QUESTIONS AND DISCUSSION POINTS

1 What are the advantages and disadvantages of an enclosed sea location for coastal tourism?
2 In what ways is the build up of marine pollution a threat to coastal tourism? In what types of location is the danger greatest?
3 In which climate zones of the world are the best natural conditions for coastal tourism to be found? Where are these zones in relation to the main tourist generating regions of the world? (*See also* Chapters 1 and 2.)

ASSIGNMENTS

1 You work for a tour operator who specialises in sun, sea and sand tours to the Mediterranean region for the UK market. Your Chief Executive wishes to diversify into summer sun, sea and sand packages in *other* parts of the world and has asked you to select the regions of the world likely to provide the ideal combination of climatic and coastal conditions for this type of holiday.

Prepare a short report (illustrated with world maps) indicating those stretches of coast where these conditions are likely to coincide, and where your company might start to search for suitable sites to develop and promote.

2 You work in a travel agency. A customer arrives who is a surfing enthusiast, and he asks you to advise him where in the world the best surfing conditions are likely to occur, and when would be the best times of year to visit these places. Write notes for this customer, listing:

(*a*) the general world locations, where the best surfing conditions are likely to be found; and

(*b*) the months of the year when the climate is most suitable for beach activities in these places.

List the range of temperatures he might expect during this period. The customer wants this information for *each* of the regions of the world you have identified under (a).

Landscape resources for tourism

LEARNING OBJECTIVES

After studying this chapter you should be able to

- list the qualities that make a landscape attractive for tourism
- assess the attractiveness of a landscape for tourists
- locate the areas of the world that have the greatest potential for scenic tourism
- appreciate the role of world conservation bodies and national governments in the protection of scenic and wildlife resources for tourism
- understand the differences between the British and the world National Parks
- locate Britain's main landscape resources for tourism.

Introduction

Tourists visit the countryside for many reasons; their motivations may be much more complex and varied than those that generate coastal tourism.

1 Visitors may travel to rural areas to appreciate the natural wonders of the world – features such as great waterfalls (e.g. the Niagara Falls) volcanic phenomena (hot springs, sulphur pools, geysers such as Old Faithful in Wyoming, USA etc), geological phenomena such as caves or rock formations (e.g. Ayers Rock), or spectacular views (e.g. across the Grand Canyon).
2 People may use the countryside in order to pursue activities that require a rural setting or that depend on rurally located resources, rather than for the scenic quality of the rural backdrop. Activities such as sailing, canoeing, potholing, shooting, climbing, hang-gliding and skiing are examples of the latter where the quality of the resource is more significant than the landscape in

which it is set, whereas activities such as cycling, horse riding and walking perhaps depend more closely on high quality landscapes.
3 Touring holidays, where the travel is the focus of the experience rather than the destination, will also be best enjoyed in a region with a variety of attractive landscapes and picturesque villages.
4 On the other hand, people may wish to visit the countryside as a destination in its own right in order to experience a non-urban way of life for a period, as a relief from the congestion and pressures of the urban environment. This may be motivated by the wish to participate in a real or imagined rural lifestyle as exemplified by holidays on working farms or dude ranches in the USA.
5 Nature tourism is a specialised, though developing, market. With the increasing interest in environmental issues, and the experience of seeing television films of animals in the wild, people now wish to see wildlife in its natural habitat rather than in the zoo or safari park setting.

6 Finally, people may indeed visit the countryside purely for the pleasure of looking at, and being in attractive rural landscapes.

Landscape elements

There are three basic geographical elements that make up any landscape.

1 The landform and geology, which determine the shape of the land and its relief. The landform also determines the presence or absence of many of the features on which activity-based rural tourism depends (e.g. caves for potholing, rocky peaks for climbing, cliffs or scarps for hang-gliding, very steep slopes for skiing etc). The other important physical element of the landscape is the water which shapes and drains the landscape, in the form of rivers, lakes and inland seas.

2 The natural vegetation of the land, and the animals that depend on it. On a world scale, this ranges from the tropical rainforest of equatorial regions, to the grassy plains and savannas of Africa, through to the forests of the north which give way to the scrub and mossy plains of the open tundra and finally to the arctic ecosystems of the polar regions. The nature of vegetation and wildlife is obviously closely related to the pattern of world climates. The landform and vegetation when untouched by man create the natural landscape and wilderness areas of the world.

3 The third element of the landscape is the presence of man. Much of the natural vegetation has been greatly modified by man through agricultural and forestry practices. The landscapes that are created by human modification and exploitation of the natural vegetation can be called the 'land use' landscape. Buildings, roads, power lines and other man-made constructions add artificial elements to the land use landscape. Human interaction with the natural features of the land has created a variety of cultural landscapes across the world, from the detailed, intimate landscapes of enclosed fields and hedges in the English lowlands, or the terraced hillsides of Southeast Asia, to the vast open landscapes of the North American prairies.

In certain circumstances each of these three elements may individually dominate the landscape, e.g. in the dry deserts, the landform is the dominant element, while the city centre is dominated by the man-made landscape. In a tropical rainforest the natural vegetation masks all the other elements. In general, however, most landscape consist of combinations of the three elements, in fact the landscape itself is the product of the interaction between the three elements. The way in which the elements combine to create particularly attractive landscapes is hard to define. Attempts have been made to assess the appeal of landscapes for recreation and tourism but it is a difficult task since 'beauty is in the eye of the beholder'. It is evident that different people have different tastes and preferences depending on their background, culture, education and personal experiences. Nevertheless, studies of the perception of and preference for landscapes do seem to show that there are certain types of landscape that appeal widely to people of westernised cultural backgrounds.

Preferences for landform landscapes

Research on landscape preferences, and, indeed tourist behaviour, indicates that landscapes with

Fig 4.1 Relative relief vs absolute relief

high relative relief are the most dramatic and most attractive to visitors. Relative relief is the difference in height between the highest point (e.g. the top of a mountain, hill or plateau) and the lowest point of a landscape (be it a river valley, lake surface or lowland plain). Relative relief thus differs from absolute relief (that is, the height of land above sea level) as it is a measure of vertical scale and degree of dissection of a landscape, rather than its altitude (*see* Fig 4.1).

A landscape of high relative relief will be characterised for example, by deep valleys, or by cliffs and scraps (*see* Fig 4.2). High relative relief provides the opportunity for long or dramatic views. The presence of water in such a landscape always adds even more to its dramatic quality, perhaps because the water surface (by definition truly horizontal) provides a sharp contrast to the surrounding hill slopes, and reflections in still water (such as lake surfaces) appear to add depth to the view in another dimension.

The fjords along the coast of Norway are a classic example of this type of landscape where the mountains plunge thousands of metres into the sea; another world-famous landscape with a very high relative relief is the Grand Canyon where the River Colorado has cut a gorge over a mile deep into the flat plains of the Colorado desert. Landscapes of low relative relief, be they undulating lowland plains, or plateau surfaces tend to afford shorter views; truly flat landscapes (therefore, with zero relative relief) provide featureless vistas or long views interrupted only by trees or buildings, such landscapes tend to be perceived as boring, though of course in some parts of the world can provide very dramatic land and skyscapes (*see* Fig 4.3).

Landforms may be described and classified according to their relative relief. Linton's system (*see* Fig 4.4) provides a comprehensive classification, combining relative and absolute relief.

Fig 4.2 A landscape of high relative relief: Yosemite National Park, California

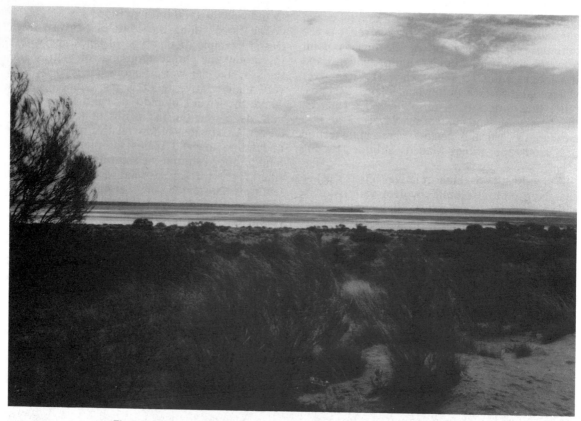

Fig 4.3 A landscape of very low relative relief: the salt plains of Australia

Lowlands	Areas below 500′ (150 m) in height
Rolling countryside	500–1500′ (150–450 m) with relative relief <400′ (120 m)
Upland plateau	1500′+ (450 m+) high with relative relief over 400′ (120 m)
Hill country	(a) 500–1500′ (150–450 m) high with relative relief over 400′ (120 m)
	(b) 500–2000′ (150–600 m) with relative relief 400–600′ (120–180 m)
Bold hills	(a) 2000′+ (600 m) in height with relative relief 400–800′ (120–250 m).
	(b) 1500–2000′ (450–600 m) with 600′+ (180 m+) relative relief.
High hills	Over 2000′ (600 m) high with over 800′ (250 m) relative relief.
Mountains	Over 2500′ with 2000′+ (600 m) relative relief.

Fig 4.4 Definitions of landform

This classification was adopted in a research project (by A Gilg of Exeter University) designed to discover people's preferences for different types of landform. A group of 50 geography students were shown a series of 38 photographs of landscapes representing the range of possible landforms. The students were invited to rate the pictures according to the strength of their preferences: the higher the score the greater the appeal of the landscape. Figure 4.5 shows the average score given to each type of landform, and clearly indicates a preference for landscapes of high relative relief.

	Average score of different landforms out of 95
Lowlands	37
Low uplands	46
Plateau uplands	47
Hill country	53
Bold hills	61
Mountains	75 – most attractive landform.

Fig 4.5 Preferences for landforms

Natural landscapes and their world distribution

Natural vegetation of the world

Throughout the world, trees will grow and dominate the vegetation wherever it is mild and wet enough to support them. The type of dominant tree species will vary with soils and climate. In more extreme climatic conditions, trees are replaced as dominant vegetation usually by smaller, tougher plants that can withstand long periods of very hot or very cold temperatures and can survive where water is rarely available (especially in hot deserts, or in freezing conditions). From the Equator to the Poles, there is a series of vegetation zones (corresponding roughly with the temperature zones shown in Fig 2.3 on page 20. A similar type of zonation vegetation is seen on mountain slopes, as the climatic changes with increasing altitude.

Generalised vegetation and climatic zones of the world

Hot climates

1 Equatorial tropical forest. Dense forest, very rich in species of both plants and animals. The climate is hot and wet, allowing for vigorous plant growth all year round.
2 Tropical savannah grasslands. Dominated by tall grasses but with some scrub and forest patches. The growth of trees is limited by the pronounced dry season. The grasslands support vast numbers of grazing animals and large carnivores that prey on them.
3 Hot deserts. Too hot and dry for even grasses to survive. No vegetation at all, or only scattered cactus or thorn scrub.

Warm temperate climates

1 Mediterranean scrub (known in different parts of the world as garigue, maquis, or chapparal).

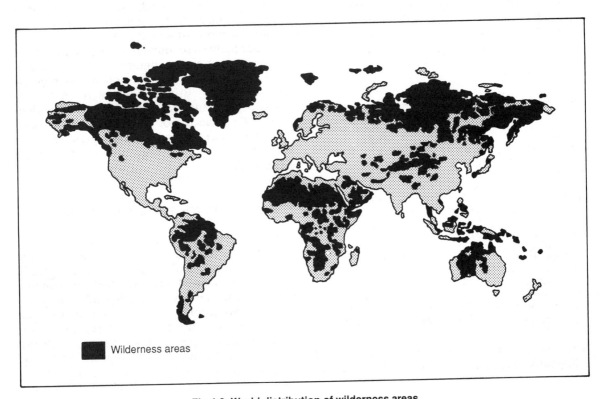

Wilderness areas

Fig 4.6 World distribution of wilderness areas

A mixture of drought-resistant, often evergreen trees and shrubs mixed with open areas of grass and herbs. Again, the prolonged summer drought limits tree growth.

2 Cool temperate climates

Temperate forests: forest lands of the wet but cooler regions. Often deciduous tree species.

3 Cold climates

Coniferous forests: needle-bearing trees adapted to withstand the cold and dry conditions of harsh winter seasons.

4 Arctic and polar climates

(*a*) Arctic and alpine tundra. Temperatures and growing season, too low for tree growth. This type of vegetation is dominated by grasses, herbs, moss and lichens.

(*b*) Cold deserts of polar regions. No vegetation.

In many parts of the world particularly where the climate is suitable for agricultural production, the natural vegetation has been replaced by agricultural plant species and thus the natural landscape replaced by a man-made landscape.

Figure 4.6 shows the areas of the world where the vegetation and natural ecosystems have been largely untouched by man, and, therefore, shows the parts of the world where wild landscapes still exist. The majority of these (over 60 per cent) are open, treeless tundra and hot desert areas (*see* Fig 4.7).

Vegetation type	% of total world wilderness
Tundra	41.7
Warm deserts/semi deserts	19.4
Temperate needle leaf forests	18.3
Tropical forests	9.3
Mixed mountain systems	4.1
Cold winter deserts	3.1
Tropical grassland/savannahs	1.5
Temperate forests (rainforest and deciduous)	1.5
Temperate grasslands	0.6
Evergreen forests (Mediterranean type)	0.4
Island systems	0.2
	100% = 48 069 951 km²

Fig 4.7 Percentage of wilderness left (1988)

The vast majority (nearly 80 per cent) of this wilderness lies in only ten countries (*see* Fig 4.8).

	Million km²
1 Antartica	13.2
2 Soviet Union	7.5
3 Canada	6.4
4 Australia	2.2
5 Greenland	2.1
6 China	2.1
7 Brazil	2.0
8 Algeria	1.4
9 Sudan	0.7
10 Mauritania	0.7

Fig 4.8 Distribution of wilderness areas

Preference for natural landscapes

Although vegetation has often been shown to be a significant factor in shaping landscape preferences few landscape research projects have explicitly investigated the strength of preferences for different types of natural vegetation cover. The preference study already referred to on page 42 grouped all non-forested wild landscapes together, and these averaged a preference score of only 50 out of 95 though when wild landscapes were combined with mountain terrain they became far more attractive. Forest landscapes on the other hand were found to be highly attractive, irrespective of the topography. This finding is supported by research done on a wider cross-section of the British population (not only students but adults, recreationists etc) who when offered the chance, not only picked out forested landscapes but overwhelmingly preferred oak woodland, the natural vegetation of most of the British Isles.

Preference for the land use landscape

Through agriculture and other forms of resource exploitation and development, much of the world's natural landscapes have been greatly modified by man. Preference for the resulting land use landscapes may well depend on people's cultural backgrounds and the type of managed landscapes that they are used to seeing in their everyday life. Gilg's study was limited to British students responding to European (including Britain) landscapes but for what it is worth it shows clearly that varied landscapes (be they varied forest and moorland or varied farmland) were liked better than urban landscapes or treeless farmland (*see* Fig 4.9).

Landscape type	Average score for different landuses out of 95 (NB the higher the score, the greater the preference)
Urban/industrial	39
Treeless farmland	42
Wild landscapes	50
Moorland (a semi natural but man-created landscape)	51
Varied forest/moor	54
Varied farmland	59
Forest	69

Fig 4.9 Preference for natural or landuse landscapes

To summarise, according to Gilg's study, mountains or any landscape with high relative relief, particularly when combined with wild landscapes or forests appear to be the most attractive, and any water feature adds to a landscape's appeal.

The conservation and promotion of tourism in wild landscapes

The next section will discuss the ways in which attractive landscapes are defined, managed and conserved, and how they are made available for tourism. The United Nations and the International Union for the Conservation of Nature and Natural Resources (IUCN) have played leading roles in promoting the management and conservation of landscapes throughout the countries of the world.

World Heritage Sites

In 1972 UNESCO set up the World Heritage Convention, designed to protect the most outstanding examples of the world's cultural and natural heritage. The Convention came into force in 1975 and by 1983 76 member states accepted the Convention and agreed to identify, conserve and protect world heritage sites. Member states also contribute to a fund whereby the poorer nations of the world can be financially aided to protect their world heritage sites.

Natural landscapes that have been accepted nationally and internationally as world heritage sites include the Galapagos Islands (with their unique fauna) the Ngorongoro conservation area in Tanzania (a dramatic extinct volcanic crater where African savannah wildlife now abounds) the Tai National Park in the Ivory Coast (one of the last vestiges of West African tropical rainforest) the Kakadu National Park in the wetlands of north Australia, the Grand Canyon of Colorado, USA, and the Nahanni National Park in northern Canada which is characterised by turbulent rivers and hot sulphur springs.

Biosphere reserves

The International Union for the Conservation of Nature and Natural Resources also aims to encourage nations to conserve their wildlife and landscapes. The IUCN advises that countries should establish a range of types of protected areas; these may vary in 'naturalness' from untouched areas of undisturbed wildlife that should be protected from any disruption by humans ('strict nature reserves') or 'National Parks' where natural habitats should be protected from all forms of exploitation other than tourism, through to 'protected landscapes' which may include landuse landscapes considerably modified by man. The two categories of protected area that have most significance as tourist resources are the IUCN's National Parks and protected landscapes. The IUCN collects world data on the National Parks of the world, on behalf of the United Nations. Figure 4.10 shows the world distribution of conserved landscapes.

International National Parks

In order to be included in the UN list of National Parks and equivalent reserves, National Parks should enjoy legal protection against all human exploitation of its natural resources. Agriculture, hunting, fishing, forestry, mining or water gathering would all be prohibited; and no residential, commercial or industrial development, road or railway construction would be allowed. The only exception would be tourism, since tourism is one of the major reasons for the existence of the Park, so road construction, hotel

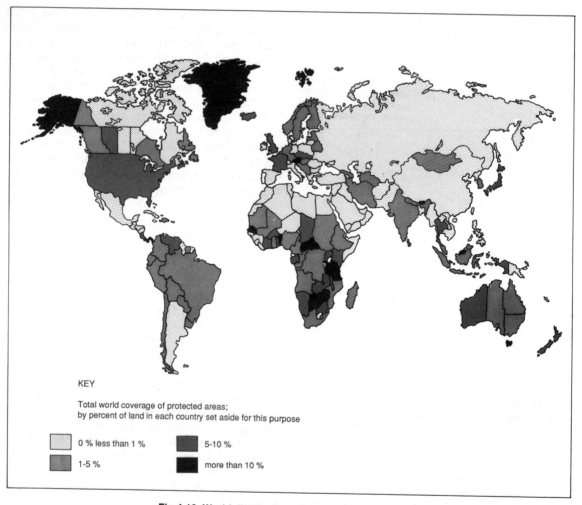

Fig 4.10 World distribution of conserved landscapes

building, provision of camp sites, interpretation centres and other services and infrastructure for tourism are allowed in internationally recognised National Parks. However, most Parks are zoned for different levels of tourist use: some areas are accessible for mass tourism; and some areas are accessible only to visitors on horseback or on foot. The National Park should be free of all resident population other than those needed to administer the Park and manage its tourism.

Although many countries of the world have designated National Parks, two regions (the USA and the Central African countries of Kenya, Uganda and Tanzania) are particularly noted for their Parks and the tourist activity associated with them.

Case study: National Parks in USA

The USA began the world National Park movement by being the first to designate a National Park, the Yellowstone National Park in 1872. A hundred years later, the USA had 38 National Parks, covering about 5.8 million hectares. The Parks cover a wide variety of types of landscape and natural features, ranging from the forested mountain landscapes of Yellowstone in Wyoming, the snowy peaks of Mount McKinley in Alaska, the active volcanoes of the Hawaiian National Park, to the low-lying tropical swamps of the Everglades in Florida. American National Parks may also be focused on particular landscapes elements such as the Sequoia and Redwood

National Parks in California that include stands of the giant trees (the biggest trees in the world), or the Carlsbad caverns in New Mexico, again the largest known cave system in the world.

The US National Parks system is extensively used for tourism with 287 million visits in 1987. Most parks contain accommodation and camp sites, though the location of tourist development is controlled and parts of the National Parks are set aside as 'Wilderness Areas' where no tourist vehicles are allowed and where the intensity of tourist use is deliberately kept very low.

In a developed and affluent economy such as the USA, the legal powers and financial resources are available to maintain the natural habitats of the National Parks in a relatively undisturbed form. In such a large country the pressures for the economic use of the land can be diverted to other parts of the territory. The main problem is the product of their success and popularity – the control and management of tourist pressures on the environment.

Case study: the East African National Parks

The African National Parks are far greater in size even than those in the United States. The National Parks south of the Sahara in Africa together cover an area of 53.6 million hectares (an area only slightly smaller than the whole of France). The abundant, and (for tourists) easily visible wildlife of the open savannah grasslands is the main reason for the Parks' designation and their main tourist attraction. Vast herds of wildebeeste, zebra and antelope mix with elephants, giraffe and buffalo. Groups of lions appear to be quite tolerant of the approach of tourists in vehicle convoys, although the weight of tourist numbers may be beginning to affect the wildlife. The threat to the African National Parks is not so much one of controlling tourism, but of managing the whole ecosystem so that the numbers of animals are maintained, and of controlling the illegal poaching of the animals (for meat, ivory, horn or skins) by the native population in response to national and international demands for these products. The occurrence of poaching directly reflects the national and international demands for these products.

Poaching in some areas has caused drastic reductions in animal populations – see Fig 4.11.

	1969	1973	1979	1980
Kabelega Falls NP (Uganda)				
Elephant	—	14 000	—	200
Ruwenzori NP (Uganda)				
Elephant	3 000	153	—	—
Buffalo	18 000	4 200	—	—
Kenya as a whole				
Black rhinos	1 800	—	1 500	—
Elephant	167 000	—	60 000	—

Fig 4.11 Loss of wildlife in East Africa 1969–1980

Illegal hunting tends to increase during periods of national and international disturbances which have characterised this part of Africa since 1964. The presence of sophisticated firearms and plentiful ammunition, plus the disruption to both local food supplies and to wildlife protection systems (generated by civil or international instability) all encourage the destruction of the animals. Another threat to the integrity of the National Parks in Africa comes from the pressure for economic developments. The economic benefits from wildlife-based tourism may in the end not be sufficient to contain the pressure for economic development (e.g. for farming or water gathering).

Thus the effectiveness of National Park designation varies from country to country although the framework for protection exists.

To summarise, international National Parks are defined by the following criteria:

1 They are authorised by the central government of the country concerned; in many countries the land of the Park is nationally owned.
2 They have legal protection from economic exploitation, backed up by having a minimum level of staff to implement the protection and conservation of the landscape and wildlife, and a defined annual budget allocated for the same purpose.
3 The national government allows or itself organises and promotes tourism within the National Park.

Protected landscapes

According to IUCN, the purpose of designating areas as protected landscapes is 'to maintain nationally significant, natural landscapes which are characteristic of the harmonious interaction of man and land, while providing opportunities for public enjoyment through recreation and tourism within the normal lifestyle and economic activity of these areas'.

Thus, in contrast to international National Parks, protected landscapes include landuse landscapes: the cultural landscapes that have evolved over time as a result of human activity over a period of thousands of years.

Many countries of the world have developed different hierarchies of protected landscapes (excluding the areas internationally recognised as National Parks). For example, Australia has a system that ranges from State Recreation Areas, through Nature Parks, Environmental Parks, Parks, to State Parks. The USA's protected landscapes include designations such as National Reserves, National Wildlife Refuges, Parks, National Historic Parks, to National Recreation Areas and other areas.

As virtually all of Britain's landscape has been much artificially modified, all the designated landscape areas are classified internationally as protected landscape, even the National Parks of England and Wales. These National Parks are not recognised as full international National Parks as they do not meet any of the international criteria set out.

The British National Parks are not nationally owned; the landscapes are extensively exploited for economic purposes and agriculture is explicitly encouraged; visitors do not have legal rights of access over the whole of the Parks – indeed, there may be policies for the constraint of recreation and tourism rather than for its promotion. England and Wales has ten National Parks and two Equivalent Areas (the New Forest and the Norfolk Broads). The corresponding landscape designation in Scotland are the National Scenic Areas: areas of national scenic significance

which are considered to be of unsurpassed attractiveness and which must be conserved as part of the national heritage. The second level designation is the Area of Outstanding Natural Beauty (AONB). These are parts of the countryside of England and Wales which, while they lack extensive areas of open country (suitable for recreation) are nonetheless of such·fine scenery that there is a national as well as local interest in keeping them so. In spite of the relative lack of opportunity for outdoor recreation, the AONBs are still the focus of much tourist activity. AONBs are also designated in Northern Ireland but there is no equivalent category in Scotland.

Stretches of attractive and undeveloped coastline may be designated as Heritage Coasts in England and Wales. In these areas there are often conflicts of interest between the conservation of the coastal landscape and its development for tourism.

Finally, certain areas whose characteristic landscape depends entirely on the maintenance of a particular traditional form of agricultural practice, are designated as Environmentally Sensitive Areas. These cover less than two per cent of the surface of England and Wales.

Figure 4.13 shows the distribution of protected landscapes and therefore the main landscape resources for tourism within Britain. The ten National Parks and the Scottish National Scenic areas are concentrated in the Upland and mountain areas of the North and West of Britain, reflecting people's preferences for landscapes of high relative relief. The two other areas of England and Wales equivalent to National Parks are landscapes where elements other than landform are dominant. The New Forest is a lowland area of mixed moorland and varied coniferous and deciduous forest, whereas the Norfolk Broads, is a series of shallow lakes and extensive navigable waterways. It is a major

Designation	Number	Area (km²)	
National Parks	10	13 745	(9% of England and Wales)
Equivalent Areas	2	662	
National Scenic Areas (Scotland)	40	10 018	(12.9% of Scotland)
AONBs (England & Wales)	37	1 708	(11.3% of England and Wales)
AONBs (N Ireland)	9	2 803	
Heritage Coasts	40	1 370	(31.05% of coastline of England and Wales)

Fig 4.12 UK areas of protected landscapes (May 1987)

KEY

National Parks (England and Wales) and National Scenic Areas (Scotland)

National Park - Equivalent Areas

Areas of Outstanding Natural Beauty

Heritage Coast

SCOTLAND

NORTHERN IRELAND

ENGLAND

1   Northumberland
2   Lake District
3   Yorkshire Dales
4   North York Moors
5   Peak District
6   Snowdonia
7   Brecon Beacons
8   Pembrokeshire Coast
9   Exmoor
10 Dartmoor
11 New Forest
12 Norfolk Broads

0   100km   N

Scale

Fig 4.13 UK protected landscapes

centre for water recreation and tourism based on boating.

The Heritage Coasts are clustered on the south and west coast. The majority of the Heritage Coasts are dramatic cliffed coastlines, again reflecting preferences for landscapes of high relative relief and the presence of water as a major feature in the landscape. The Areas of Outstanding Natural Beauty are also mostly located in the south and west of England (i.e. south and west of a line drawn from the Dee to the Thames). This leaves the heavily populated and industrialised centre and eastern quadrant of England relatively undersupplied with high quality landscape resources.

QUESTIONS AND DISCUSSION POINTS

1 To what extent is tourism a threat or a benefit to the international National Parks?
2 Why are British National Parks ineligible for recognition as international National Parks?
3 What features make the landscape shown in the photograph below attractive for scenic and wildlife tourism?

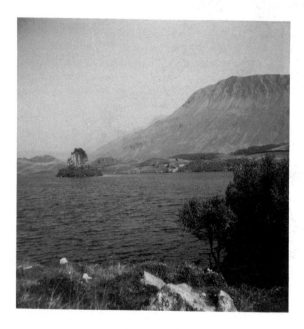

ASSIGNMENTS

1 Select a tour company brochure selling scenic holiday tours (e.g. a 'lakes and mountains' brochure). Analyse the content of the photographs of landscapes in the brochure. What landform, landuse, and natural vegetation features do the photographs depict? How effective are these pictures likely to be in selling the holidays?

   You have been asked to redesign and update the brochure for next season. Would you suggest any changes to the illustrations? If so, what changes would you recommend?

2 A group of American tour operators (specialising in tours for Americans to American National Parks) have arrived in Britain for a study tour of the British National Parks. You are a tourism officer employed by one of the British National Park authorities. You have been invited to give a welcoming speech to the party and show them something of your National Park. The brief you have been given for your speech is:

   (a) to explain the British system of landscape and wildlife protection to the party; and

   (b) to outline the tourism potential, tourism policies and tourist development in British National Parks. (You may use your own park as an example where appropriate.)

   Draw the party's attention to the similarities and differences between the British and American National Park systems.

   Write notes for your speech. (You may decide yourself which National Park Authority you work in. Reference should be made to the appropriate National Park plan, where available.)

CHAPTER 5

Historic and cultural resources

LEARNING OBJECTIVES

After studying this chapter you should be able to

- define a historic or cultural resource
- explain why tourists are attracted to historic and cultural resources
- understand the processes by which historic resources have survived, and some of the problems facing the organisations who are responsible for maintaining them for future tourist use
- locate the major world concentrations of historic resources
- appreciate the importance of modern cultures as tourist resources.

Introduction

Culture may be defined as 'improvement by mental or physical training'; in other words it denotes intellectual development. Thus, the cultural resources of a nation, race or religion are of two basic types.

1 The physical expression of intellectual development: the art, architecture, literature and even artificially created landscapes and townscapes, created by a race or nation now or in the past. Historic resources are the surviving physical remnants from past civilisations. Places associated with significant historical, religious or mythical events may also be regarded as cultural resources even though the place may have physically changed out of all recognition or have no architectural evidence of past events.

2 The living expressions of existing cultures: the performing arts (music, dance, drama), clothes, social habits, traditions and customs, the cuisine and language, the religion and religious rites that form the way of life of the different peoples of the world today. All these, of course, are a result of the history and development of those people.

Both these two types of resource are of great importance for tourism.

Historic resources

Tourists find these resources attractive for several reasons.

1 Tourists may simply be attracted by the **age** of ancient relics of past civilisations and at the technological achievements of those ancient cultures. This is a particularly important factor for North American visitors to Western Europe. The first sustained European colonisation of America dates only from about the beginning of the 16th century, so these ex-European colonies are obviously without physical traces of West European culture from before this date. Americans must, therefore, come to Europe in order to experience the cities and buildings of their own cultural background dating from before 1500 AD.

Many people, apart from the North Americans go to marvel at the extreme age of buildings and artefacts, and the technical ability and physical skills of the people that constructed them without the aid of any modern machinery, whether it be Stonehenge, the Egyptian pyramids (built about 4500 years ago) or the 15th and 16th century cities of the Incas in which the stones were cut with such accuracy that the walls needed no cement.

2 Tourists of varying cultural backgrounds may enjoy visiting historic sites purely for the appreciation of the **beauty** of the art and architecture. For example, it is the beauty of the Greek temple at Sounion, set on a dramatic promontory that attracts visitors to it in preference to the many other temples accessible from Athens. Similarly, the Taj Mahal in India, named by many as the most beautiful building in the world, attracts increasing numbers of both Indian and international visitors.

3 Visitors may be attracted to buildings and places for their **historic meaning** rather than their visual appeal. The Viking excavations in York reveal fascinating details of the social life of the ninth century inhabitants which can stimulate the imagination of the visitors to the sites. Similarly, places associated with great historical or mythical exploits and events can be of great interest; visiting Mycenae in Greece with its association with Agamemnon and the Trojan wars adds an extra dimension to the reading of the stories of Odysseus in Homer's Iliad.

In Britain, Stratford-upon-Avon is visited for its association with Shakespeare rather than for its aesthetic qualities. Places such as Runnymede or the battlefields of Flanders in Belgium may hold the tourists' interest simply because they are the locations of events of great political significance.

Similarly, places may hold great religious meaning.

How do historic features survive?

There are certain geographical factors which enable ancient buildings to survive.

Protection from atmospheric weathering

The stonework of ancient buildings is subject to the same process of weathering as the rocks which break down to form the sand and pebbles of the beach (see Chapter 3). Buildings from the past will only survive if this process of weathering is slow. The dry, unpolluted air of the desert has had little effect in weathering the granite monuments in Egypt, although even here, more weathering can be observed on the monuments near Cairo where there is some slight rainfall than the statues in the drier parts of Egypt. Even limestone and marble rock which is very susceptible to weathering in a mild, damp climate such as the British Isles may survive undamaged for thousands of years in a dry Mediterranean climate such as Athens. Many of the stone carvings on British cathedrals dating from the 15th century have needed considerable restoration in recent years, whereas the sculpture on the frieze of the Acropolis were still in excellent condition after thousands of years when removed by Lord Elgin to Britain in the 19th century.

More recently, however, air pollution caused by an increase in sulphur dioxide in the atmosphere has accelerated these processes of weathering in both Britain and Greece. In 1975 UNESCO concluded that air pollution had already had a significant detrimental influence on the buildings and monuments of the Acropolis and in 1977/8 some controls on the use of high sulphur domestic fuels were introduced in Athens in an attempt to reduce the level of sulphur dioxide in the air. In spite of these efforts, considerable restoration work has been necessary. The industrialisation and spread of atmospheric pollution to the hitherto undeveloped countries of the Middle East and Central Asia are a substantial threat to the survival of existing and potential historic tourist attractions in these areas.

Archaeological and historic remains may be protected from atmospheric weathering by being covered with the accumulated dust and vegetation of the years. Their preservation depends on the presence or absence of oxygen.

In temperate latitudes, archaeological remains are protected and preserved by being buried under the fragments of rock and soil created by erosion and weathering and deposited by soil creep and rainwash. In Britain, Roman villas dating from before 450 AD have been excavated from beneath nearly two metres of rock waste (representing an accumulation of about 0.3 m per 200 years). As oxygen is present in the soil all but the stonework has decayed.

In totally oxygen-free environments, such as in acid bogs, or on the sea bed, wood, leather and metal may not decay. This may allow the recovery of well-preserved objects such as the Mary Rose, the flagship of Henry VIII, which, when subsequently preserved and restored using modern technology, became a major tourist attraction.

Changes in settlement patterns

Settlements are located at particular sites for many reasons. For example, towns may be located at sites that were easy to defend, or they may be market centres for rich agricultural regions; they may be sited close to highly localised physical resources (e.g. water for power, sandy beaches for tourism, minerals for industrial use etc.) or they may develop at crucial points along routeways such as ports or river crossings. Settlements that retain this function continue to grow and thrive and the old buildings at their original core are renewed and replaced as technological demands change. If, however, there is a change in these geographical factors (e.g. if a river on which a port is situated silts up) the settlement may be bypassed by more modern development rather than being rebuilt.

Thus, the original street layout and many of the original buildings may not be destroyed by more modern development, though if the site is abandoned completely then the fabric of the buildings will decay and their condition will depend on their age and on the weathering factors mentioned above. The seven cities of Delhi were built by successive Moghul rulers between 1193 and 1648 and each abandoned as a new seat of government was built. The ramparts of the oldest city are incomplete whereas the last two cities, dating from about 1540 and 1640 have most of their buildings intact. Most of the seven cities have now been surrounded by modern development as the suburbs of Delhi spread out, but the sites themselves remain untouched.

Barely a hundred years after the last city of Delhi was being built in India, the industrial revolution was underway in Britain. The early industrial developments in the Ironbridge Gorge in Shropshire were sited there because industry depended on water for both power and transport at the time. However, the discoveries of Abraham Derby at his iron works in Coalbrookdale in the 1760s changed the whole basis of industry and the subsequent industrial developments took place on the major coalfields. This left the Ironbridge sites abandoned until the recent interest of historians in industrial archaeology led to their excavation and the interest of tourists led to its restoration and development as a tourist attraction. Many of the major historic towns of Britain were also bypassed by the industrial revolution. Towns such as York, Winchester, Norwich and Wells had important commercial, ecclesiastical or administrative functions in medieval times but have retained much of their medieval character, since, while they retained a local significance as a market centre, they were located well away from the centres of growth during the industrial revolution. Chester, sited at a critical crossing point of the Dee, was originally an important port in Roman and medieval times but was replaced by Liverpool as the major port for the northwest of England as the River Dee progressively silted up. Modern industrial development thus bypassed Chester and its centre survived much 20th century redevelopment. A similar pattern of events occurred at Bruges (a major commercial centre of the medieval world) which was overtaken as a port by cities such as Antwerp. In this way Bruges has retained much of its medieval character. These historic towns were not industrialised but over the centuries they still retained some economic functions as a local administrative or market centre so that the buildings retained some economic use and were, therefore, occupied and maintained in good repair rather than being abandoned to decay. However, in the 20th century a major problem facing these historic tourist centres is finding new economic uses for the buildings in order to pay for the escalating cost of the upkeep of the ageing buildings. The small scale of the buildings and the tortuous medieval street patterns with difficult access make them unattractive for many modern office, commercial or even residential uses. Their medieval character and inaccessibility, which form their major tourist attraction, make them totally uneconomic locations for any other activity other than residential use or tourism.

Venice is facing this problem today; although the major palaces on the Grand Canal are reasonably well maintained, many of the other buildings (which individually may not be of outstanding architectural significance but together make up the distinctive character of the city) are empty and decaying. The problems of subsidence and flooding make the whole situation worse as it raises the cost of maintenance.

Retaining and continuing traditional uses

In contrast to the problems discussed above, some buildings have survived relatively intact because they have retained their original use, and have been maintained but little modified through the centuries. The ancient universities of Oxford and Cambridge, the great cathedrals and churches and some of the historic country houses which are family homes in the English countryside are examples of this in Britain.

Major world distribution of historic features

Early civilisation

Modern tourists are fascinated by relics associated with early man. Some of the earliest human fossils (1½ million years old) were found in the Olduvai Gorge (south of Lake Victoria in Tanzania, East Africa) but early man quickly spread to many parts of the world.

The first urban civilisations, that have left remnants of buildings for posterity, date from the period 3500–1500 BC. It is believed that urban civilisation started in the arid but fertile alluvial valleys of the Tigris and Euphrates, a region known as Mesopotamia that is now part of modern Iraq.

The Iran-Iraq war of the 1980s and the crisis in the Gulf in 1990 has inhibited any tourist development of these sites. However, there was a series of scattered civilisations (*see* Fig 5.1) that

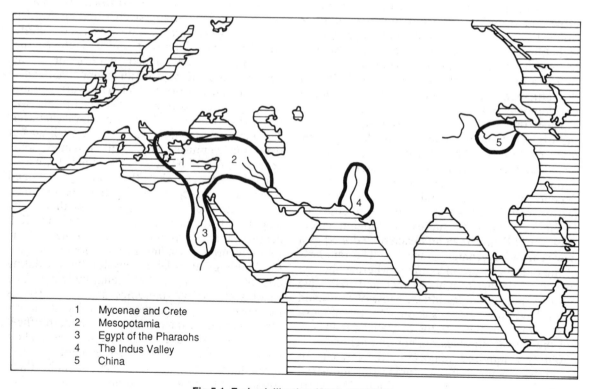

1	Mycenae and Crete
2	Mesopotamia
3	Egypt of the Pharaohs
4	The Indus Valley
5	China

Fig 5.1 Early civilisation (3500–1500 BC)

flourished in similar environments at about the same time, some of which have been exploited as tourist attractions. To the west of Mesopotamia the main centres were along the Nile valley (the Egyptian pharaohs in 3000–1000 BC) and circled round the Aegean Sea (Mycenae, Crete and Troy).

The archaeological sites of this period which lie to the east of Mesopotamia have not been fully developed for tourism due to modern political instability or restrictions. Notable ancient civilisations are located in the Indus valley (in modern Pakistan) and in northern China.

The classical world

The civilisations of this era spread, developed, evolved and were replaced, until in the period 1000 BC to AD 500 there was a more or less unbroken chain of empires which made up the 'classical world' (*see* Figs 5.2 and 5.3). This formed a zone of civilised life in Europe and Asia from the Mediterranean to the Pacific coast of China, some of which is roughly bounded by the Tropic of Cancer (23.5° N) and 40° N. Particular regions within this zone came to prominence at different times during the 1500 year period.

Each had its own particular style of architecture and many of the great historic monuments of the Mediterranean and Middle East date from these centuries. In general, the surviving buildings are built on a lavish scale and consist of public buildings, temples, palaces and tombs of kings and leaders, all expressions of the civilisation's wealth and power, and illustrating the peaks of artistic skills and technical achievements.

The smaller scale, less substantial buildings of the ordinary citizens rarely survive intact in other than exceptional circumstances as occurred at Pompeii where the entire Roman town was engulfed in and preserved by the lava and ash from the volcano, Vesuvius. The greatest

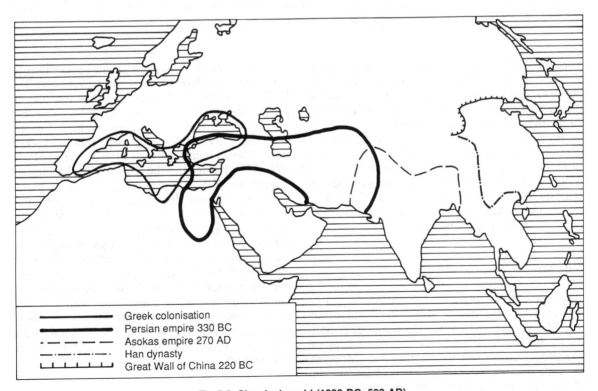

Greek colonisation
Persian empire 330 BC
Asokas empire 270 AD
Han dynasty
Great Wall of China 220 BC

Fig 5.2 Classical world (1000 BC–500 AD)

Fig 5.3 Roman world (1000 BC–500 AD)

concentrations of historic remains are inevitably centred on the core of each empire. Thus, the Aegean region is rich in Greek buildings, Iran in Persian buildings, and Italy in Roman constructions, though examples are found throughout the territory of each empire. For example, notable Roman ruins are seen in even the farthest flung corners of the Roman world such as Hadrian's Wall in Northumberland, and the coliseum in Tunisia, North Africa. Similarly, the Great Wall of China was built during the period 300–100 BC, at the northernmost limits of the Han empire.

The age of migrations

The classical world, with civilisations based on stable, urban communities came to an end around the fifth century AD, when the nomadic peoples from the north of Asia (e.g. tribes such as the Angles, Saxons, Huns, Goths and Mongols) became dominant over wide areas of Europe and Asia. The rural and nomadic way of life of these peoples left few major built monuments for posterity. The only areas of urban civilisations to withstand or adapt to these invasions were the Byzantine empire (which covered the territory of present-day Greece and Turkey) and the Chinese kingdoms which were eventually reunified in the sixth and seventh centuries with the emergence of the Tang Dynasty, which survived from 618 to 907 AD. However, the period of the age of migrations also saw the spread of two major religions that now dominate the culture of much of the present-day world: Christianity (from first century AD) and Islam from 632 AD. As these religions spread from their origin in Israel and Saudi Arabia, substantial buildings such as churches, monasteries, and mosques were constructed (*see* Fig 5.4). Again, the best of each culture's artistic and technical skills were invested in the buildings, many of which attract tourists to them purely for their beauty, in addition to those who visit them for religious purposes and on pilgrimages.

V ——— Viking influence c. 850 AD
H ·—·—· Hindu empire c. 640 AD
– – – – Christendom c. 600 AD
■■■■■ Islamic world c. 750 AD
— — — Tang dynasty 750 AD

Fig 5.4 Civilisations 500–900 AD

The recovery of Europe

Medieval times

From about 950 AD there was a re-establishment of urban-based civilisations in Europe, which developed in parallel with economic change, population growth and the creation of wealth by trade. The period was typified by the use of the small rival city states, for example in Italy, dominated by cities such as Florence, Naples and Milan and by the rich merchant cities such as Venice, Genoa, Pisa and Dubrovnic.

Further north in Europe too, a similar form of political and economic organisation developed which created the wealth of historic city centres that tourists now can enjoy. On the western and northernmost fringes of Europe, however, society was characterised by the establishment of feudal monarchies and the major heritage of this period is the scattering of defensive strongholds and castles built by the conquering feudal rulers in the nation states of England, France, Portugal, Scandinavia and Spain.

14th–16th centuries

The Renaissance, a period spanning the 14th to the 16th centuries, was a time when the great wealth generated by trade allowed the aristocracy and the rich merchants to become patrons of the arts. Their wealth was expressed in the architecture and art of the cities, much of which have survived intact, particularly in those cities bypassed by the subsequent development of the industrial revolution in Europe from the 17th century onwards. The most outstanding examples are, of course, the buildings and the art in the churches and galleries of Florence and Venice.

17th century to the present

Once again, the outstanding architectural features of more recent years tend to be the religious buildings or homes of the rich and powerful, who built themselves new homes and palaces on a grand scale using the best architects and designers of the period. On the other hand, few settlements retain the essence of the character of the times, because (apart from Victorian cities developed in new locations during the industrial revolution) the overall settlement pattern stabilised, and sites have been continuously occupied. Thus, towns grew organically with a mixture of buildings of different dates and styles, with new development replacing or modernising the older buildings. However, there are major exceptions, for example, the towns based on the early development of the tourist trade, which sprang up in hitherto undeveloped locations, such as the spa town of Bath, and many Georgian and Victorian seaside resorts which characterise the style and taste of their period. Similarly the ghost towns of the new world which sprang up very rapidly with the development of particular economic resources (e.g. in the California gold rush) and were completely abandoned once they become obsolete, for example, as resource was worked out or lost its value or economic relevance. In California, most of the 19th century gold rush town remains deserted ruins but some have been preserved as tourist attractions (such as Old Sacramento and Columbia State Historic Park).

There has been a growing interest in the history and architecture of the industrial revolution, and many of the northern industrial towns of Britain have begun to preserve, renovate and market their industrial heritage for tourism, e.g. Gladstone Pottery Museum in Stoke-on-Trent, the Black Country Museum in Dudley, and the promotion of the whole city of Bradford; industrial conservation and tourism has also been built into many of the dockland redevelopment schemes in Britain, for example the Arnolfini, the SS Great Britain and the Watershed (all in Bristol) the maritime museums and other attractions in Cardiff and in Swansea.

Historic resources of the New World

Many peoples of the New World (i.e. outside Europe and Asia) have very ancient origins. It is maintained that the Aborigines of Australia represent the oldest unbroken culture of the world of about 40 000 years. But many of these peoples of the new world were nomadic hunter/gatherers, living in small groups in ecological equilibrium with their environment. Thus, these cultures, in spite of their immense age, leave few buildings or monuments as historical resources.

However, the more urban-based civilisations of Central America were one exception. The ancient Mayan culture was at its peak around AD 300 but extended on to between 800 and 900 AD. Their major centres are located mainly in present-day Mexico, but their influence also extended into Guatemala and Honduras.

In later years the urban civilisations of the Toltecs around the 11th and 12th centuries and the Aztecs from the 13th century dominated Mexico, while in the central Andes during the 15th century the Inca empire extended over a region 320 km wide and 3200 km long, covering parts of present-day Ecuador, Peru, Bolivia and the northern parts of both Chile and Argentina.

The world distribution of historic resources is thus very patchy. The greatest wealth of historic resources exists in the western Mediterranean from Italy, through the Aegean to the Middle East. These regions retain well preserved remnants of the most ancient civilisations, which are complemented by rich examples of the art and architecture of later periods of history too. China can also boast a similar wealth of historic resources.

Some of these regions have the wealth and political stability to both protect and develop their historic resources for the benefit of the tourist. In the other areas, however, political instability not only inhibits the development of tourism but also more critically it may threaten the very survival of the historic features themselves.

Many historic sites and cultural properties are included on the list of World Heritage Sites and enjoy the same support and protection as the natural landscapes referred to in Chapter 4. Examples are drawn from every historic period from the archaeological ruins at Moenjodaro in the Indus valley in Pakistan, the Egyptian pyramids, the rock-hewn churches in Lalibela in Ethiopia, the Maya site of Copan in Honduras, Chartres Cathedral, the historic centre of Florence through to the Auschwitz concentration camp which was run by Nazi Germany in Poland during World War II.

Living cultural resources

World pattern of cultures

It is clear that much of Western Europe has a similar historic background, shares a religion, has a common basis for language (dating from the Latin of the ancient Roman empire) and a similar political way of life. This relative unity is, however, made up of a myriad of regional differences – regional both in terms of the differentiation between the countries of Western Europe and in terms of more local differences within countries. These variations in language and dialect, in cuisine, dress and customs and traditional events have led in recent years to a much greater consciousness of regional, ethnic and provincial identity (leading sometimes to political expressions of regional independence, for example, the Basque separatist movement in Spain and, to some extent, the Welsh and Scottish Nationalists in Britain). These regional variations are of great significance for tourism. Travellers within Europe find such variations attractive in that they are novel and interestingly different from their own regional culture, but reassuringly similar in that the basic way of life, manners, customs and style of life is the same as their own. Tourists can thus be assured that the local cuisine or customs will not be offensive or repellent, neither will the tourists' normal behaviour be liable to misinterpretation by the local residents.

Outside Europe there are much wider variations in culture. In the areas of European colonisation of the New World many of the indigenous nomadic races and their cultures have been more of less wiped out so that very little of their authentic culture remains. This is very much the case in North America and Australia. Similarly other parts of South America, Africa and the South Pacific have had Western values superimposed so that indigenous cultures have been stifled, suppressed or so undervalued that much has been lost, and what remains is in danger of being trivialised for the benefit of the tourist.

On the other hand, the Eastern cultures of the Islamic, Hindu and Buddhist worlds are less influenced by westernisation. Indeed, some countries such as Burma are still virtually closed to the outside world, and some have only recently been opened to Western influence. Travel in and out of Japan has only really developed since the 1960s and China's disrupted 'open door' policy dates only from the 1980s. These cultures, founded on the three main types of religion, are based on very different beliefs, traditions and codes of behaviour, which may inhibit tourism development. Strict adherents to Islam, for example, will not consume alcohol and will expect women to both dress and behave modestly in public. Thus, the Islamic fundamentalist states (e.g. Libya, Iran and Saudi Arabia) do not welcome Westernised tourists, whose behaviour is often not compatible with Islamic beliefs. Buddhism and Hinduism are inherently more tolerant religions, and some regions have deliberately managed and marketed their religion and culture for tourism, the island of Bali being a classic example.

However, there is still a great potential for mutual misunderstanding between tourists and hosts. This is particularly the case in Japan, a country which superficially appears very Westernised but whose society is based on fundamentally different customs and values. Individualism, unconventionality and self-expression do not fit comfortably into the Japanese way of life. The convention of politeness and the unwillingness of the Japanese to say 'no' directly to a request that cannot be met, and the formalities of bowing etc. can lead to misunderstanding and frustration.

Modern cultural events as tourist attractions

There are many international events that attract large numbers of tourists that have no origin in history and are not particularly associated with any one regional culture. These events are of three basic types; sporting events, arts festivals and commercial events. The sporting events include, of course, the Olympic Games, World Championships and regional events such as the Commonwealth Games, Asian Games and so on. These events trigger off extensive capital investment in both sports facilities and the associated infrastructure of communications and accommodation. Many cities hosting the Games use the opportunity to market themselves as subsequent tourist destinations and take advantage of the sports facilities to develop tourism. The locations of the Winter Olympics with the associated upgrading of infrastructure are often enhanced as winter sport centres after the

Games are over (e.g. Sarajevo). In spite of the cost of putting on the Games, there is still intense competition to host them. Annual arts festivals, on the other hand, tend to be associated with specific locations, and specialise in specific arts; for example, Edinburgh in the theatre, Glyndbourne and Bayreuth in staged opera, and Cannes in films.

Lastly, commercial events are one-off or annual events designed to promote a region or a product. They may attract the business traveller but also cater more widely for the leisure tourist too, e.g. the World Wine Fair, the Munich Beer Festival, and in past years the Festival of Britain in the 1950s and Expo '67 in Montreal.

QUESTIONS AND DISCUSSION POINTS

1 Which country in Europe has the widest range of historic resources of different ages?
2 Explain the processes that are leading to the loss of historic resources. How can historic features be protected from destruction?
3 Locate the historical resources that are effectively out of bounds for tourism due to modern political problems.

ASSIGNMENTS

1 Your tour company wishes to develop new European tours with a special interest in history. You have been asked to construct a 14-day itinerary to include sites characteristic of each main period of European history. Write a brief report to your chief executive, outlining your suggested itinerary and explaining the reasons for your choice of stops, showing how your selection represents each main period of European history.

2 The local council of your home town is considering promoting the town's tourist potential. You have been commissioned by them to (a) make assessment of the historic and cultural resources of the town and (b) make recommendations to the council as to whether or not the historic resources have the potential for this form of tourist promotion, and whether the council should go ahead with their planned promotion campaign.

Write a brief report for the Chairman of the Leisure and Tourism Committee of the local council, assessing the historic resources of the town, and advising the committee on the course of action they should take.

World Patterns of Tourist Travel

Introduction

The first two parts of this book have identified the world locations of the major tourist generating and destination regions. This third part considers the patterns of tourist travel between them. It seeks to answer the following questions:

1 How do transport systems evolve to link tourist generation regions with the attractions tourists wish to visit (i.e. their destinations)?
2 How are national, international and global tourist routes affected by the geographical characteristics of the earth?
3 How do tourists use these routes? Can we discern any general patterns of tourist travel between the tourist-generating and destination regions of the world?
4 Can the world be divided into coherent tourist regions on the basis of the distribution of tourist generation regions, the destination areas and the flows of tourists between them?

In general, transport routes and systems evolve (or are planned) to enable three main types of tourist movement to take place: a flow of tourists to the coast; a flow of tourists to and between urban areas; and a flow of tourists from the towns to the mountains and countryside. But on both the national and international scales, the overriding influence of the climate imposes a

clear directional (i.e. towards the Equator) influence on these flows: tourists in the the Northern Hemisphere tend to travel south, while those in the Southern Hemisphere tend to travel north towards the warmer and sunnier climates. This, together with the evidence presented in Parts 1 and 2 suggest that the world can be divided into four major tourist regions:

1 Europe and the Mediterranean basin;
2 North America, plus Mexico and the Caribbean;
3 East Asia and the Pacific; and
4 The remainder of the world's economic periphery (i.e. South America, Subsaharan Africa, South Asia and the Middle East).

These four functional tourist regions are clearly distinguishable in terms of tourist activity (both in overall volume and directional flow) but the regions are very large: they cut across the boundaries of the continents and overlap the division of the world into the economic core and periphery. In order to subdivide the world into more manageable geographical units, the remainder of this book is organised according to the more traditional units of the continents, rather than the four functional tourist regions of the world. However, this presentation should still allow the functional relationships between different parts of the world to become apparent.

CHAPTER 6

Transport for tourism

LEARNING OBJECTIVES

After studying this chapter you should be able to

- understand the political and economic factors that influence the development of route systems and transport services
- be aware of the geographical factors that constrain transport networks
- be able to assess the suitability of different modes of transport for different client groups
- understand and be able to explain time differences and time zones
- locate the main European rail routes and European airports.

Introduction

A tourist cannot make use of tourist resources unless they are accessible: a transport system of some sort must link the tourists' home to their desired destination. The transport system consists of:

1 the **means of transport** (vehicles such as cars, trains, aircraft); and
2 the **network of routes** along which the vehicles travel (e.g. roads, railway tracks, air and sea lanes). The speed of travel of the vehicles along the network will govern journey times. At certain points these separate networks come together to provide interchange nodes where the traveller may change from one mode of transport to another.

Each form of transport will have different advantages in terms of speed, comfort, cost and convenience, and travellers will make appropriate choices between modes. On multi-mode journeys, the time taken to change modes at the transport nodes is perceived as part of the journey time. Therefore, improving the capacity and efficiency of the interchange facilities to handle passengers can make a significant contribution to the reduction of journey time.

Provision of transport networks on land

Although circumstances vary from country to country, it is generally true that the public sector (i.e. Central Government or local authorities) provide most of the investment in road and rail networks. This has not always been the case, for example, the railways in Britain were originally provided by private companies during the industrial revolution, but the scale of investment in new motorways and high speed rail tracks is now so great that private companies find it difficult to raise the capital.

Public sector provision

It is, therefore, the transport planning policies and decisions of world governments that are currently crucial in making destinations available to tourists. However, land transport networks are primarily designed to meet the needs of the commercial, industrial and commuter traffic that uses the network alongside the tourists. Only where tourism makes a significant real (or potential) contribution to a region or to a country's economy will the transport infrastructure be designed specifically to meet the needs of the holidaymaker. Governments also take the environmental impact of new road and rail developments into account and these considerations may have some influence on public investment decisions. Thus, the nature and geographical patterns of routes between tourist generating and destination areas depend not only on tourists' preferences and desires but also on the perceived balance of national costs and benefits and on the other political factors that influence governments' transport planning policies. At international level, the provision of through routes traversing more than one country will depend on the co-ordination of different national transport policies.

There are two processes by which public sector transport investment decisions are made; an incremental process by which a network is slowly adapted bit by bit in response to the needs of tourist and other traffic, and a comprehensive process by which a new transport network (or major new elements of the network) is designed in a co-ordinated way in conjunction with new tourist developments and constructed in a methodical manner to a clear plan. The incremental process could be summarised as follows:

1 tourists 'discover' and visit an area using roads designed for local economic needs;
2 the private sector responds by providing more accommodation and tourist attractions, and tourist numbers increase;
3 congestion builds up on the existing road network, particularly at nodes and settlements on the route;
4 piecemeal road improvements at the worst congestion points;
5 increased tourist (and non-tourist) traffic flows in response to gradually improving accessibility;

6 more congestion and eventual decision to add new roads (e.g. the motorways);
7 congestion of motorways; and
8 improvement of motorways.

Transport improvements have followed the growth of tourism. This process is well illustrated by the growth of tourism and improvement of the road network in southwest England. The region has always been one of the most popular holiday destinations in Britain, but road access to the peninsula has developed in a distinctly piecemeal fashion. Road improvements began with the construction of bypasses at bottlenecks and the widening of other congested sections. Major feeder motorways (M4 and M5) linked the region to the main tourist generating areas before a distributor motorway (from Bristol into the southwest peninsula) had been constructed. The M5 was only later gradually extended to Exeter.

In contrast, the French planning system makes comprehensive planning much easier, and there have been several major integrated tourism developments.

Case study: Comprehensive planning in the Languedoc-Rousillon region of France

This region lies on the French Mediterranean coast, extending from the mouth of the Rhône westwards to the Spanish border. Before 1960 it was a backward, rural area with an ailing local economy and poor communications but with extensive underdeveloped sandy beaches. In the early 1960s, the French Government decided that the region should be developed, in order to stimulate and diversify the regional economy and to provide new tourist opportunities. A comprehensive plan was produced in 1964. Improving access and developing the tourist potential of the area were major elements of the plan but all aspects of the region's development were considered, including, for example, its agriculture, afforestation and wildlife conservation. The plan proposed five major concentrations of tourist accommodation, linked by expressways to a motorway located a little way inland. The additions and improvements to the local road network were conceived at the same time as the new tourist development, making the whole project a coherent, integrated unit. The original plan has progressively been implemented (though with some modifications in 1969 and 1972) in a systematic and orderly way, resulting in an increase in tourist bednights in the period 1968–79 from 16 million to 39 million.

The process followed here is simply one of central government recognising the opportunity for tourist growth and taking the risk of making a major investment, followed by the systematic development and promotion of the scheme. In this case tourism growth has followed the process of development. Sustained tourist expansion does not always occur. The Italian Government tried to increase tourism in the extreme south of Italy by improving motorway access, but tourism has not grown as much as expected.

The modernisation and extension of rail networks is another area of public sector involvement. Again, the need to balance social and environmental considerations against commercial objectives makes public provision more appropriate, though in the 1980s in Britain the railway system was being prepared for privatisation. Europe has the densest rail network in the world, with over 140 000 km of track, built in the 19th century, on a radial pattern from the capital cities to the frontiers. This network is currently being modernised.

A major programme of public investment in high-speed rail tracks is underway in the 1990s

Fig 6.1 European high-speed rail links (existing and planned network 1989)

which will eventually result in a more co-ordinated international network of high-speed rail links in Northern Europe and a series of key routes to the Mediterranean (*see* Fig 6.1). By 1988 France had already completed their new high-speed line from Paris to Lyon, allowing TGVs (Train à Grande Vitesse) to run from Paris to Switzerland and the Côte d'Azur. West Germany, too, is making major public investments in its rail system, with a specific aim of improving its north-south links.

Private sector provision of land routes

The problems of raising enough capital and obtaining high enough returns quickly are so great that the private sector now plays little part in the provision of roads and railway networks. Even though tolls are charged on many public road systems (for example, 3200 km of interstate highways in USA are toll facilities and tolls are also payable on many European motorways) the revenue is not sufficient to yield the profit required by private investors. Private companies do sometimes provide small scale tourist railways as attractions at the tourist destination (e.g. the Snowdon mountain railway) but their function is more to provide a leisure experience than a means of transport.

The influence of physical factors on road and rail networks

Surface transport routes often follow river valleys in order to take advantage of the relatively gentle gradients and level land on the valley floor. Very marshy or mountainous areas are the greatest barriers to land transport, but expensive engineering (e.g. viaducts, bridges, tunnels) can overcome most of these problems. In Europe, the Alps and the Pyrénées are the major mountain barriers that obstruct the dominant north-south flow of tourists to the Mediterranean.

The major routes between France and Spain avoid the Pyrénées by skirting round the coast at either end of the mountain chain, but the Alps form a more intractable barrier and routes from Germany and Northern Europe to Italy and Yugoslavia are funnelled through a relatively small number of passes which are potential bottlenecks.

The approaches to the passes can be long and steep and in winter may be closed due to the weather (*see* Fig 6.2). In a few locations (e.g. Gt St Bernard Pass, St Gotthard Pass, and on the Chamonix-Courmayeur route at Mont Blanc) tunnels have been constructed that are passable during the winter but may occasionally need wheel chains on the approach roads in the worst of the snow.

Railways can climb at only very gentle gradients, and are much more limited in their choice of

	Country	Height (m)	Maximum gradient	Winter conditions
Passes				
Gt St Bernard	Switzerland/Italy	2473	1 in 9	Usually closed Oct-June
Simplon	Switzerland/Italy	2005	1 in 9	Occasionally closed Nov-April
St Gotthard	Switzerland	2108	1 in 10	Usually closed Mid Oct-June
Splugen	Switzerland/Italy	2113	1 in 7½	Usually closed Nov-June
Brenner	Austria/Italy	1374	1 in 7	Usually open
Tunnels				
Gt St Bernard	Switzerland/Italy	1827		
Mont Blanc	France/Italy	1218		
St Gotthard	Switzerland	1157		

Fig 6.2 Alpine passes and tunnels

available routes through mountainous areas. In deeply dissected country, numerous bridges, viaducts, cuttings and tunnels are needed and are very expensive to build and maintain. The Alps still form a major barrier to the development of the European rail network, although rail links do cross the mountains, e.g. via the Lotschberg and Simplon rail tunnels. Major technical and financial problems must be overcome before such lines can be converted for high speed trains.

Short stretches of water are generally more easily surmountable and can be crossed by bridges or tunnels for both road and rail transport. The Severn Bridge which carries the M4 from South Wales to Avon, has had an important effect on the economy of South Wales (including tourism) and has made the Pembrokeshire National Park and the beaches of the Gower Peninsula much more easily accessible from England. The level of traffic is so great that in 1990 a second Severn crossing is planned, that will also link into the motorway system. However, the weather can also occasionally disrupt road traffic here, as the bridge may be closed for safety reasons, for example during spells of very windy weather. In this case, the railway link to South Wales passes under the Severn in a tunnel and avoids this climatic disadvantage.

The Channel Tunnel is due to open in 1993. It is one of the most ambitious engineering projects ever attempted, which aims to overcome the barrier of the sea-crossing between England and France, and link the British road and rail systems with those of Europe. It is also one of the few major route developments which was planned to be financed by the private sector.

It is clear that networks of fixed routes on land evolve through the interplay of economic, political, physical and climatic factors, and generally depend on public investment. The interaction between governments' economic, transport and tourism policies has a crucial effect on the way in which routes are provided.

Provision of transport networks on the sea and in the air

Sea and air routes do not need to be constructed, and there are relatively few physical constraints on the movement of ships and planes. The sea and the air are freely available, and cost nothing

to use; nevertheless, ships and aircraft may be required to follow specified air corridors and sea lanes for safety and environmental reasons. The direction and pattern of use of the lanes depend on the location of the transport interchanges (which are sea and airports) and the volume of traffic flows along the routes depends on demand for travel.

The operators will favour particular routes that are the most economic in terms of operating costs. Usually, the most economical route is the shortest. The shortest route between two places on the earth's surface is known as a 'great circle route'.

Great circle routes

The shortest route between Quito in Ecuador and Nairobi in Kenya is across the Atlantic along the line of the Equator. The shortest distance from London to Valencia (in Spain) is due south following the Greenwich meridian (0° longitude). The Equator and the Greenwich Meridian both divide the world into equal halves; lines such as the Equator that cut the world into two equal hemispheres are called Great Circles, and they can extend in any direction (east-west, north-south, north-west to south-east and so on). Using a globe, the course of the great circle route between any pair of places can easily be traced. But because of the distortions to shape and location caused by projecting the outlines of the world's continents from the curved surface of the globe onto a flat sheet of paper, a straight line drawn between two map locations is not necessarily a great circle route and may not be the shortest distance between them. Both ships and aircraft have the freedom to follow great circle routes.

Jet streams

Wind speeds can also affect operating costs of air travel, strong head wind by increasing fuel consumption and a tailwind reducing it. Aircraft generally fly at high altitudes (10–17 000 metres) – well above the influence of surface winds.

In certain parts of the world there are winds of very high velocity blowing in the 10–15 000 metre height zone. These are the jet streams,

Key

A Winter position of sub-tropical jet stream
B Area of activity of the polar front jet stream
C Equatorial jet stream
→ Direction of jet streams

Fig 6.3 Jet streams

and the wind can reach speeds of over 400 km/hr, equal to the greatest speeds ever recorded at ground level. Aircraft can take advantage of the jet streams on some routes. The equatorial jet stream occurs at about 15 000 metres, and blows from the east across South Asia in the SW monsoon season. The sub-tropical jet stream occurs in a relatively narrow zone around the Poles between 12 000 and 15 000 km above the earth's surface and blows from the west, but it occurs in a relatively narrow zone around the Poles between 20 and 35° N and S. The polar jet stream also blows round the Poles from the west, at about 10 000 km and takes a variable path between latitudes 35 and 65° (*see* Fig 6.3). Where air routes coincide with the jet stream bands, and the aircraft travels in the same direction as the jet stream, the journey time can be substantially shortened.

Airport location

The site requirements of an airport are relatively straightforward. It must have:

1 enough flat land with space for 3000 metre runways and all the ancillary services and buildings
2 no tall buildings or high land on the approaches
3 a suitable local climate, i.e. with steady prevailing winds (as aircraft must take off into the wind), little turbulence, or fog.

The problems of airport location stem more from the incompatible need to

1 be a long way from the urban population that the airport serves in order to reduce the impact of aircraft noise on the residents; and
2 be as close as possible to the city centre so that the airport is accessible and the time advantages of air travel are not squandered by a slow and inconvenient journey to the airport.

This will generate major conflicts in a densely populated area, such as the London region, where the demand for more airport capacity is great, but there is strong resistance by local residents to any proposal for an additional airport in any specific place. In London's case, proposals for a new airport at sites such as Maplin and Cublington were each rejected in turn on environmental grounds, and London still has no new international airport, although Stansted is currently being expanded to fill the gap.

However, a small airport catering specifically for business travel has been located in inner London itself. It is only environmentally acceptable because its use has been limited to a particularly quiet short take-off and landing aircraft (the Dash −7) that can approach over the Thames. An inner city airport would have been unthinkable before this particular technical development. New airports are extremely costly to build and once again investment on this scale has normally come from the public sector.

Sea transport and port location

The age of long-distance sea passenger transport is past. Ships are simply too slow to compete with air transport over long distances. Britain is entering a period of port decline and many port facilities, such as London, Bristol, Swansea, Cardiff, are being redeveloped for leisure boating and have completely lost their passenger and freight transport function. The only passenger ports that are thriving are ferry ports that cross short stretches of water directly linking surface routes on each shore.

Ferries usually keep to relatively sheltered coastal waters, and are not subject to the full rigours of the weather of the open oceans. Nevertheless, winter conditions in the storm wave environments of the world (*see* Fig 3.3 on page 34) can be severe at times. Hovercraft and even ferry services from British ferry ports are occasionally disrupted.

Provision of the transport service

Once a network of land, sea and air routes has been provided, competition between transport modes begins, and transport services develop. The private sector has a much more important role in providing transport services than in creating the infrastructure. Once a variety of services can be provided, and the process of consumer choice begins and there is competition between transport modes and between the providers of services.

Travellers have varying requirements: the businessman needs quick reliable transport, preferably with space to work; the elderly need comfort; the student needs cheap travel, while the family with young children need a flexible and spacious travel mode that can adapt to the children's immediate needs. Modes of transport can be divided into independent means of travel (controlled by the individual tourist) and mass travel (where tourists travel together in groups to and from a common origin and destination).

	Independent	Mass
Cycle	X	
Car	X	
Coach		X
Train		X
Plane	*	X
Boat	*	X

* Boats and planes can be individual modes of transport for the those who can afford one.

Fig 6.4 Classification of modes of travel

Mass travel is less convenient as it usually involves at least one change of mode but it is normally cheaper than independent travel would be over the same distance.

Car travel

The tourist normally owns and controls this form of transport. The road network is extensive, and apart from toll routes, the motorist does not pay directly for the use of the system (payment is usually indirect via fuel or road tax). This provides car users with a unique level of freedom; they can control every aspect of their journey – its speed, duration, the route, the destination and the flexibility to change any of these at will during the journey itself. Finally, it is the only extensively used means of transport in which the traveller can complete the journey door to door without changing transport mode.

With all these advantages, it is not surprising that car transport is the dominant mode of travel for all world tourism. Road transport accounts for 77 per cent of all world international arrivals (particularly intra-regional travel) and in most developed countries, car transport similarly dominates the domestic tourist scene.

The main drawback of car travel to the tourist is the relatively low average speed of travel. Different countries have different speed limits, e.g. motorway speed limits are 100 kph in the Netherlands, 120 kph in Spain, and 130 kph in France and Germany. But average speeds are usually lower, and in congested conditions can be very low indeed (e.g. under 18 kph in Central London). The journey time and the fatigue experienced by the driver, as much as the cost of fuel, are the main constraints that limit the range of carborne tourist traffic. For the European, 1000 km appears to be a critical distance. Beyond this, too great a proportion of the holiday is taken up with getting to the destination and this tips the balance in favour of a faster, though in some respects a less convenient, form of mass transport.

Coach travel

As coaches use the same road networks, coach travel is almost as flexible as car travel in the choice of routes and destinations available, though the size and weight of the vehicle make some routes (particularly narrow scenic country lanes) and destinations (such as the streets of historic towns) inaccessible. The coach operator, therefore, can tailor the coach tour or scheduled service to the needs of the tourist. But the fact that coach travel is a form of mass transport immediately makes it less attractive to the user, though it is a relatively cheap form of transport; and scheduled services are mainly for non-car owners. Coach travel is ideally suited for two forms of tourist travel:

1 circuit tours; and
2 transfer of mass tourists, e.g. airport to hotel, airport to city centre.

Coach travel is generally the cheapest form of long-distance mass travel, but is, perhaps, the least comfortable.

Rail travel

Rail travel was the dominant form of mass public transport before the car age in the developed economies, and still remains the main travel mode in less developed countries, such as India. It is significant, however, that as affluence increases and car ownership extends through the population, rail travel declines. In spite of being a faster mode than the passenger car (the average speed of high-speed train services is 250 kph, though such trains are capable of 400 kph) its great limitation is the range of routes available. Train services are limited to the network of tracks, which usually form a radial pattern from the major conurbations, reflecting the spatial needs of freight, commuter and business traffic rather than holiday tourist flows.

It has been noted that railways are generally publicly owned and run, so the nature of the network, the cost (and level of subsidy) and type of service provided depends on government policy. France and Germany lead Europe in terms of investment in and subsidy of public transport and France is actually extending its range of high-speed train routes (TGVs). In France the use of the railway system (excluding the metros) has increased (in terms of passenger km) by 27 per cent between 1974 and 1984. In Britain, on the other hand, subsidies for public transport were gradually withdrawn during the 1980s, reinforcing the downward trend in tourist usage of trains.

Trains are on the decline as transcontinental passenger modes. The huge investment needed to convert long-distance routes for high-speed trains is not justified by the current numbers of passengers. Canada is cutting its government funding for the railways and in 1989 services were cut by 50 per cent. The long-distance routes are disproportionately affected with the trans-Canada services falling from 14 to 3 a week. The 4500 km journey took over three days, and is no longer viable. In Australia a similar coast-to-coast journey of 4000 km (Sydney to Perth) takes nearly 66 hours, totally uncompetitive with air transport both in terms of time and cost, and even slower than the same journey by coach.

Rail travel is competitive with road and air transport in a relatively narrow distance band. Air transport begins to challenge rail on journeys of two hours duration or more, but rail is competitive on journeys up to 500 km in distance (and five hours in duration). It is thought that when the high-speed rail network in Europe is complete, rail transport will be competitive with air services on several intercity routes (*see* Fig 6.5).

Journey	Fastest time in 1990	Fastest time on completion of high-speed rail network
Brussels – Amsterdam	2 hr 41 min	1 hr 28 min
Frankfurt – Munich	3 hr 46 min	3 hr 00 min
Rome – Milan	4 hr 05 min	3 hr 05 min
Paris – Amsterdam	5 hr 07 min	2 hr 48 min
London – Paris	5 hr 12 min	2 hr 30 min
Barcelona – Madrid	6 hr 13 min	3 hr 00 min

Fig 6.5 European intercity rail journeys

Air transport

A small proportion (12.5 per cent) of the world's tourists travel by air. Even though it is still only used by a minority of tourists, air transport has revolutionised the geographical pattern of world travel since 1960. Tourism has changed from a local to an intercontinental activity. It has created tourist industries in destinations hitherto untouched by the physical, social or economic impacts of tourism. In the mid-1950s the journey by ocean liner between Britain and Australia was measured in terms of weeks; in 1990 the same journey by air lasted less than 24 hours. The subsonic Jumbo Jet (the Boeing 747) flies at over 1000 k/h and supersonic aircraft can reach speeds of 1950 k/h. Concorde has cut the journey time between London and New York from about six hours to only three, making it possible for businesspeople to travel there and back in a day.

The speed and range of air travel gives rise to a problem for the traveller that no other form of transport is able to. Air travel can take the tourist from one time zone of the world to another in a matter of hours, much faster than the body can cope with. It takes several days for the body's rhythms of waking and sleeping to adjust to a new pattern of day and night. The fatigue experienced during this period of adjustment is known as jet lag. It is most clearly felt when travelling to the opposite side of the world where the time difference between the tourists' home and their destination is the greatest.

Time zones

Pictures from outer space make it easy to visualise the world as a globe, spinning on its axis (one revolution being equal to a day) and orbiting round the sun (one complete circuit in one year). At any given moment, the part of the earth closest to the sun will be experiencing midday,

and the point furthest away will be at midnight. Figure 6.6 shows the distribution of day and night when it is midday in London (which lies on the Greenwich Meridian 0° longitude). At this exact moment, the time in Leningrad (30° E) is 14.00 hrs and in Tokyo (140° E) it is just after nine pm (and travellers from London to Japan must get used to a pattern of day and night which is almost the complete opposite to that which their bodies are accustomed). In Toronto (80° W) it is just before seven in the morning. Each 15° of longitude experiences exactly one hour's difference in solar time. For convenience, the world has been divided into time zones roughly corresponding to each 15° longitude band, and each with generally one hour's difference in time between them (see Fig 6.7). The boundaries of the time zones follow lines of longitude closely, but may deviate where administrative boundaries lie close to that line (for example, in Africa the time zone boundary follows the Sudan/Ethiopia and Uganda/Zaire borders instead of the line of longitude, and in North America it deviates to follow some state boundaries). It is much more convenient for one

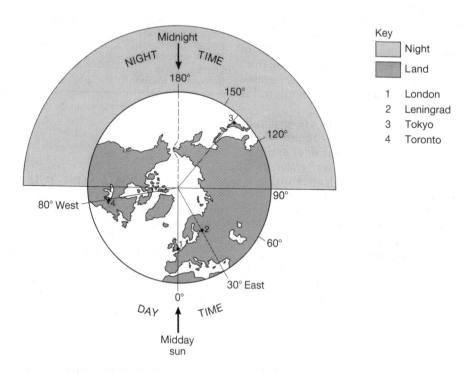

Fig 6.6 World distribution of day and night (when it is midday in London)

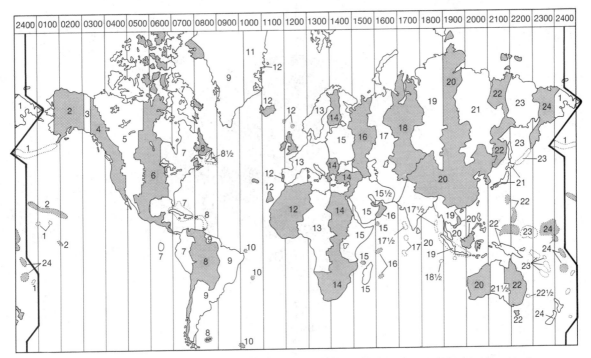

| 2400 | 0100 | 0200 | 0300 | 0400 | 0500 | 0600 | 0700 | 0800 | 0900 | 1000 | 1100 | 1200 | 1300 | 1400 | 1500 | 1600 | 1700 | 1800 | 1900 | 2000 | 2100 | 2200 | 2300 | 2400 |

Fig 6.7 World time zones (giving the time in hours, in each zone when it is midday in London)

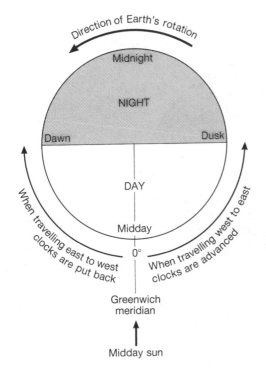

Fig 6.8 Time adjustments around the world

administrative unit to lie within one time zone.

As travellers go eastward and pass from one time zone to another they must adjust their watch one hour forward, and when they travel west, they must put their watches back one hour (*see* Fig 6.8). The only occasion when the whole world is experiencing the same day is when it is midday in London (*see* Figs 6.6, 6.7 and 6.8). From that moment the new day starts to sweep clockwise (westwards) round the world (*see* Figs 6.9 and 6.10). When travellers cross the International Date Line (180°) from east to west they will step ahead into the next day; when they cross it from west to east they move into the day before (*see* Fig 6.10).

The calendar on the Asian side of the international date line is always one day ahead of the American side. The location of the International Date Line was agreed in 1884. The line corresponds more or less with the 180° meridian, passing through the empty Pacific ocean. The occasional deviations in the line away from the 180° meridian allow some groups of Pacific islands to all lie in the zone of the same calendar day.

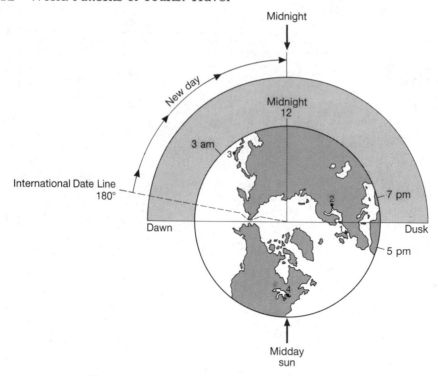

Fig 6.9 Spread of a new day (west): dawn in the Pacific and midday in Toronto

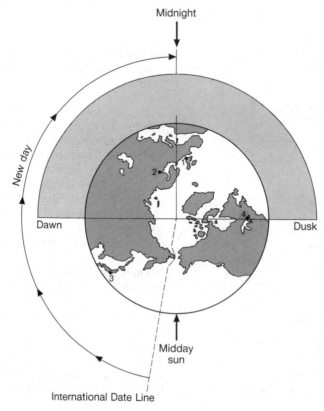

Fig 6.10 Spread of a new day (east): midday in the Pacific and dusk in Toronto

---

EC airports listed by category

Category 1 Hub airports

Belgium:	Brussels-Zaventem
Denmark:	Copenhagen-Kastrup/Roskilde
West Germany:	Frankfurt/Rhein-Main, Düsseldorf-Lohausen, Munich-Riem
Spain:	Palma-Mallorca, Madrid-Barajas, Malaga, Las Palmas
Greece:	Athens-Hellenikon, Salonica-Micra
France:	Paris-Charles de Gaulle/Orly
Ireland:	Dublin
Italy:	Rome-Fiumicino/Ciampino, Milan-Linate/Malpensa
Netherlands:	Amsterdam-Schiphol
Portugal:	Lisbon, Faro
UK	London-Heathrow/Gatwick/Stansted, Luton

Category 2 Regional airports

West Germany:	Hamburg-Fuhlsbüttel, Stuttgart-Echterdingen, Cologne/Bonn
Spain:	Tenerife-Sur, Barcelona, Ibiza, Alicante, Gerona
France:	Marseille-Marignane, Nice-Côte d'Azur, Lyon-Satolas, Basle-Mulhouse
Ireland:	Shannon
Italy:	Naples-Capodichino, Venice-Tessera, Catania-Fontanarossa
Luxembourg:	Luxembourg-Findel
Portugal:	Funchal, Oporto
UK:	Manchester-Ringway, Birmingham-Elmdon, Glasgow-Abbotsinch

Category 3
Includes all other airports officially open to international scheduled services.

Fig 6.11 Europe's hub and spoke airports
(*Source: European Commission.*)

Spatial distribution of air traffic

Most air traffic movements are concentrated in the more populated parts of the world, where there is the densest provision of airports serving that population.

Most countries have at least one major international airport capable of handling intercontinental traffic, and some of these have developed into major interchanges where many long-haul routes intersect, e.g. London, Frankfurt, Singapore and New York. London Heathrow handled over 34 million passengers in 1987. Frankfurt is Europe's second airport with 22 million. The smaller British regional airports (the runways of which may not be long enough to receive the jumbo jets) specialise in holiday charter flights or provide services into Heathrow (or Gatwick) to connect with the international flights. This pattern of 'hub' and 'spoke' airports is more firmly established in the USA, but Europe is also evolving this pattern (*see* Fig 6.11). The bulk of international air traffic in Europe flows between the hubs, but as congestion increases, the secondary airports are beginning to take a more important role. Manchester, with 8.5 million passengers in 1987, was Europe's most important 'spoke' airport, followed by Barcelona and Hamburg. Many of the smaller airports have ambitious expansion plans, and the patterns and flows of air traffic may change and grow rapidly as total traffic increases and deregulation, plus the implementation of the Single European Act, take full effect.

Sea travel

It has been noted that the only major passenger transit role of sea transport is that of short sea (ferry) crossings in island nations, and local inner city ferry services for cities such as Venice and Sydney that have waterways in the heart of the urban area. In these cities, ferries provide both commuter and tourist transport. Ferries may be boats of traditional design, or hydrofoils where greater speed is required.

In general, boat travel has a greater leisure and tourism role than a transport role.

Cruising

Cruising is one of the forms of tourism in which the travel element is an integral and essential part of the holiday experience. The cruise ship is basically a floating hotel; passengers can enjoy the attractions of luxury hotel service while they are travelling between ports of call. The world market for cruising is quite small (3 to 3.5 million in 1987/8) but in style, cruising is essentially a form of mass tourism; while 800 berth vessels were cost-effective in the 1970s, the normal size in the 1980s was for 1500 berth vessels and in the late 1980s vessels double that size were being planned. These ships either leave from a home port, or in order to save days sailing to the cruise destinations, passengers may fly to the port of embarkation in the cruise destination are ('fly-cruises').

The main world locations of cruise activity are in the three island-studded, enclosed seas that by geographical accident are found in favourable subtropical or Mediterranean climatic regions and are also close to major tourist generation areas. These three seas are the Caribbean, the Mediterranean and the South China/Pacific, adjacent to the American, European and Australian/New Zealand/Japanese markets respectively. The more northerly coasts and en-closed seas, e.g. Alaska, China coast, Norwegian coast and Baltic are visited by cruise ships in the summer season but numbers are negligible compared to the three major regions. Cruising in the Mediterranean has been long established (for nearly 100 years) but the political difficulties of Suez crisis in 1956/7 led to the temporary cancellation of Mediterranean cruises and both cruise ships and cruise businesses were transferred to the Caribbean.

Although the Mediterranean has partially recovered, the Caribbean has been the most important world region for cruising since the late 1950s. Initially ships departed from New York but from 1970 Miami took over as the leading Caribbean cruise port.

Not surprisingly, Caribbean cruising is completely dependent on the American market. American tourists are, however, also very important to the Mediterranean cruise business, which suffered a second major setback in 1985/6 after a Mediterranean cruise ship (the Achille Lauro) was attacked by Arab terrorists who killed an American tourist on board. American cruise visitors decreased from 75 000 pa before 1985 to virtually nil thereafter.

The main cruise circuits in the Mediterranean area are

1 The Western Mediterranean
2 Eastern Mediterranean/Aegean – Greek Islands (sometimes linked to the Holy Land and Egypt). Piraeus, Venice and Genoa are the most used start/finish points.
2 North Africa and the Canaries (a winter circuit).

The Pacific cruise business is geared to the Australian, New Zealand and recently developing Japanese markets, though some fly cruise passengers come from North America and Europe. Trips to the islands of the South Pacific embark from Australian or New Zealand ports, but many of the cruises of the South China Sea start from Singapore or Hong Kong.

QUESTIONS AND DISCUSSION POINTS

1 What is a great circle route? Why is it normally advantageous for sea and air routes to follow them as closely as possible. Under what circumstances would boats and planes not follow them?
2 What is the most used mode of transport for tourism in the world? What advantages make it so popular?
3 Most major airports are located a considerable distance from their city centres, except in certain coastal cities. Why is this?

ASSIGNMENTS

1 A client has booked a trip to Australia through your travel agency. He has been given the following details of the journey (all local times):

Depart London Airport	on Monday	at	2235 hrs
Arrive Singapore	on Tuesday	at	2220 hrs
Depart Singapore	on Friday	at	0040 hrs
Arrive Cairns, Australia	on Friday	at	0900 hrs
Depart Cairns	on Friday	at	1030 hrs
Arrive Brisbane	on Friday	at	1250 hrs

The client is totally confused as to the length of time he will be travelling in the plane and the amount of time he will have at the stopover locations.

Explain to him:

(a) the length of time he will be flying on each leg of the journey; and

(b) the length of time he has in Singapore (and how many *full* days of sightseeing he will have there).

2 A businesswoman, books a return trip from London to San Francisco. Her schedule is as follows:

Outbound: Depart Heathrow 0900 hrs on Wednesday
Arrive San Francisco 1155 hrs on Wednesday
Meeting 1500 hrs on Wednesday in San Francisco

Return: Depart San Francisco 1720 hrs on Thursday
Arrive Heathrow ? (time to be calculated)
Meeting in London 1430 hrs on Friday.
(*All local times*)

Her meeting in the United States is expected to last two to three hours. Advise the client on

(a) How much time she will have in the plane on the outbound journey to read her notes and prepare for the meeting;

(b) How much time she will have for sightseeing in San Francisco before she returns; and

(c) How long she will have to sleep on the plane on the return journey, and whether she will return in time for the London meeting.

CHAPTER 7

The growth and distribution of world tourism

LEARNING OBJECTIVES

After reading this chapter you should be able to

- list the factors that influence travel within and between countries
- locate the main world tourism generating and destination regions
- distinguish between inter- and intra-regional travel
- identify the four functional tourist regions of the world
- understand the logic of different subdivisions of the world into different tourist regions.

Introduction

The location of an affluent urban area alongside a region with attractive tourist resources, linked together by transport routes and networks, will trigger off the flow of tourists between them. The most powerful flows will be towards the most attractive, accessible and popular destinations.

These travel patterns occur on a domestic, international and inter-regional scale; various factors influence these directional flows of tourists.

Factors affecting domestic tourist flows

The directional flows of domestic tourists within a country will depend on the location of its natural resources and on the distribution of its population. However, each of the resources described in Chapters 2 to 5 generates a characteristic pattern of tourist travel.

1 A major wave of tourist travel flows outwards from the urban areas to the coast, often to the nearest (or most accessible) available coast, sometimes seemingly irrespective of its environmental quality (e.g. the residents of Manchester and Liverpool visit Blackpool, and the eastenders of London traditionally travel to Southend-on-Sea). As Britain is an island, the flow to the coast is multi-directional from the cities, though with a general southerly bias towards the best combinations of climate and beaches.

2 A second, though far smaller, wave of tourists flows outwards from the cities towards the countryside and mountains. Again, in Britain this is fairly multi-directional, though this time with a bias towards the west (and northwest) towards the landscapes of upland Britain.

3 The third tide of tourist travel is in the opposite direction and represents the movement of rural and provincial residents into the conurbations for the cultural attractions and entertainments of the city centre.

4 The fourth stream of tourists takes place

between the cities, representing travel by business and cultural tourists and people visiting friends and relatives. This interchange of tourists utilises the web of transport routes that evolved to meet the needs of commercial and industrial transport and the significant volumes of this element of tourist travel may be camouflaged by the even greater volumes of non-tourist traffic.

Superimposed on all these patterns on tourist movement is a general trend of travel towards better (i.e. warmer, sunnier or drier) climatic conditions. In Britain this results in a strong concentration of tourism in the south and south-west. Thus, in the Northern Hemisphere, the flow is essentially towards the south, and cultural, historic or landscape resources need to be of outstanding quality to draw tourists northwards against this tidal flow to the south. Of course, in the Southern Hemisphere, the pattern is reversed: in Australia and New Zealand, tourists tend to drift northwards for the better weather.

International tourist flows

The same factors influence travel between countries, and, once again, climate appears to play a dominant role in shaping patterns of international travel.

Contrasts in climate would seem to be the most important factor that triggers off tourism worldwide. The main tourism generating areas are located in the northerly or mid latitudes that have cool and variable climates. The main tourist flows in both Europe and North America are north-south to the warmer and more reliable climates in the regions on their southerly borders (in Europe to the Mediterranean, and in North America to Florida and the Caribbean). The most clear-cut example of this type of travel is shown by the Scandinavians; in 1985 one quarter to one third of their travel outside the Scandinavian region is in the form of package holidays to the Canary Islands during the winter when hours of daylight (let alone hours of sunshine) in the northerly latitudes are very limited indeed.

Once again, it should be noted that in the Southern Hemisphere, the parallel trend is northwards. In Australia, for example, the residents of Melbourne and Sydney tend to travel north to the Queensland coast and beyond for their winter sun holidays, while New Zealanders

may visit the Pacific islands to their north. On a world scale, therefore, the trek towards more favourable climates generates travel towards the Equator. However, in addition to the climate, other factors influence the direction, volume, mode and frequency of travel between countries. These are

1 Distance between countries. The tourist flows between two countries are likely to be bigger, the closer together the two countries.

2 Natural and man-made attractions. Tourist travel will be triggered off between countries if one can provide the attractions (e.g. beaches, landscapes or historic resources) that the other country lacks.

3 Communications. Travel between countries will be encouraged where good transport infrastructures exist. Tourism will flourish particularly where travel between countries can take place without a change of mode of transport (e.g. entirely by car).

4 Relative costs (cost of living and exchange rates). If two countries have significantly different costs of living, tourism flows will be encouraged from the more expensive country to the country with the lower cost of living.

5 Cultural links. Other things being equal, travel is more likely to occur between countries with some common cultural link (e.g. a common language or religion, shared political history).

6 Political factors. The long-term political stability of a country will make it a relatively more attractive destination both for investors in tourism and for the tourists themselves.

Distance

The majority of international tourist movements takes place between adjacent countries. Figure 7.1 lists some examples of countries in the world's economic core, showing the proportion of their international visitors that originate from countries with whom they have a common border.

As the distance a tourist travels increases, so the financial cost and the time taken for the journey tends to increase. The tourist must weigh these disadvantages of long-distance travel against the attraction of the far away destination. This 'friction of distance' may lead the tourist to choose a similar type of destination that is closer

Country	% international tourists from adjacent country/ countries	Name(s) of adjacent country/countries
North America		
Canada	87.0	USA
USA	62.8	Canada, Mexico
Europe		
Austria	66.3	West Germany, Italy, Switzerland, Yugoslavia, Hungary, Czechoslovakia
Belgium	57.2	Netherlands, France, West Germany
Italy	56.7	France, Switzerland, Austria, Yugoslavia
France	53.3	West Germany, Belgium, Spain, Italy, Switzerland
Spain	43.9	France, Portugal

Fig 7.1 Tourism between adjacent countries

to their home country in preference to the true long-haul destination, however attractive its character might appear to be.

Thus, the volume of tourist traffic will decrease with distance away from the tourist generating area. This relationship is known as the **distance-decay factor**.

Natural and man-made attractions

The lack of a particular type of attraction in a generating country may also trigger off significant flows of tourists to countries where those resources exist in abundance. For example, tourists from the Netherlands (appropriately known as the 'low countries' owing to the fact that most of the country lies below 200 metres, and much is below sea level) flock to Switzerland and Austria. The Alps are the second most important destination for Dutch travellers; 19 per cent of the Dutch visited France in 1985, followed by the Alps (Austria and Switzerland), with a 17 per cent share of Dutch holiday destinations abroad.

Germany has a very limited coastline in relation to its size, and the coast it has is in the north. This creates a strong demand among Germans for holidays in the coastal resorts of the Mediterranean countries. Britain's pageantry (particularly that associated with the Royal Family) attracts visitors from countries that lack such historic traditions or do not have monarchies.

Communications

Good transport links between countries is a prerequisite for the exchange of tourists between them. Where international borders cross land areas, road transport is the dominant mode of travel; road networks designed to meet local or industrial needs may predate tourist development and allow exploratory road travel by tourists (*see* Chapter 6). The Costa Brava in Spain was 'discovered' in this way by French visitors driving south across the border in the 1950s. It was only after the tourist potential of the costas was recognised that the roads were improved and airports built. Similarly, car-borne visitors driving from Europe towards Greece along the Adriatic highway found the attractions of the Yugoslavian coast worthy of more than a stopover visit.

Road transport is by far the dominant means of transport for tourism worldwide. Seventy-seven per cent of world international arrivals are by road, and only 12.5 per cent by air, and 10.5 per cent for rail and boat together. In Europe, too, car transport dominates travel between countries (ranging from 60–80 per cent of visits). The same pattern holds for North America, where the bulk of international trips are by road; in 1987, 67 per cent of the visitors from USA to Canada went by road, and 66 per cent from Canada to USA.

Long-haul travel is on the other hand essentially airborne, and relies on either charter flights (purpose-designed for tourists and tailored to the short/medium-haul destinations for mass tourism) or scheduled flights. The networks and infra-structure of the scheduled flights are designed to meet the locational needs of commerce and business, linking urban and industrial centres rather than specifically the tourist generating regions with far-flung and less developed tourist destinations.

Relative costs

The relative purchasing power of the currency of a given country is a reflection of the strength of that country's economy and its standard of living. Prices to the consumer (and, therefore, to the tourist) will vary considerably between different countries. Travel will be inhibited to countries where consumer prices are relatively higher than in the home economy, while tourists will get better value for money if they travel to a country where consumer prices are lower than at home. Figure 7.2 shows the relative purchasing power of the pound in 1986 compared to other countries (values of the index above 100 indicate countries where goods are relatively more expensive than in UK, and below 100 indicates relative cheapness).

Country	Index
More expensive than UK	
Denmark	141
West Germany	127
France	119
Netherlands	115
Irish Republic	113
Belgium	110
Luxembourg	101
Less expensive than UK	
Italy	98
Spain	84
Greece	77
Portugal	68

Fig 7.2 Relative purchasing power of the pound sterling 1986

With changes in exchange rates, and varying inflation rates, the relative purchasing power of currencies will vary over time. For example, in terms of the pound's relative purchasing power, Italy became steadily less attractive to UK visitors over the period 1981–86, while the relative difference between Greece and UK remained the same over the whole period. Countries like Denmark and West Germany became increasingly expensive for British visitors.

	Index					
	1981	1982	1983	1984	1985	1986
Denmark	111	116	120	122	122	141
West Germany	102	106	115	115	111	127
Italy	72	75	83	86	85	98
Greece	73	78	78	79	74	77

Fig 7.3 Relative purchasing power of the pound 1981–1986

Such price differentials can strongly influence patterns of travel particularly where destinations are closely competitive, leading tourists to switch from one destination to the comparable but now somewhat cheaper alternative. However, changes in travel behaviour seem to take effect over a period of about one to three years after the change in relative prices.

Price differentials can also make destinations in the world's economic periphery very attractive to tourists from the economic core. The standard of living may be relatively much lower in the countries of the economic periphery, but costs of labour and costs of living are also low. If the countries of the periphery can overcome the economic problems of providing a tourist infrastructure at an acceptable standard, then the relative cheapness of holidays there may draw large numbers of tourists from the countries of the economic core. The zones of the economic periphery lying adjacent to the tourist generating regions of the world's economic core have certainly experienced an influx of tourists; for example, Mexico and the Caribbean (both on the fringe of the periphery) are major destinations for the North American market, while Turkey and North Africa (also on the fringe of the periphery) compete directly with countries of Southern Europe for the Mediterranean holiday trade. In the Pacific region, the countries of the periphery (e.g. Indonesia, Thailand and the economically under-developed islands of the Pacific) attract significant numbers of Australasians and Japanese.

Cultural links

There are three types of cultural links that influence travel between countries.

1 Countries with a shared cultural background are more likely to generate tourism between them. The Scandinavian countries share their Viking history, and between 33 and 50 per cent of their visitors come from other Nordic countries.
2 Patterns of immigration into a country will create cultural links between the receiving country and the immigrants' original homeland. The immigrants may wish to travel back to visit families left at home and vice versa, and the descendants of immigrants tend to be drawn to explore the countries where their ancestors once lived. The United States was peopled by immigrants, initially from Europe; from Britain, Germany and Ireland up to 1860, to which were

added Scandinavians in the period 1860–1890, and Eastern and Southern Europeans from 1900–1914. In more recent years (since the 1960s) the immigrants have come mainly from Southeast Asia and Latin America. Apart from the slave trade, virtually no migrants came from Africa, and few from the Middle East. American overseas tourism appears to reflect these cultural links.

3 Past colonial links. Until their independence, many of the Third World countries were governed as colonies of European nations. The colonial power often imposed its language on the colony as well as its general style of education, culture, currency and political organisation. Some of these characteristics have been retained by the independent states even though the members of the colonial power have long since left. This may make the country an attractive destination for tourists from the original colonial power. The flow of tourists between France and its ex-colonies in French West Africa and North Africa illustrates this point. Similarly, there are significant flows of the Dutch to Surinam, the Belgians to Zaire and the British to former colonies in East Africa and Asia. These flows of tourists reflect the traces of the political geography of past eras.

Political factors

The current political geography of the world exerts a powerful control on tourist flows between countries.

Political conflict or co-operation between nations can inhibit or encourage tourism. Wars, terrorist campaigns or any form of political instability may immediately deter tourists temporarily or for a longer period of time. The memories and suspicions bred of past conflicts, and longer term ethnic rivalries can also inhibit tourism between countries, e.g. India and Pakistan; Greece and Turkey – both pairs of adjacent countries with a long-term history of conflict reflected in a smaller than expected travel flow between them.

Countries may also erect financial and legal barriers to travel which may have profound effects upon international travel patterns. Until the 1989 upheavals in Eastern Europe, the travel restrictions imposed on both visitors and residents by the then communist countries reduced east-west travel in both directions to a mere trickle.

Less drastic but still influential financial and legal barriers such as restrictions on foreign currency allowances, and access to visas may just as effectively control travel between certain countries (e.g. throughout the Central and South American countries).

On the other hand, political decisions may be made that facilitate and even encourage travel between countries or groups of countries. The Scandinavian countries have co-ordinated many of their laws and customs regulations, which allow virtually complete freedom of travel for Scandinavians between their countries. The Single European Act is designed to have the same effect eventually on the EC.

All these factors will combine in different ways to shape and modify the overall patterns of world regional and inter-regional tourism. The flows of tourists between any specific pair of countries and, indeed, pairs of regions in the world will be a result of the interplay of these factors, although there must be the predisposing conditions for tourist generation in the one country, and tourist attractions (be they climatic, scenic, historic etc.) must exist in the other.

Regional patterns of tourism

Chapter 1 located the tourist generating regions of the world as Europe, North America and parts of the Pacific (the world's economic 'core'). Chapters 2–5 located the main tourist resources of the world and showed that there are major concentrations of attractive resources in the Mediterranean basin, Central America and in the Caribbean. Chapter 6 and the first section of this chapter identified the factors that trigger off and encourage flows between any pair of tourist generating and destination areas. This next section will describe the overall world patterns of tourist arrivals at destinations that represent the outcome of this interplay of geographical factors, and on the basis of these patterns of tourism, the functional tourist regions of the world can be identified (see Fig 7.4).

The four functional tourist regions of the world are:

1 Europe and the Mediterranean: a region of high tourist activity with major tourist flows south to the coasts of the Mediterranean basin.

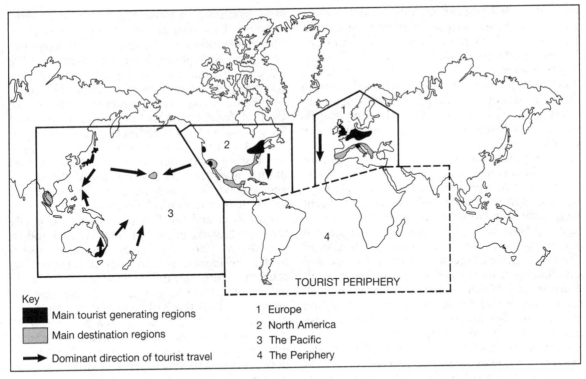

Key

■	Main tourist generating regions
▨	Main destination regions
➡	Dominant direction of tourist travel

1 Europe
2 North America
3 The Pacific
4 The Periphery

Fig 7.4 The four main tourist regions of the world

2 North America plus Mexico and the Caribbean: similar in many ways to Europe with dominant southerly flows of tourists to Florida, Mexico and the Caribbean.

3 East Asia and the Pacific: a region of much lower tourist activity but where tourism is growing very rapidly indeed. Due to the huge size of the Pacific Ocean, relatively few tourists travel right across it and the strongest tourist flows are around its edge – between the countries on the 'Pacific Rim' (again in a predominantly Equatorwards direction). A second flow takes place from these countries towards the centre of the Pacific, to island holiday destinations.

4 The remainder of the economic periphery: Subsaharan Africa, Central and South America, the Middle East and South Asia. The level of tourist activity is very low indeed due to factors such as political instability, inaccessibility, poverty and poor tourist infrastructure.

When tourist arrival data is grouped according to the World Tourist Organisation regions (*see* Fig 7.5), it is clear that Europe has always been the dominant international tourist destination of the world (the boundaries of these statistical regions are shown in Fig 7.6 on p 83).

Region	% world international arrivals					
	1950	1960	1970	1980	1985	1989
Europe	66.6	71.0	74.7	70.0	65.5	61.9
North America	24.6	21.4	16.1	12.5	11.8	13.4
Caribbean and Latin America	5.2	3.8	3.0	7.2	6.1	6.3
Middle East	0.8	2.0	1.7	2.0	3.3	2.9
Africa	2.0	0.6	1.4	2.2	3.5	3.8
Asia/Australasia	0.8	1.2	3.1			
East Asia & Pacific				5.6	9.0	11.1
South Asia				0.6	0.8	0.7

Fig 7.5 Evolution of regional patterns of world tourism

Functionally Europe extends into the Mediterranean basin with all its wealth of tourist resources (climatic, coastal and cultural) and Spain, the south of France and Italy are the main Mediterranean destinations, with each country having over 25 million tourist arrivals in 1987, while another 22 million tourists filter into the eastern half of the Mediterranean and spread through Yugoslavia, Greece and, more recently, Turkey.

The southern coast of the Mediterranean is much less popular, though functionally, North Africa is part of the European tourist region, as many of its visitors come from Europe and its destinations compete with other Mediterranean coastal resorts.

The second major functional tourist region of the world is North America (*see* Fig 7.4). While 62 per cent of world international arrivals were concentrated in Europe, only about 10 per cent were located in North America. However, these figures, with their emphasis on international travel, perhaps give a misleading impression of the overall scale of the dominance of Europe and distribution of tourist activity in the world. Both Europe and North America are regions with large, affluent and mobile populations (376 million in Europe, 245 million in USA); but because Europe is politically divided into many small countries, much of the tourist movement in the region is expressed as international travel. In contrast, the United States of America consists of 50 states (many of which are larger than most European countries) and interstate travel is recorded as domestic tourism: in 1988 US citizens made 1241 million person trips of over 160 km from home, of which 840 million were holiday trips, indicating a volume of tourist activity on the same scale as that in Europe.

It is the differences in the political history of the two regions – which has left Europe divided in many small independent political units, but resulted in the political unity of the USA – that gives rise to the apparently enormous difference in levels of tourism as shown by international tourist statistics. As in Europe, the main generating region of North America is in the north (particularly between the Eastern Seaboard and the Great Lakes), while the major tourist resources lie to the south. The major destination regions are the states of Florida, Texas and Southern California, while Mexico and the Caribbean islands also attract very substantial numbers of Americans and Canadians. Thus, parts of Central America and the Caribbean are functionally part of the North American tourist region (*see* Fig 7.5 on p 81).

Of the remaining regions of the world, the most significant in terms of international tourist arrivals is East Asia and the Pacific (*see* Fig 7.4). This region includes the economic 'core' countries of Japan, Australia and New Zealand (*see* Fig 1.2 on p 6), but also the rapidly industrialising countries of Taiwan, South Korea, Singapore and Hong Kong. The average growth rate of GDP of Asian countries throughout the worst of the recession of 1975–85 has been consistently of the order of five to seven per cent per annum – far outstripping the performance of the economies of the other 'non-core' countries of the world, and, indeed, far above the growth rates of many of the main core market economies too.

East Asia and the Pacific accounts for nearly ten per cent of all world international tourist arrivals, and, not surprisingly, the region shows by far the highest growth rates of international tourism in the world. In 1984 and 1985 international tourism was growing by 11 per cent per annum; by 1987 this had increased to 15 per cent per annum and in 1988 had reached nearly 18 per cent per annum. This compares to annual growth rates of tourist arrivals of generally between five and seven per cent in Europe and America over the same period of time.

The generating and destination areas of the Pacific region are far more widely dispersed than in Europe or North America. Hawaii is the main destination and is located right in the centre of the Pacific, while the other significant destinations are scattered in an arc along the south and east sections of the 'Pacific Rim' (*see* Fig 7.4).

The remaining regions of the world (i.e. Central and South America, Subsaharan Africa and the Middle East, and South Asia) are similar in terms of their political instability, generally poor economic performance and low levels of tourist activity. This suggests that they might be considered together as the fourth functional tourist region of the world; a peripheral region, both in economic and tourist terms (*see* Fig 7.4). The continents of this region together account for barely seven per cent of all international tourist arrivals, and their relative poverty generates little international travel from within their own regions. They are spatially separated from the main generating regions and depend on long-haul travel from the developed world for international arrivals. Although the long-haul market is growing, it still accounts for a relatively small proportion of total world international travel.

Fig 7.6 World tourist regions

Thus, the countries of these regions lie outside the spheres of influence of the three main tourist generating regions of the world's economic core. They are mostly in the first phase of tourist development (*see* Chapter 1), and few have even any significant domestic tourism, except perhaps for India, Brazil, Argentina and South Africa. They lack any tourist infrastructure, therefore, and their poverty denies them the resources to develop the necessary facilities for international tourism.

The general political instability of these regions also inhibits any coherent planning for tourist development, even though the foreign currency it would generate could benefit their ailing economies. Travel to the continents of the periphery is also inhibited by potential visitors' perceptions of them as prone to natural disasters, such as droughts, floods and famine, and prone to political disturbances, such as civil wars, border strife and coups. All these factors result in very small numbers of international tourists in these peripheral destinations – less than five million in Subsaharan Africa, and two million in

the Indian subcontinent, and six million in Latin America.

These fundamental problems are experienced in all the regions of the economic periphery but there are spatial variations. The main sub-regions of the periphery are shown on Fig 7.6 and consist of:

1 Subsaharan Africa which extends from the southern parts of the Sahara to the Cape of Good Hope.
2 The Middle East. Syria, Iran, Iraq, Saudi Arabia, the Gulf States.
3 The Indian Subcontinent and Indian Ocean.
   (*a*) Mainland countries: Burma, Bangladesh, the Himalayan states, India, Pakistan and Afghanistan.
   (*b*) The Indian Ocean Islands, including Sri Lanka, the Seychelles, the Maldives, Mauritius, Madagascar.
4 Latin America
   (*a*) Central America: Belize, Costa Rica, El Salvador, Guatemala, Honduras, Nicaragua and Panama.

(*b*) South America: the whole continent from Columbia to Argentina.

These general patterns of world tourism are shown more clearly in Fig 7.7 where the WTO regional statistics are regrouped to match the four functional tourist regions of the world.

Functional regions	% world tourist arrivals	% world tourist receipts
Europe and Mediterranean basin	**64.74**	**54.06**
N Europe	5.96	9.89
E Europe	12.50	1.10
W Europe	22.07	22.09
S Europe	21.86	18.69
N Africa	2.35	2.29
North America, Central American + Caribbean	**16.87**	**23.42**
N America	12.56	17.44
C America	1.82	2.35
Caribbean	2.49	3.63
East Asia and Pacific	**11.35**	**14.31**
The Economic Periphery	**7.04**	**8.25**
S America	2.03	2.26
Subsaharan Africa	1.38	1.05
Middle East	2.90	3.97
S Asia	0.73	0.97

Fig 7.7 Functional tourist regions of the world. Regional pattern of world tourist arrivals and receipts (WTO 1988).

These four functional tourist regions (Europe, North America, the Pacific region and the periphery) are relatively clearly separated tourist systems: most international travel takes place within these regions (i.e. as intra-regional travel) with the dominant flow of tourists towards the Equator within each separate region (*see* Fig 7.4). Up to 1980, about 80 per cent of all the world's international tourism was intra-regional. The remaining 20 per cent was long-haul inter-regional travel, mostly east-west travel between the three main generating regions (i.e. Europe, North America and the Pacific). During the 1980s the pause in the growth of world tourism (*see* Chapter 1) did not inhibit the expansion of long-haul travel, and by 1987 inter-regional travel accounted for between 30 and 40 per cent of arrivals in the three main tourist regions. At the same time, long-haul travel continued to develop in the tourist regions of the economic periphery, for example, into Africa and South Asia.

Thus, the boundaries of the functional tourist regions are becoming more blurred with time as linkages between the regions strengthen. If these trends of increasing inter-regional travel continue, it may be more appropriate to divide the world into just three tourist zones: the economic core; the periphery and a transitional zone between (*see* Fig 7.8). With increasing east-west long-haul travel, the whole of the world's economic core may become one major interlocking tourist system. The adjacent edge of the world's economic periphery is essentially a destination zone for the generating regions of the core, receiving large numbers of tourists from the core. It represents, therefore, a transition zone, which is gradually expanding towards the heart of the economic periphery as new destinations are promoted. The remainder of the periphery still remains relatively isolated from the tourist systems of the core, with its tourism depending on a small but growing band of long-haul travellers from the core, or on small, isolated pockets of tourist development (e.g. southern Brazil, South Africa) within its own borders.

It is clear that patterns of world tourism are evolving over time and that the boundaries of the tourist regions of the world are changing as long-haul tourism grows. The remainder of this book presents the information on individual countries on a different and perhaps less volatile basis. For convenience, therefore, the remaining chapters are organised around the traditional division of the world into continents which do not necessarily coincide with the functional tourist regions of the world (*see* Fig 7.9). It is hoped that this presentation will allow different approaches to the identification of tourist regions to be made and that it will not obscure the fundamental functional relationships between different parts of the world.

QUESTIONS AND DISCUSSION POINTS

1 What factors influence the direction and volume of tourist travel between two different countries of the world?
2 Referring to Fig 7.5 on p 81, describe how the

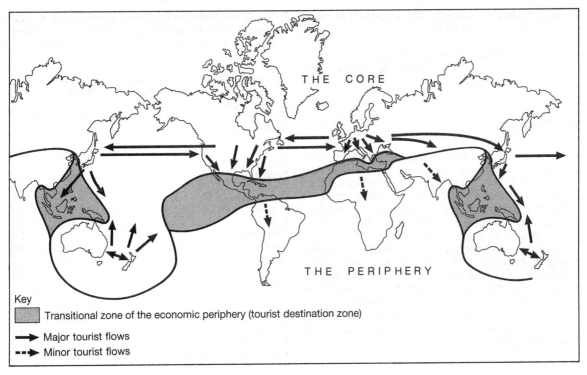

Fig 7.8 'Core-periphery' tourist regions of the world

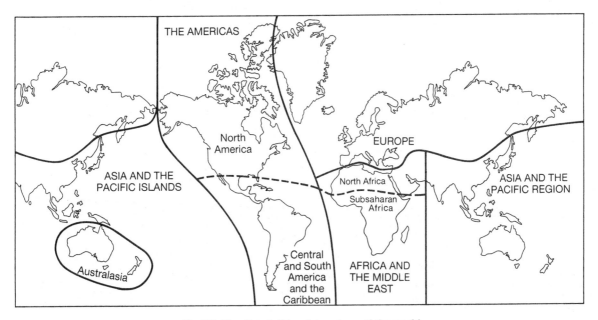

Fig 7.9 'Continental' tourist regions of the world

regional pattern of world tourism changed between:
  (a) 1950 and 1970; and
  (b) 1970 and 1988.
Explain the reasons for these changes.

3 On what basis can the world be divided into different tourist regions?

ASSIGNMENTS

1 You work for the British Tourist Authority (or an American or Australian equivalent – you may choose which one). Your job is to organise the international promotion of your country and to advise inbound tourist operators on their international advertising. Your department has recently expanded and you have appointed several new staff.

Prepare short briefing notes for the new members of staff, outlining the target areas for marketing your country in the next year. List the countries in your own region that will be targeted, and identify the other regions of the world (and the main countries within them) in which you will be actively promoting your country. Explain the reasons for this plan to your new staff.

2 Study the table below showing arrivals of foreign tourists at the Greek frontier in 1989. Suggest some possible explanations for this pattern of arrivals.

% of foreign tourist arrivals (1989) Country of origin	
Austria	3.1
Belgium	1.9
Cypus	1.3
Denmark	3.7
Finland	3.0
France	5.6
FR Germany	19.4
Ireland	0.7
Italy	6.7
Netherlands	5.0
Norway	0.8
Spain	1.2
Sweden	3.1
Switzerland	1.6
Turkey	0.5
UK	19.1
USA	3.3
Yugoslavia	4.3
Rest of World	15.7

Europe

Introduction

This section of the book seeks to answer the following questions.

1 What is the distribution of tourist resources in Europe, and how are they used for tourism?
2 What is the tourist role of each European country; where are their resorts; who visits them and why?

Chapter 8 outlines the structure, climate and tourist resources of Europe and the broad flow of tourist travel within Europe. The established Mediterranean destinations of France, Italy and Spain are described in Chapters 9 to 11, while the evolving destinations in the eastern half of the Mediterranean coastlands (i.e. Yugoslavia, Greece, Turkey, Malta and Cyprus) are dealt with in Chapters 12 and 13. These Mediterranean destinations are in competetition with the resorts along the North African coast. (The latter may be thus considered functionally as part of the European tourist region but are discussed in Part 5.)

One of the major inland destinations of Europe is the Alpine mountain chain. The core of the mountains are in Switzerland and Austria and are discussed in Chapter 14, although the outer fringes of the Alps are dealt with in the chapters on France, Italy, Yugoslavia and Germany. The main tourist generating regions of Europe are discussed in Chapters 15 (Benelux and Germany), 17 (the UK and Ireland) and 18 (Scandinavia).

The tourist resources of Eastern Europe and Russia are briefly described in Chapter 16. At the time of writing (1990), the economic and political geography of this part of Europe was undergoing major changes and its undoubted tourist generating potential has yet to be realised.

CHAPTER 8

Europe

LEARNING OBJECTIVES

After reading this chapter you should be able to

- identify the main physical, climatic, cultural and political regions of Europe
- locate the most important tourist regions of Europe
- explain the relationship between Europe's structure, climate and resources and its pattern of tourism
- describe the general patterns of tourist routes and tourist movements within Europe
- explain the relationship between a country's European location and the mode of transport used by its tourists
- appreciate the influence of economic, political and cultural factors on the development of tourism within Europe.

Introduction

Europe is one of the world's most highly developed tourist regions, both in terms of levels of domestic tourism and in terms of international tourist activity, accounting for 62 per cent of all international tourists in 1989. When defined in terms of systems of tourist travel, the European region includes the UK, Scandinavia, mainland Europe and all the countries bordering the Mediterranean basin: this chapter will discuss European tourism on this basis. The patterns of tourism within each country and sub-region of the continent of Europe will be described in the following chapters, while the countries of North Africa and the Middle East that have a Mediterranean coast will be described in detail in Part 5 (pp 231–246). The patterns of tourist movement within Europe are influenced by physical factors on the one hand and by economic and political factors on the other.

Physical factors influencing tourist flows

The north of Europe is characterised by high concentrations of highly urbanised and industrial populations who live in cool temperate, highly variable climates. To the immediate south lies a comparatively undeveloped region with a climate that could be considered ideal for tourism encircling an enclosed sea: the Mediterranean.

This juxtaposition of regions of such contrasting character has led to the evolution of a massive two-fold tidal flow of tourists. First, a north to south flow both on a national scale (reflected in the domestic tourism of each country) and on an international scale predominantly to the Mediterranean. Second, there is a major coastward flow, again internationally mainly to the Mediterranean but also at domestic levels to the available coastline within each national boundary.

These north to south coastward flows are seasonal, with the main summer peak but with a secondary less significant winter peak flow to the southernmost coasts only. Superimposed on these major flows are further resource-based tourist movements:

1 a double seasonal flow to the mountain regions of Europe in the summer for scenic tourism and in winter for winter sports; and
2 an all-season flow into the cities throughout Europe for cultural, historic and business tourism, and a complementary flow of local urban populations out of the cities to the tourist attractions in the cities' own region or hinterland.

These tourists travel along corridors that are partly constrained by physical barriers: southward road and rail flows are concentrated on routes through the mountain barriers such as the Rhône corridor in France and the main passes through the Alps. Once the coast is reached, the flow of tourists tends to be spread via routes running along the main tourist coasts (e.g. from Marseille, west along the Spanish coast to Alicante and Malaga and east to Livorno and beyond; the N2 motorway running the length of the Italian Adriatic coast which is mirrored by the Adriatic highway on the Yugoslavian side).

Political and economic factors influencing tourist flows

Chapter 7 has listed the economic and political factors that influence tourist flows between countries. In the past, of course, the major political divide was between the Western European democracies and the communist bloc of Eastern Europe, which inhibited travel into and out of the communist countries.

Evolving economic and political structures and affiliations are leading to new patterns of tourism in Europe. The political geography of Eastern Europe has been transformed since 1989: barriers to travel between the countries belonging to the European Community (the EC) have progressively been reduced, while movement of Scandinavians between Scandinavian countries is free of all restrictions.

Other historic political relationships may facilitate or inhibit the development of cross-border tourism, for example, the French outnumber other European arrivals in their ex-colonies of Algeria, Tunisia, and Senegal (originally the administrative centre for the whole of French West Africa) whereas long-standing conflicts, (e.g. between Turkey and Greece) may still be reflected in low levels of travel between the country.

Physical resources of Europe

In very general terms, Europe can be divided into three main physical zones (*see* Fig 8.1), which are characterised by very different types of tourism. These regions are:

1 The Mediterranean basin – the focal point of the southward flow of summer tourists.
2 The mountain chains that form the east-west spine of central and southern Europe. This region is the magnet that draws the dual seasonal flow of summer scenic tourism and winter sport tourism. It is also the region that divides the Mediterranean basin from
3 The industrialised lowlands of the northwest margins and of continental Europe. This region is the focus of business tourism and the area that generates day tourism to the local coast and countryside.

Each of these regions will be discussed: the following sections will describe the physical resources that have some relevance for tourism.

The Mediterranean basin

Physical character

Figure 8.1 shows that the description 'basin' is very appropriate, as apart from in the southeast sector (Tunisia, Libya and Egypt), the Mediterranean sea is encircled by mountains and uplands, with generally only a narrow strip of coastal lowlands (the strip of land that has the true Mediterranean climate). This structure reinforces the factors that protect the marine environment of this enclosed sea, sheltering the Mediterranean from the influences of Atlantic weather and wave patterns.

Climate

The general characteristics of the Mediterranean type of climate make it ideal for tourism. The summers are hot (generally averaging over 21° C)

Fig 8.1 Structure of Europe

yet the relative humidity is low enough to maintain a comfortable environment for many forms of tourism for most of the time. However, the daily temperature range is high (up to 11° C) with temperatures climbing to over 30° C at the hottest time of day (mid to late afternoon). This limits active pursuits during this 'siesta' period, although the diurnal temperature range at coastal resorts may be slightly less due to the moderating influence of the sea and the cooling effect of sea breezes. The summers are very sunny with cloudless skies throughout the sustained and reliable summer drought.

Even the winters have potential for tourism, as in many parts of the Mediterranean the temperatures in December and January rarely fall below

10° C and although the rainfall is concentrated in autumn or winter, it frequently occurs in intense bursts with clear, sunny skies in between. Much of the Mediterranean enjoys more than four hours' sunshine a day in December, and the greater part of the French and Spanish Mediterranean coast has less than ten rain days on average in January. Total amounts of rainfall range between 385 mm pa and 900 mm pa. The area that experiences this type of climate is shown in Fig 8.2.

It can be seen from the map that the Mediterranean basin extends over 3000 km east-west from the fringes of the Atlantic to the heart of the continental land masses of Asia, the Middle East and Africa, and extends roughly from

WESTERN · CONTINENTAL

MARITIME

SA

SA/D

	Mediterranean
	Mountain
SA	Semi arid	D	Desert

Fig 8.2 Europe's climates

latitude 31° N to 46° N, a north-south extent of more than 1500 km. Thus, within the broad climatic pattern described above, some variation in temperatures and rainfall is to be expected over so wide a region. The temperatures tend to increase not only to the south but also to the east of the Mediterranean basin. In summer the more land-locked eastern Mediterranean may be up to 2° C warmer than the Western Mediterranean which is more open to the influences of the cooler, moister Atlantic weather systems.

The north-south temperature variations are more clear-cut; for example, the July average in Venice is 24.1° C, whereas in Djerba (on the North African coast) which is more or less due south of Venice, the summer average climbs to around 27° C.

The islands of the Mediterranean show a further variation in their patterns of temperature. The surrounding sea warms more slowly than land in the summer but retains its heat and, therefore, cools down more slowly in winter. This has the effect of marginally depressing the peak summer temperatures of the islands, but conversely it also has the effect of keeping the winter temperatures a little higher than those of the adjacent mainlands. The smaller the island, the more pronounced is this effect. Thus, some

of the Mediterranean islands have important winter holiday trades (e.g. in 1988 Malta received 18 per cent of its visitors between November and February).

The second major variation in climate over the whole Mediterranean region concerns the distribution of rainfall. The total quantity of rainfall generally decreases to the east and south, whereas the length of the summer drought increases from two months in Marseille in the south of France, to three months (June–August) on the Spanish coast, six months (April–September) in Athens and the Greek islands, and to nine months (February–October) in Alexandria. Not surprisingly, the total annual hours of sunshine increase across the Mediterranean in parallel with the increasing length of the summer drought (*see* Fig 8.3).

The Mediterranean type of climate thus has great tourist appeal and the whole coast of the Mediterranean basin enjoys its benefits, although Fig 8.2 shows that it is experienced on only a relatively narrow coastal zone. In the southern Mediterranean, the Mediterranean climate rapidly gives way inland to the deserts of continental Africa, while in the north and east the proximity of the European and Asian land masses cause the climate inland to become rapidly more extreme in temperatures. The mountain ranges in Yugoslavia, the Apennines and the Alps all generate orographic rainfall, leading to sharp increases in rainfall inland away from the narrow Mediterranean coastal belt.

The Mediterranean coast and sea

The Mediterranean, as noted in Chapter 3, is one of the world's enclosed seas. Thus, the low tidal range (one metre at its very highest on the coast of Provence, South of France, and at the head of the Adriatic) combined with small waves (generally between 1 and 1.25 metres in height and seldom exceeding 2.75 metres in the winter storms) make tourism easy to provide and manage.

However, there are environmental problems arising from the fact that the sea is virtually completely enclosed, which may threaten the future of coastal tourism in the region. The Mediterranean Sea loses water from its surface due to intense evaporation throughout the hot

Place	Number of months' summer drought	Mean annual total hours sunshine	Mean annual total rainfall (mm)
French Mediterranean coast	2	2201	575
Malaga	3		600
Athens	6	2737	396
Alexandria	9	3119	217

Fig 8.3 Climatic variation in the Mediterranean

summer months; this is replaced by rivers, but more importantly, from inflow of sea water from the Atlantic through the Straits of Gibraltar. A little Mediterranean water flows out at sea floor level under the incoming current but this exchange of water is such that the Mediterranean water is completely exchanged only once in 75 years. Therefore, any pollution in the Mediterranean is relatively rapidly concentrated (by the evaporation) and only very slowly dispersed into the Atlantic.

There are about 350 million people living in the countries bordering the Mediterranean Sea, all discharging waste into the sea, either directly or via the main rivers such as the Po and Rhône which both flow from the main industrial areas. In summer, 100 million tourists add to the problem. The waste includes some noxious industrial waste, but consists mainly of sewage runoff, which contains chemicals such as phosphates that plants need for their growth. The UN Environmental Programme shows that 85 per cent of urban effluent is discharged into the Mediterranean without previous treatment. In addition to this, it was estimated that in 1977 over one million tonnes of plant nutrients (from agricultural fertilisers washed from the fields into the rivers) were carried into the sea.

In particularly warm, still conditions the concentration of pollutants may build up in particular locations where the normal currents are slow to mix the sea and river water (e.g. at the head of the Adriatic). The surface water temperature in a normal August may reach 23–24° C; the combination of high water temperatures with the build up of chemical pollutants many of which are in fact plant nutrients may trigger off the very rapid growth of small sea weeds and microscopic plants (algae) that float and multiply in the sea water by feeding on these dissolved plant nutrients. These 'algal blooms' were responsible for the green slime that developed

in the sea off the Italian Adriatic resorts in the summer of 1989, and made sea bathing extremely unpleasant.

The other form of marine pollution that has an immediate effect on tourism is oil pollution. Very little of the Mediterranean is free of oil pollution as oil tankers regularly cross the sea from Suez and North Africa to the Atlantic. Over two million tonnes of crude oil a year is spilled into the Mediterranean during loading and unloading and tank cleaning operations.

Additional forms of pollution, for example from industrial processes, may be less immediately visible, but in the long run may have serious effects on health and thus inhibit tourists from bathing.

The mountain chains of Central and Southern Europe

Figure 8.1 shows that the mountain core of Europe consists of (east to west) the Pyrénées, the Cevennes (in the Massif Central), the Alps and the Carpathians. Three fingers of upland areas extend southward from this core into the Mediterranean region, namely the Iberian plateau with the Sierra Nevada of Andalucia forming its highest point, the Apennines that make up the spine of Italy and finally the chain of mountains that run north-west to south-east through Yugoslavia, Albania, Bulgaria and Greece before being submerged to form the Greek Islands in the Aegean Sea. The Alps rise to over 4500 metres and dominate Southern Europe.

The core of the Alps consists of ancient mainly igneous rock, which when glaciated gives rise to jagged peaks and deep 'U' shaped valleys – dramatic landscapes of very high relative relief. The middle slopes may be wooded but towards the snow line the coniferous forest gives way to low growing vegetation adapted to conditions that are too cold for the growth of trees. The igneous Alps are flanked by and interspersed with mountains of limestone (e.g. the Jura, Dolomites, and further south the Dalmatian and Greek uplands), which in their southern extensions give rise to the typical limestone mountain or 'karst' scenery of dry valleys, rivers that disappear underground, extensive cave systems and barren mountain tops. Thus, the variety of mountain resources of Southern and Central Europe provide a wealth of choice for scenic and activity (i.e. climbing, walking, caving) holidays in summer in spite of the fact that the climate with its summer or autumn rainfall peak would appear to be less than ideal for tourism. It is, however, the winter climate that provides the second major tourist resource of these mountain regions. Even the southernmost extensions of the mountain systems have enough snow for the development of some winter sports centres, for example, in the Pyrénées the snow line descends to 1000 metres in mid-winter, and ski resorts have also been developed in the Sierra Nevada of Southern Spain and in the Apennines of the Italian peninsula. However, the major international winter sports centres are located in the mountain chains of continental Europe, where the continental high pressure system builds up and stabilises in winter, giving long spells of very cold, calm weather with clear skies and high amounts of sunshine. The effects of altitude and continentality thus combine to produce ideal conditions for the accumulation and maintenance of better quality snow over a longer winter season than in the more southerly mountain chains. The Alps are, therefore, the primary centre for international mountain tourism in Europe with many resorts that perform the dual function of providing for both summer scenic and for winter sports tourism.

Further north in Europe, suitable snow cover does exist at progressively lower altitudes, e.g. in the Black Forest in Germany which rises to 1500 metres, the Harz (up to 1125 metres) and at 900 metres in the Cairngorms in Scotland. These regions, however, tend to cater for more localised domestic winter sports demand, as towards the north and western margins of Europe the climate becomes progressively windier and more variable (and thus less suitable for skiing) due to the increasing influence of depressions sweeping in from the Atlantic.

The lowlands of the north and west margins of continental Europe

The interior of continental Northern Europe has an extreme climate with very cold winters dropping below −30° C in January (e.g. Warsaw) and warm summers (19° C Warsaw, July) but the climate here suffers from a summer peak of rainfall associated with thundery, unstable weather conditions that develop over continental northern Europe. The rainfall peaks between May and August; Warsaw receives 87 mm rainfall in July alone. This reduces the tourist appeal of the climate of this part of Europe particularly in comparison to the adjacent Mediterranean climate.

It has been noted that the western margins of Europe experience an extremely variable climate dominated by the influence of cyclones moving northwest from the mid Atlantic over northwest France, Britain and Northern Europe. These depressions caused by the process of mixing of moist Atlantic air with other air masses, bring cloudy weather with bursts of heavy rain, periods of freshening winds and showers, interspersed with spells of sunshine, all in quick succession. From time to time, however, the western margins of Europe may experience the sort of weather more typical of continental Europe – or indeed the Mediterranean – as the more stable air masses associated with these types of climate temporarily shift towards Britain. These can bring periods of intense cold weather in winter or conversely spells of hot, dry and sunny weather in summer, such as in the 'drought' years of 1976, 1989 and 1990 in the UK. It is the variability and unreliability of this type of climate that reduces its tourist appeal; it is virtually impossible to provide good long-term forecasts, so that tourists booking summer holidays in advance risk the chance of picking on a spell of wet or unsettled weather. In spite of this there is still a substantial flow of domestic tourism to the coasts of the countries of the 'western maritime' zone but more and more this is of the short break, second holiday or day-trip type of tourism. Those who are able to take up international travel will be lured south to the reliable and predictably perfect summer weather of the Mediterranean region. Thus, the contrasts in the climate of Europe is one of the major factors which generates the north to south flow of tourists from Northern Europe to the Mediterranean coast.

Patterns of tourist movement in Europe

There are two main concentrations of population in Europe: the first extends through the main industrial area of the Northern European lowlands stretching from Britain in the west through northern France, Benelux, East and West Germany to Czechoslovakia and Poland in the east. The second (and the only major concentration of urban and industrial development south of the mountain spine of Europe) is located on the north Italian plain. These are the major tourist generating regions of Europe (*see* Fig 8.4).

Car travel is the most important mode of tourist travel in Europe, dispersing tourists from these major population concentrations to the tourist receiving areas. Figure 8.5 shows domestic and international holiday travel habits and demonstrates the dominance of car travel to be a consistent pattern in most European countries, with the French at 81 per cent showing the highest rate of usage of the car.

Train travel only plays a significant part in countries such as Spain and Portugal which have lower than normal car ownership rates, or countries such as France with particularly good, fast intercity rail services.

Predictably it is only countries which are wholly islands (e.g. Ireland) or which have much island territory (e.g. Greece and Denmark) that utilise boats to any great extent. These countries and those located in the periphery of Europe are

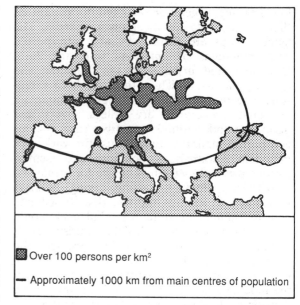

□ Over 100 persons per km²

▬ Approximately 1000 km from main centres of population

Fig 8.4 Major tourist generating areas of Europe

the only countries to rely significantly on air transport for their main domestic and international holiday travel (e.g. UK, Netherlands, Luxembourg and Denmark to the north, and Greece on the southern periphery). It is, however, road travel that dominates European holiday travel. In 1986 68 per cent of all international and domestic holiday trips throughout Europe as a whole were made by car.

The main international flows of tourists from the main generating areas of Northern Europe

	Car	Coach	Train	'Plane	Boat	Motorbike	
France	81	7	15	6	2	2 ⎫	Mediterranean
Portugal	76	16	17	3	3	1 ⎪	territories. (Road
Italy	73	11	15	5	5	2 ⎬	and rail transport
Spain	70	12	16	5	2	– ⎭	dominant)
Belgium	77	7	6	10	1	2	
West Germany	61	7	16	17	3	1	
Netherlands	70	14	8	14	5	6	
Luxembourg	62	15	10	19	4	–	
Denmark	59	4	14	18	11	3 ⎫	Island countries
UK	59	14	11	24	8	– ⎪	(ferry travel
Ireland	51	6	11	31	18	1 ⎬	important)
Greece	78	0	4	13	25	1 ⎭	

Northerly countries over 1000 km from most of the Mediterranean coast (air travel important) {Belgium, West Germany, Netherlands, Luxembourg}

Fig 8.5 Transport used by Europeans on holiday 1986: % of residents' holiday trips (domestic and international) by mode of transport

are constrained by the mountain barrier to which they are attracted and through which they have to pass to reach the goal of the Mediterranean coast. Traffic is concentrated into the easiest north-south crossings of the Alps and considerable congestion may be experienced on the main routes at peak times.

The Rhône valley forms the major artery taking traffic via the Autoroute du Sol from the Paris region (and the western end of the Northern European conurbations) southwards round the western end of the Alps to the coasts of the western Mediterranean. The Rhine rift valley similarly forms a dominant north-south corridor of movement from the low countries and Germany to the northern slopes of the Alps. Here traffic either swings west to join the Rhône-Soâne route southwards to the French or Spanish Mediterranean coasts or filters more directly south through the Alpine passes or tunnels into northern Italy for access to the Italian and Yugoslavian coasts. Once the Mediterranean has been reached, tourists are dispersed via routes that hug the coast, keeping to the narrow strip of coastal lowlands (*see* Fig 8.6).

To the west, unbroken motorways run the length of the Spanish coast from the French border to Málaga, and to the east via the Côte d'Azur and North Italy. The western and Adriatic coasts of Italy are accessible from the Côte d'Azur and the north Italian plain, and the Adriatic highway runs along the length of the Yugoslavian coast from Trieste to the Albanian border. Visitors can conveniently filter off these motorways directly into the coastal resort of their choice, though the proximity of major through routes running parallel to the coast may cause problems to local traffic, cutting off locals from the coast itself.

In spite of the convenient access by road to the Alpine and Mediterranean resorts, there is a limit to the distance and time that tourists are prepared to spend driving to their destinations. According to the Geneva-based International Touring Alliance, over 70 per cent of all leisure car trips in Europe are between 500 and 1000 km in length. Southern Spain, the toe of Italy, Greece and Turkey lie outside the 1000 km range of travel from the Northern European tourist generating area (*see* Fig 8.4 on page 94). Significantly it is only Spain, Greece and Turkey of all the countries of mainland Europe that have

a significant proportion of international tourist arrivals by air (*see* Fig 8.7), although, of course, the tourist areas cut off from the tourist-generating areas by sea, namely Britain, the Mediterranean islands and the countries of the North African coast also have a high proportion of incoming tourists arriving by air.

In those Mediterranean countries that rely on air transport for the bulk of their tourist arrivals, the developments for international tourists tend to be clustered in zones around the international airports, while in the countries of mainland Europe where car travel is the dominant mode of arrival, the tourist developments tend to be much more evenly spread through the attractive parts of each country.

General patterns of tourism in Europe

The Mediterranean basin is the dominant destination region of Europe with 132.9 million international tourist arrivals to the countries bordering the Mediterranean Sea in 1988. The greatest volume of mass tourism (99.4 million arrivals) is concentrated in the northwestern part of the Mediterranean (in France, Spain and Italy). The second important sub-region of the Mediterranean is the northeast section (Greece, Yugoslavia, Turkey plus the islands of Malta and Cyprus) with 22.4 million arrivals. This subregion has experienced two spurts of growth in tourist arrivals, firstly in the decade 1960–1970 when its share of Mediterranean arrivals jumped from 5.4 per cent to 11.6 per cent, and more recently in the period 1980–1985 when its market share rose from 13.9 per cent of all arrivals in the Mediterranean basin to 16.2 per cent (a growth rate of over 40 per cent, way above the growth rates of 13 to 18 per cent experienced in the other sub-regions of the Mediterranean). The tourist flows to the African and extreme east coasts of the Mediterranean are negligible in comparison. In 1988, the southwest Mediterranean (i.e. the Islamic countries of Morocco, Algeria and Tunisia) received only 7.2 million arrivals and only 3.1 million visitors travelled to the southeast, (i.e. Libya, Egypt, Israel and Lebanon – countries where international conflict, civil wars and terrorist activity are currently occurring or have only relatively recently died down).

Fig 8.6 European motorway routes

KEY

⑫ air

34 road

Fig 8.7 European tourist arrivals: % arrivals by air and road

After the Mediterranean, Central Europe is the second most important tourist destination area with 48.2 million international arrivals in 1988. The Alps, of course, are a major attraction, with 28.2 million international visitors to Switzerland and Austria alone. Northern Europe received 23.5 million visitors.

Finally, Eastern Europe whose tourist resources consist mainly of the Carpathians (the eastern extension of the mountain chains of Southern Europe) and inland lakes and seas, such as Lake Balaton in Hungary and the Black Sea, received 43 million international tourists in 1988. This represented mainly travel between members of the communist bloc, as freedom of travel between Eastern and Western Europe was not possible before the upheavals in Eastern Europe in 1989.

Political and cultural factors and their influence on patterns of tourism

The three main cultural and political regions of Europe are Western Europe, Moslem countries and the countries of Eastern Europe. Western Europe consists of Christian cultures, market economies and stable parliamentary democracies; and most countries of Western Europe are members of the EC.

The European Community (EC)

Belgium	Italy
Denmark	Luxembourg
France	Netherlands
Germany	Portugal
Greece	Spain
Ireland	UK

Fig 8.8 The twelve members of EC

There are relatively few constraints on travel between these countries, although until the end of 1992 and the full implementation of the Single European Act, there are still passport controls and differential rates of tax on goods necessitating customs controls. The Single European Act, or to give it its full title, 'The Single (Internal) Market of the European Community (EC)' defines the Single Market as 'an area without internal frontiers in which the free movement of goods, persons, services and capital is ensured'. As the Community evolves towards this situation, there will be changes in patterns of tourist movement throughout the 12 countries but the outcome may be simply an increase in total levels of tourism rather than its spatial redistribution. The overall effect may be simply to reinforce trends which are already well established.

The EC have, however, attempted to influence the spatial distribution of tourism more explicitly in two other ways. In 1986 the Community agreed to improve the seasonal and geographical distribution of tourism, by encouraging member countries to stagger holidays, to reduce congestion and also to promote social, rural and cultural tourism. More specifically member countries are invited not to encourage further tourist development in saturated areas, and to promote areas which have spare capacity.

The EC can aid the implementation of these policies directly through financial instruments such as the European Regional Development Fund, the ERDF, whose overall objective is to help correct imbalances in regional development, that is, to aid regions whose economic development is slow or declining. As tourism is one means of regional development and the ailing regions are likely to be those with spare capacity for tourism and not suffering from tourist congestion, grant aid and financial assistance to tourism can fulfil both sets of objectives. Tourism projects accounted for 166 million ECU of ERDF expenditure in the period 1975–84. (N.B. 1 ECU in 1984 = £0.6013.) Grants to member states over this period are shown in Fig 8.9.

Although the amounts of grant are small in the context of total (government and private sector) investment in tourism, these grants help support policies for the relocation of tourism.

The regions benefitting from this tourist investment are in the peripheral, mainly rural, regions of Europe (North and West Britain, the toe of Italy and the Greek Islands) or in certain depressed industrial areas of central Europe and in the Midlands and North of England.

The Eastern Bloc

Up to the autumn of 1989 the countries of Eastern

	Million (ECU)
Belgium	6.71
Denmark	0.74
West Germany	13.02
Greece	7.73
France	4.33
Ireland	0.27
Italy	34.90
Luxembourg	1.59
Netherlands	2.38
UK	94.67
Total	166.38 m

Fig 8.9 European Regional Development Fund – Tourism Grants 1975–84

Europe were all communist countries, with centrally planned economies but each country having differing levels of freedom of travel and of affiliation to the Soviet Union.

Yugoslavia was expelled from the communist bloc in 1948 and has operated independently from the USSR, yet up to 1989 has retained communism as a means of government. The country has been open to western tourists since 1961. Albania is also a communist country independent of the USSR, but, in contrast to Yugoslavia, has been completely closed to Western travellers. There are signs, however, that Albania is starting to change and take in tourists. The rest of the communist world, which had been under the tight control of the USSR is undergoing profound changes as a consequence of the policy of *glasnost* introduced in the USSR in 1986. In the autumn of 1989 the Warsaw Pact countries of East Germany, Poland, Czechoslovakia, Hungary, Bulgaria and Rumania abandoned communism and started the process of transition to market economies and democratic forms of government. These countries up to 1989 had experienced severe controls on international travel by their citizens, and imposed strict controls on incoming Western travellers. Given longer term political stability the removal of these restrictions may eventually have very profound effects on patterns of tourism throughout Europe, as new destinations are made available and accessible in Eastern Europe to Western travellers and a total population of over 110 million Eastern Europeans become more mobile to travel west as soon as their economic situation allows it.

The USSR itself may be facing a long period of political and economic readjustment, and similarly, the patterns of tourism that will emerge will take time to change and evolve into new spatial patterns.

The Islamic World

Islamic religious attitudes do not favour the promotion of Western-style sun, sea and sand tourism. Nevertheless, sporadic pockets of tourist development designed for the Western market have been established in the more politically stable countries of Morocco, Algeria and Tunisia although the association of Tunisia in 1985 with Palestinian terrorism has constrained further rapid development of tourism. The core of the political instability within the Islamic world centres on the long-running conflict between the Jewish State of Israel and the surrounding Arab/ Islamic countries of Syria, Jordan, Lebanon, Saudi Arabia, Egypt and Libya. The conflict has existed since Israel was established in 1948, though the focus of the conflict has shifted. In the 1980s Egypt and Israel were not involved in conflict, whereas Lebanon had disintegrated into civil war. Thus, the potential for coastal and cultural tourism in this part of the region remains relatively undeveloped of all the countries in this region, Turkey is the most likely to undergo major changes in the near future. Although 95 per cent of Turks are Moslems, Turkey is an atheist State, and seems to identify itself more with the Western European style of economic and political organisation than those typical of the other Islamic countries. It is becoming politically more stable, and has expressed its desire to become integrated into Europe. In parallel with these changes, Turkey has been 'discovered' by Western tourists and in the 1980s it experienced the most rapid growth in international tourist arrivals in the whole European region. However, tourism to the Moslem countries of the southeast Mediterranean has been further disrupted by the 1990–1991 Gulf crisis.

Economic factors and their influence on patterns of tourism

Chapter 7 discussed the significance of differences in standards of living, exchange rates and relative costs in encouraging tourist flows between countries. Given the location of the major physical resources, and the political divisions within Europe, cost and price factors do influence specific destination choices. These factors have encouraged and reinforced the southward flow of tourists from the affluent Northern European countries to the relatively less developed economies in the south, for example, Spain, Portugal, Greece and Turkey. Cost factors also influence the distribution of tourists between these countries. The Economist Intelligence Unit estimates that over half the changes in the travel shares of competing Mediterranean destinations in the period 1980–1987 were due to changes in the relative cost of holidays in each destination. The success of the Northern European countries in adapting their economies to post-industrialisation, and the relative rates of economic development of the southern countries will, no doubt, influence the choice of specific geographical location of future tourist usage in the main destination regions of Europe.

QUESTIONS AND DISCUSSION POINTS

1 Study the figures in the following two tables. Which physical, political and economic factors help explain the pattern of tourist arrivals to Tunisia?

Tourist arrivals in Tunisia 1986

Nationality	Arrivals (000s)
French	411.6
West German	330.5
British	124.4
Italian	58.7
Scandinavian	71.8
Swiss	34.0
Belgian	38.5
Dutch	46.0
Austrian	26.5
Spanish	17.1
Yugoslav	4.0
Luxembourg	2.4
Algerian	297.5
Libyan	3.9
Moroccan	6.7
USA	6.3
Canadian	2.4
Middle Eastern	22.4
African	5.8
Other	21.9
Total	1532.3

Tourist arrivals in Tunisia by mode of transport 1986 (000s)

	By air	By sea	By road
European	1084.5	40.5	10.3
North African	42.4	2.7	263.0
Middle Eastern	21.7	0.2	0.7

2 In what ways might the activities of the European Community influence the pattern of tourism in Europe?

3 A variety of reasons help to explain the movement of tourists between the countries of Europe. Some of these reasons are listed below. Can you rank them in order of importance? Are there any other factors that influence tourist flows that are not included here?
- Distance between countries.
- Differences in cost of living.
- Convenient routes between countries.
- Differences in climate between countries.

ASSIGNMENTS

1 Divide into groups of two.

One of you works for a tour company based in London. Your chief executive is presenting a paper at an international conference in Genoa in Italy at Easter. He has asked you to make his travel arrangements for him. Outline the modes of transport and the routes that he might choose from. Recommend the route and mode that you think might best meet his travel needs. List the factors that influence your decision.

The other member of the pair works in the AA Overseas Routes Unit. A party of students who share a car and are based at a college in South Wales also wish to attend the same conference, and have asked for your advice on how to get to Genoa. Outline the choice of routes open to them, and recommend a route that you think would be most suitable to them. List the factors that influenced your decision.

As a pair, compare these two lists. Explain any similarities and differences in your lists.

2 You work for the Economic Regional Development Fund of the European Community. You have just received two requests for grant aid for major tourist projects, one in Merseyside in the northwest of England, and the other from Sicily in southern Italy. The applications are for equal amounts of money. You only have enough money left in your budget this year to fund one of the projects.

Identify the tourism and development objectives and policies of the EC and ERDF. Make a reasoned recommendation of which project should be granted aid.

CHAPTER 9

France

LEARNING OBJECTIVES

After reading this chapter you should be able to:

- assess the tourist potential of the climatic, landscape, historical and cultural resources of France
- distinguish the regional distribution of these geographical resources and their development and use for tourism
- demonstrate a knowledge of the main tourist resorts and tourist centres
- understand the role of France in the general pattern of European tourism
- be aware of the problems of seasonality and congestion in French tourist destinations and on the routes to them.

Introduction

France is characterised by a variety of tourist resources: different types of coast and climate, attractive, unspoilt rural areas, mountains, a wealth of historic and architectural sites and the cultural attractions of French nightlife and regional cuisine. With such a varied choice, it is not surprising that the majority of the French take holidays in their own country. There is, however, a spatial imbalance between the distribution of the tourist resources and the location of the resident population: the greatest concentration of natural resources lie in the south of the country in upland and Mediterranean France while the most densely populated industrial areas of France are in the lowlands of the north and northeast, and around Lyon in central France.

The French domestic market is large, with an estimated 52 million holidays being taken in

Fig 9.1 Regions of France

1988, and is still very highly peaked in August. This inevitably leads to great congestion on the routes (the E1/N6 and N7) running south from Paris through Lyon via the Rhône Valley, to the Mediterranean coast at Marseille. The Côte d'Azur to the east of Marseille has long been the most popular holiday region for the French. Some of the other regions are relatively economically backward compared to the more densely populated and industrialised lowlands of northern France. The highly centralised French planning system has systematically developed certain rural regions for tourism, e.g. the Aquitaine, parts of the Central Massif and Languedoc/Rousillon, in order to encourage regional economic development. These projects have focused on the needs of the huge domestic market rather than those of foreign tourists. Paris, the Côte d'Azur and the Alps are still the most popular destinations for the international visitor to France. 38.3 million foreign tourists visited France in 1988, making it the leading European international tourist destination.

Physically France can be divided into five tourist resource regions (*see* Fig 9.1):

1 The lowlands of the north and west (the Seine, Loire and Garonne basins).
2 The Channel and Atlantic coasts, including the Brittany peninsula. Both these two regions experience the variable western maritime climate.
3 Upland France. This consists of a series of uplands running from the Pyrénées in the south west, via the central Massif to the Alps and its associated ranges in the east. All these areas have the harsher climate characteristic of upland areas.
4 The Mediterranean coast.
5 The island of Corsica.

The lowlands of north and west France

The Paris basin

This region consists of the Seine basin with the Paris conurbation (the Ile de France) at its centre. To the northeast of Paris, the open, flat landscapes of Picardy and the Nord rise gradually to the border with Belgium. To the east of Paris the lowlands give way to a series of scarps and vales, and then to the plateau of Lorraine. To the south, the Seine valley rises gradually into the

gently rolling countryside of Burgundy. The chalk plateau of Normandy lies to the west of Paris. The countryside of the Paris basin is pleasant though unspectacular; it provides for the daily and weekend recreation of the city, rather than for tourist needs. International tourists tend to bypass the countryside of this region on their way south.

Paris itself is, of course, another matter. The Ile de France received 34 per cent of the foreign arrivals at French hotels (amounting to six million visitors) and 41 per cent of all foreign hotel bednights in 1987. A similar number of French tourists also stayed in hotels in Paris that year. Paris has a wealth of cultural and historic attractions such as Notre-Dame Cathedral, Montmartre, the Opera, the Champs Elysées, the Arc de Triomphe, and the Eiffel Tower. The museums and galleries, such as the Louvre and the Musée d'Orsay are also world-famous, and the cafés, theatre, nightlife and shops all add to the attraction of the city centre as a tourist destination. There are also attractions, both ancient and modern on the outskirts of Paris. For example two modern theme parks (Asterixland and Mirapolis) are located on the northern fringe within 40 km of the centre, and a third Disney World is due to open in 1992, and the Palace of Versailles, built in the 17th century, is located even closer to the city centre, on the southwestern edge of the city. Within an 80 km range of Paris there are additional attractions such as the Palace of Fontainebleau, Chartres Cathedral and the vineyards and caves of the Champagne region.

Paris also has an expanding range of exhibition and conference facilities. It is a leading centre for international conferences and business tourism due to the combination of high quality facilities, city centre attractions and good accessibility.

The Charles de Gaulle airport will increase its importance as a rail, air and road communications hub as the European high-speed rail network is developed and the airport terminal capacity is increased.

The Loire valley

The Loire river rises in the central Massif, flows north towards Paris, and swings west at Orléans to reach the Atlantic at La Baule. The lowland landscape of the area, known as the Garden of

France, is quietly attractive with agricultural land in the valley bottom and vineyards on the upper slopes. The historic resources are the major tourist attraction: over 120 châteaux are strung along the river, often sited on a prominent bluff or spur overlooking the valley. They range from defensive medieval castles through to renaissance residences to the classical houses of the 17th and 18th centuries. The main concentration of châteaux lies between Angers and Orléans. A significant number are now hotels, and many more have additional attractions: for example, Chambord (the largest château of the region) has a game reserve, the fortress-like Chaumont displays a range of horse-drawn vehicles, Villandry has superb formal gardens, and Saumur has a porcelain museum and a classical equitation centre.

The coastal lowlands of the Vendée and Poitou-Charentes link the Loire to the Aquitaine basin. They are a mixture of wooded lowlands, open plateau landscapes and moorland, making the transition from northern arable landscapes to the southern pastoral economy, and from the cool and variable north European weather to a sunnier and warmer western maritime climate.

The Garonne basin: the Aquitaine

There is a strong contrast in the landscapes and tourist attractions of the head waters, middle valley and coastal section of the Garonne basin. The sandy coastal lowlands of Les Landes are dominated by coniferous forests. The middle Garonne valley, the home of the Bordeaux wine, is an undulating rather monotonous landscape. These are rather low-key tourist areas, but the edges of the valley, e.g. in the Dordogne to the north of the river provide some more attractive landscapes. Most of the tourist facilities of the region are concentrated on the coast.

The Channel and Atlantic coast

Atlantic coast of Aquitaine

This stretch of coastline from Biarritz to the mouth of the Garonne has two geographical advantages favouring tourism and one disadvantage which until relatively recently has inhibited the development of its tourist potential. Of France's non-Mediterranean coast, this region has the advantage of the best climate for seaside tourism. Bordeaux has an August average temperature of 21° C and only 771 mm of rainfall a year (though the maximum is in July). Biarritz has 1231 hours of sunshine between April and September (compared to the French Mediterranean with 1800 hours). The region also has the advantage of a long (270 km) stretch of virtually unbroken sandy beach, backed by sand dunes. The drawback, however, is the relative inaccessibility of the beach. The dunes have caused the internal drainage to form shallow lagoons and marshes which are difficult to cross. The dunes (up to 10 km wide, and 100 m high) are an additional barrier and the Baie d'Arcachon is the only major natural gap through them.

A plan for the integrated tourist and rural development of the area was drawn up in 1967, and an inter-ministerial commission set up to co-ordinate the development, which was mainly financed and implemented by the private sector. The plan divided the coast into 16 sectors: nine zones to be developed for tourism (beach, lakeside and watersports activities), separated by seven 'green zones' where landscape and wildlife were to be conserved and measures taken to protect the fragile dune systems from recreational pressure. The development areas include the conservation of existing resorts such as Arcachon and Biarritz, the redevelopment and expansion of existing settlements (e.g. Lacanau where 22 000 new bed spaces, golf facilities and entertainment centres have been added, and Hossegor-Capbreton where there is now a 700-berth marina) and the creation of new resorts such as Moliets (*see* Fig 9.2). Facilities were developed and extended both on the coast and for water sports on the freshwater lakes behind the dune belt. The new accommodation was designed to meet the modern needs of the French domestic market. By 1982, 28 per cent of the bed spaces were in campsites; the serviced sector (guest houses and hotels) accounted for only just over 13 per cent of bed spaces, whereas 46 per cent were provided as second homes for French families.

Tourism in the region grew steadily since the development began. Hotel bednights remained fairly stable through the recession years of the 1980s while camping in the region continued to grow (from 13.4 million nights in 1982 to 15.6 million in 1987).

The Atlantic coast of the Loire and Brittany

Between the mouth of the Garonne and Nantes there are many seaside resorts both fashionable and for families, with good sandy beaches. But the climate becomes cooler and less sunny towards the north, and the region does not support mass tourism on the same scale as Aquitaine or the Mediterranean.

Brittany

The peninsula is similar structurally and physically to southwest England: the core of the region is infertile granite moorland but the effect of marine erosion on this type of rock creates a magnificent rugged coastline, consisting of bold cliffs and rocky headlands, with caves, stacks and cliffs, interspersed with coves and sheltered bays where fine sandy beaches and dune systems accumulate.

The isolation and backward economy of the region has led to long-term depopulation, though the area has a strongly independent cultural identity. The economy has depended on agriculture and fishing though attempts have been made to diversify the economy and living standards have slowly been rising.

Tourism is significant in the local economy, but it is a region that is declining in popularity. In 1983 the region received 9.1 per cent of French summer holidays, but in the period 1985–87 its total number of hotel bednights (French and foreign) declined slightly, while the total number of camping bednights (French and foreign) dropped from 12.8 million in 1982 to 11.1 million in 1987. Of these, only about a quarter were overseas visitors (in the past, mainly from UK, and the Benelux countries). The climate and relatively isolated position of the peninsula may explain why the region's tourist industry is not growing. The climate is mild due to its maritime situation, but it is humid, drizzly and quite windy, with rain all year round, although total amounts of rain are fairly low (822 mm near Brest, and about 1180 mm on the inland moors). The summer average temperatures do not rise much above 17° C and Brest has 1190 hours sunshine between April and September. Thus, climatically

the region is not able to compete with the Aquitaine, let alone the Mediterranean coast.

The Channel coast

This region also has the typical variable western maritime climate (770–1025 mm rainfall per annum, with average maximum temperatures in the range 18–20° C). There is a string of resorts along the coast (e.g. Dunkerque, Calais, Boulogne, Le Touquet and Deauville) catering for local demand from the Paris region and day-trip visitors from England. But this region also suffers from Mediterranean competition and shows the familiar problems of a declining serviced sector and outdated tourist infrastructure, just like the resorts on the English side of the Channel.

Upland France

The Pyrénées

The French-Spanish border runs east-west along the crest of this 400 km mountain chain. The mountains rise to over 3300 metres, but are only 50–80 km wide. The landscape is varied, with well wooded valleys, deep gorges, lakes and craggy mountains. The Pyrénées National Park connects with the Ordesa National Park on the Spanish side of the border. Thus, the landscape is an important tourist resource, but there is also enough winter snow to support ski resort development. The central Pyrénées normally have 100 days of snow cover at 1200 m and 170 days at 1800 m. A series of ski resorts have been developed: Font-Romeu, Aulus-les-Bains, Bagnères-de-Luchon and Superbagnères (a high altitude greenfield site) on the eastern section of the Pyrénées, and a second group of resorts on the northern edge of the National Park (including La Mongie, a modern resort, Barèges and the main centre at Cauterets – see Fig 9.2). In 1987, the Pyrénées had 10 per cent of total French ski lift capacity, and 13.5 per cent of the winter sport resort bed spaces. But it took only 8 per cent of the total market share. Another tourist resource of the area are the spas based on mineralised springs. This aspect of tourism is reflected in many of the place names like the spa town of Ax-les-Thermes and also places such as Aulus-les-Bains and Les Eaux-Bonnes.

The central Massif

This upland area (bounded by the 300 m contour) makes up one sixth of France. Its average height is 900 m but it rises to 1800 m in places. Its landscape is varied but the harsh climate inhibits the development of mass tourism. The major landscape resources are:

1 The Cevennes National Park, an area of monotonous granite moorlands which produce more dramatic landscapes on their eastern edge, where the mountains overlook the mouth of the Rhône Valley, and are deeply dissected by steep-sided ravines. From the summit of Mont Aigoual the land drops 1200 m in a distance of only six km.
2 The limestone plateaux and gorges of the Grande Causses area on the western edge of the Cevennes National Park. The river Tarn runs through a dramatic gorge here.
3 The puys of the central Auvergne. The term 'puys' refers to the 70 extinct volcanic cones that rise from above the plateau of the Auvergne. Some are regular craters with circular rims, some simply the remaining core of the volcano, standing out as precipitous towers of rock that are sometimes capped by a church or monastery. This scenery is found in the Puy de Dôme area of the Parc des Volcans d'Auvergne to the west of Clermont-Ferrand.

The climate of these uplands is variable, as it lies at the junction of Atlantic, continental and Mediterranean influences, but its height keeps temperatures low. Above 900 m, snow may lie between 30 and 100 days, and only three months a year are frost-free. Rainfall may reach over 2000 mm per annum, though the Mediterranean flanks are much drier. The region is economically backward, with a declining upland agriculture, and has long been considered France's most serious problem area. Integrated rural development schemes have been promoted since 1962 aimed at both improving the local economy and protecting the fragile landscape. In some areas (e.g. the inner zones of the Cevennes National Park) access is restricted and camping prohibited, but elsewhere tourism is promoted in three ways, by:

1 the support of rural landscape-based tourism;
2 the support of thermal spas (the central Massif has one third of all French spas) e.g. at Vichy;
3 the development of ski centres (e.g. Mont Dore). However, the snow cover and terrain cannot compete with the Alps or Pyrénées, and only two per cent of France's ski lifts are located here;
4 the creation of integrated holiday villages with a range of accommodation and sports facilities (e.g. swimming pools, boating and other activities).

In spite of these developments tourism in the region is still fairly low key. The core of the region (Auvergne and Limousin) received only about 5% of French hotel bednights and 2.5 per cent of French and foreign camp bednights in 1987.

The French Alps

The southwest end of the Alpine chain is located in France (*see* Fig 9.2). The mountains drop from Mont Blanc (4807 m) in the north, through the Haute Savoie, the Savoie (around 3000 m) to the Basse Alps in Provence (2–3000 m) in the south. Although summer visitors outnumber winter sports tourists, the region is better known for its ski facilities. The average snowfall in the northern section is over 3 metres at 1500 m altitude but in the Basse Alps the average snow depth is only 2.5 m at the same altitude. The main season is February and March, but the season normally begins in early December and runs through to the end of April. Lower altitudes throughout the French Alps may get as much snow but it is more variable and the season is less reliable. If the effects of global warming continue to grow, the variability of snow cover at each end of the season is likely to increase.

The French Alps have been a winter sports centre since before the Second World War. The region now accounts for 82 per cent of all French ski lift capacity and over 480 km of ski piste. Eighty-one per cent of all winter sports holidays in France were located in the Alps. The original resorts, such as Chamonix and Megève were developed before 1939 and were based on existing climatic or thermal resorts. A second generation

Fig 9.2 Tourist resources of southern France

Alpine winter sports resort

1 Chamonix
2 St Gervais
3 Megève
4 Val d'Isère
5 Tignes
6 Les Arcs
7 La Plagne
8 Courcheval and Meribel
9 Les Menuires
10 Alpe d'Huez
11 Les Deux Alpes

Resorts in the Pyrénées

12 Font Romeu
13 Ax les Thermes
14 Aulus les Bains
15 Luchon
16 Superbagnères
17 La Mongie
18 Barèges
19 Cauterets
20 Les Eaux Bonnes

Key

Land over 1500 m

Coastal lagoons

* National Parks

of resorts were based on expanded villages at higher altitude, e.g. Courcheval and La Plagne. These are large centres with over 30 000 bed spaces. Since the 1960s, high altitude greenfield sites have been developed for smaller modern purpose-built integrated ski centres. These have been located adjacent to new ski runs with the best slopes and reliable good quality snow. The traffic system segregates pedestrians, skiers and motor traffic; indoor sports facilities are included and the settlements are designed to cater for summer landscape, climbing and activity holidays as well as for winter sports.

The most significant of these centres (with up to 20 000 bed spaces) include: Morzine-Avoriaz and St Gervais in the Haute Savoie; and Les Arcs, Tignes, Méribel, Les Menuires, Alpe d'Huez and Les Deux Alpes in the Savoie region.

Like the other major regional tourist developments in France, the accommodation provided is geared more to the tastes of the domestic market than for overseas visitors. In 1988, 45 per cent of the bed spaces were in rented chalets or apartments and 30 per cent in second homes for the French. Only 11 per cent were in hotels.

The Mediterranean coast

This region receives more tourists than any other part of France. Its climate is the main attraction;

	Average temperature °C	Average rainfall mm	Average relative humidity %
January	7	48	68
February	8	38	64
March	10	46	62
April	13	51	60
May	16	48	59
June	20	25	57
July	22	15	54
August	21	23	57
September	19	66	63
October	15	94	69
November	11	79	70
December	8	56	70

Total annual rainfall – 589 mm.
Total annual hours of sunshine – 2000 hours.
Average number of rainy days per annum – 100 days.

Fig 9.3 Marseille's climate

it has the most suitable weather for sun, sea and sand tourism of all the French coasts.

Due to its northwesterly location in the Mediterranean basin, the region has a shorter summer drought than, for example Greece, and this reinforces the problems of seasonality that are characteristic of French tourist destinations.

The region also has much of cultural and historic interest. Well preserved ancient Roman buildings are found in the lower Rhône, for example, the Roman theatre and arch at Orange, the arena and Temple of Diana at Nîmes, and the Roman city at Arles. Medieval castles such as at Perpignon, walled cities (e.g. Carcasonne), cathedrals (e.g. Aix-en-Provence) and other buildings such as the 12th century bridge at Avignon are abundant throughout the area. Many of the famous artists of the 19th and 20th century lived and worked in the eastern part of the region, and are commemorated here. The Matisse Museum, Renoir's house and Picasso museums are located in the Antibes-Nice area, and Cézanne's home is in Aix-en-Provence. The living culture of folklore, carnivals and festivals (ancient and modern) add to the distinctive regional character. The dramatic landscapes of the Cevennes and the Basses Alpes provide the back drop to the region, but after the climate it is the coast that is the most important tourist resource of Mediterranean France. The coast can be divided into three zones (see Fig 9.1):

1 The French Riviera, from the Italian border to Marseille.
2 The Camargue (the delta at the mouth of the Rhône) between Marseille and Nîmes.
3 The Languedoc-Rousillon coast which runs from Nîmes to the Spanish border.

These areas are very different in their physical characteristics, and in the style of tourism that has been developed.

The French Riviera

This riviera consists (from east to west) of the coasts of the Départements of Alpes-Maritimes (the Côte d'Azur), Var, and Bouches du Rhône. The Alps protects the coast from cold winter and spring winds, e.g. the Mistral, that blow from the centre of the continent, so the coastal strip enjoys a mild winter climate that encourages some winter tourism. The coastal belt is narrow. The Côte d'Azur has many rocky promontories and cliffs interspersed with small bays and safe yachting harbours (e.g. Cannes). Most of the beaches are pebbly. From the very beginning of European tourism (from the Grand Tours of the 17th and 18th centuries) the Côte d'Azur has been a fashionable area, though it first became popular as a winter resort rather than for summer tourism. When the railway from Paris reached Nice in 1865 and sea bathing became popular, summer tourism grew rapidly, and the rich and famous bought land for their private villas and apartments and there is little land available for new development. The resorts are stylish and exclusive with luxurious grand hotels, nightlife and casinos (e.g. at Cannes and in the tiny independent state of Monaco). More recently, conference facilities have been added (e.g. at Nice in 1985). This section of coast is more or less at capacity. The coast of Var (stretching from St Raphaël to Bandol) has better sandy beaches (e.g. at St Tropez and the Iles d'Hyères); it has also been developed more recently and has facilities and accommodation for the mass market. Self-catering and camping resorts are located between St Tropez and St Raphaël, and Le Lavandou is a new resort with a casino and all facilities, (see Fig 9.2).

The French Riviera thus caters for all sections of the sun, sea and sand market, and in 1987 received a third of all France's camping bednights (French and foreign visitors) and about 14 per cent of the hotel bednights.

The Camargue

The lowlands of the Rhône delta occupy the 90 km stretch of coast between Marseille and Aigues-Mortes (south of Nîmes). It is a desolate, marshy area of inaccessible reed beds and shallow brackish lagoons. Wild white horses and bulls (reared for the bull rings in Provence) roam the marshlands, and wildlife such as duck, heron, flamingo, ibis and egret abound in a 15 000 ha nature reserve. The region caters only for very specialised tourism as the coast, with its shifting dunes and watercourses is too unstable for coastal tourist development.

The Languedoc-Rousillon coast

Until the 1960s, this coast was hardly developed for tourism. The sweeping dune coastline is separated from the mainland by a series of marshy lowlands and shallow lagoons. The largest is the Etang de Thau, 20 by 13 km and 25 m at its deepest. The lagoons were infested with mosquitos. In 1960 the French Government initiated the tourist development of the area by building access routes, clearing the swamps and eradicating the mosquitos, as part of a co-ordinated regional development programme (see Chapter 6).

Tourist accommodation and facilities were concentrated in five centres; Grau du Roi (located north of Sète), Thau, Valras-Gruissan, Leucate-Barcarès, and Canet-Argelès, each of 40–50 000 bed spaces (see Fig 9.2). Some were based on the original small resorts but others were completely new, developed in conjunction with a range of beach and water sports facilities (using both the lagoons and the sea). The bulk of the accommodation provided is self-catering (camping, apartments and second homes). The tourist centres are separated by woodland and undeveloped nature reserves.

The region caters more for the domestic market than for international tourists, and accounted for about ten per cent of all (domestic plus foreign) camping bednights in 1987, but only four per cent of foreign visitors hotel bednights.

Corsica

Corsica is 170 km from the Côte d'Azur. It is the most mountainous of all the Mediterranean islands, with a variety of landscapes from Corsican pine forests to deep valleys and stony deserts. The east is low lying with lagoonal plains along the coast while the rest of the coast is a mixture of red cliffs and yellow sandy beaches. Being an island, its temperatures are a little less extreme than on the nearby mainland (see Fig 9.4) though its summers are a little drier.

The island has fairly poor communications with the mainland (ferries operate from Marseille, Toulon and Nice), and very few tourists make the crossing. In 1987 only 137 000 French and 150 000 foreign visitors stayed on the island.

	August		January	
	Max	Min	Max	Min
Corsica (Ajaccio)	28	16	13	3
French Mediterranean coast (Nice)	31	15	18	0

Fig 9.4 Comparison of temperatures on Corsica and on the French Mediterranean coast (average temperatures °C)

The French domestic market

Many of the new tourist developments in the regions of France have been designed with the domestic, rather than the international market in mind. The French domestic market is not typical of Western Europe as a whole. It is characterised by:

1 a much lower level of foreign tourism than most other Western European countries. In 1988 only 17 per cent of French holidaymakers travelled outside France (generating only 13 million foreign trips from a population of about 55 million people). This by definition means than 83 per cent of French tourism (which in 1988 was 52 million holiday trips) is accommodated in France itself.

2 a very pronounced peaking of holiday travel. The main French school holidays are in July and August with only short breaks at Christmas, in February and at Easter (*see* Fig 9.5).

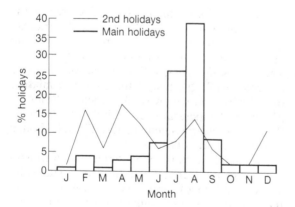

Fig 9.5 French seasonality of holidaymaking

3 a strong reliance on the car as a means of holiday travel. Eighty-one per cent of all (domestic and foreign) holiday trips in France were by car.
4 a higher level of holiday taking amongst the urban population than among rural residents. In 1985 up to 83 per cent of Parisians took a holiday, and 64 per cent of the residents of the other major cities. Only 40 per cent of the rural population took a holiday. All these factors combine to create acute peak period congestion on the roads leading from the cities to the resorts and to overcrowding in the destination regions.

The French make little use of hotels for their city, coastal or rural domestic holidays, preferring rented apartments, camping, visiting friends and relatives or using their own second homes, though hotels are a little more popular for winter sports and touring holidays. The French do use hotels on their foreign trips, as shown in Fig 9.6.

	%
Hotels	19
Visiting friends and relatives	33
Camping and caravans	22
Rented accommodation	17
Second homes	7
Holiday village	4

Fig 9.6 Accommodation used by the French for domestic and foreign holidays

French holiday destinations

About half of the French summer tourists make for the coast, and a quarter to the countryside. An additional 17 per cent favour the mountain regions. In winter the proportions change to 17 per cent to the coast for winter sun holidays, 28 per cent to the countryside and nearly 40 per cent to the mountains for winter sports. This pattern is reflected in the popularity of the destination regions of France for domestic tourism.

Geographical region and corresponding tourist statistical region	Number of arrivals at hotels and campsites (in millions) 1987
The Mediterranean coast (Côte d'Azur and Languedoc/Rousillon (1 and 2)	18.8
The Alps (Rhône/Alpes (3))	8.2
Paris (Ile de France (4))	5.9
Aquitaine (5)	5.5
Brittany (6)	4.5
Pyrénées (and part of central Massif (7))	3.8
The remainder of the central Massif (Auvergne and Limousin (8))	2.8

NB The tourist statistical regions do not match perfectly with the physical regions (*see* Fig 9.8).

Fig 9.7 Most popular regions of France for the French

Key

▒ Upland areas

Statistical regions
1 Côte d'Azur
2 Languedoc/Rousillon
3 Rhône/Alps
4 Ile de France
5 Aquitaine
6 Brittany
7 Pyrénées
8 Auvergne and Limousin

Fig 9.8 Statistical and physical regions of France

French outbound travel

It has been noted that only a small proportion (17 per cent) of the French take their holidays abroad. The majority travel by road: only five per cent of the French take a package holiday, and only six per cent travel by plane. It is not surprising that the adjacent countries of Spain and Italy benefit most from French foreign summer holidays, these two countries together receiving 40 per cent of such trips. Long-haul destinations, such as USA, Asia in summer and Mexico, the French Caribbean Islands and French Polynesia for winter sun holidays are increasing in popularity. However, Spain (including the Canaries) is still the most popular winter sun destination. The UK ranks second (behind West Germany) as a destination for French business travel, and fifth in popularity as a summer holiday destination.

Foreign visitors to France

The numbers of foreign visitors to France has grown steadily, from about 30 million arrivals in 1980 to nearly 40 million in 1989. The spatial flow of visitors has remained fairly stable over this period, with about a quarter coming from West Germany, 17 per cent from the UK, 11 per cent from the Netherlands, and 8 to 9 per cent from each of Scandinavia, Belgium, Italy and Switzerland. The French Riviera is by far the most popular destination region (with about 35 million hotel and camping bednights in 1987) followed by Paris with 15.5 million hotel bednights alone, followed by the Alps, Aquitaine and Languedoc-Rousillon each with over six million hotel and camping bednights. Visiting friends' homes and rented accommodation are also popular forms of accommodation. The 'gîtes' are particularly popular with the UK market. They are self-catering holiday homes, often old farmhouses in the country, and in 1989 there were over 23 000 available.

Conclusion

It is evident that the less popular regions of France have the capacity and potential to take more tourists whereas the most popular regions such as the French Riviera are very congested at peak periods. There are signs, however, that the French might be prepared to change their traditional pattern of domestic holiday taking and spread the demands on facilities and accommodation over a longer summer season.

The opening of the Channel Tunnel will improve communications between UK and France, but it remains to be seen as to whether it will alter existing travel patterns or merely confirm the current flows.

QUESTIONS AND DISCUSSION POINTS

1 What distinguishes the French approach to the development of coastal and rural resources for tourism?
2 Rank the different sections of France's coastline in order of popularity and explain the reasons for the different levels of tourist use.
3 Why is France the leading tourist destination country in Europe?

ASSIGNMENTS

1 Mr & Mrs Driver live in Reading and are planning a three-week summer camping/caravan holiday in France, for themselves and their two children (aged 9 and 13). They have never driven on the Continent before and they are anxious to avoid the worst congested roads. They want a leisurely holiday away from the crowds but with plenty of outdoor activities for the children. They would like to see a variety of French historic attractions and regional cultures, but they also want to spend some time on the beach. Suggest a three-week itinerary for the family, specifying their route to and through France and a departure date that would avoid the worst congestion but also give them good weather.

2 You are the editor of a UK travel trade journal. You are planning an issue on the appeal of the UK to the French. Write a brief editorial note explaining the characteristics of the French holiday market and French holiday and travel tastes. Outline the difficulties that UK tour operators face when trying to market their tours and attractions to the French. Indicate the extent to which travel improvements between UK and France might affect the appeal of the UK to the French.

CHAPTER 10

Italy

LEARNING OBJECTIVES

After reading this chapter you should be able to:

- assess the tourist potential of the climatic, landscape, historical and cultural resources of Italy
- distinguish the regional distribution of these geographical resources and their development and use for tourism
- demonstrate a knowledge of the main tourist resorts and tourist centres
- understand the role of Italy in the general pattern of European tourism.

Introduction

Tourism has been a well established industry in Italy for over one hundred years. The country has a huge diversity of tourist attractions ranging from its climate, coast, lakes and landscape, to its historic cities and winter sports resorts. These attractions draw in a high level of international tourist traffic, making Italy a leading world destination, with a total of 55.1 million foreign arrivals in 1988, including day-trippers, accounting for about a fifth of all the tourist arrivals in the Mediterranean region.

Tourism is, therefore, a major source of foreign currency for Italy and a major generator of jobs in the Italian economy, and the support for tourism is regarded as a high priority. However, northern Italy is one of the few highly developed industrial regions of the Mediterranean and the large domestic, urbanised population seeks to share the use of the national and cultural tourist resources with the international visitors. This leads to problems of congestion overuse and deterioration of the quality of the resources, particularly in the north of Italy, whereas the tourist resources of the south remain relatively underdeveloped and underused.

Physical resources

Italy is naturally divided into four major physical units each with a different range of tourist resources and different climatic conditions (*see* Fig 10.1). The three main regions are from north to south:

1 the southern slopes of the Alps (northern Italy).

2 the north Italian plain, drained by the river Po which flows into the head of the Adriatic sea (Turin to Venice).

3 The Apennines, a mountain range of lower altitude than the Alps, but forming the structural spine of peninsular Italy (Parma to Lecce).

The fourth physical unit is
4 the coast and the surrounding seas.

Fig 10.1 Regions of Italy

The Italian Alps

Italy's share of the Alps consists of the south-facing slopes of the main Alpine peaks and the southerly pre-Alps which descend into the Po basin (*see* Fig 10.2). The area has the typical alpine climate with a summer precipitation maximum and cold, sunny winter conditions which allow the formation of good quality snow fields. However, the sheltered southerly aspect and the mass of the Swiss and Austrian Alps protect the Italian mountains from the coldest north winds which originate in the centre of Europe in winter. There are three subsections of the Italian Alps:

1 West of Lake Maggoire. Here, Italy's border with Switzerland and France follows the highest peaks and corresponds to the watershed between the Po to the east and the Rhône to the west. The mountains decrease in height from the spectacular sharp peaks of Mont Blanc (4807 m) in the north to Mt Argentera (3250 m) in the south, where they form the backdrop to the Italian Riviera of the Ligurian coast. The Gran Paradiso National Park, noted for its rare animals and plants, is situated close to the French border. The main skiing centres are concentrated in the Val d'Aosta region, made accessible via the routes that run up the valley from Turin to the Mont Blanc tunnel and the Little St Bernard pass (both to France) and to the Great St Bernard pass (to Switzerland). Although ski centres are extensively developed on the French side of the frontier, many French people visit the Val d'Aosta due to its accessibility and to the French speaking inhabitants. The main ski centres are Cervinia and Courmayeur.

2 The central section: the Italian lakes. This subregion is characterised by superb glacial landforms but the geology gives rise to fewer spectacular peaks (other than Ortles and Adamello). The distinctive tourist attraction, is the series of lakes that lie in deep steep sided 'U' shaped valleys gouged out by glaciers in the ice age. In this region the glaciers flowed from north to south (from the centre of the Alps), and left piles of moraines at the valley mouths as they melted. These moraines blocked the valleys and ponded back the lakes. The location of the lakes in sheltered south-facing valleys has given them an unusual climatic advantage and has led to their development as tourist resources. Tempera-tures here all year round but especially in winter are much higher than they normally should be; this is reflected in the vegetation of palms, citrus trees and olives which flourish here but are more typical of a southern, more truly Mediterranean, climate. A series of international resorts such as Baveno on Lake Maggiore and Limone on Lake Garda have developed along the lake shores; 65 per cent of the bednights were taken up by foreign visitors in 1985, many of whom are Germans attracted to the motor boating. Else-where, the climate of the lakes region is more typical of the continental north with very cold winters and July temperatures climbing over 20° C. The summer rainfall peak tends to occur in sharp bursts often associated with continental thunderstorms.

3 The eastern Alps: the Dolomites. The landform consists of a mixture of resistant rock mixed with more easily eroded material which, through glacial action, produces a very dramatic mountain landscape with a series of spectacular sharp peaks (such as Marmolada), interspersed with tiny but extremely beautiful alpine lakes. The region is cut by the N-S valley of Val di Adige, which is followed by the motorway route from Verona to the Brenner pass. There are major concentrations of winter sports and summer scenery and climbing resorts in the Dolomites, e.g. Madonnadi Campiglio (in Trentino), Val Senales (in Alto Adige) and Cortina d'Ampezzo (in Veneto). It is particularly accessible to and popular with West German tourists, as this part of Italy is also German speaking, but it is also rapidly increasing in popularity in the domestic market.

The north Italian plain

The Po basin is the industrial heart of Italy; it contains the major conurbation centred on Milan and its hinterland (*see* Fig 10.2). The region as a whole has over 22 million inhabitants. It is also a fertile agricultural area though subject to flooding in the lower reaches of the Po. The climate has continental overtones with quite extreme tem-peratures (in Milan the average January tempera-ture drops to 1.9° C with over 100 days of frost, though the summer temperature rises to an average of 23.9° C in July). It is mainly a domestic tourist generating area but with the normal VFR

Fig 10.2 North Italian plain

and business tourism associated with developed urban areas. The Adriatic end of the region is, however, a major centre of Italy's cultural and historic tourism based on Venice, Padua and Verona, but also with fine architectural attractions in towns such as Bologna, Ferrara, Parma and Modena.

Venice

Like Florence and Rome, Venice is very rich in renaissance art treasures but it has a unique additional attraction. The medieval character of its winding alleyways, open piazzas and canal system is totally unspoilt. The only means of getting about the city is by boat or on foot, as there are no motor cars. This gives the tourist a unique experience of living in a pre-industrial city, although it can be very crowded with pedestrians in the peak season. These very qualities, however, make the city totally unsuitable for most economic activities other than tourism. The consequent problems of preserving the city have been discussed in Chapter 5.

The Apennines and peninsular Italy

The Apennines form the backbone of peninsular Italy. The mountain chain runs NW-SE for most of its 500 km length, until it reaches Sicily, where the orientation of the mountains changes abruptly to an E-W structure. It can be divided into three physical zones.

1 The North (located in Tuscany, Marches and Umbria (see** Fig 10.3).** This region is made up of unstable, softer, easily eroded rocks, reaching only 1669 m (Mt Magiorasca) to 2140 m (Mt Cimone). Nevertheless, the climate is cold enough in winter to produce snow in enough quantity and quality to support ski centres for the domestic market, e.g. at Abertone (near Mt Cimone). The tourist development of this part of the Apennines is, however, focused on the urban areas fringing the more fertile Arno basin, with historic town centres such as Pisa, Lucca, Pistoia, Prata, to the north and Siena (site of the Palio), Perugia, (an ancient Etruscan city) Orvieto, Spoleto and Assisi to the south. But, of course, the main focus of cultural tourism in the region is in Florence.

The unspoilt city centre is full of 12th to 17th century buildings; the Uffizi Gallery contains one of the most outstanding art collections in the world, including famous paintings by Leonardo da Vinci, Botticelli and Michelangelo. The Accademia di Belle Arti houses the Michelangelo Statue of David, and other works of art abound in the churches and historic buildings.

For such a southerly, Mediterranean location, the climate of the Apennine chain is relatively harsh; most of the mountains receive more than 1200 mm rainfall a year, and on the higher peaks this reaches 2000 mm (even as far south as the mountains of Calabria). Only the islands of Sardinia and the coastal lowlands and the heel of Italy have the typical long (three to four month) summer drought. The rainfall is, however, concentrated in autumn and winter and can be intense and violent, as demonstrated by the storms which caused the Arno to burst its banks and damage so much of Florence's art treasures in the mid-1960s. This relatively heavy rainfall is orographic in nature, caused by the Apennines blocking the path of west flowing moisture laden Atlantic air which penetrates into the Mediterranean basin in autumn and winter. Temperatures, however, are more characteristically mediterranean, though the 'hot south' only truly begins south of Rome.

2 Central Apennines of Latium, the Abruzzi and Molise (see** Fig 10.3).** This region consists of some ranges of harder rock which give rise to the forest-clad mountains of Gran Sasso in the Abruzzi, (2913 m). The 300 km² National Park here is noted for its landscape and wildlife, particularly for a species of bear unique to Italy. Elsewhere the landscape is one of pastoralism and thin forest but with many abandoned upland villages due to long-term emigration to the north and to more local urban centres. International tourism is mainly confined to Rome, though modest winter sports (e.g. Terminillo), holiday resorts (catering for the domestic market) and unspoilt historic settlements are widely distributed.

Rome is a major historic, artistic and cultural centre, and is the site of the Vatican, the centre of the Roman Catholic faith. This busy, modern city also abounds with historic ruins, particularly from ancient Roman times, but it has many fine renaissance and baroque buildings too.

3 The deep south. Campania, Apulia, Basilicata, Calabria and Sicily (**see** Fig 10.3). The landscape

Fig 10.3 Italy's regions

is an attractive and varied one of well wooded, deeply dissected plateaux, mountain chains, and smaller steep-sided blocks with the bare, karst landscape typical of limestone areas at their summit. There is also evidence of recent volcanic activity, at present dormant at Vesuvius (Naples) but still active in Sicily (Mount Etna) and in the islands off Sicily (Stromboli, Vulcano and Lipari). Cultural tourism is centred on Naples (close to

Pompeii and Herculanium) and Paestum, famous for its Greek temples.

The Mezzogiorno

This region as a whole remains unspoilt as it has been bypassed by the industrial revolution. The economy of the far south of Italy has long been underdeveloped, with the population suffering from high unemployment and a low standard of living. The region lacks industrial infrastructure, has a backward agriculture on land suffering from erosion.

The regions of the south have experienced emigration for many years, resulting in abandoned agricultural land and deserted villages in the mountain areas. Since 1950 a special ministry, the Cassa per il Mezzogiorno, was given responsibility for promoting the development of the south. This has included the implementation of water management, reafforestation, some industrial development and provision of power and transport infrastructures so that now the Mezzogiorno is linked to the north by fast motorways. Although the bulk of the aid has gone into these developments, investment in tourism infrastructure has been encouraged by grants and loans in the hope that a well developed tourist industry would create suitable jobs and inject money into the local economy. The EC has also contributed to the cost of these projects (*see* Chapter 8). By the early 1980s 65 000 additional hotel rooms had been provided but these tended to be in large capital-intensive enterprises rather than in locally run establishments. Although much of the region contains much unspoilt mountain scenery and magnificent deserted beaches, in some places the local coastal scenery has sometimes been poorly managed: for example the proliferation of unplanned and uncontrolled second home development has spoilt some areas, whereas in others (e.g. Sicily) tourism has been developed near industrial zones in order to take advantage of the improved infrastructure. The number of tourists visiting the area remains low and is only slowly increasing. However, this is due as much to the peripheral location of the region as to the mismanagement of tourist development within it. The southern tip of peninsular Italy is well outside the 1000 km limit for car travel (*see* Chapter 8), and is thus too far for carborne travellers from the population centres of Northern Europe; it must, therefore, rely on air transport and compete with destinations such as Greece, Turkey and Spain which may be either environmentally more attractive to the potential visitor, or much more competitively priced.

Sicily is a mountainous island, whose interior is desert-like, whose relief is dominated by Mount Etna and whose population lives on the coast. It is rich in art and history, with, for example, Greek temples at Agrigento, Roman ruins at Syracuse, and a medievel castle at Catania, and has some good sandy beaches and resorts such as Palermo, Taormina and Cefalu. In spite of these resources, the island is underdeveloped for tourism, with less than four per cent of Italy's tourist arrivals.

Sardinia is another of Italy's Mediterranean islands which is visited by even fewer tourists. Much of its 1200 km coastline is still undeveloped, and is a sequence of white sandy beaches, cliffs and promontories. Its exposure to the British market during the 1990 World Cup football competition may make the island a little better known to potential tourists.

The coast

All the coastal lowlands have lower rainfall than the interior of Italy (under 800 mm) and experience the more characteristic Mediterranean climate, but the coast is relatively unevenly developed. It can be divided into sub-regions (*see* Fig 10.1) each with a different physical character and different balance of tourist development:

1 the Ligurian coast (between the French border and Pisa);
2 the Tuscan and Roman coasts (Pisa to Rome);
3 the Amalfi coast (Naples area);
4 the coast of the far south (Palermo to Lecce); and
5 the Adriatic (Lecce to Venice).

Ligurian coast – the Italian Riviera
(*see* Fig 10.2)

This stretch of coast is backed by mountains, in the west by the Alps and eastern stretch (from Genoa to La Spezia) by the Apennines. The coast is characterised by cliffs, interspersed with sandy bays, though many of the shores are rather pebbly. Many of the bays form excellent yacht harbours such as Portofino and Rapallo. The coast is sheltered by the mountains, which protect the coast from cold continental air, keeping winter temperatures up. The January average temperature at Genoa is 8.4° C and frosts are hardly known; Diano Marina is one of the significant winter resorts. Land for tourist development is at a premium and many of the best sites have already been developed for tourist accommodation or private villas, since many settlements have been tourist resorts for over 150 years. The current pattern of tourism development is, however, varied, from classy 'up-market' resorts, and larger noisy centres of activity, to quieter fishing villages.

The Tuscan and Roman coasts

The crest of the Apennines moves inland, and wider coastal lowlands have developed in places. The alluvial plains are sometimes fringed by coastal dunes which produce fine, wide sandy beaches, for example Massa and Viareggio in the north and the beaches serving Rome in the south.

The Amalfi coast

This stretch of coast varies in character from the lowlands north of Naples and the Gulf of Salerno, the islands of Ischia and Capri to the high cliffs south of Salerno. In the coves, sandy bays have been developed. This stretch of coast includes some famous resorts such as Capri, Sorrento, Positano and Ravello, but some are now very overcrowded or at capacity.

The coast of the south

The coast of the far south of Italy has the best climate for coastal tourism, very varied coastal landscape yet it remains relatively under-developed, with uncrowded beaches and unspoilt villages interspersed between small resorts such as Maratea. The climate of Sicily is even more conducive to coastal tourism, with under 700 mm rainfall per annum and July temperatures reaching 25.7° C. The south coast of the island has wide sandy beaches, while the islands off the north coast provide opportunities for underwater fishing, yet again the development of resorts and provision of bed spaces is limited.

The Adriatic coast

In the southern section from Pesaro to Foggia, the hilly coast is dominated by softer rock, eroded into low cliffs by the Adriatic. The main seaside resorts are relatively small (e.g. Guilia-nova, Silvi Marina, Francaville and Vasto). The Abruzzi coast is popular with Roman holiday-makers particularly for camping. The main

modern, mass tourist development occurs on the short stretch of the northern Adriatic coast between Ravenna and Pesaro where the alluvial lowlands of the Po begin to open out, and the shallow Adriatic has accumulated extensive coastal dune systems, providing continuous, huge sandy beaches. With plentiful level coastal land for development of modern hotels, a string of modern international resorts have grown up to cater for the demands of mass tourism, for example Rimini, Riccione, Cattolica, Milano Marittima, and Cesanatico (see Fig 10.2). The coast at the head of the Adriatic is also dominated by coastal deposition of sand, but here the dunes and spits tend to enclose tidal or inland lagoons. The lagoons may inhibit tourist access but nevertheless the coast is extensively used at the resorts of Lido di Jesolo, Bibione and Caorle.

Spatial patterns of tourism

The bulk of Italy's tourist accommodation is concentrated in the four provinces of the north of the country: Trentino/Alto Adige, Veneto, Emilio Romagna and Toscano (see Fig 10.3). Here the location of mountain, coastal, cultural, social and business tourist resources coincide, and are most accessible to both the domestic and international markets. In 1985, two thirds of Italy's hotels were concentrated here (in contrast to only 16.7 per cent in the centre and 13.5 per cent in the south of Italy). Camping facilities are proportionally more important in Marches, Abruzzi and Latium, whereas rented accommodation plays a more significant role in the limited stock of bed spaces in Calabra and Apulia.

The spatial pattern of tourist arrivals and bednights mirrors this pattern, though there are some differences between the domestic and international patterns (see Figs 10.4 and 10.5). Domestic tourism tends to be relatively short-haul and predominantly within the tourist's region of residence, because the coasts of northern Italy have a good summer climate, the population tends to travel to their nearest coastal resorts instead of travelling further south. Thus, the most heavily populated regions of Lazio, Emilio Romagna, Veneto, Toscano (all with local coastal resources) and Lombardia (with local scenic and winter sports resources) each receive about 10–11 per cent of the domestic market.

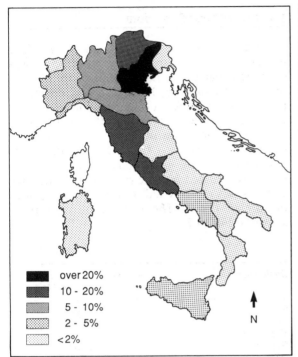

Fig 10.4 International tourist travel in Italy (tourist nights)

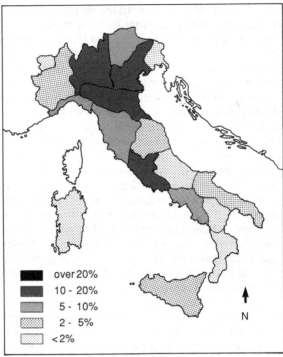

Fig 10.5 Domestic tourist travel in Italy (tourist nights)

The international market (though still strongly concentrated in the north which receives 60.4 per cent of international arrivals) is especially focused on Veneto (20 per cent international arrivals 1984), but Toscano (centred on Florence) and Alto Adige (predominantly a winter sports region) both receive 13–14 per cent each; the Rome region ranks fourth with about 11 per cent of international arrivals. This reaffirms the fact that the Italian lakes, mountains and cultural resources are more popular with international tourists than with the residents. Forty-five per cent foreign visitors chose Italy for artistic and historical attractions, 43 per cent for its climate, 27 per cent for its natural environment and, significantly, a third chose Italy for the possibility of combining several activities.

Conflicts between domestic and international tourists

The Italian domestic market is large; 36.3 million holidaymakers in 1984 compared to 19.2 million foreign visitors. Although there is not the massive road congestion due to the 'rush to the Mediterranean' coasts as there is in France, the Italian domestic market is similarly very strongly peaked in July and August. Sixty-five per cent of domestic coastal holidays and 51.5 per cent of all domestic and foreign bednights are taken in these two months in 1985. This leads to problems of congestion both in the cities and in the coastal resorts. The peaking of holiday demand also creates the problem (for the tourist industry) of relatively low overall occupancy rates, the highest gross occupancy rates being 42 per cent in Lazio, 35.3 per cent in Tuscany, 32.1 per cent in Liguria and the lowest in the centre and far south (17.6 per cent in Abruzzi, 17.6 per cent in Basilicata, 19 per cent in Calabria).

International tourists

The highest proportion of foreigners crossing the frontier into Italy in 1987 came from the adjacent countries of Switzerland, West Germany, France and Austria. However, perhaps as many as half of these are day excursionists or in transit. The latter category would cover car tourists from France and Central Europe travelling east to Yugoslavia and Greece, or residents of Central Europe travelling west through Italy to the coasts of France or Spain. Considering just the staying visitors, these come from a wide range of countries, reflecting the wide appeal of cultural tourism, but the West German market dominates, particularly in the accessible Veneto and Alto Adige regions. Not only do more West Germans visit Italy but they stay longer than any other nationality, when measured in terms of average length of stay at registered accommodation. It must be remembered though, that many long-haul travellers, for example from USA, Japan and even Northern Europe, may spend over a week in Italy but split the time between the three major cultural centres of Rome, Florence and Venice (thus depressing the average length of stay figures). Recent surveys showed that each nationality favours the particular elements of Italy's range of tourist attractions that complement their own domestic resources. Thus, over half of the visitors from land-locked Austria make their way to the Adriatic beaches, a quarter to the cities but only 10 per cent to the mountains. Fifty per cent of the French visit the cultural attractions of the cities and only a quarter go to the coast. The British tend to concentrate on the cultural attractions of Venice but also visit Emilio Romagna, Toscano and Campania.

Italian outbound tourism

A relatively small number of Italians take their holidays outside their country. In 1985 it was estimated that three million trips of four nights or more were taken by Italians abroad, compared to a domestic market of 36.3 million arrivals in 1984. The varied nature of Italy's resources mean that most tourist tastes can be met at home. Nevertheless, the Italians' increasing purchasing power generated by an improving economy, coupled with the relaxation of exchange controls has recently led to a very rapid growth of foreign travel. The distribution of trips is shown in Fig 10.7.

Destination	Numbers of vacation trips made by Italians 1985
France	602 000
Spain	551 000
Yugoslavia	457 000
Greece	295 000
UK	139 000
W Germany	120 000
Switzerland	113 000
Austria	103 000

Fig 10.7 Italy: outbound tourism

The distances travelled are generally short (nearly 50 per cent travelled less than 500 km)

	Number of arrivals at frontiers 1987		Number of arrivals at registered tourist accommodation 1987	Arrivals at registered tourist accommodation 1987	Average number of nights spent 1985	Total bednights 1987
	%	(million)	(million)	(%)	(nights)	(%)
West Germany	18.2	9.6	7.1	33.3	7.1	44.8
France	17.1	9.0	2.1	10.1	3.6	7.3
USA	2.6	1.4	1.9	9.2	2.5	5.1
UK	3.7	2.0	1.4	6.5	5.0	6.6
Austria	10.4	5.5	1.3	6.3	6.2	7.1
Switzerland	19.7	10.4	1.2	5.8	5.7	6.4
Spain	0.9	0.5	0.8	3.7		1.6
Netherlands	2.4	1.3	0.6	2.7		3.6
Japan	1.3	0.7	0.5	2.3	2.3	0.9
Belgium	1.7	0.9	0.5	2.2		2.5
Others						
Total		52.7	21.32			106.34 million

Fig 10.6 Overall pattern of international tourism to Italy

but the proportion of longer haul travellers to countries other than those adjacent to Italy is rapidly growing. In 1982 24 per cent travelled over 1000 km, whereas in 1985 this had grown to 32 per cent.

Conclusion

In terms of the evolution of its own domestic and outbound tourism, Italy is in the early stages of the third phase of development (*see* p 6, Chapter 1). At this stage, mass outbound tourism becomes widespread, following the establishment of a mass domestic market in Phase 2. If Italy conforms to the pattern set out in Chapter 1, then growth in domestic tourism may slow down (as outbound tourism grows). This may ease some of the problems of increasing congestion in Italian resorts. It is unlikely that international tourism to Italy's coastal resorts will expand greatly due to the strong price competition from other Mediterranean destinations. On the other hand, the quality and range of Italy's historic and cultural attractions is unique and they will inevitably maintain their attractiveness to international travellers. The challenge of conserving the historical cities and managing their visitors is ever present.

QUESTIONS AND DISCUSSION POINTS

1 Italy's tourist product is very varied. Is there any evidence available to suggest which of its resources (beaches, landscapes, historic or climatic) are the most popular?

2 Do you think Italy is well-placed to withstand competition from recently developing Mediterranean destinations such as Greece and Turkey?

3 Why do you think the attempts to develop tourism in the far south of Italy have not met with great success?

ASSIGNMENTS

1 You work for a tour company that specialises in city break holidays in Europe for the UK market. You have been asked to update and rewrite their brochure for Italy. Select at least four cities with potential for city breaks and assemble notes on their history, historical and cultural resources, their location, accessibility and climate. Suggest the client groups that might find these cities attractive, and indicate the seasons (and specific months of the year) during which time these tours might be most successful. Prepare a draft of the text of the new brochure for one of these cities.

2 A 48-year-old widow is planning a two-week holiday in Italy with her 19-year-old daughter. She is interested in landscape painting and art in general but also enjoys relaxing on the beach. Her daughter is more interested in meeting other young people. They cannot agree on a venue and have come to your travel agency for advice on which parts of the Italian coast might meet their needs and to see if you can suggest a resort that they both might enjoy. Prepare some notes that might help them arrive at a decision.

CHAPTER 11

The Iberian peninsula: Spain and Portugal

LEARNING OBJECTIVES

After reading this chapter you should be able to:

- assess the tourist potential of the climatic, landscape, historical and cultural resources of Spain and Portugal
- distinguish the regional distribution of these geographical resources and their development and use for tourism
- demonstrate a knowledge of the main tourist resorts and tourist centres
- understand the role of Spain and Portugal in the general pattern of European tourism
- be aware of some of the problems of over-development on the Spanish coasts
- locate and explain the particular tourist appeal of Spain and Portugal's island territories.

Introduction

Spain is the focus of Mediterranean mass coastal tourism, and is one of the world's leading destinations. Tourism to Spain has grown rapidly in the post war era from under three million in the 1950s to 35 million in 1988. Tourist development is strongly concentrated on Spain's Mediterranean coast and Mediterranean island possessions, for example, the Balearic islands. The Atlantic coast of the Iberian peninsula is relatively undeveloped for tourism: Portugal received only about six million foreign tourists. The greatest concentration of tourism on Iberia's Atlantic coast is in the Algarve in the south of Portugal. The hot, arid plateaux of the interior of the peninsula attract relatively few tourists in spite of their historic and cultural attractions. Both Spain and Portugal possess islands in the Atlantic off the coast of West Africa that are far enough south and,

Fig 11.1 The Atlantic islands

therefore, have mild enough winters to attract visitors for winter sun holidays. Madeira (32° N) belongs to Portugal, while the Canary Islands (28° S) are part of Spain (*see* Fig 11.1).

Growth of tourism in Spain

Spain was virtually unknown as a tourist destination in the period between the First and Second World Wars. The country was poor and the economy was further disrupted by its civil war of 1936–1939. Meanwhile, Italy, the Côte d'Azur and the Alps were prospering as Europe's main resort areas. In the early 1950s the first wave of carborne tourists from France explored the Costa Brava, found the climate attractive, the beaches deserted and the cost of living low. Tourism grew steadily from 1.26 million in 1952 to 4.19 million in 1959. The Spanish Government recognised the contribution tourism could make to its economy and encouraged tourist development in a variety of ways, for example, with

loans for the construction of hotels.

In 1959 the economy was opened up for foreign investment, and the peseta was devalued, making Spain an even more attractive destination compared to the Riviera of France and Italy. The private sector in Spain responded very rapidly, and in the early 1960s new hotels, villas and apartments were built all along Spain's Mediterranean coast in a rather uncoordinated and unplanned manner. The volume of tourism quadrupled from six million in 1960 to 24 million in 1970. The expansion of air transport accelerated this growth by opening up Spain to the Northern European market, particularly Britain, although in 1970, 63 per cent of Spain's visitors still came across the border by car causing congestion on the coastal routes, (particularly in July and August). Tourism had a significant effect on the Spanish economy, creating jobs (half a million in the mid 1960s and one million by 1975) and generating foreign earnings. Tourism accounted for a quarter of the value of Spain's exports in 1975. Not surprisingly, the Spanish government continued to support tourism, although the accelerating and uncontrolled growth led to the destruction of forests and loss of environmental quality and to problems of tourists arriving to find hotel developments incomplete and with poor infrastructure. The continued concentration of development on the Mediterranean led to a shift in the distribution of the Spanish population away from the interior towards the costas and the Balearic Islands. By the mid 1970s, when the growth of tourism was checked slightly, Spain already had an extensive stock of large modern hotels tailor-made for the needs of the mass market. Exchange rates still made Spain an attractive destination for the British. In spite of the recession, tourism resumed its growth, and the industry continued to cater for mass tourists from the middle and lower class social groups. The growing prosperity of the Spanish, political changes in their country, (for example the re-establishment of democracy and their entry into the EC in 1986) and the over-development and congestion on the coast and the bad behaviour of some visitors has led to some conflicts between tourists and residents.

In spite of this, however, tourism became even more important to the economy: it employed 11.5 per cent of the labour force, contributing 44.6 per cent of the value of Spain's exports in 1986, and 11 per cent of GDP. Although increasing numbers of Spaniards are beginning to travel abroad, the country enjoys a huge surplus of income from tourism over Spanish expenditure on tourism abroad. However, the profitability of tourism is declining, and there is a need to upgrade and diversify both the tourist industry and the economy as a whole. Efforts are being made to promote conferences and to open up new areas away from the islands and congested Mediterranean coast, and to provide a wider variety of types of holiday.

The tourist regions of Spain

Spain can be divided into two broad tourist regions: the coast and the interior, the former very heavily used for sun, sea and sand tourism, and the latter hardly visited although it abounds with cultural and historic attractions. The landscapes and climate of the interior make it a less varied and less attractive tourist destination than the interior of France.

The interior

Most of the Iberian peninsula is over 500 m. It consists of a high plateau with flat, monotonous skylines, divided into basins by east-west mountain chains that stand out above the plateau surface (*see* Fig 11.2). It has a hot semi-arid climate and maximum temperatures rise to over 30° C in Madrid in midsummer. The uplands consist of dry, dusty ridges and rolling plains, but where irrigation is possible the valleys are green and fertile.

A semicircular rim of mountains frame the plateau on its northern, eastern and southern edges. These ranges are known as the Cantabrian and Iberian mountains and the Sierra Nevada (in Andalucia). The plateau gradually drops in height from these mountains to its western edge in Portugal. The plateau is cut into two basins by the Central Sierras running east and west across its middle.

The Cantabrian mountains

These run parallel to Spain's north coast, and they drop sharply to the Atlantic to form a steep, cliffed coastline. Turbulent rivers have cut deep valleys in their northern flanks. The valleys are steep – often dropping over 2500 m in a distance of 1632 km. The hillsides are green and lush as the region lies in the path of moist Atlantic weather systems.

The region has its own distinctive cultural resources. In Galicia (at its western end) there are many medieval monasteries, religious houses and chapels associated with the 'way of St James', the Christian pilgrims' route to the town of Santiago de Compostela. The Basque country with its unique language and independent traditions lies to the eastern end of the region.

The Iberian mountains and the Central Sierras

The Iberian mountains form a more diffuse upland block at the eastern edge of the plateau of central Spain, while the granite mass of the Central Sierras rises to over 1400 m. The landscapes are much drier and more barren.

The basins and plateaux to the south of the Central Sierras have a hot semi-arid climate, and maximum temperatures rise to over 30° C in Madrid in midsummer. The only part of the

Fig 11.2 Regions of Spain and Portugal

interior that receives any significant tourism is Madrid (the political and cultural capital). It is both a historic and modern industrial city of three million people. Over ten per cent of domestic tourism is centred here. Foreign visitors may come for business tourism but also for cultural tourism. The city is the home of the Prado Museum, one of the world's most famous art galleries. The town of Toledo (60 km to the south of Madrid) is another major cultural and historic attraction. It was a regional capital from Roman times, (218 BC-300 AD), during the rule of the Visigoths and during the following period when Spain was ruled by invading Arabs (the Moors) who introduced Moslem culture and architecture in the period 712–1035 AD. When Christianity was re-established, Toledo became the wealthy capital of the Kingdom of Castille until Madrid replaced it as capital in 1561. Thus modern development has been diverted away

from Toledo, so it has survived virtually intact, and its narrow, winding streets, free of wheeled traffic, retain their medieval character. It is one of Europe's finest unspoilt medieval towns, even on par with Venice.

The Sierra Nevada mountains of Andalucia

These form the southern rim of the plateau, and include Spain's highest peaks (over 3800 m).

The ranges extend over 125 km inland to the Guadalquivir valley, but are highest in the south and drop steeply to the Mediterranean coast, forming the backdrop to the Costa del Sol, and protecting it from any cold northerly weather influences. The mountains are rounded, smooth domes but in places their flanks are deeply dissected by spectacular valleys and gorges. Snow lies between November and May (above 2000 m), allowing winter sports developments, e.g. at Solynieve 34 km from Granada. The eastern end of the mountain chain (inland of the Costa Cálida between Almeria and Cartagena) is very hot and dry with a treeless and desolate pink and ochre landscape of gorges, badlands and rolling plateaux.

Andalucia has a long history with many of the settlements in the Guadalquivir valley having Roman origins. But it owes much of its particular cultural and architectural character to Moorish influence. The Islamic Moors arrived in Gibraltar (its name derived from the Moorish name Djebel al Tarik) in 711 AD, and ruled most of Spain for several centuries, their occupation of Andalucia coming to an end in 1492 when Granada finally fell to the Christians. The region is rich in Moorish architecture such as the Grand Mosque (La Mezquita) in Córdoba, and the Alhambra Palace, a 13th-14th century fortified palace built of pink stone, in Granada. Seville is famed for its bullfighting and its April Fair when flamenco dress, music and dancing underline the special culture and character of the region.

The Pyrénées.

The only other inland location that attracts foreign tourists in any significant numbers is the Pyrénées. The Spanish side of the mountain range has similar landscapes to the French side (see Chapter 9). This area is visited for both summer and winter sports holidays (some resorts offer skiing for up to six months of the year). The main ski resorts are Baqueira Beret and La Molina-Supermolina.

However, Spain is synonymous with sun, sea and sand holidays, and foreign tourism is highly concentrated on a few coastal regions (see Fig 11.3).

The Mediterranean coast

The Costa Brava

This is the stretch of coast running from the French border to Blanes, 60 km north east of Barcelona. Its climate is similar to that of

	Foreign tourists using hotels %	All accommodation %
Balearic islands	40.7	22.6
Canary Islands	17.7	18.4
The Mediterranean Coast		
Northern section (Catalonia/Costa Brava)	15.2	20.6
Middle section (Valencia)	8.3	16.2
Southern section (Andalucia/Costa del Sol)	11.7	13.2
All the rest of Spain	6.4	9.0

Fig 11.3 Distribution of foreign tourism in Spain (1986)

	Av temp °C	Rainfall mm	RH%	Average sun hours per day
January	8.7	35	68	5
February	10.3	38	65	6
March	11.4	44	68	6
April	14.0	46	66	7
May	17.2	33	66	8
June	20.8	33	64	9
July	24.0	27	65	10
August	24.1	38	69	9
September	21.6	34	73	7
October	17.1	72	71	6
November	12.9	44	70	5
December	9.3	28	67	4

Fig 11.4 Barcelona's climate

Fig 11.5 Costas Dorada and Brava

Barcelona (*see* Fig 11.4). 'Costa Brava' means 'wild coast'. It is wild in that the scenery is rugged. The coast is spectacular, with cliffed headlands alternating with small sandy beaches in the coves and bays backed by steeply sloping hills. Some relatively quiet beaches may be found, but it is generally very intensively developed for tourism (*see* Fig 11.5). The large modern resorts consist of multistorey hotels and apartments and are very crowded (e.g. Lloret de Mar and S'Agaro). Some remain relatively unspoilt, for example Tossa (which was originally a Roman city with 12th century walls). Many of the original settlements were fishing villages that have been expanded by the addition of hotels, villas and apartments, e.g. Rosas and Estartit. All these resorts plus major centres like San Feliu and Blanes, are dominated by tour operators providing package tours mainly for the British and German markets (*see* Fig 11.6). Elsewhere, the development consists of sprawling settlements offering villa and campsite accommodation, catering for the independant and individual tourist. The number of villas built as second homes is growing rapidly, particularly on the steep hillsides overlooking the sea. The region has over 25 per cent of all Spain's campsites and these cater particularly for the French who drive the short distance across the border along the

A17 motorway to the Costa Brava. Longer distance travellers arrive via the international airport at Barcelona or the more local Gerona airport which was opened in 1967.

Origin of visitors	% of all foreign visitors to hotels
West Germany	35.3
France	17.6
UK	12.1
North America	2.5
Other	32.5

Fig 11.6 Foreign visitors to the Costa Brava 1986

The Costa Dorada

This is the stretch of coastline south from Barcelona to Tarragona (*see* Fig 11.5). It has fine sandy beaches and has a gentler landscape than the cliffed and rocky Costa Brava. The motorway and railway run close to the coast, often cutting off the beach from the settlements inland. Tarragona has many well preserved Roman buildings and retains much of its original Roman plan. In 1984 the province of Tarragona had 14 per cent of Spain's campsite bed spaces, with a total of 51 000, but only 2.5 per cent of Spain's hotel bed spaces. The province is thus providing accommodation to appeal to French taste. Hotel visitors are more likely to come from Britain or West Germany. Catalonia as a whole (the combined Costa Brava and Costa Dorada regions) has 45 per cent of all Spain's campsite accommodation, reflecting the needs of the nearby French market.

Costa de Azahar

This extends from Viñaroz over 180 km south to Cap de la Nao (*see* Fig 11.2). It is an unbroken strip of lowland, again flanked by the motorway and railway. The coast is fringed by pine-clad dunes and long, sandy beaches, which are sometimes cut off from the mainland by lagoons, and hotels are scattered along the coast with no

really large resorts. The region has only two per cent of Spain's accommodation but again the majority (three fifths) is in the form of campsites and apartments to cater primarily for the French market.

The Costa Blanca (The White Coast)

This runs from Cap de la Nao to Alicante (*see* Fig 11.7). The coastal plain is interrupted by the northern ridges of the Andalucian mountains as they run into the sea. In the northern section, white cliffs are interspersed with white shingle and sand beaches, but south of Altea the coast levels out and there are larger beaches of fine, white sand, for example Benidorm has two major beaches, one 3.2 kms long and the other of 1.6 kms. To the south, the beaches become a little more pebbly. The biggest and best beaches

Fig 11.7 Coasts of southern Spain

have all been developed since the 1960s, and the majority of the accommodation is in hotels. It is dominated by English-speaking visitors (the British make up 21 per cent of all foreign hotel visitors and 11 per cent are North Americans). Only about six per cent of hotel visitors come from France and Germany. Benidorm is the largest resort and it caters for this market well, with British food available, and a wide range of entertainments (e.g. bingo, entertainment parks, discos, nightclubs, and a selection of land and water sports). The region has also been popular for the development of foreign-owned second homes (villas or apartments) which are used by the owners firstly as holiday homes and then as retirement homes. In 1986 there were about half a million along this stretch of coast, of which about a third are British-owned and a quarter are West German.

The southernmost section (the coast of Murcia, south of Alicante) is sometimes known as the Costa Cálida. Here the coastal lowlands disappear as the mountains meet the sea. It has few resorts and can be extremely hot and dry in the summer.

The Costa del Sol

This coast runs from Almeria to Gibraltar (*see* Fig 11.7) and is backed by the mountains of the Sierra Nevada which rise to 3440 metres. It has many fine beaches, and the climate is appreciably warmer and sunnier than the Costa Brava. Average temperatures reach 26° C in July and August in Málaga, and the summer drought is complete between June and August (15 mm only). Almeria averages over 10 hours of sunshine a day for four months (May to August). The region is densely populated and has a substantially urbanised or suburban tourist landscape. Nearly 70 per cent of the accommodation is in the form of hotels and apartments and the region is swamped by budget-priced packages, though there are some luxury hotels, and many foreign-owned second homes. The main resorts – Torremolinos, Benalmadena Costa, Fuengirola, Marbella and Estapona – are linked to the airport at Málaga by the coastal road. Again, the hotels of the area are most popular with the English-speaking visitors (17.5 per cent of hotel visitors come from UK and 10.8 per cent from North America). The Andalucian mountains inland from the coast contain a wide variety of tourist attractions but are not so popular as the coast.

The Atlantic coast of Spain

Although the main concentration of tourist development is along the Mediterranean coast, the Atlantic coast has great potential for development (*see* Fig 11.7). The Costa de la Luz runs from Gibraltar to the Portuguese border and consists of the lowlands at the mouth of the valley of the river Guadalquivir. Sand dunes extend along the coast, impeding the drainage of the river and creating extensive marshy areas inland (Las Marismas). This is designated as the Coto de Doñana National Park on account of its exceptional wildlife, but there may be conflicts between the need to conserve the wildlife and the pressures for the tourist development of this stretch of coast. Cádiz and Jérez (from where sherry originated) lie at the mouth of the valley; Seville and Córdoba are towns which have many Moorish buildings, such as the eighth century Mosque at Córdoba, and are both steeped in Andalucian culture (characterised by flamenco music and dancing, bullfighting and religious festivals).

The North Atlantic coast

The coastline has many fine beaches and is quite popular with Spanish domestic tourists but has very little international tourism. Because the coast is open to Atlantic weather the climate is cooler (with average summer temperatures below 20° C) and much wetter, with rainfall all year round, than the Mediterranean coast of Spain. Sunshine hours average seven a day in mid summer (compared to 12 hours in Almeria). The landscape is lusher and greener than the Mediterranean and the coast is largely undeveloped and uncrowded.

The Balearic Islands

This group of islands is in the Mediterranean, nearly 200 km south of Barcelona and 240 km due east of the Valencian coastline. The total area of the archipelago is 5014 km^2 and the coastline is 1240 km long. The largest of the islands is Majorca (*see* Figs 11.2 and 11.8) and is the main centre of tourist activity.

These islands are Spain's most important tourist area with 3.6 million foreign visitors in 1986. Eighteen per cent of all of Spain's tourist

	Area km²	% of land area of the archipelago	% of coast-line of the archipelago	% hotel bednights 1985	Airport	Flight time from London
Majorca	3660	73	45	80.9	Palma	2 hrs 15 min
Minorca	686	14	23	5.4	Mahon	3 hrs 30 min
Ibiza	593	11	17	13.0		3 hrs 30 min
Formentera	94	<2	<15			

Figure 11.8 The Balearic Islands

accommodation is located here, consisting mainly of hotels and apartments (26 per cent and 22 per cent respectively of Spain's total stock) but very few campsites. This selection of accommodation is tailored to the needs of the British and West German markets. The islands rely heavily on the British market, which accounts for 32 per cent of all visits to hotels and over half the total number of visitors though the proportion varies from island to island (*see* Fig 11.9). The British connection with the islands is longstanding. The island of Minorca was occupied by the British between 1708 and 1802, and there is a substantial and well-integrated resident British community on the island and a considerable proportion of the 9000 plus second homes on the island are owned by British people who may eventually retire there and thus further add to the resident British community.

	% tourists to		
	Majorca	Ibiza (incl visitors destined for Formentera)	Minorca
UK	41.9	52.3	76.7
West Germany	28.9	29.1	14.4
France	6.0	0.6	–
Switzerland	3.5	2.3	1.3
Netherlands	3.0	3.3	2.0
Norway	3.2	0.3	1.2
Denmark	2.9	2.0	0.9
Italy	2.6	5.1	0.6
Sweden	2.3	0.3	1.6

Fig 11.9 Foreign visitors to the Balearic Islands: Tourists by nationality and island of arrival 1986

These cultural and historical links with the islands are one explanation of their popularity with British tourists and their natural resources have reinforced the connection. The islands have a typical Mediterranean climate (*see* p 29, Chapter 2). The summer temperatures, which (rise to 25° C in July and August) are intermediate between those of Barcelona (to the north) and Athens to the east. Their maritime location makes them a little less extreme, i.e. wetter and more humid than Athens in the summer, but slightly milder and drier in the winter, making them more attractive for winter visits. The coastline is varied, consisting of rocky cliffs, deep inlets, and good harbours interspersed with fine sandy beaches of different sizes and character. Some are large and heavily developed and commercialised, while others remain isolated and deserted. Tourism is dominated by sun, sea and sand package holidays, although the landscapes also have tourist potential. For example, in Majorca there is a band of rugged mountainous terrain in the northwest of the island, extending 16 km in from the coast (*see* Fig 11.10). Its highest peak rises to 1459 m. There are high, almost vertical cliffs where the mountains jut into the sea. The peaks occasionally get snow in winter but they protect the rest of the island from cold NW winds in winter. The land to the southeast of the mountains is lower and is covered with almond orchards which flower in February. It is formed of less resistant rock that has been eroded by the sea to form two wide bays where the island's best beaches are situated (at Palma in the south and Alcudia in the north). These are the most intensively developed, e.g. the 1.6 km Playa de Arenal, east of Palma, and are backed by multistorey hotels and apartments, with all the entertainments and facilities to suit British holiday tastes. The east coast of Majorca is made of limestone and has slightly fewer and rather smaller beaches in a series of coves between rocky headlands. The south coast is

Fig 11.10 Majorca

much more cliffed and is the least developed for tourism.

The islands plan to diversify their tourist product with the development of active sports facilities such as golf courses and yacht moorings. It is, however, the very success of the tourist industry in meeting the needs of the mass sun, sea, sand package market that has led to environmental and economic problems. Sixty per cent of the islands' GNP comes from the tourist industry.

The economy of the islands is over-dependent on tourism, and relies too much on just the British and West German markets which together account for 80 per cent of all visitors. The spending levels of British tourists are low, hotel profit margins have been declining and some new apartment developments have been badly built, threatening the beauty of the landscape. Majorca's season lasts from May to October with nearly 13 per cent of visitors coming in the winter months, yet only 40 per cent of its hotels are open in the off-season. The other islands have a far shorter summer season, with nearly 40 per cent of their visitors arriving in July and August, and negligible winter seasons. An additional pressure is for second home development (both for the developing domestic Spanish market and for foreigners). By 1981, numbers of second homes had risen to near two million. Flats and apartments are concentrated in the coastal and resort areas, but many smallholdings in the interior have been aquired by hobby farmers and used mainly for holidays rather than for agriculture. These problems have led the Balearics Government to consider imposing much greater control on new development, and it plans to both diversify and upgrade the tourist product, and also to support the other industries of the islands (e.g. textiles in Ibiza, and leather and footwear in Minorca).

The Canary Islands

These islands lie off the African coast well outside the Mediterranean basin, and the area has a sub-tropical climate (*see* Fig 11.1 on p 125). The islands are considered in this chapter because they are politically and economically integrated with Spain. In terms of tourist perceptions, the islands are primarily a winter sun destination that compete with other longer haul sub-tropical locations rather than with the Mediterranean.

The islands are ancient volcanoes, and some of the mountains are extinct craters. Many of the beaches are made of black sand derived from the volcanic deposits.

The winter climate and coast are the main tourist resources, as the January maximum temperature can rise above 20° C and the winters are dry. The low rainfall and high visitor populations, however, lead to problems of water supply and an expensive desalination plant is required to obtain supplies from seawater. In 1989 over 1.4 million visitors arrived on Tenerife and a similar number on the island of Las Palmas. Most of these visitors were from the UK or West Germany, who stay in hotels and apartments.

Domestic tourism in Spain

The coastal resorts of Spain cater for the domestic market as well as international visitors, but do not suffer from such intense congestion as in France or Italy where international and domestic demands coincide. This is because the Spanish domestic market is small by Western European standards. Only 44 per cent of Spain's 39 million population took any sort of holiday away from home, of which, however, 90 per cent were in Spain. Thus, Spain appears to be in Phase 2 of the evolution of its own domestic and outbound tourism (*see* p 6, Chapter 1), with a comparatively small but rapidly growing domestic market and only a very small minority of the population travelling abroad. Domestic tourists generally stayed in cheaper accommodation (approximately 30 per cent with friends or relatives and only 21 per cent in hotels). So, again, domestic tourists do not yet compete directly with international visitors. On the other hand, domestic holidays are strongly peaked in August – the Spaniards, like the French, have a tradition of taking one long holiday in August – and this may lead to temporary conflicts of interest between domestic and international tourists. Fifty-seven per cent of all domestic holidays were to the coast but few Spaniards visited the Balearics or the Canary Islands. The Costa de Azahar, Costa Blanca and Andalucia were the most popular destinations overall, but the north coast (particularly Galicia) is far more popular with domestic tourists than with foreign visitors.

Spanish outbound tourism

Outbound tourism is as yet little developed, and shows the following characteristics of an immature but rapidly growing market.

1 Numbers are low. Only 2.5 million Spaniards visited Portugal in 1986, 1 million to France and 0.5 million to Italy. Many of the visitors to Portugal were transit tourists, often on shopping trips.

2 Numbers of outbound tourists are growing rapidly. Growth rates (even in the recession of the 1980s) were in the range of 30 to 57 per cent to Portugal, Greece, Morocco, Turkey and Tunisia (all the relatively cheaper Mediterranean destinations). Lower growth rates were recorded for Spanish visitors to the relatively expensive destinations such as France, Italy and UK.

3 Few Spaniards travel by plane. Eighty-eight per cent of Spanish outbound tourists left Spain by car, and only nine per cent went to longer haul destinations by plane. Coach travel is important and package coach tours abroad are popular. The majority of trips are fairly short, i.e. to adjacent countries. Much of the genuine long-haul air travel is still business tourism (40.7 per cent of Spanish visitors to Canada and 44.5 per cent to Japan were business travellers).

Portugal

The country can be divided by the Tagus into two climatic regions; the north, dominated by cooler, moist Atlantic weather and the south where the climate and vegetation are more Mediterranean in character.

The north coast of Portugal (the Costa Verde) averages 1270 mm rainfall a year, while on the windward (west-facing) slopes of the mountains inland, the total may reach over 2500 mm a year. Lisbon (on the Tagus estuary) has 708 mm a year and two months (July and August) of drought. Faro, on Portugal's southern coast, has only 453 mm a year with a three-month dry period. In the south average maximum temperatures rise to 28° C in the summer drought, while Lisbon's average midsummer temperature is around 22° C.

Physically the country is divided into:

1 the uplands and plateaux
(*a*) the mountains of the north (Minho and Tras os Montes). These are located inland of the Costa Verde.
(*b*) the plateaux of Beira and Alentejo (the edge of the Spanish Meseta). The Beira plateau is located inland of the Costa de Prata, while Alentejo is east of the Lisbon coast.

2 the lowlands
 (*a*) the coastal lowlands and plains
 (*b*) the Tagus valley

The uplands

The mountains of the north rise to 780 m in Minho, and the Tras os Montes to over 1500 m. The landscapes are interesting rather than dramatic. The unspoiled, rugged granite uplands of Minho are well wooded with maritime pines and offer opportunities for walking and climbing, while the Tras os Montes is a monotonous treeless plateau dissected by deep valleys. The Beira plateau has more tree cover (pine and chestnut) and rises southwards to the more striking landscapes of the Estrela mountains. The rolling Alentejo plateau (rising to only 400 m) is a richer, arable agricultural landscape.

These regions form Portugal's interior, and tend to be dry and hot in the summer, as the plateaux rise to merge into the Meseta across the Spanish border. There are many unspoilt historic settlements, e.g. Estramoz and Portalegre, and the fortified hill towns along the border are of particular interest. These date from the 12th century and many such as Elvas, have impressive medieval fortifications. Evora is another 12th century town that became Portugal's second most important city in the 17th century and has much magnificent architecture of the period.

In spite of these attractions these parts of Portugal are hardly visited by international tourists, with less than two per cent of Portugal's foreign visitors.

The coast

The coast is the main tourist resource, and it can be divided into four zones (*see* Fig 11.2).

1 The Costa Verde (The Green Coast). The coast is green with forests and lush vegetation but the rainfall that supports the vegetation limits the tourism. The coastal plain is between 1.6 and 8 km wide and extend into the Douro valley inland of Oporto. The valley sides are terraced vineyards where the port wine is produced. There is a cluster of resorts with good sandy beaches around Oporto but the region attracted only 9.2 per cent of Portugal's total tourist

bednights in 1986 and 4.3 per cent of foreign tourists.

2 Costa de Prata (the silver coast). This extends from Espinho (just south of Oporto) to Estremadura. The coast is flat, fringed with mobile sand dunes which have ponded back the River Vouga to form saltmarshes and lagoons at Aveiro.

These are now drained by a maze of canals and Aveiro has been likened to Venice and its surrounding countryside to Holland. The town had been a significant fishing port in the 16th century before the river mouth became choked with sand.

The most important historic town inland is Coimbra, Portugal's third largest city with one of Europe's oldest universities (dating from the 16th century). Elsewhere along the coast there are long sandy beaches but the resorts are quite small and are more spread out. The climate is more Atlantic than Mediterranean and the region attracted 12 per cent of Portugal's tourist bednights in 1986, but only 3.5 per cent of foreign visitors. These northern coasts cater mostly for the growing domestic market.

3 The Lisbon coast (Costa Lisboa and Costa Dourada). This is in the climatic transition zone towards a more Mediterranean climate. The coast is low lying with long beaches, some of which are more intensively developed both for staying visitors and day-trippers from Lisbon e.g. Cascais, Estoril, which has a casino, nightlife and a range of land-based sports, and Troia which is a modern tourist beach complex of hotels, restaurants, nightclubs, golf and watersports facilities. Lisbon itself has an excellent natural harbour and the site has been settled since pre-Roman times. Its cathedral dates from the 12th century and its Moorish quarter from the medieval period. But its wealth expanded with Portugal's overseas trade and the city was added to and partly rebuilt in the 17th and 18th centuries. It is still a thriving commercial and business centre: it attracts many domestic and international business tourists, but also all year round short-stay cultural visitors. The average length of stay is low at two to eight days for international visitors, but the visitors are high spenders and there is a good stock of upmarket accommodation (over 40 per cent of all Portugal's five-star hotel rooms are in Lisbon). Elsewhere in the region there are also good camping facilities.

There are a number of historical sites inland

that are accessible from Lisbon, such as Sintra, Queluz and Mafra. Much of the countryside inland of the Lisbon and Dourada coasts is forested with cork oak trees and is a centre of cork production. This region with its varied cultural and coastal attractions took 23 per cent of Portugal's bednights and drew its international tourists from a wide variety of generating countries.

4 The Algarve. This stretch of the southern coast of Portugal dominates Portugal's tourist industry, taking 40 per cent of bednights, and attracts most of the country's foreign tourists. It faces the Atlantic (*see* Fig 11.7) but because of its southerly aspect is relatively sheltered from Atlantic depressions. It has a long, warm and dry summer with virtually no rainfall June–August. Summer maximum temperatures rise to 28° C, though the average temperatures are lower than the Mediterranean. Nevertheless, it is well developed for coastal tourism. The beaches are extensive and sandy. The western section (from Faro to Sagres) is continuously developed with little land left for new development. High rise hotels, villas and apartments line the coast with particularly large concentrations of hotels in Portimao, Albufeira and Loulé. The accommodation is dominated by budget quality facilities to meet the needs of the relatively low spending British package visitors. This, plus the unplanned nature of the resorts and the speed with which they were developed, has led to some deterioration of environmental quality. The greatest number of campsites are at Lagos and Villa Real (at either end of the coast).

With over half of the international arrivals, the Algarve is by far the most popular region of Portugal among foreign visitors. The economy of the region relies particularly heavily on the British market. British holidaymakers accounted for 51 per cent of all the nights in hotels, boarding houses and apartments, and most British visitors (73.4 per cent) came on package tours. Faro is the Algarve's international airport, and the primary gateway for package tourists. Spanish day-trippers come across the border by road.

Madeira

Portugal also possesses a sub-tropical Atlantic island located 650 km west off the Moroccan coast (*see* Fig 11.1). Madeira is 57 km east-west,

and 22 km north-south. Two-thirds of its territory is mountainous and the coast is precipitous, with mainly shingle or boulder beaches. Its climate is its main resource (*see* Fig 11.11). The best season is April to June but it does have all year round tourism.

	Av temp °C	Rainfall (mm)	Peak months for	
			Non-Iberian tourist arrivals	Arrivals from Spain and Portugal
Jan	15	86		
Feb	15	91		
March	15.4	86	*	
April	16	51	*	
May	18	28		
June	19.2	10		
July	21	2		
Aug	22	2		*
Sept	21	30		
Oct	20	102		
Nov	18	119	*	
Dec	16	81		

Fig 11.11 Funchal's climate and seasonality of tourism

The island has mild winters and warm, dry summers. The relatively dry climate, the growing local and tourist demands and the small catchment area of the island has led to problems of water supply. The best season is April to June but Madeira does have all year round tourism. This is made up of two distinct groups of tourists with contrasting seasonal patterns of demand.

Visitors from Spain and Portugal come to the island for their summer holiday, so there is a pronounced peaking of Iberian visitors in August. Other visitors from Europe, and particularly from Scandinavia, see the island more as a winter sun destination and there is a double peak of these visitors: the months of March/April and November each record over 25 000 non-Iberian visitors, while in summer (May to August) these visitor arrivals drop to around 15 000 a month. Northern European visitors prefer to travel to other resorts in the Mediterranean with better beaches during these summer months. When these patterns are superimposed it is clear that, in spite of the attractive climate in late spring, May is the month the island receives fewest tourists.

Madeira depends heavily on the British and West German markets, which together account for about a third of the islands visitors, with another 17 per cent from Scandinavian countries.

The island has had historical connections with Great Britain, associated with the trade in Madeira wine. In the 18th century the wine merchants built their mansions on the islands and let them for the winter season. Modern tourism on the island did not expand until the airport was built at Funchal in the 1960s, but the topography has constrained tourist growth. The island is short of flat coastal land suitable for tourist development, including an airport. Madeira was originally served by air via the military base on the neighbouring small island of Porto Santo but this was an unsatisfactory arrangement and Funchal airport was built in the 1960s, but required major engineering work to create a long enough runway.

In spite of these problems, Madeira is Portugal's third most important tourist region (after the Algarve and Lisbon regions) for international tourists.

The Azores

This is a group of nine islands (the largest, Sao Miguel being a little bigger than Madeira) located in the Atlantic 1500 km west of Lisbon, further north than Madeira. Consequently their climate is a little wetter, windier and cooler than Madeira, and tour operators perceive them to be summer destinations only. International tourism has hardly been developed, due to their limited accessibility by air. The majority (70 per cent) of the visitors are domestic tourists from mainland Portugal who come on internal Portuguese flights. The average length of stay of visitors to the islands is short (only three days), and the total number of visitors is around 100 000 a year (representing only 3.4 per cent of Portuguese domestic tourism and 0.7 per cent of Portugal's foreign visitors in 1986).

Domestic and international tourism in Portugal

The domestic market is as yet small: only 26–30 per cent of the 11 million population have taken annual holidays away from home since 1979. In 1986, only eight per cent went abroad. The

regional pattern of domestic tourism is a little different from that of international, with the northern coastal regions having more appeal for the Portuguese (*see* Fig 11.12).

Region	Foreign %	Portuguese %
Costa Verde	4.3	15.8
Costa de Prata	3.5	13.4
Lisbon Coast	21.1	28.7
'Mountains' (inc North and Beira Plateau)	0.7	9.7
'Plains' (inc Alentejo plateau)	1.0	6.0
Algarve	51.1	16.7
Madeira	17.6	6.3
Azores	0.7	3.4

Fig 11.12 Distribution of tourists (1986)

The volume of tourism in Portugal

Portugal receive around 16 million frontier arrivals, but this includes a large number of day visitors from Spain, and only 6.6 million were classed as tourists in 1988. Under 4 million foreign visitors arrived at registered tourist accommodation.

Tourists from	Tourist arrivals at Portugal's frontier
Spain	45.1
UK	16.1
France	8.5
West Germany	7.9
Netherlands	4.1
USA	2.9
Italy	2.1

Fig 11.13 Tourist arrivals at Portugal's frontiers (1988)

By European standards, international tourism is as yet small scale in Portugal, but it has a particular importance for the British market, offering package tours to a near Mediterranean environment at very competitive prices.

Conclusion

Although the size of the tourist industry of Spain and Portugal is very different, the two countries show significant similarities. Tourist development in both countries is heavily concentrated in relatively small regions, where the sheer volume of tourist numbers and the level of development may be beginning to reduce the quality of the holiday experience. Yet in other parts of each country, tourism is hardly developed: both have empty stretches of Atlantic coast and an abundance of inland cultural resources.

Both countries also have immature, but rapidly growing, domestic markets, and both are just beginning to expand their outbound tourism.

QUESTIONS AND DISCUSSION POINTS

1 To what extent is it true that the combination of climate, coast and accessibility explains the spatial distribution of tourism in Spain and Portugal?
2 It has been suggested that over-development and environmental problems have led the Spanish 'costas' into crisis. Do you consider this to be true — if so, what should be done to overcome the problems?
3 Do you expect Spain to increase or decrease its share of Mediterranean coastal holidays in the future? Explain the reasoning behind your answer.

ASSIGNMENTS

1 You work in a travel agent that serves an inner city area. A young couple come in. They have never been abroad before and have saved up for their first holiday in Spain but they are muddled about where the various 'costas' are and what each 'costa' is like. Briefly explain to them where each of the Spanish 'costas' is located and what characteristics typify each one. Suggest at least one resort in each of the 'costas' that the young couple might like to choose for their holiday.

2 You work in the planning and development section of a major tour operator. The company sells a wide range of different types of holiday including cultural, activity and special interest holidays but currently has no tours of these types in Spain or Portugal. You have been asked by the chief executive to assess the potential of inland Spain and Portugal for one of these types of holiday. Write a brief report:

   (a) locating and describing the chief resources for either cultural, activity or special interest holidays;

   (b) identifying any constraints imposed by climate, lack of infrastructure, difficulties of accessibility etc. on the development of such tours; and

   (c) making recommendations as to which destinations/regions might be worth promoting.

CHAPTER 12

Yugoslavia, Albania and Greece

LEARNING OBJECTIVES

After reading this chapter you should be able to:

- assess the tourist potential of the climatic, landscape, historical and cultural resources of Yugoslavia, Albania and Greece
- distinguish the regional distribution of these geographical resources and their development and use for tourism
- demonstrate a knowledge of the main tourist resorts and tourist centres
- understand the role of Yugoslavia, Albania and Greece in the general pattern of European tourism
- be aware of the impact of political events on the development of tourism.

Introduction

Tourism in these three countries is of a smaller scale and lower intensity than in France, Spain or Italy. In 1988 Yugoslavia attracted 9 million visitors and Greece 7.7 million – modest totals indeed if compared to the 90 million tourists that visit France, Spain and Italy together. On the other hand, the eastern half of the Mediterranean is now a serious competitor to the older established tourist centres of the Western Mediterranean. It has a hotter and longer summer season than the Western Mediterranean, the cost of living is lower and the coasts are relatively undeveloped. These advantages more than offset the greater travelling distance from the tourist generating regions of Northern Europe.

Tourist development in Yugoslavia and Greece has spread eastwards through the region from its beginning at the head of the Adriatic. Yugoslavia was opened to mass tourists in the 1960s, and Greece from 1974 and Turkey followed from

1982 (*see* Chapter 13). In each country the promotion of tourism had to wait for certain political changes to take place, and for improvements in accessibility. Once these had been achieved, tourist flows increased dramatically. By 1990, Yugoslavia's tourist industry had reached maturity and required updating to meet changing tastes, while in Greece, tourism was well established and still actively expanding.

Yugoslavia

Introduction

Yugoslavia has a wide range of natural resources for tourism, but international tourism is very strongly focused on the coast. However, it is the climate and scenery that are the main attractions rather than the beaches: most of the coast is rocky or shingly, but it enjoys a particularly sunny Mediterranean climate. In comparison to other Mediterranean destinations the country attracts a higher proportion of older, childless couples from higher socio-economic groups, rather than young couples or families with young children. Only 12 per cent of its visitors in 1986 were under 24 years of age.

Although Yugoslavia is in competition with destinations such as Spain, it thus offers a slightly different product and attracts a more specialised market. On the other hand, Yugoslavia (like Spain) relies heavily on the West German and British markets. Seventy-one per cent of Yugoslavia's foreign visitors arrive by car, relying on the Adriatic Highway for access down the coast. Most cross the border from Italy via the Milan-Trieste Highway. The country also has a strong domestic market, with more domestic tourists than international visitors. However, foreign tourists are crucial to its faltering economy as they contributed 15 per cent of the country's foreign exchange earnings in 1987.

Yugoslavia's physical resources

Yugoslavia has a land area of 255 800 square km and is about the same size as the UK, but it has a population of only 22½ million. It is predominantly a mountainous country of remote and unspoilt scenery; and can be divided into four main physical regions (*see* Fig 12.1):

1 the Adriatic Coast;
2 the limestone mountain chain that runs parallel to the coast down the length of the country
3 the Yugoslav section of the Alps
4 the inland plains of the Danube and Sava

The Adriatic coast

The coastal zone consists of a very narrow belt of land (only 1 to 60 km wide) that enjoys a true Mediterranean climate. In Split, the July and August temperatures hover around 25° C and although there is no complete summer drought, the climate is particularly sunny. Split enjoys an average of 2658 hours of sunshine a year, with 115 completely cloudless days and only 102 rain days a year. The coast is rugged and rises quickly inland to bleak bare mountain slopes. Most of the beaches are rocky or shingly as they are made of limestone, a rock which does not yield a sandy sediment. There are no big wide sandy beaches like the ones found on the Italian side of the Adriatic. The Dalmatian coast of northern Yugoslavia is fringed by 1000 islands, which are the submerged crests of limestone ridges running parallel to the mountain chain inland. Many are small and uninhabited but some of the larger islands are developed for tourism and are connected by ferry to the mainland.

The greatest concentration of resorts is on the coast of the Istrian peninsula (*see* Fig 12.1). The larger resorts, including Umag, Porec, Rovinj and Opatija, each had over one million foreign tourist nights in 1985. Centres such as Vrsar, Pula and Rabac each had half a million nights. Most of the resorts' modern hotels are grafted on to older settlements such as small medieval towns, e.g. Umag, fishing villages, such as Porec, or even older settlements. The town of Pula was a Roman military and administrative centre in second century BC, and still possesses major Roman monuments such as the Amphitheatre, and the Temple of Augustus. On the other hand, Medulin and Rabac are essentially modern developments attached to small villages.

Tourists from Northern Europe reach the Istrian resorts via the airports at Pula and Ljubljana further inland, but the majority, from Germany and Italy, come by road. In fact, Istria

Fig 12.1 Main regions and provinces of Yugoslavia

is so close to the Italian border that most of the resorts offer coach or hydrofoil daytrips to Venice.

The Dalmatian coast between Opatija and Split is much less intensively developed, with a series of smaller more widely spaced resorts. Foreign tourists outnumber domestic tourists in most of the resorts north of Split, due to their accessibility by road from the Italian border. Split is an ancient town but with modern commercial port and university functions. Its airport also serves the resorts of Central Dalmatia. There is a second concentration of resorts south of Split, along the 'Makarska Riviera', and on the nearby islands of Brac, Hvar and Korcula. The coast is still essentially rocky with small coves and pebbly beaches, and some of the more secluded beaches on the islands are reserved for

naturists. There are also naturist centres on the Istrian peninsula, and along the coast south of Dubrovnik.

Although many of the resorts have historic cores, Dubrovnik is the only example of a medieval town preserved in its original state. The old city is enclosed by high walls and ramparts. It owed its medieval wealth to trade with Italy but was conquered and ruled by the Venetians between 1420 and 1797. Modern hotels have been built along the coast outside the old city. Like Split, it enjoys a particularly sunny climate (averaging 2584 hours of sunshine a year). The airport at Dubrovnik is the gateway to the southernmost part of the Yugoslavian coast (southern Dalmatia and Montenegro). The beaches here are bigger and are of coarse sand, and the dense concentrations of hotels at Budva,

Becici, Petrovac and Ulcinj are more heavily used by domestic tourists than by overseas visitors. Seventy per cent of the overseas visitors (and 82 per cent of foreign tourist nights) are concentrated on the coastline of Yugoslavia as a whole. Most of Yugoslavia's coastal tourist zone lies within the Republic of Croatia (*see* Fig 12.1).

The mountain spine

The mountain chain that backs the coast extends to 60–100 km inland, and averages 600 m in height, though substantial areas reach 1500 m. The mountains, running parallel to the coast in a NW-SE direction, lie at right angles to the prevailing winds and receive much more rainfall (totals of over 2500 mm) than the coast. The temperatures are lower, and the weather is quite harsh in winter as the climate is continental rather than Mediterranean. The mountains are made of limestone and have the typical 'karst' landscape of underground rivers, cave systems (e.g. at Postojna) and dry valleys. Thus, although the climate is wet, there is little surface water and the mountains appear dry and barren. Further inland, the geology changes, and rivers flow on the surface. Here the uplands are clothed with forests and pastures which provide a more attractive mountain landscape. The Plitvice National Park lies on the edge of the limestone zone, and consists of a series of 16 lakes linked by cascades and waterfalls, set in beech, spruce and fir forests. The hotels that fringe this park, and resorts such as Zabljak (set in the heart of another National Park characterised by deep gorges, canyons, forests and lakes) provide opportunities for two-centre holidays, for example linking Opatija and Plitvice in the north, and Zabljak with Ulcinj or Petrovac in the south. Sarajevo, which lies inland from the Montenegro riviera has also been promoted in this way, capitalising on its mountain landscapes for summer holidays and on its sports facilities (developed for the 1984 Winter Olympics) for winter holidays.

The Yugoslav Alps

A small section of the European Alps extends into northern Yugoslavia. Triglav is the highest peak (2863 m). The jagged peaks and flat-bottomed valleys create a much more dramatic mountain landscape than the limestone mountains further south. The lower slopes of the Yugoslav Alps are forested, merging into alpine pastures above the tree line. Lakeside resorts such as Bled and Bohinj have similar climatic advantages to the Italian lakes – the average July temperature at Bled is 21° C. These resorts are popular in summer, and are also promoted for two-centre holidays, for example Bled with Umag, Dubrovnik or the Dalmatian islands. Kranjska Gora is both a summer and winter sports resort, and ski facilities have also been developed at Planica. The lower cost and less crowded facilities make them very competitive with the winter sports resorts in Switzerland, Austria and Italy.

The inland plains

The northeasterly corner of Yugoslavia consists of the monotonous plains of the Danube. These plains merge into the expanses of the Hungarian plains to the north. The climate is continental, with cold winters down to minus 0.2° C in Belgrade, and warm summers averaging 22.7° C in July. The interior is also relatively dry; the capital, Belgrade, has only 687 mm rainfall a year. Belgrade is the commercial and communications centre of the interior. The modern city has grown around a historic core, but it is mainly a centre for cultural, commercial and business tourism.

The development of tourism in Yugoslavia

In some ways, the development of tourism on the Yugoslav Adriatic coast parallels that of the French and Italian rivieras. Much of Yugoslavia's coastal territory came under Austrian rule from 1813 to 1918 and resorts such as Opatija were visited by the Austrian Court. From 1880 to 1900 the Istrian peninsula and the Dalmatian coast were among the most fashionable tourist regions of Europe, while the Dubrovnik riviera became very popular with the French and Czechs during the inter-war period.

International tourism was disrupted by the Second World War, after which Yugoslavia was established as a communist state in 1945 and restrictions were imposed on movements into and out of the country. Yugoslavia was expelled from the communist bloc in 1948 but international tourism did not resume until 1961. Freedom of movement within Yugoslavia was not allowed until 1965, when the Adriatic Highway was opened and carborne tourists began to visit the country for one or two nights at first, in the Yugoslav Alps and later on the Istrian peninsula, and along the Dalmatian coast. This stimulated the provision of motels and campsites. The domestic market also began to grow in the mid 1960s encouraged by the socialist system of providing organised holidays for workers. From 1966 to 1970 there was a systematic development of the coast with hotels and holiday villages. Tourism grew at 20 per cent per annum until foreign arrivals reached six million in 1973. Growth slowed down in the 1970s due both to the world economic situation and to the federal government's inconsistent tourist policies. In the 1980s arrivals began to increase again but the provision of new accommodation failed to keep up with the expansion, leading to shortages of suitable accommodation. Since President Tito died in 1980, there have been growing internal political problems concerning the nature of the Yugoslavian Federal Government and the level of independence of the countries' republics and autonomous provinces. The economy has performed badly; rapid inflation and numerous devaluations of the dinar have led to a decline in domestic tourism, while the advantages of devaluations to foreign tourists have been cancelled out by internal inflation. As a result, the tourist industry in Yugoslavia has stagnated. In 1987 it still received only about six million genuine holidaymakers. In the absence of strong, co-ordinated national planning Yugoslavia's tourist industry is likely to suffer in the face of competition from Greece and Turkey. However, in 1988 the federal government proposed a new tourism development strategy which aims to enlarge and modernise its accommodation, and to diversify into water sports, landscape tourism, hunting, health and business tourism.

Supply of accommodation and patterns of use

In 1986, hotels, holiday villages and motels made up a quarter of the stock of bedspaces, and were used mainly by airborne package tourists mostly from UK, USA and Switzerland. Twenty-seven per cent of the bedspaces were campsites; and 63 per cent of the bednights were accounted for by foreigners, mostly West Germans, French, Austrians and Dutch. A third of the stock of accommodation is in the form of private houses, half of which are used by domestic tourists, as are the holiday camps. As yet there are few self-catering units or rented apartments available. The accommodation stock does not really meet the needs of overseas tourists. The stock is mostly located on the Adriatic coast but tourists need to be attracted inland in order to spread the benefits of tourism to all of the provinces.

The three main sources of foreign tourists are the neighbouring countries of West Germany, Italy and Austria (31 per cent, 13 per cent and 9 per cent of foreign visitors respectively in 1987). Most cross the border by car, and stay in campsites or private accommodation. Their average length of stay declined through the worst of the recession; because of their mobility and flexibility of accommodation, such tourist markets are volatile as they can change their plans easily and visit another country if political or economic conditions in Yugoslavia looked unfavourable. On the other hand, these visitors do show high levels of repeat visits and loyalty to particular regions. The charter market from Northern European markets (including the UK) is more consistent and reliable. The UK market contributes 7.8 per cent of Yugoslavia's foreign visitors and is the fourth most important market. About another ten per cent come from the Eastern European countries such as Czechoslovakia. The economic and political changes in these countries in the 1990s will dictate the development of their tourism to Yugoslavia.

Conclusion: Yugoslavia

The natural resources of sea, climate and unspoilt countryside have been shown to be Yugoslavia's main attractions, followed by safety and reasonable prices. However services such as entertainment, sports, shopping and facilities were seen as unsatisfactory, particularly the shortage and poor range of goods in shops; this resulted in the relatively low levels of foreign tourist expenditure. This in turn denies Yugoslavia the hard currency so desperately needed by its ailing economy. The communist party voted to end its political monopoly in 1990, and at the same time the federal structure of government appeared to be failing, with individual republics seeking greater independence. The management of Yugoslavia's economy and the resolution of internal political conflicts are critical for the growth and development of its tourist industry.

Albania

This communist country has been politically and economically isolated from the West for many years, but in 1990 it was cautiously beginning to open up to Western travellers.

The country is physically and climatically similar to Yugoslavia and Greece, as it occupies the stretch of coastal territory between them. The coastal plain varies in width, reaching 50 km inland in places, (considerably wider than the coast strip of Yugoslavia), and has more sandy beaches than Yugoslavia. Inland the well-forested mountains rise to over 2500 m. Three large lakes (Shkodres, Ohrid and Prespan) lie on the Albanian-Yugoslav border in the mountain region. Resorts do exist, for example there are beach hotels south of Durres, and Pogradec is a resort on Lake Ohrid (see Fig 12.2), but the cultural and historic resources have great potential for tourism. The local people still wear traditional dress in the rural areas and there are few cars. Historic towns range from the picturesque museum towns of Gjirokaster and Berat, with their 14th century citadels, to the ancient ruins of Butrint (dating from the fourth and third centuries BC). In short, the country has great potential for tourism if the political situation allowed it to develop. Individual tourists and Americans have not been admitted to the country for many years although limited package tours are available. In 1990 tourism is still at the pioneering stage in Albania, as Albania was the last of the European communist countries to challenge communism and consider moving towards a more open society.

Greece

Introduction

Although Greece has been the focus of small-

scale historical and cultural tourism for many years, mass tourism is a more recent phenomenon. The trickle of post-war cultural tourists (mainly from the USA) was checked in 1967 when there was a coup d'etat and a military dictatorship took over the government. This inhibited the growth of mass tourism at a time when it was developing rapidly elsewhere in the Mediterranean. It was not until 1974, when the country returned to democratic rule, that there was a sustained growth of tourist numbers. Since then sun-loving tourists have flooded into Greece, particularly to the islands: Greece was seen as an attractive, unspoilt and competitively priced alternative to the increasingly congested Spanish resorts.

The climate and island beaches are now the country's main tourist resource rather than the ruins of ancient cities and temples of classical Greece. Although Greece relies heavily on the British and German markets, the country does attract a wide range of different types of tourist from a large number of European countries. It is thus better placed that Yugoslavia to benefit from the resumption in growth of European mass tourism in the 1980s. Moreover, the country has been politically and economically more stable than Yugoslavia in the 1980s. The Greek tourist industry is as yet still relatively small (8.5 million visitors in 1989) but is still growing and is capable of adapting to new demands and changing tourist tastes.

Fig 12.2 Tourist resources of Greece and Albania

Greece's physical resources for tourism

Eighty per cent of Greek territory is mountainous. The limestone mountains that run NW-SE parallel to the coastline through Yugoslavia and Albania continue into peninsular Greece, and form its backbone. They gradually become lower from the north of Greece towards the south, and the islands are the submerged peaks of the mountain chain as it subsides into the Aegean sea. The coastline is broken by gulfs and inlets.

The surface area of the country is only 131 994 square km but it has an exceptionally long coastline of 15 320 km. The island and coastal territories of Greece enjoy a typical Mediterranean climate with a long summer drought and average July temperatures everywhere over 27° C. All parts have at least 2300 hours of sunshine a year, and some islands receive over 3000 hours annually. The mountainous west is much wetter and the north of Greece has a more continental climate.

Greece can be divided into four mainland

Fig 12.3 Regions of Greece

regions and five groups of islands (*see* Fig 12.3):

1 Mainland Greece
  (*a*) Northern Greece (Macedonia, Thessalonica, Khalkidiki, Kavalla and Thrace);
  (*b*) Central Greece (Epiros, Thessaly and Central Greece);
  (*c*) Athens region (Attica and Euboea); and
  (*d*) The Peloponnese.
2 The Islands
  (*a*) Ionian islands (including Corfu);
  (*b*) Cyclades;
  (*c*) Sporades;
  (*d*) Dodecanese (including Rhodes); and
  (*e*) Crete.

Mainland Greece

Northern Greece

This strip of land consists of the southernmost extension of the Carpathian mountains, and the lowlands of the Vardar and Nestos rivers which flow southwards into Greece from across the Yugoslavia and Bulgarian borders. The coast possesses many good sandy beaches, and the Khalkidiki region is being developed for mass tourism for the nearby Yugoslavian market, and for package tourists coming in via Thessalonica

airport. However, the Yugoslavian market declined in the late 1980s due to that country's severe economic problems, and northern Greece is being marketed more actively in other countries. The countryside is green and well wooded, and the mountains of Macedonia are particularly beautiful. It is rich in archaeological sites, but is still quiet and unspoilt, and the region accounted for 11 per cent of foreign overnight stays in 1986. Nearly half the accommodation is the form of campsites and rented rooms.

Central Greece

The Pindhos mountain range forms the central backbone of Greece and divides Epiros (in the west) from the lowlands of Thessaly to the east (*see* Fig 12.2). The limestone mountains themselves are stony and sparsely vegetated in spite of the higher rainfall on their west-facing slopes. Much of Epiros is, however, thickly wooded, and the land drops away to the Ionian coast where there is a mixture of good sandy beaches, estuaries and lagoons. Thessaly is also a fertile agricultural region, overlooked in the north by Mount Olympus (the home of the immortal gods of classical Greece). One of the most dramatic historical sites of the region, however, dates from Byzantine times. A series of sheer-sided rock columns rise from the plain to the northwest of Larissa. Monasteries have been built on top of each of 24 pinnacles. They date from the 4th to the 15th centuries, and the monastic community is known as Meteora. Central Greece is as yet relatively little used by tourists, and in 1989, Central Greece and Thessaly received 4.5 per cent of the country's total foreign overnight stays, and Epiros only 0.5 per cent. These areas are more popular with domestic tourists than with foreign visitors, with about 20 per cent of domestic hotel nights in 1989.

Athens and the surrounding region

The capital, Athens is a major tourist destination, taking 14 per cent of the country's overnight stays by foreigners, and has 17 per cent of the stock of hotel beds. It is easily accessible via the international airport, and its port (Piraeus) links it by ferry to most of the islands. It is a modern, industrial and increasingly polluted city but is dominated by the Acropolis perched on its rocky promontory overlooking the city. There are remains from every period of Greek history here, and the old town (the Plaka) spreads around the foot of the Acropolis. The modern city provides modern, luxury shopping, restaurants and nightlife. The whole of the coastline of the peninsula running southeast of Athens is well developed for tourism. The 70 km stretch of coast that extends from Piraeus to Cape Sounion is called the Apollo Beach. A series of resorts along the coastline provide beach tourism and for water sports, and a variety of accommodation (from rented rooms to modern luxury hotels) is available. The east coast of Attica (Cape Sounion north to Oropou) is similarly fairly intensively developed (*see* Fig 12.2). Athens and its region has declined in popularity as other parts of Greece have been opened up. The island of Euboea (Evia) lies to the north of Athens. It is linked to the mainland by road and ferry and provides a greater variety of busy resorts and unspoilt villages with quiet beaches. The landscape is also attractive, with wooded mountains and varied lowlands, but this region too has suffered a decline in tourist nights in the 1980s. The region abounds in archaeological sites. Delphi is one of the most beautiful of the ancient Greek sites, and is located inland, 176 km northwest of Athens. It was .built on the southern slopes of Mount Parnassus, overlooking the coast. During the day it is busy with coach trips from Athens.

The Peloponnese

This is a large peninsula linked to mainland Greece by a narrow neck of land (six km wide) at Corinth. The core of the peninsula is a barren limestone plateau with mountains up to 2400 m high. It is scattered with archaeological sites such as Mycenae and Tiryns (dating from the 14th century BC), Epidavros (site of the well preserved Greek theatre), Olympia (the site of the original Olympic Games) and the ruined Byzantine city of Mistras. The west coast has some big sandy beaches but is relatively undeveloped for tourism. The east coast (linked to Athens by both road and ferry) is a series of bays, beaches and rocky promontories. The region receives about eight per cent of the country's tourism and is increasing in popularity. However, the adjacent islands of Aegina, Hydra and Spetse were promoted for tourism early and are visited by day-trippers

from Athens. They contain 5.5 per cent of Greek holiday accommodation stock, but like the other old established tourist regions of mainland Greece, are losing tourists (with a drop of over half a million visitors between 1981 and 1986).

The Greek islands

About 60 per cent of Greek tourist nights occur on the islands. Island tourism appears to be of two contrasting types: certain islands are extensively developed for package tours, for example Corfu, Crete and Rhodes, and others cater for independent visitors travelling from island to island. There also appears to be some regional specialisation in that certain nationalities favour particular islands, e.g. the British concentrate on Corfu, the Germans in northern Crete and the Scandinavians in Rhodes. The islands can be divided into five groups.

1 The Ionian Islands. This group includes Corfu, Levkas, Cephallonia, Ithaca and Zante (Zakinthos), and is located off the wetter west coast of mainland Greece. Corfu is green and well vegetated and has many beautiful beaches. The town of Corfu has retained its medieval character; the Venetians occupied the island in the 16th and 17th centuries and fortified the town between 1553 and 1558.

The island has 6.5 per cent of the total stock of Greek hotel beds and received nearly 9.8 per cent of all tourist bednights to Greece in 1989. It meets the needs of the package tour market.

Corfu caters primarily for the UK market: 27 per cent of all UK visitors to Greece stay in Corfu while no more than eight per cent of any other country's visitors stay there. The international airport at Corfu receives visitors from Northern Europe. The other islands of the group are less intensively developed but share Corfu's wooded green character and its abundance of medieval (rather than classical Greek) buildings. Zante also has an airport and the other islands are linked to the mainland by ferry. Accommodation is biased towards camping and rented rooms (60 per cent of the stock of rooms on these islands).

2 The Cyclades. This group of islands spreads over the Aegean Sea to the southeast of Athens. The islands are wild, rocky and barren, some of which show the remnants of decaying volcanic activity, for example Santorini is the eroded crater of an extinct volcano, and hot springs are found on Kythnos and Kimolos. The landscapes of the islands are characterised by barren hillsides, olive groves and vineyards, unspoilt sandy beaches, churches and chapels, square white-washed cottages and windmills. Historic remains are abundant. Delos was a sacred island (supposedly the birthplace of the God Apollo) in ancient Greek times and is covered in ruins of temples and monuments. One of the most splendid Byzantine churches dating from the fifth century AD is found in Paros, and Byzantine paintings exist in many of the smaller churches in Naxos. Venetian castles from the medieval period were built on islands such as Paros and Andros. Most of the islands are accessible by boat from Athens. Tourism is generally small-scale and many of the islands and their beaches are quiet and unspoilt. The Cyclades as a whole received two per cent of all Greek tourist overnight stays in 1986 but have six per cent of the total stock of Greek holiday accommodation, 56 per cent of which is in the form of campsites and rented rooms: only four per cent of the bedspaces are in hotels. However, Milos, Poros, Santorini and Mykonos are accessible by air. Mykonos is the biggest tourist centre and has a more cosmopolitan atmosphere, particularly popular with the gay community. It has 75 per cent of the total tourist nights spent in the Cyclades.

3 The Sporades and the Aegean Islands. The Sporades (Magnesia) lie off the east coast of Thessally and the Aegean islands (Lemnos, Lesbos, Chios and Samos) are larger islands in the eastern Aegean close to the Turkish coast.

The Sporades are more fertile and green than the Cyclades. Their coasts are a mixture of rocky promontories, coves and sandy beaches, many of which are most easily accessible by boat. The islands are increasing in popularity and there is active nightlife with clubs, discos and tavernas. There are few big hotels, and the accommodation again is mainly small guest houses, rented rooms and campsites. The bigger Aegean islands are connected to Athens by air as well as by boat. They have abundant pine woods and olive groves, and also many good sandy beaches, though some are pebbly. Lesbos and Chios have many medieval castles dating from the 9th to the

15th centuries. Like the Cyclades, these islands have around six per cent of Greek tourist accommodation but receive only three per cent of total overnight tourist stays.

4 The Dodecanese. This group of 12 islands is to the southeast of Athens, and is close to the Turkish coast. The islands provide contrasting tourist attractions from the big hotels and sophistication of the busy islands of Rhodes and Kos to the smaller, quiet and less developed islands of Tilos, Halki, Astipalea and Kassos.

Rhodes is the biggest tourist centre of Greece. It took 22 per cent of all the overnight tourist stays in 1986, and has ten per cent of the country's tourist accommodation much of which is in the form of hotel bed-spaces. It is increasingly popular and, even through the recession of the 1980s, tourist nights increased by nearly three million. The island has an international airport and is well suited for the package tour market. It is one of the best developed islands in the Mediterranean and provides nightlife, casinos, watersports and sightseeing trips. The island is not particularly scenically outstanding but its beaches and climate (suitable for winter and summer tourism) are its main resources. The average temperature in January is 16° C and rises to 29° C in July. Rhodes is particularly favoured by West Germans and 21 per cent of all German visitors to Greece stay there. A similar proportion of Austrian and Swiss tourists go there. The Scandinavians also favour this part of Greece, (46 per cent of Swedish visitors to Greece, 56 per cent of the Norwegians and 31 per cent of Danes prefer Rhodes). This island is not so popular with the UK market: only 16 per cent of the UK visitors to Greece stay in Rhodes.

5 Crete. Crete is the third major tourist centre in Greece (of similar scale to Athens and Rhodes). It is the most southerly of the Greek islands, and among the hottest, both in summer and winter. The island has varied and attractive scenery (the mountains, with deep valleys and dramatic gorges, rise to over 2400 m) and a coastline of cliffs and rocky promontories interspersed with good sandy beaches. Although the climate, coast and scenery are its main attractions, Crete has a wealth of archaeological remains. It was the centre of Minoan culture from 2600–1100 BC and there are many remains of their palaces and tombs. The Romans and Byzantines (395–823

AD) also left many buildings and the castles of the medieval Venetian occupation are superimposed on more ancient settlements. The greatest concentration of tourist development (with hotels and modern facilities) is on the northern coast of the island: Hiraklion is the biggest centre with plenty of nightlife and the nearby international airport to attract package tourists. Crete as a whole has nearly 11 per cent of Greek tourist accommodation with an emphasis on hotel accommodation rather than rented rooms or campsites. Seventeen per cent of all Greece's overnight tourist stays were spent in Crete. The island is also particularly popular in the West German and Dutch markets.

Conclusion: Greece

Greece offers a very varied tourist product, and attracts visitors from many different countries (*see* p 86). It is a country for the young and active tourist (70 per cent are between 16 and 40 years old). The British market is of increasing importance to the Greek tourist industry, increasing from 14 per cent of arrivals in 1971 to 19 per cent in 1989. Although the numbers of Americans visiting Greece is slowly increasing, its share of the market has dropped from a quarter in 1971 to around seven per cent in the late 1980s. This was partly a response to terrorist activity (a TWA aeroplane was hijacked at Athens airport in 1985, and Athens has a continuing reputation for poor airport security). The Americans are among the few nationalities that visit Greece mainly for its antiquities, although 35 per cent of the Japanese, 25 per cent of Italians and 41 per cent of Spanish mentioned the historic resources as reasons for visiting Greece. However, the majority are attracted by the climate, this being particularly true of the British market (62 per cent of the British visited for the climate and only three per cent for the historic resources of the country). It has been noted that different nationalities congregate in the particular regions and islands which appear to specialise in meeting their needs, with the Spanish and Americans concentrating on Athens

and the British, West Germans and Scandinavians on particular islands. On the other hand, younger backpackers of all nationalities participate in 'island hopping' holidays so as to travel through many different parts of Greece. The French, too, do not appear to frequent the popular centres: although 19 per cent of French tourist nights were spent in Athens, 49 per cent were spent outside the main popular centres. Italian visitors to Greece also showed the same pattern of tourism.

QUESTIONS AND DISCUSSION POINTS

1 In 1990, great political changes were underway in Yugoslavia and Albania. How may these changes affect international tourism to these countries?
2 Tourism is heavily concentrated in four regions of Greece (Corfu, Crete, Rhodes and the Athens area). Rank the other regions of Greece in order of their tourist potential.
3 Is the growth of tourism in Greece likely to be a greater threat to the tourist industry of Spain or to that of Italy?

ASSIGNMENTS

1 You work in a travel agency and the following people have enquired about tours to Yugoslavia and Greece:

(*a*) A middle-aged, middle-class, childless couple of limited means, who are looking for a seven-day seaside holiday.

(*b*) A group of students who plan to go backpacking for at least four weeks in their summer vacation.

(*c*) A couple who are in their early thirties and they have two children aged four and seven. They usually go to Spain for two weeks but fancy something a bit different this year.

(*d*) A newly retired couple (one was a dentist, the other a school teacher). They have both been to Athens before and they want a stimulating but physically relaxing holiday to celebrate their retirement. They can be away from home for up to three weeks.

Select appropriate resorts/itineraries for each group and suggest the best time of year that each client might take their holiday.

CHAPTER 13

Turkey, Cyprus and Malta

LEARNING OBJECTIVES

After reading this chapter you should be able to:

- assess the tourist potential of the climatic, landscape, historical and cultural resources of Turkey, Cyprus and Malta
- distinguish the regional distribution of these geographical resources and their development and use for tourism
- demonstrate a knowledge of the main tourist resorts and tourist centres
- understand the role of Turkey, Cyprus and Malta in the general pattern of European tourism
- be aware of the influence political and cultural factors have on the nature and location of tourism.

Introduction

Tourism in this part of the Mediterranean basin is still on a small scale compared to the tourist industries of Spain, France, Italy, Greece or Yugoslavia. Turkey, with 3.7 million visitors in 1988 is the leading destination of the eastern Mediterranean. The countries of the region have suitable coastal and climatic resources to meet the growing and changing demands of Western tourism but political and cultural factors have dictated the scale, location and development of Western-style tourism in each country.

Tourism to Cyprus began early (in the 1960s) but was totally disrupted by later political events. On the other hand, Turkey's tourism could not begin until its internal political environment became more favourable.

Turkey

The development of international tourism in Turkey is a recent phenomenon, as the country was only opened to mass tourism from 1982. Turkey's tourism began to grow (from a base of 1.3 million in 1982) at 29 per cent per annum to an estimated 3.5 million foreign arrivals in 1988. This rapid expansion was triggered off by two factors:

1 the achievement of **internal political stability** and the installation of a government that welcomed the economic benefits of tourism.
2 a **receptive Western European market** that was ready to explore more exotic and unspoilt destinations further afield for sun, sea and sand holidays.

The political and economic background

Turkey was disrupted by internal political instability and conflict through the 1970s and this culminated in a military coup in 1980/81. A period of Westernisation and democratisation of the Turkish Government and the economy followed, and civilian rule was established in the elections of 1983. The new government was committed to further political and economic reform; the country applied for EC membership and sought closer links with Europe. Ninety-seven per cent of the population are Moslems, although the social structures of the Islamic state were abolished in the 1920s and the state is now atheist. Islamic fundamentalism has not so far inhibited the country's move towards Westernisation, although the Government is beginning to put more emphasis on religion. The Turkish Government is committed to the promotion of tourism for its economic and employment benefits. In 1988 foreign tourism yielded over US $2 billion, representing about 20 per cent of total exports in 1986/7. The Government has offered incentives to investors in the tourism sector, and has encouraged the construction of tourist installations, for example by providing loans and investment subsidies, certain customs and tax exemptions, reduced gas, water and electricity prices etc. It is expected that in response to those measures, the accommodation capacity will have doubled in the period 1988 to 1991 (from 135 000 to 283 000 bedspaces). Foreign investment in the Turkish tourist industry has also taken place. However, the speed of the new development has led to some of the problems experienced in Spain in the 1960s, i.e. uncontrolled, environmentally poor quality development, incomplete hotels and construction in progress at resorts and inadequate roads, power and water shortages.

These difficulties, plus the after-effects of the Gulf War in 1991, may deter some tourists, but the exotic oriental image, the coast and climate and relative lack of sophistication may be factors that attract the more adventurous tourist.

Turkey's physical resources for tourism

Ninety-seven per cent of Turkey is physically part of Asia, and only three per cent (the lowlands of Thrace on the west side of the Dardanelles) is part of Europe.

The coast

Turkey has a coastline of about 8000 km, with plenty of beaches, though there are few really long stretches of sand. Almost everywhere the coast is backed by spectacular mountain scenery. The coast is divided into four main areas: (*see* Fig 13.1):

1 The Black Sea Coast
2 The coast of Thrace and the Sea of Marmara
3 The Aegean coast
4 The Mediterranean coast.

Most of the modern resorts that cater for the package tourist are located on the southern half of the Aegean coast (between Izmir and Marmaris) and the western section of Turkey's Mediterranean coast (from Marmaris to Alanya) These resorts are served by the three airports at Izmir (Adnan Mendres), Dalaman and Antalya.

The holiday resorts evolved in the 1960s and 1970s for the Turkish domestic market (as Turks were not then allowed to travel abroad because of tight exchange controls). Hence, they have a good supply of apartments, pensions and small hotels. Larger hotels catering for the new Western package-tour market were grafted onto these existing resorts.

Fig 13.1 Regions of Turkey

The Aegean coast

The main attractions on the northern half of this coast are the historic sites of Troy and Pergamon. Along the 'olive coast' (as the stretch from Lesbos to Izmir is known) there are some small resorts with villas and apartments such as Foca, set along a coast of coves and bays. Some beaches are only accessible by boat. Izmir is a modern city, and an important port, but has many hotels. Between Izmir and Kusadasi many of the bays are filled with high density, low-grade holiday townships and holiday homes with beach access. Many of these homes lack basic services (water, power, sanitation) and were built by local speculators for the domestic market. Better quality development designed for the international tourist has been grafted on to towns such as Kusadasi and Bodrum. Kusadasi is another port town, a lively resort that functions as a centre for trips to the ancient Greek and Roman city of Ephesus, founded in the 13th century BC. Ephesus has very well preserved ruins and is perhaps the most outstanding of the ancient Greek sites along this part of the Aegean coast. It attracts over one million visitors a year.

Prienne, Miletus and Didyma are also important ancient Greek coastal sites which also receive substantial numbers of visitors (100–200 000 per annum) (*see* Fig 12.2).

Bodrum is a second major tourist centre, and the harbour is dominated by the 15th century crusader castle. Accommodation is primarily apartments, pensions, and small hotels, and some of the new building has suffered from the speed of development. Marmaris has a longer sand and shingle beach, set in a deep fjord-like inlet, and has some larger hotels.

In 1987, the Aegean coast ranked second in Turkey in its accommodation capacity with 26 000 beds but this stock will rise to over 77 000 beds when all those planned and under construction are complete.

The Mediterranean coast

This is sometimes known as the 'turquoise coast'. The major resorts along this stretch of coast include Fethiye, Kas, Antalya, Side and Alanya (*see* Fig 13.1). The bigger hotels are concentrated in Alanya and Antalya, and this region will become the leading concentration of accommodation when all proposed developments are complete to provide 82 000 beds.

There are many historical sites in the region, for example, one of the best Roman stadiums is at Perge, and there is an outstandingly well preserved Greek theatre (dating from the second century AD) at Aspendos, which receives 250 000 visitors a year. The coast from Alanya to the Syrian border is less accessible and hardly developed for Western tourism: between Alanya and Mersin the mountainous coast provides spectacular scenery and has great tourist potential. There are historic sites of all dates (Paleolithic, Hittite, Roman, Byzantine and Crusader) reflecting the region's location in the centre of the ancient world and its successive colonisation by most of the ancient civilisations (*see* Chapter 6).

The coasts of Thrace and Marmara

In the late 1980s, the region had the greatest accommodation capacity of all Turkey's regions, (with 36 500 bed spaces) but will soon be overtaken by developments along the Aegean and Mediterranean coasts. The Thracian side of the sea of Marmara is rolling countryside, and the south coast is more mountainous and forested with some good sandy beaches. The resorts cater mainly for the domestic market, for example Erdeck and a new luxury resort being developed at the readily accessible site of Klassis.

However, Istanbul is the major centre of the region, and was Turkey's capital in Roman and Byzantine times and during the Ottoman Empire which was at its peak in the mid-16th century. The city has many splendid historical buildings such as the Topkapi Museum (once the residential palace of the Ottoman emperors), mosques, and the Byzantine church of St Sophia. The major attractions receive 1.5 to 2 million visitors a year. Istanbul is thus a centre of cultural tourism but also has a significant level of business tourism, although Ankara has now superseded Istanbul as the country's capital. Istanbul airport is one of the main gateways into the country – one of three Turkish airports with scheduled international services.

The Black Sea coast

This region has good weather, but is much more variable than the Aegean and Mediterranean climates, and is thus relatively less attractive as a location for beach tourism. The coast is mountainous and dramatic and there are some good sandy beaches, but the resorts are small and the accommodation rather basic – mainly country inns developed for the domestic Turkish market in the 1950s, 60s and mid-1970s. The scale of tourism and speed of development is very much lower here than on Turkey's southern and eastern coasts. (Only 3500 bed spaces existed in 1987.)

The interior

Central Anatolia

The Anatolia peninsula is a vast high plateau (mostly 1–2000 m high) with a mixture of agricultural and forest landscapes. Two of the country's national parks are visited by overland coach trips. These are Pamukhale and Goreme (in Cappadocia).

Pamukhale, inland due east of Kusadasi, covers the scarp on the side of the Menderes valley. Warm springs saturated in calcium compounds issue from the rock and deposit pure white calcite as the spring water flows over terraces from pool to pool. Tourists bathe in the warm pools, but there is a danger that they will cause erosion damage to the terraces. The landscape of the Goreme valley is very different. The rock here is soft, volcanic material which has been eroded into fretted ravines, cones, chimneys and pinnacles (many surmounted by caps of slightly harder rock). The strangeness of the environment is emphasised by the fact that cave dwellings, churches and rock cities have been carved into the rock. These dwellings date from 400 BC including early Christian monastic settlements. Some of the rock carved dwellings are still inhabited, as at Soganli, but most have been evacuated due to the danger of rockfalls as the natural process of erosion continues. The Cappadocian region is relatively inaccessible but still attracts 500 000 visitors a year. The Anatolian mountains are high enough for good winter snow cover and several of the more accessible locations have been developed for skiing, for example, Bursa which serves the Istanbul region in the north, and Saklikent (48 km north of Antalya) in the south. There is enough snow here in spring (March and April) to combine skiing with beach holidays at Antalya (where the Mediterranean Sea is warm enough for bathing at this time of year). Most of the ski resorts cater for domestic tourists but there is significant potential for international tourism too.

Eastern Anatolia

The interior has a continental climate with great extremes of temperature (25° C in July down to minus 6° C and minus 18° C in January at Kars) and a summer rainfall maximum. The region is inaccessible and very rarely visited by foreign tourists, but it has desolately beautiful landscapes and scattered historic towns. There has been some political and ethnic unrest in the region between Turks and Kurds. Turkey has some common borders with Iraq and Iran, and the region suffered some disruption in the aftermath of the Gulf War.

Communications

An inadequate transport system is one of the factors limiting the spread of tourism through the country: the motorway system is poor, and there are many narrow, unsealed roads, although there are good bus services between the main cities. Due to the distance factor and the lack of good road access from Europe, most foreign tourists arrive by air, so the coastal tourist developments are mainly serviced accommodation and are limited to sites easily accessible from the existing airports. There are very few campsites, as so few tourists come by car. The only major land border crossings occur in the east with visitors from Syria, Iran and other Middle Eastern countries.

There is very little ferry traffic from Greece into Turkey, the poor communications perhaps reflecting the long-standing poor political relations between the two countries. Some opinion in Turkey would favour the development of new airports at Bodrum to serve the Aegean coast better, and another charter airport on the east Mediterranean (between Antalya and Mersin) to encourage the opening up of this stretch of coast.

Inbound tourism

Statistics on tourism in Turkey are patchy. It is estimated that about 2.9 million foreigners visited

Turkey in 1987, plus 1.25 to 1.5 million expatriate Turks returning for holidays (see Fig 13.2).

	Arrivals at frontiers (000s)	Nights spent in registered accommodation (%)
West Germany	524	39.0
Yugoslavia	344	0.9
UK	267	7.1
Greece	174	0.8
France	169	13.1
Iran	166	–
USA	131	3.3
Italy	102	4.6
Austria	76	5.3
Poland	56	1.5
Rest of Middle East	395	–
Total	2.8 million	8.3 million

Fig 13.2 Foreign visitors to Turkey 1987

The resident population of Turkey is around 50 million and it was estimated that the domestic market was between 2.6 million and 6 million in 1987.

Cyprus

Cyprus is the third largest island in the Mediterranean, after Sicily and Sardinia, with an area of 9216 km^2 (see Fig 13.3). It has a typical Mediterranean climate, but its easterly location gives it a prolonged hot dry season, and temperatures rise to 30° C between mid-May and mid-September. The winter, however, is more changeable, with periods of disturbed weather lasting several days as depressions pass over the island from west to east, but the weather stays mild (around 16° C on average) so the island is promoted as both a winter and summer destination. The island's north coast is rocky and is backed by the limestone Pentadactylos mountains which rise to 1000 m. The south coast has more sandy beaches interspersed with small coves. Coral Bay (west of Paphos) and Ayia Napa (on the southeast coast) are the largest and most popular beaches. Ayia Napa was a small fishing village and has a scattering of large hotels along its coast. The main settlements (Paphos, Limassol and Larnaca) also cater for beach tourism but have additional

Fig 13.3 Regions of Cyprus

cultural attractions e.g. Roman remains (at Paphos and Limassol) Crusader Castles (e.g. Kolossi Castle also in the Limassol area) and abundant old churches and monasteries in the rural villages. The Akamas peninsula is an unspoilt nature reserve, and the Troodos mountains (rising to 1900 m) provide opportunities for walking and horse-riding activity holidays. Platres is the main mountain resort. Cyprus thus has all the resources of climate, coast and landscape to make it an ideal all year round tourist location: tourist arrivals to the whole island reached nearly one million in 1987, but the development of tourism in Cyprus has been strongly influenced by political events.

The island's population is made up of Cypriots of both Greek and Turkish origin. It was a British colony up to its independence in 1960, and Britain still retains a military base at Akrotiri. Violence associated with the independence campaign and the ensuing political problems slowed down the early development of tourism in the 1960s when some other Mediterranean destinations were beginning to expand. Tourism grew more rapidly in the next decade, increasing from 25 700 in 1960 to a thriving 274 100 in 1973. Much of this expansion took place in the north of the island, with 65 per cent of the bed spaces concentrated in the two north coast resorts of Famagusta and Kyrenia.

In 1974 the tourist industry in Cyprus was disrupted by political events: a coup d'etat occurred, and the Turkish army invaded the island. After a brief period of warfare a *de facto* partition of the island took place: the northern part of the island (37 per cent of the territory) was taken over by Turkish forces, and the south remained a contracted Republic of Cyprus (*see* Fig 13.3). Major population movements followed, with Greek Cypriots living in the north moving south. Many were hotel owners who abandoned their properties and businesses in the north coast resorts. In parallel, Turkish Cypriots living in the south moved into the northern Turkish-controlled part of the island. While this readjustment was taking place, tourism to the island slumped in 1975 to only 47 000 visitors. The political situation has since stabilised and in 1983 the northern territory was unilaterally declared the Turkish Republic of North Cyprus, but it is not recognised by the international community and no other governments have consulates there. In 1990 there are still tight border controls: visitors to north Cyprus are not allowed south, and tourists in the south are only allowed north for day-trips (in daylight hours). The International Hotel Association advised professional bodies in tourism not to cooperate with North Cyprus and the north is only accessible by air via Turkey (Istanbul or Izmir).

These political events have led to a complete change in the nature and location of the tourist industry in Cyprus: in 1990 the south has replaced the north as the major centre of the tourist industry with just over one million arrivals in 1988, while the scale of tourism in the north (230 000 visitors 1988) has not yet reached the volume of 1973.

Tourism in the Republic of Cyprus (Southern Cyprus)

After partition in 1974, the south was left with virtually no facilities but a trained, experienced personnel and a potentially loyal clientele. The accommodation stock in the south was located in Nicosia and the hill resorts in the Troodos mountains: very little was on the coast. Nicosia airport, which had served the whole island, was in Turkish-occupied Cyprus, and Cyprus Airways was left with no aircraft or airport. Air access was limited to the military bases until a replacement airport was swiftly constructed at Larnaca. Because of the importance of tourism to the economy, the Government strongly supported the rebuilding of the tourist industry with state loans for new hotel building, support for Cyprus Airways, and provision of further training and tourism infrastructure. Almost all the new development in the south has been at coastal sites. Limassol is now the largest resort, with 11 600 beds in 1987, Larnaca is expanding rapidly, and new hotels have opened at Paphos since the new airport was completed in 1984. The speed and urgency of this reconstruction has led to some poor quality development, for example ribbon development, incomplete building, poor infrastructure such as unfinished roads and lack of sewage, and this has spoilt some locations, as witnessed by the unsightly seafront at Limassol. But tighter controls on development were

introduced in 1983 to improve the quality of provision and to encourage investment in entertainments, attractions and basic infrastructure to complement the expansion of tourist accommodation. Two completely new purpose-built tourist resorts have been built at Paralimni and Ayia Napa in the southeast of the island, designed to meet modern tourist needs.

The Cyprus Government has tried to promote the island as an upmarket prestige destination in order to attract the higher spending visitor and until recently has restricted charters to the island. By 1985, 27 per cent of the new accommodation completed (and 41 per cent of hotel construction in progress) was in the four- and five-star category: of the rest, the balance has been in favour of apartments rather than one- to three-stars hotels. Efforts are being made to diversify the island's tourist product by promoting conference, cultural tourism and the hill resorts in addition to beach tourism. In the 1980s the prices have been higher in Cyprus relative to some other mass-market Mediterranean destinations, and Cyprus has not wanted to enter into the mass-market. Nevertheless in 1986, restrictions on charter regulations were eased, allowing some UK operators to introduce charter flights from the UK regional airports.

Inbound tourism

Cyprus relies heavily on the UK market – about one third of all visitors come from UK in 1987. Scandinavians have increased from three per cent of arrivals in 1977 to 21 per cent in 1987, and other Northern Europeans, e.g. West Germans, Irish, Austrians and Swiss (i.e. from areas of poorer climate) form the balance. However, 89 000 Lebanese visited Cyprus in 1985, Cyprus being a geographically close refuge from their own political problems, and a substantial number of Greeks also came, reflecting the political and cultural links between Greece and the Greek Cypriot parts of the island.

Tourism in the Turkish Republic of Northern Cyprus

In 1975, the north of Cyprus was faced with the reverse of the situation in the south: the north had a plentiful stock of coastal accommodation, but with few experienced staff to run the hotels and no established market. The revival of the tourist industry has been slow. Tourist arrivals crept to 113 000 by 1978 but the world recession hit tourism in the north of the island badly, due mainly to the fact that north Cyprus relies very heavily on the Turkish market, and the lean years of 1978–84 correlated with a slump in Turkish arrivals. By 1988, 80 per cent of arrivals still came from Turkey. The accommodation stock (dating from the 1960s) neither met the needs of the Turkish market (who stay mainly with friends or in the cheaper accommodation) or the potential West European market. The non-Turkish market is gradually recovering, with the UK and German market (10.6 per cent and 13.3 per cent of arrivals in hotels respectively) slowly increasing in importance.

In 1987, a more co-ordinated plan for the development and promotion of tourism was set up with incentives for both local and foreign investors, for example, low rents of state land, tax concessions for the first ten years of operation, repatriation of profits for foreign investors). This has encouraged new hotel development, with an increase of about 2500 beds within a year. Most of the new development was in the four- and five-star category, and located in the old established coastal tourist areas (the Kyrenia coast and the north of Famagusta). The standstill in tourist development between 1975 and 1987 has meant that North Cyprus has not suffered from the sort of over-development and poor quality environment that has been typical of some of the other Mediterranean mass destinations. Given better communications, it still has great potential to meet modern tourist needs, though it has to prove its ability to attract the West European market.

Malta

The islands of Malta and Gozo are tiny (316 km²) and together they are smaller even than the Balearic island of Ibiza. Malta's location (93 km south of Sicily and 290 km north of the North African coast) gives it a latitude as southerly as Crete or Cyprus, and therefore among the most southerly tourist destinations in the Mediterranean. The summer temperatures are high in spite

of the moderating effect of the surrounding sea, but the heat is tempered by cooling sea breezes. Between June and September temperatures range from minima of 18–29° C to maxima of 33–36° C. Annual rainfall is only 670 mm, and the summer season (April-September) is dry. The islands have around 800 000 tourists a year (1987) and, like the Balearics, rely very heavily on the UK market which provides nearly two thirds of its visitors. The links with the UK date from 1800 when British occupation began but tourist links continued after the islands became an independent republic in 1964. The climate coast and the landscape are the main tourist resources. The islands are low, gently undulating limestone plateaux, with the terraced hillsides giving the landscape a distinctive character. The south and east coasts are good for water sports in the sheltered inlets that are drowned valleys. The west coast is more cliffed and craggy and has a few sandy beaches. Tourism in the island grew rapidly in the 1970s (20–30% growth per annum) and led to some problems of poor quality development and water shortages. It had the image of a low cost volume charter destination. Its over-reliance on the UK market led to problems in the recession of the 1980s. Non-UK European visitors declined in the early years of the recession (the late 1970s) but this did not hit the UK market until 1981–84 when the numbers of British visitors fell by half. At the same time the Maltese economy became stronger making the island less competitive for the British market. However, numbers have recovered in the late 1980s and Malta has been promoted for winter and off season tourism. In 1988, 18% of its trade was in Winter (November-February) and 43% in the shoulder months of March-June and October. Accommodation has been improved to meet modern needs; self catering bed spaces have increased five fold between 1979 and 1989. Apartments and holiday complexes have also grown significantly.

QUESTIONS AND DISCUSSION POINTS

1 With reference to the development of tourism in Turkey, Cyprus and Malta, discuss the influence of history, religion and political affiliations on the location, nature and development of modern tourism.

2 What competitive advantages and disadvantages does the tourist industry in Cyprus (or Malta) experience in comparison with other Mediterranean island destinations?

3 To what extent does the development of tourism in Turkey in the late 1980s parallel that in Spain in the early 1960s?

ASSIGNMENTS

1 You are the tourism specialist in a planning consultancy. The Turkish Government has commissioned your firm to prepare a report advising them of the dangers of rapid and unplanned coastal tourist developments and the alternative approaches to tourist development that the Government might adopt. Your brief is to write a report:

(*a*) outlining the current level and distribution of tourism in Turkey;

(*b*) assessing the environmental problems that tourist development has caused to date;

(*c*) with reference to the experience of other European countries (e.g. Spain), predicting the possible long-term effects (on the environment, on tourists themselves and on tourist businesses) of uncontrolled expansion and growth of tourist developments; and

(*d*) indicating the choices open to the Turkish Government concerning the type of tourism it wished to encourage and ways of avoiding the problems associated with the rapid expansion of tourism.

The Mediterranean as a whole (Chapters 9–13)

2 You work for a company called 'Two by Two' that specialises in two centre holidays in the Mediterranean for the UK market. These holidays consist of one week in an attractive inland landscape setting and one week on the coast. Your current range of holidays does not seem to be holding its popularity and the company is concerned that the centres chosen are not ideal. Therefore, the directors of the company have asked you to prepare a report outlining the features that the UK visitor finds most attractive in inland landscapes and in coastal locations. The report should also identify at least one pair of locations (towns or small regions of countries) in the Mediterranean that exhibit these ideal characteristics as closely as possible. The two locations must, of course, also display climates suitable for sun, sea and sand and activity holidays respectively. The centres must be easily accessible from Britain and close to each other.

Your report should present evidence for your conclusions and a full justification of your choice of centres.

3 Your company designs special interest cruises in the Mediterranean. The chief executive has been approached by two groups requesting quotes for special cruises.

(*a*) The head of history at a sixth form college has asked the company to suggest an itinerary for a fly cruise illustrating the pre-Christian history of the Mediterranean, but in order to explain the history clearly to the children he has asked if the cruise could visit sites of historical interest in their correct historical sequence (i.e. the oldest first and the more recent last). Is it possible to construct an itinerary that meets this criterion? School finances dictate that the cruise cannot be more than ten days.

(*b*) A group of wine and cookery clubs have asked for a Mediterranean fly cruise illustrating the best of the regional variations in wine and cuisine for the connoisseur. The itinerary must also include plenty of time to relax or to participate in active pursuits. Draw up a draft itinerary for discussion with the club representatives.

The Alps: Austria and Switzerland

LEARNING OBJECTIVES

After reading this chapter you should be able to:

- assess the tourist potential of the climatic, landscape, historical and cultural resources of Austria and Switzerland
- distinguish between the regional distribution of these geographical resources and their development and use for tourism
- demonstrate a knowledge of the main tourist resorts and tourist centres
- understand the role of Austria and Switzerland in the general pattern of European tourism
- be aware of regional variations in the development of winter sports resorts throughout the whole alpine chain
- understand the problems and opportunities afforded by the double tourist season in many alpine resorts.

Introduction

The Alps are the dominant mountain range in Europe. The core of the range runs almost east-west, but they curve southwards at their western end and drop down towards the sea to form the mountains backing the French and Italian rivieras. At their eastern end they gradually decrease in height until they are separated from the Carpathians by the widening valley of the Danube. Most of the Alps fall within Swiss and Austrian territory, but the southern section is divided between France and Italy, while the northern slopes just overlap into Germany; the far southeast extends into Yugoslavia. Most of the tourist developments are concentrated in the High Alps, which form the spine of the mountain chain and run from France, through Switzerland

and into western Austria (*see* Fig 14.1). The landscapes and landforms are the major tourist resource: the flat-floored, steep-sided valleys rise to craggy peaks, producing dramatic landscapes of sometimes 1200 metres relative relief, and steep slopes suitable for ski runs. The mountain climate is characterised by cold, sunny winters but cool, wet and cloudy summers. This climatic regime enables the region to be developed for winter sports, while summer tourism takes place in spite of the less than ideal summer weather. Nevertheless, the volume of summer tourism is much greater than the winter sports trade measured either in terms of visitor numbers or in tourist nights.

There is, however, some significant regional variation in the nature of tourism and tourist developments throughout the Alps. In the

Fig 14.1 The Alps

western Alps the tourist centres are bigger, (some over 40 000 beds), and many (for example in France) are purpose-built high altitude tourist settlements completely separate from the original villages.

While the French resorts cater primarily for their own domestic market, the tourist centres in central and eastern Switzerland and in west Austria are generally on a smaller scale, often consisting of small hotels and other accommodation units integrated into traditional valley villages. European travellers have significant regional preferences. Both Austria and Switzerland rely heavily on the West German market but far more Germans visit Austria; the French prefer their own resorts but those who do cross into Italy, stay in the Alps of west Italy, while German visitors to Italy congregate in the Alto Adige. Dutch visitors clearly prefer Austria to Switzerland

while Belgians visit the two countries in roughly equal numbers. British and Italians show only a very slight preference for Austria. These patterns of tourist movement relate as much to historic factors, common languages and road communication routes as well as economic factors.

The structure and landscapes of the Alps

The High Alps form the core of the mountain chain but they are one of four physical regions, each of which has a different landscape character:

1 the High Alps;
2 the Calcareous Alps;
3 the Alpine Foreland and piedmont lakes; and
4 the Jura.

The High Alps

These mountains are made of resistant crystalline rocks which form the highest peaks, e.g. the needle-like peaks of the Aguille Rouges (3650 m), the pyramidal peak of the Matterhorn (4477 m) or sometimes more rounded summits (e.g. Mont Blanc 6087 m). The slopes are often very steep (frequently over 40°) and screes readily form. Some of the highest regions (over 2750 m) retain permanent snow and ice and some glaciers flow from these icefields. The longest glacier is 32 km long but most have retreated in the last century, and global warming might prolong this trend. The landscape is deeply dissected by wide U-shaped valleys gouged out by glaciers in the last Ice Age. The flat valley floors are cultivated, while forests clothe the valley sides. Above the tree line (at about 2000 m) alpine meadow plants can grow and are seasonally grazed. These are the classic Alpine meadows that provide a profusion of flowers such as anemones, gentians, saffrons, crocuses and edelweiss, in the spring, though the growing season is short (only 6–13 weeks). Above 2000 m it is too cold for plant growth and the meadows merge into high altitude rocky wastes.

The landscapes thus have an attractive mixture of farmed and wild landscapes with forests everywhere an important element. They also have extremely high relative relief with dramatic and craggy skylines. Sometimes there are small lakes in the valleys. All these characteristics combine to give an ideal and very attractive landscape for tourism (*see* Chapter 4). In winter the High Alps normally receive over seven metres of snow, which lies for up to six months. Snowfall is heavy everywhere above 1375 metres. The region thus has the resources for winter sports too.

The Calcareous Alps

These limestone mountains flank the High Alps to both north and south. On the north side they form the Bernese Oberland (dominated by the Jungfrau and Eiger) which merge eastwards into the northern ranges of the Tyrol, while on the southern flanks they make up the Dolomites (which run into Italy).

The landscapes range from tabular masses with dramatic white cliffs, scarps and terraced slopes, to frayed skylines with sharp peaks. Where the limestone rock is particularly soluble they produce the classic karst landscapes of gorges, caverns, underground rivers and high-level, stony, desert-like landscapes devoid of surface drainage. Some of the ranges are high enough to retain icefields and glaciers (e.g. in the Bernese Oberland). Again, the landscape and climate provide the ideal resources for both summer and winter tourism.

The Alpine Foreland

This extends to the north of the central core of the mountains, and is made up of softer rock which creates a varied landscape of relatively low dissected hills and less deeply cut valleys. There are many examples of glacial deposits, i.e. where the glaciers of the Ice Age spilled out from the High Alps. The region is fertile farmland, and is more densely populated than the High Alps. The major landscape features and tourist resources are the string of 'piedmont' lakes that are located at the foot of the Calcareous Alps, (e.g. Lakes Geneva, Thun and Lake Lucerne).

The Jura

This mountain range is much lower than the Alps. It lies on the outer (north westerly) edge of the Alpine Foreland. The French/Swiss border follows the SW-NE trend of the mountain ridges and valleys. The landscape is not so dramatic as the Alps, though some of the rivers flow in deep gorges where they have cut across the ridges.

Climate

The characteristics of mountain climates have already been described in Chapter 2. The Alps have a continental climate (i.e. of cold, dry winters and unsettled, mild summers) but modified by altitude. A major area of high pressure builds up over Central Europe in winter giving the sunny, dry, still weather so suitable for winter sports, though fog may form in these conditions over the Alpine Foreland. In spring the high pressure system breaks down and depressions crossing the Mediterranean may coalesce with those tracking over Northern Europe to create an area of low pressure north of the Alps. Under these conditions local winds may suddenly develop like the warm, dry Föhn wind that blows from the south. It is often funnelled along the courses of N-S valleys. It is particularly common in spring and causes very rapid snow melt and a danger of avalanches. Sometimes the wind causes violent squalls over the piedmont lakes on the north flanks of the Alps.

The highest rainfall occurs in the summer when afternoon thunderstorms may occur. Precipitation increases everywhere with altitude but the west-facing (windward) slopes get twice as much as leeward slopes at the same height. Some sheltered spots may be very dry, for example the upper Rhône valley (in the Swiss Canton of Valais) which is in the rain shadow of the Mount Blanc massif, and receives only 609 mm precipitation. It is so dry in summer that the crops need irrigation. On the other hand, exposed west-facing slopes may get over 2450 mm a year. Snow lies longer at the higher altitudes but this again is modified by aspect: the south-facing slopes are sunnier but snow cover is less prolonged than on the colder north-facing slopes which are often in deep shadow all day. The valleys in the High Alps experience a high diurnal range of temperature in winter. The air warms up in the daytime, but at night the heavy cold air drains into the valley bottoms and the temperature drops sharply. This fact, combined with the effect of aspect on sunshine, has led to valley settlements (and tourist accommodation) being located on the sides of valleys on south-facing slopes.

There are some general regional patterns of variation in the climate. The western Alps, which are more exposed to depressions from the Atlantic and Mediterranean are wetter and slightly milder than the eastern end of the mountain chain. The climate becomes steadily more continental from west to east. In eastern Austria the summers are quite hot and rainy, while the winters are very cold indeed.

Agriculture and the development of tourism in the Alps

The physical environment of the Alps does not favour agriculture, but it was the main industry of the mountain region. The original settlements evolved to meet the needs of a peasant agricultural population. Alpine agriculture is very labour-intensive and farms were relatively small, with an average size of about six hectares in 1960. Agriculture has become increasingly marginal and unprofitable, leading to outmigration of the young and depopulation of the remoter valleys. Tourism has always been seen as a means of supplementing incomes and providing employment in these problem areas, and the Swiss and Austrian governments have supported tourism for this very reason. Alpine tourism began by farming families letting rooms to tourists and combining tourism with agriculture, and this initiated the tradition in both countries of small scale family-run tourist businesses though few are combined with farming now.

The first tourists to the Alps came to Switzerland to see the landscape in summer. In the early 19th century, a wealthy, foreign elite (especially the English) visited the lakes to enjoy the scenery. In Chopin's time, Interlaken was just a row of hotels but he noted (with some annoyance) that 'every other person was English'. The British also popularised mountaineering holidays, and resorts such as Chamonix and Zermatt developed as climbing centres. With the arrival of the railway in the Alps in the 1870s, tourism expanded further, and thermal spas such as St Moritz and Bad Ischl became fashionable. Although skiing was introduced from Norway in the 1870s and skating from Holland in the following decade, summer visitors dominated Alpine tourism until the 1920s, when the first Winter Olympics were held in Chamonix in 1924. Ski facilities began to spread, particularly in Switzerland, and the first French resorts (Alpe D'Huez, Tignes and Val D'Isere) were established in this phase of rapid growth. Although skiing centres still catered for a small wealthy elite, winter tourism accounted for as much as 14 per cent of overnight stays in the Tyrol by 1924, and while British visitors dominated the Swiss industry at the time, most of Austria's pre-war visitors came from east and southeastern Europe. The economic depression, the Second World War and its political aftermath completely disrupted these travel patterns. Switzerland (still relying on a Western European clientele and having been neutral in the War) recovered quickly with a rapid expansion of tourist accommodation outside the established centres; in 1950 Switzerland still dominated Alpine tourism while Austria was rebuilding her tourist industry. This was done with great speed and success and by 1955 Austria had overtaken Switzerland as the premiere Alpine tourist region (*see* Fig 14.2) while France rapidly developed its own resorts from 1960 onwards.

Million tourist bednights (domestic and foreign)		
	Switzerland	**Austria**
1934	12	–
1945	14	–
1950–51	–	19
1955–56	20	31.6
1960–61	–	50.7
1965–66	29	70
1970–71	–	96.5
1975–76	31	105.0
1980–81	–	121.3
1985–86	34	113.3

Fig 14.2 The growth of tourism in Austria and Switzerland 1934–87.

Tourism in both countries appears to have stagnated in the 1980s, partly due to the recession and competition from other destinations, but also because countries have been relatively slow in modernising and changing their accommodation stock to meet modern needs (for example for self-catering and high quality hotel accommodation). The fact that tourist businesses are small, and have limited access to capital for such modernisation, has also constrained expansion. In both countries, summer landscape-based tourism has shown the greatest decline while winter sports holidays are still growing steadily. A series of mild winters with late and poor quality snow in the late 1980s has caused further problems. If this trend is a foretaste of the effects of global warming (rather than just a short-term climate swing) then the ski resorts may have to face shorter and more unreliable seasons in the future.

Switzerland

Switzerland's territory covers most of the central section of the Alps. The country includes parts of the four main physical regions of the Alps, each of which have different landscape and tourist characteristics. These are:

1 The High Alps – the Cantons (i.e. the administrative areas) of Valais, Tessin and Grisons in the far south of Switzerland;
2 the Calcareous Alps – the southern parts of the regions of Berne, Central Switzerland and Eastern Switzerland, and divided from the High Alps by the Rhône and Rhine valleys;
3 The Alpine Foreland – most of the remainder of Switzerland; and
4 The Jura – in the northwest of Switzerland the border with France follows the crest of these mountains.

The High Alps

The characteristic landscapes of the High Alps have been described above. The region is divided into three sections: Valais; Tessin (Tecino); and Graubunden (the Grisons).

Valais

This region consists of the wide valley of the river Rhône, and the mountain block known as the Pennine Alps which increases in altitude towards the south to the peaks of the Matterhorn and Mount Rosa (Switzerland's highest mountain at 4634 m).

The Swiss/Italian border follows the crests of the mountains, but this massif forms an impenetrable barrier to communications, though there are passes that carry cross border routes around the west (the Great St Bernard) and the east (the Simplon) which end the mountain block (*see* Fig 6.2 on p 65). The mountains are high enough to retain permanent snow and ice fields, and summer skiing is possible on the glacier plateau, which is at 3500 m on the ridge between the Matterhorn and Mount Rosa. These icefields can be reached by ski lifts from Zermatt, an old established climbing and skiing resort. The main skiing season here runs from early December to mid-April, and the centre has a variety of skiing and non-skiing activities as well as nightlife. The other main ski developments of the Pennine Alps are based on Saas-Fee; Verbier, a large, modern and mainly self-catering resort with good facilities for beginners through to more experienced skiers, and the quieter family centres around Champéry (*see* Fig 14.3).

The Rhône valley forms the northern boundary of the Pennine Alps. It is a wide structural trench which is followed by the river Rhône as it flows westwards from its source in the Rhône glacier (located just north of Gletsch). The valley is also followed by the main road and rail

Fig 14.3 Switzerland's tourist areas

Key

— International boundary

▓ Land over 2000 metres

)⟮ Passes

* Swiss National Park

≡ The Engadine

○ Winter sports resorts

THE VALAIS
1 Champéry group
2 Verbier group
3 Zermatt group
4 Crans–Montana

GRAUBUNDEN
5 Arosa
6 Davos
7 Klosters
8 St. Moritz group

BERNESE OBERLAND
9 Diablarets group
10 Gstaad
11 Adelboden
12 Grindelwald group
13 Bettmeralp

CENTRAL SWITZERLAND
AAR MASSIF/
14 Engelberg
15 Andermatt

GLARUS ALPS
16 Sargans group
17 Flims group

arteries between the Swiss Alps and France: the French influence is reflected in the fact that the region is partly French-speaking. The valley is sheltered from rain-bearing westerly winds by the Pennine Alps, and it enjoys a particularly dry and sunny climate, suitable for vineyards, peach and apricot orchards. The Crans-Montana development is situated on the dry and sunny south-facing slope of the valley. This is one of the biggest Alpine tourist resorts in Switzerland with a mixture of substantial hotels, self-catering apartments and plenty of nightlife. In the Valais area as a whole, 87 per cent of the beds are self-catering, and the region accounts for 15 million bednights. Domestic visitors match the numbers of foreign tourists.

Tessin (Ticino)

This part of Switzerland looks towards Italy: it is Italian speaking, and its southerly aspect and latitude give it a milder climate and a slightly more Mediterranean character than the northern Alps. A major transalpine route runs through the region linking Zurich (via Andermatt and the St Gotthard Pass) to the valley that runs south through Tessin to the head of Lake Maggiore and the north Italian plain. The High Alps are less massive in Tessin, reaching only just over 3000 m. The landscape has less densely forested hillsides, with extensive beech and sweet chestnut woods as well as the characteristically alpine coniferous forests. In the south it is mild enough for peaches, citrus fruit and vines to flourish. The far south of the province (in the Lake Maggiore and Lake Lugano region) is physically part of the Italian Lakes region, and has a similar pattern of essentially summer tourism based on the lakeside resorts such as Locarno, Lugano and Ascona. In 1986 Tessin was the fourth ranking Swiss Canton in terms of supply of bed spaces, but it attracted only five million bednights (a third of the number in Valais, Grisons and Berne). Self-catering accommodation forms three-quarters of the stock of bed spaces. The majority of visitors are foreign tourists as the domestic market takes up only 35 per cent of the total bednights.

Graubunden (the Grisons)

This is a high, rugged isolated mountain region. The valley bottoms do not fall below 1100 m while most of the mountains are over 3000 m high, and some have permanent snow fields and glaciers. It is a major summer tourism region but there are also clusters of relatively high altitude ski resorts, for example, (Davos is at 1564 m and Arosa at 1700 m, and the ski season is consequently a little longer than the resorts in the west. In the Grisons the season runs from the beginning of December to the end of April. Chur is the hub for a cluster of resorts including Klosters (a quiet, expensive and exclusive resort), Davos (originally a health resort and now a well established ski centre but with few facilities for young people) and Arosa (a modern resort located on a sunny SW facing valley shoulder with a wide range of ski and non-skiing facilities), (see Fig 14.3).

The Grisons mountains are cut by a confusion of 150 valleys: the biggest valley is the Engadine, a major trench up to a mile wide which cuts through the mountains from SW to NE, i.e. from the head of Lake Como northeast to the Austrian border. For most of its length it is drained by the River Inn which flows NE into Austria, and eventually to the Danube. St Moritz is situated in the upper Engadine Valley where a series of small lakes adds to the attraction of the scenery. The valley sides are covered with juniper scrub and pine, larch and birch forests. The wide, flat valley floor is cultivated meadow land. St Moritz was originally a health spa, based on the local mineral springs, but is now a large and expensive ski resort. It has all facilities and nightlife, but there are smaller and quieter resorts in the valley, e.g. Celerina and Zuoz. Below Zernez the Inn passes through a narrow gorge before emerging into the wider Lower Engadine valley. The landscape here is outstanding, making the region important for summer tourism as well as winter sports. The spectacular scenery of the Swiss National Park lies to the SE of Zernez and it has a wealth of alpine wildlife, such as ibex, chamois, deer and marmots.

After Valais, the Grisons has Switzerland's second biggest concentration of bed spaces, and receives roughly the same number (15 million) of visitor nights. Seventy-five per cent of the stock is self-catering accommodation. In the hotel sector, winter tourism bednights just outnumber summer bednights.

The Calcareous Alps and the Pre Alps

The landscape of the limestone Alps is significantly different from the High Alps (*see* p 161).

The region is split into three tourist regions:

1 The Bernese Oberland. This is in the south of the Canton of Berne. It is one of the most intensive tourist regions in Switzerland because it is the most easily accessible of the major mountain blocks. The Rhône valley allows access from the south and west, while on its northern flanks, routes penetrate deeply into the mountains up the series of parallel glacial trenches that run N-S towards the higher peaks.

The crest of the mountain range runs parallel to the Rhône valley, from the sheer rock faces of the Diablarets (in the SW) to the peaks of the Jungfrau and Eiger (in the NW) that tower over Interlaken. The 17 km long Aletsch glacier descends from the southern flanks of the Jungfrau massif. Most of the resorts in the western half of the range are quiet, good for families and suited to all levels of ski skills. One exception is Gstaad which is fashionable, expensive and glamorous. The resorts in the easily accessible valley to the south of Interlaken, such as Grindelwald, Wengen, Murren and Lauterbrunnen, are highly developed for summer tourism as well as winter sports.

The general pattern of tourism is similar to that of Valais: three-quarters of the stock of bed spaces are self-catering, (though only half the bednights). The Berne Canton as a whole receives about 15 million tourist nights, half of which are generated by the domestic market and half by foreign visitors.

2 The Aar Massif of central Switzerland. This is located between Lake Lucerne and Andermatt, and is divided from the Glarus Alps by the Reuss valley which carries the N-S route from Zurich to Andermatt (and via Tessin to Italy). The valley is spectacular, particularly in the Scholleren gorge. The main resorts are grouped around Andermatt, with its lively nightlife, and Engelberg.

3 The Glarus Alps. Tourism here is on a relatively small scale compared to the Bernese Oberland. The main centres are at Flims and Sargans, and are quiet, with good ski facilities.

The Alpine Foreland

This is a lower region, with more gentle rolling landscapes. But a series of piedmont lakes lies at the foot of the high mountains, at the junction of the Alpine Foreland and the Calcareous Alps. These lakes with their backdrop of dramatic mountain landscapes make them ideal locations for summer tourism, and many lakeside resorts have been developed, such as Interlaken and Wilderswil between Lakes Thun and Brienzer, and Lucerne and Weggis on Lake Lucerne. Lakes Leman, Zurich and Constance are in slightly gentler landscape settings. Zurich is Switzerland's second city and is a centre of banking and business, so attracts business rather than holiday tourism. Geneva (on Lake Leman) is also an international centre and is the site of the headquarters of many international organisations mainly due to Switzerland's neutrality and stable economy. Geneva, therefore, attracts many foreign visitors (both holiday and non-holidaymakers), and relies more heavily on hotel accommodation than the rest of Switzerland. Zurich and Geneva each attract around five million tourist bednights.

The Jura

The landscapes in this region are attractive but not as spectacular as the main Alpine chain, nor is the snow season so prolonged. The Jura is the least visited part of Switzerland, and mainly caters for the domestic market. It is, however, the centre for watchmaking, one of Switzerland's traditional industries.

The volume of tourism in Switzerland

Tourists in Switzerland are of four types:

1 Domestic tourists;
2 Foreign staying visitors;
3 Foreign day visitors who are based in another country and make a day-trip into Switzerland and return to their original starting point; and
4 Direct transit visitors. These are visitors passing through the country on their way from their home to another holiday destination – essentially north Europeans on their way to the Mediterranean.

As Switzerland does not collect statistics on border arrivals it is difficult to assess the size of the different markets.

Domestic tourists

Switzerland's population is around 6.5 million and, as shown in Chapter 1 (*see* Fig 1.8 on page 9), is an affluent population with a high propensity for holiday taking. Figure 1.8 would suggest a domestic market of around 2.3 million people. More reliable bednight data shows the domestic market is substantial, generating 40.1 million bednights in 1987, and accounts for 54 per cent of all tourist bednights in Switzerland. The majority of these (61 per cent) were in self-catering accommodation (chalets, apartments, campsites). The large stock of apartments have been built largely in response to the demands of the domestic market.

International staying visitors

Estimates suggest that international arrivals have stabilised at between 11.5 and 12 million in the mid-1980s, reaching 11.7 million in 1988, although bednights have fallen over this period from 36.8 million in 1982 to 34.4 million in 1987.

International visitors have responded to the recession by reducing the length of their visit to Switzerland rather than cutting it out. Lengths of stay are quite short as Switzerland is a relatively expensive destination due to the strength of the Swiss franc against other European currencies in the 1980s. The Germans, Dutch and Belgians tended to stay longest (with average stays of over five days) but these visitors favour the use of the cheaper self-catering accommodation rather than hotels. As most come by car they are mobile and independent and can take advantage of self-catering facilities. Intercontinental travellers (from USA and Japan) showed the shortest stays in 1985 (2.2 and 1.8 days respectively) and virtually all stayed in hotels. British and French visitors showed an intermediate pattern (averaging around four days in Switzerland, with the majority staying in hotels).

The relative stagnation of Switzerland's international tourist trade may be due to competition with new Mediterranean package summer destinations and the opening up of less developed rural and coastal summer destinations in the long-haul sector.

Day visitors and transit visitors

Very little information is available on these types of visitors. Estimates suggest that in the mid 1980s, Switzerland attracted about 85 million day visitors and roughly five million transit visitors each year, who contributed 13 per cent of tourist receipts in 1985.

Origins of international visitors

Figure 14.4 shows that Switzerland relies very heavily on the West German market. Apart from that, the country attracts visitors from a wide

	Bednights in hotels	Bednights in supplementary accommodation	Total bednights	Total bednights
	(million)	(million)	(million)	%
West Germany	6.2	8.0	14.43	41.7
Netherlands	0.8	2.1	2.98	8.6
UK	1.8	0.8	2.66	7.7
France	1.6	1.0	2.60	7.5
USA	2.3	0.2	2.57	7.4
Belgium	0.8	1.0	1.83	5.3
Italy	1.1	0.4	1.41	4.1
Japan	0.6	–	0.65	1.9
Austria	0.4	0.1	0.51	1.5
Spain	0.3	0.1	0.35	1.0

Fig 14.4 Foreign tourist nights in Switzerland (1987)

range of both northern and southern European countries, reflecting the special nature of Switzerland's resources. No other European country (other than Austria and the Scandinavian territories) has mountain scenery or winter sports resources of the scale and quality of Switzerland. Austria and Scandinavia on the other hand have an abundance of snow and mountains and make a negligible contribution to Switzerland's international visitors.

Seasonality of tourism

Although landscape tourism is declining in popularity in Switzerland, the summer is still the busiest time of year. In 1985 30.4 per cent of domestic and international tourist nights were in the peak summer months of July and August, while 23.5 per cent of nights were in the peak winter months (February and March). This pattern is more marked when international visitors are considered alone: in 1987 20 per cent of international bednights were at the height of the winter season while about 33 per cent were at the summer peak. Winter tourism (both domestic and international) is, however, continuing to expand. The hotel sector has a relatively steady trade all year (at around three million nights a month), but it is the self-catering sector that absorbs the seasonal peaks. In February this sector accommodates five million bednights, and 7.5 million nights in August, but demand drops

	1985 domestic & international bednights (%)	1987 foreign bednights (%)
January	8.78	9.7
February	10.89	7.8
March	10.46	11.6
April	8.03	10.2
May	4.40	4.6
June	6.60	7.2
July	14.40	12.5
August	15.99	17.0
September	8.70	8.6
October	6.14	5.0
November	2.19	2.2
December	3.33	3.7

Fig 14.5 Switzerland's seasonal pattern of tourism

back to under a million in the off-peak months of May, November and December. Thus, in spite of all year round tourism, some sectors experience very low occupancy rates.

Regional patterns of tourism

The high mountain regions dominate Switzerland's tourism. The Cantons of Valais, Graubunden and Berne each had about 15 million tourist nights in 1986, with the latter Canton being the most popular region for foreign tourists (*see* Fig 14.7). The rural regions of Tessin and Vaud, and the cities of Zurich and Geneva each only had between four to five million nights each, while the other parts of Switzerland had very low levels of tourism. The hotel sector is only one element of the total accommodation stock but the spatial distribution of hotel nights also underlines the popularity of the mountain areas (*see* Fig 14.6).

	Total hotel bednights (million)	Foreign share (%)
Mountain resorts	13.1	54
Lake regions	7.4	60
Big towns	6.0	80
Other areas	7.4	44

Fig 14.6 Switzerland's tourist destinations

Tourism in the economy

The Swiss have a high propensity to travel and are relatively high spenders on outbound tourism: in 1984 they made 6.2 million trips abroad, spending 37.5 million nights out of Switzerland. Sixty per cent of these (and 56 per cent of trips) were to European Mediterranean countries to enjoy the coastal resources that Switzerland lacks. In 1985 they spent 7280 million Swiss francs, but international tourism to Switzerland yielded 10 120 million Swiss francs in receipts, so Switzerland has a favourable balance of tourist trade of 2840 million Swiss francs. International tourism is very important to Switzerland's economy, providing eight per cent of the national income and employment for 14 per cent of the

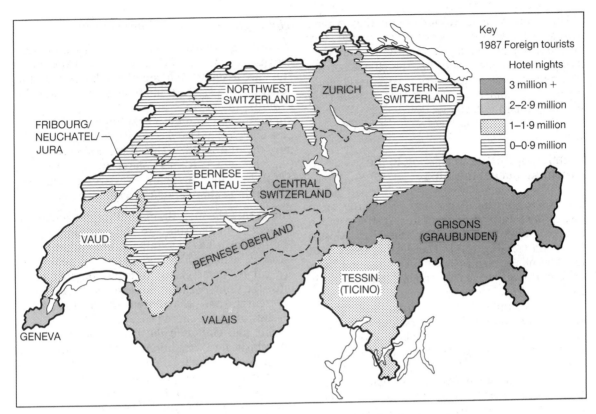

Fig 14.7 Switzerland's distribution of foreign tourism

population in the early 1980s. Tourism has been promoted by the Swiss Government because it is the only economic alternative to agriculture in the mountain regions, although it does create problems in the sensitive alpine environment and has caused some disruption to local communities.

Austria

Austria is twice as big as Switzerland but the two countries each have about the same area covered by the Alps – roughly 8000 square miles of mountain territory in each country. Austria's tourism is very strongly concentrated in its Alpine region, and the total volume of its tourist industry is much greater than that of Switzerland. The Austrian Alpine regions receive roughly twice as many visitors and tourist nights as the Swiss Alps.

The scenery and resources of the Alpine regions of the two countries are similar (*see* pp 160–2 for an overall description of the Alps) though it has been noted that the climate of the Austrian Alps is a little more extreme (slightly dryer, but colder in winter and warmer in summer) than the Swiss section.

Location of Austria in relation to the structural units of the Alps

The spine of the Alps runs eastwards from Switzerland into Austria. The Austrian-Italian border follows the crest line of the High Alps to the south (*see* Fig 14.1). The northern slopes of the Alps fill the territory of the Austrian provinces of Vorarlberg, the Tyrol and Salzburg (*see* Fig 14.1).

The River Inn (which flows from the Engadine on the Swiss border in the west cuts these provinces in half, and the river valley separates the High Alps to the South from the Calcareous Alps and Pre Alps to the North.

The Alps gradually decrease in height as they drop away into central Austria. As in Switzerland and Italy, there are strings of lakes at the foot of the mountains, although they are on a smaller scale in Austria. These lakes form the Salzkammergut lake district on the northern flanks of the Austrian Alps and the lakes of the Drau Valley in Carinthia to the south.

The north and east of Austria (the provinces of Upper and Lower Austria, and Bergenland) belong to different physical regions, i.e. to the Danube valley and the southern edge of the Bohemian mountains and the edge of the Hungarian lowlands.

In summary, the physical regions of Austria are as follows:

1 The High Alps; and
2 The Calcareous Alps – the provinces of Voralberg, Tyrol and Salzburg;
3 The remainder of the Alps, the Alpine Foreland and piedmont lakes – the provinces of Carinthia, Styria and the southern parts of Lower and Upper Austria);
4 The Danube Valley; and
5 The Bohemian Massif – Lower and Upper Austria
6 The edge of the Hungarian basin – Bergenland.

The High Alps and Calcareous Alps

Vorarlberg Province. The north and west of the province borders the Rhine and Lake Constance, and has a milder climate than the rest of the Austrian Alps. The mountains rise gradually towards the Tyrol, but are traversed by an important W-E routeway that follows the Arlberg pass and a tunnel carries the Paris-Vienna railway into the Inn valley. This route links Germany (via the upper Rhine valley) to the Austrian Tyrol, making this part of Austria relatively accessible to the German market.

The Tyrol. The most dramatic Tyrolean mountain scenery is in the south of the province, in the High Alps. The mountains are rugged and massive, with glaciers and pyramidal peaks and are cut by great glacial trenches running north into the Inn Valley. Resorts such as Ishgl, Obergurgl, and Mayrhofen lie in the upper reaches of such valleys (*see* Fig 14.8).

Ishgl and Galtur in the Patznauner valley are unsophisticated, traditional centres with good facilities for families. Winter tourism accounts for more than 65 per cent of tourist nights. Obergurgl, Hochgurgl and Solden are in the Otztal valley. Obergurgl has some large hotels (50–100 rooms) but it is a traditional and friendly resort with a long skiing season from early December to the end of April. It is visited for both summer and winter tourism. Hochgurgl is a small, purpose-built ski resort built on the French style, i.e. separate from original settlements. Solden is more isolated but is located on a sunny south-facing slope; it is also patronised by winter and summer visitors, although winter visitors outnumber summer tourists in the Otztal region of the Tyrol as a whole. It is one of most intensive tourist areas of Austria, with over one million overnight stays (excluding camping) in 1985. Mayrhofen in the Ziller valley is a gregarious, lively resort with some nightlife, and is very popular with British visitors. It has summer skiing for experienced skiers on the Hintertux Glacier and is also promoted for walking and summer sports. Other resorts in the same valley offer skiing for all standards. The valley has tourism all year round and is another intensively visited area, with over one million tourist nights in 1985.

Another of these major N-S orientated glacial troughs is used by a major N-S route (via the

Fig 14.8 Austria's tourist areas

Brenner pass) linking Austria with Italy. Thus, the Inn valley, at the heart of the Austrian Tyrol, is at a crossroads of major E-W and N-S routes through the Alps, making this part of the Alps readily accessible. Routes to the north also make it easily accessible from the German city of Munich (via the Inn Valley).

Innsbruck is strategically sited where these routes cross, and the site has been inhabited since Roman times. The old city was established in 1180, and there are many medieval streets and buildings. There are also good ski facilities, including the Olympic course, used in the 1964 and 1976 Winter Olympics, and at Igls there are bobsleigh events. The area received 1.4 m tourist bednights in 1985.

The Calcareous Alps to the north of the Inn Valley give a different landscape of white, craggy rockfaces and screes above dark green forested slopes. These landscapes form the backdrop to unspoilt resorts such as Ellmau, Söll and Westendorf which are all summer and winter resorts. The Kitzbühel area is also in this section of the Alps (*see* Fig 14.8). This cluster of resorts includes Kirchberg, a big, international resort with some larger hotels (up to 100 rooms), varied skiing and lively nightlife. This valley also

has tourism all year round and is a major centre of the region (over one million visitor nights in 1985).

The valley of the Upper Inn is a continuation of the Swiss Engadine, but the valley changes in character and widens into a very broad, flat-bottomed trench below Innsbruck. Major routes follow the valley northwards towards Germany through a gap in the Calcareous Alps.

Salzburg Province. The Hohe Tauern is a massive block of High Alps that lies south of the Inn, to the south of Salzburg province. The mountains, which are part of the crystalline Alps, extend further into the province of East Tyrol. The range includes Austria's highest peaks (e.g. the Gross Glockner rising over 3700 m) and offers opportunities for summer skiing on high level glaciers. The mountains form one of the most visited areas of Austria, with tourism spread evenly throughout the region: mixed summer and winter tourism occurs on the western half, for example in the Pinzgau area near the spectacular Krimml waterfalls, but winter tourism is more important east of Badgastein (another major centre with over one million visitor nights).

The Alpine Foreland and piedmont lakes. The

landscape is more subdued and less dramatic than the High Alps and receives relatively few visitors. The exception is the city of Salzburg, in the far north of its province. It is a tourist centre in its own right (with 1.4 million tourist nights in 1985). It has splendid architecture, is famed as being the home of Mozart and is the location of an important music festival. The Salzkammergut lake district straddles the Salzburg-Upper Austria border. The lakes are set in low forest-clad mountains and the lakeside resorts, e.g. St Gilgen, St Wolfgang and Strobl on Lake Wolfgang, cater for summer tourism which is concentrated in July and August. Austria's summer tourism has been declining in the 1980s, and areas such as the Salzkammergut and Carinthian lake districts have been hardest hit.

The remaining regions of Austria attract relatively few staying foreign tourists, though the east is experiencing an increase in the already high level of day-tripping. Vienna is the only major focus of tourism. The site has been settled since medieval times and St Stephen's Cathedral dates from 1258. Vienna retains some narrow streets reminiscent of its medieval past but the city reached its peak in the 18th century as the centre of the Hapsburg Empire.

Hofburg was the town residence of the Hapsburgs while the palace of Schonbrunn (a palace on the scale of Versailles) was their other residence. The Spanish Riding School, where the white Lipizzaner stallions perform dressage displays to music, still retains the classical methods of horse training of the period.

Vienna is still the capital and cultural centre of Austria. The many museums, including the Kunsthistorisches Museum (the museum of fine art), and the Vienna State Opera reflect its continuing association with the arts.

It ranks fourth in the league of European city tourism (after London, Paris and Rome), and in 1985, received 5.5 million overnight stays.

The volume of tourism in Austria

Like Switzerland and other countries that have many land border crossings, Austria does not collect data on foreign frontier arrivals. However, estimates suggest that in 1985 the total number of foreign arrivals was of the order of 130 million

(of which 93 per cent came by road). Eighty per cent of all arrivals were holidaymakers, five per cent business tourists, two per cent shoppers and 13 per cent people visiting friends and relatives.

These tourists fall into the same four categories as do those to Switzerland (*see* p 166), i.e.:

(*a*) Foreign staying visitors;
(*b*) Foreign day visitors; and
(*c*) Direct transit visitors.

Rough estimates indicate that about 50 million arrivals were day visitors, mainly from West Germany, 15 million staying visitors (also predominantly from West Germany) and the very high number of 50 million were direct transit holidaymakers on their way from Northern Europe to the Mediterranean coast. This reflects the location of Austria in relation to Europe's tourist generation and destination regions, and the fact that good N-S and E-W routes can be found through the Alps in Austria. Austria's road system is good, and it has no tolls, though the peak summer loads do cause bottlenecks in parts in July and August.

The political changes in Eastern Europe that began in 1989 may, if sustained, eventually allow countries such as Poland and Czechoslovakia to develop outbound tourism. Austria might be expected to benefit from an increase in day shopping trips from Czechoslovakia, and eventually to increased transit traffic from Central Europe to the Mediterranean.

Domestic tourism

Austria's tourism is more accurately measured by arrivals and bednights at registered tourist accommodation. In 1987, 85.6 million bednights were generated by foreign visitors and about 28 million from the domestic market. Although Austria's population at about 7.5 million is larger than Switzerland's, Austrians have a much lower propensity to travel, both internationally or at home. This has had an indirect effect on the structure of accommodation that left Austria at a competitive disadvantage in the late 1980s. In the past, the small domestic market has favoured the use of private rented rooms rather than self-catering accommodation, and Austria lacks the enormous stock of self-catering apartments that Switzerland now has. Self-catering accommodation is now rapidly expanding in Austria in response to changing international demand but by 1985 it still only made up six per cent of the total accommodation stock.

Domestic tourism originates mainly from Vienna and is heavily concentrated in the east of Austria. Only 10 per cent of domestic tourists visit the Alpine western provinces.

International staying visitors

Although the total number of staying visitors to Austria at 18.2 million in 1989 is much higher than the number visiting Switzerland, the two countries share a similar general pattern of tourism: the numbers of staying visitors to Austria have stabilised in the 1980s, but the average length of stay has declined (e.g. from 6.5 nights in 1981 to 5.5 nights in 1987). Summer tourism is declining, while winter sports holidays are still expanding (from 30 per cent of all tourist nights in 1975 to 40 per cent in 1985). Austria is now Europe's leading winter sports destination.

As shown in the following table, Austria relies even more heavily on the West German market than does Switzerland.

Country	Foreign arrivals at tourist accommodation (%)
West Germany	53.1
Netherlands	7.7
Italy	6.0
UK	4.7
France	4.3
Switzerland	4.1
USA	3.7
Belgium	2.3
Sweden	1.9

Fig 14.9 Foreign staying tourist to Austria (1989)

While West Germany contributes over half the number of visitors, 80 per cent of Austrian's bednights come from just three markets – West German, Dutch and British – and Austria's tourist industry must, therefore, be very dependent on the health of the economy in these three countries.

Spatial pattern of tourism

It has been noted that international tourism is very strongly concentrated in the mountains in the west: 66 per cent of Austria's visitors stayed in the provinces of Tyrol, Salzburg and Vorarlberg in 1986. The distribution of the accommodation stock mirrors this problem (*see* Fig 14.10).

	(%)
Tyrol	31.4
Salzburg	16.7
Vorarlberg	6.4
Carinthia	17.5
Styria	9.4
Upper Austria	8.3
Lower Austria	5.9
Bergenland	1.8
Vienna	2.6

Fig 14.10 Regional distribution of tourist beds in Austria (1985)

Seasonality

Like Switzerland, Austria has a double peak of tourism through the year, but Austria's peaking is more marked than in Switzerland, and Austria's smaller domestic market does not even out demand to the same extent.

	% of bednights at registered accommodation	
	International	Domestic
January	9.1	7.1
February	10.3	11.1
March	8.9	8.7
April	4.8	5.7
May	4.2	6.4
June	8.4	8.6
July	17.3	14.6
August	18.2	16.3
September	8.9	8.8
October	3.2	5.1
November	1.1	3.2
December	5.6	4.4

Fig 14.11 Seasonality of domestic and international tourism in Austria (1985)

The summer peak of demand is high (nearly 20 million bednights in August 1985). The high season in winter is February (nearly 12 million bednights). In spite of the double tourist season, occupancy rates are still quite low (24.1 per cent in 1985).

Conclusion

Swiss and Austrian territory covers the heart of the Alps and alpine tourism is concentrated here but the French, German, Italian and Yugoslavian sections of the Alps also have significant winter and summer tourism too, each with its own special character. Each country meets the winter sports needs of many of its domestic tourists but each has a slightly different niche in the international market. As the popularity of winter sports increases, all will face the problems of regulating the growing impact of skiing on the delicate alpine ecosystem (perhaps the greatest problems being experienced in the high level resorts that provide skiing to the door). All countries too share the problem of a declining summer market, and managing the sometimes incompatible demands for more ski developments with the need to conserve the landscape for the summer visitor.

QUESTIONS AND DISCUSSION POINTS

1 List the major physical regions of Switzerland *or* of Austria. Identify the dominant type of tourism associated with each region.

2 The development and organisation of winter sports tourism in Switzerland is different from that of Austria. Describe these differences and explain how and why they have occurred.

3 A double (i.e. winter and summer) tourist season would be seen as an advantage to many tourist destinations. Why is it sometimes perceived as a problem in Austria and Switzerland?

ASSIGNMENTS

1 You work in a travel agency in Birmingham and customers are beginning to think about their bookings for winter sports holidays. The following people come in asking for your advice on suitable European winter sports resorts that might meet their needs:

(*a*) A teacher who will be taking a school party (of 30 11–12 year olds, mostly beginners) on a winter ski holiday.

(*b*) A family of four. The mother is an experienced skier while her husband is a keen sportsman but has never skied. Their two children, aged 11 and 14, have both started learning to ski on artificial ski slopes in the UK. The whole family is also keen on many other indoor and outdoor sports.

(*c*) Two single businesswomen in the 28–35 age group who are both experienced skiers.

Make notes for each group of clients, selecting suitable resorts, suggesting the best time of the season they might go and the best routes and means of transport they should take.

Central Europe: Benelux and Germany

LEARNING OBJECTIVES

After reading this chapter you should be able to:

- assess the tourist potential of the climatic, landscape, historical and cultural resources of Benelux and Germany
- distinguish the regional distribution of these geographical resources and their development and use for tourism
- demonstrate a knowledge of the main tourist resorts and tourist centres
- understand the role of Benelux and Germany in the general pattern of European tourism
- be aware of the impact of changing economic and political circumstances on patterns of tourism.

Introduction

Four countries (Belgium, The Netherlands, Luxembourg and Germany) form the heart of the tourist generating region of Europe. Physically, these countries, plus the five Eastern European states, make up the non-Mediterranean core of mainland Europe (*see* Fig 8.1 on p 90). Benelux and Germany consist of three major physical units.

1 The Northern European plain. A low lying undulating region, where features of glacial deposition dominate the landscape. The plain extends from Belgium, the Netherlands, through north Germany to northern Poland.

2 The Northern European uplands. Flat topped uplands which are tilted and rise gradually from the Harz and the Ardennes in the north to the foothills of the Alps in the south. They give rise to gently rolling forested landscapes, which become more dramatic where the uplands have been cut by broad valleys, or eaten into by more deeply incised valleys. These uplands extend through the territories of Luxemburg, southern Belgium and southern Germany.

3 The Alps. The mountain chain essentially runs east-west. The Alps make up only a very small part of German territory.

The combined population of Belgium, Holland, Luxembourg and Germany was over 100 million in 1988. It is a major tourist generating region as the population has a relatively high standard of living. The countries abound with unspoilt towns and other cultural and historic resources, but are poorly endowed with coasts and climate for mass beach tourism. The 'low' countries also lack mountainous territory. Together these factors generate a very special pattern of both inbound and outbound tourism (inbound tourism mainly to the historic towns and cities and outbound tourism to destinations that complement the domestic natural resources). However, the reunification of Germany in 1990 marked the end of one political era and heralded a period of profound political and economic change: new patterns of tourism may evolve in response to these changes.

Benelux

The three countries of Benelux are small, but densely populated (*see* Fig 15.1). Together, their area is less than a third (but their total population is nearly one half) of that of the UK.

Country	Area in km²	1986 population (million)	Population density (persons per km²)
The Netherlands	40 844	15.57	351.1
Belgium	30 513	9.86	323.1
Luxembourg	2 586	0.37	142.9

Fig 15.1 Benelux population

All three countries are relatively affluent. The Dutch and Luxembourgers have high propensities to travel (at 58 per cent) and, because of the small size of their countries, a high proportion (63 per cent) of this travel is to foreign countries. Most domestic destinations are within a few hours' drive. In comparison, the Belgians tend to stay at home: only 40 per cent of their population take holidays away from home, although 56 per cent of these trips were to foreign destinations. The natural resources of all three countries are easily accessible for day leisure trips and are intensively used by both domestic day-trippers and by day excursionists who cross the border from neighbouring countries.

The landscapes have a very individual character but are subdued. The climate is slightly drier than that of UK or northern France but is still a far from ideal tourist environment. It is not surprising, therefore, that most international tourism to the Benelux countries is urban-based.

Climate

The region has a western maritime type of climate, and lies in the path of frequent North Atlantic depressions, giving mild changeable windy weather. Variations of climate within the region are related to the topography. The climate becomes cooler and wetter as the land rises towards the south of Belgium and into Luxembourg, while the strength of the wind is particularly noticeable in Holland's flat exposed landscape. The summers tend to be drier and warmer than in the UK, particularly away from the coast: in Holland the rainfall decreases from 820 mm per annum on the coast to only 560 mm inland. But summer rainfall is still frequent enough to limit the country's potential as an international destination.

The physical regions of Benelux

The countries are also known as the 'Low Countries' which aptly reflects their generally subdued relief and low altitude: much of The Netherlands is actually below sea level (*see* Fig 15.2). There are three physical regions:

1 The coastal sand dune belt. The coastline of The Netherlands and Belgium is sandy throughout its whole length and is backed by a belt of massive sand dunes, which average 6–12 m high (but sometimes rise to 60 m) and may extend

Fig 15.2 Regions and tourist resources of Benelux

2–4 km inland. The dune belt is breached only by the Rhine delta. Elsewhere, they protect the low plains from inundation by the sea. Belgium's coast is almost continuously developed for seaside resorts, and the central Dutch coast is heavily used for day-tripping from the nearby Amsterdam and Rotterdam conurbations.

2 The inland plains. These were originally marshy areas but were progressively drained to create very fertile agricultural land. In the Netherland's drainage-channels, canals and lakes were created and windmills used to pump the water out and later land was even reclaimed from the sea. As the land dried out it shrank below sea level and dykes and sea defences were built to keep the sea out. All these features combine to create the distinctive 'polder' landscape of the Netherlands.

The landscape thus has a very special quality but is exceptionally flat and is not greatly valued for tourism except where the bulbfields (located between Leiden and Den Helder) add colour and interest. However, it is an ideal setting for cycling which is very popular in The Netherlands, and the waterways are extensively used for boating. The Netherlands has 883 marinas, mostly in the Friesland lake district and around Amsterdam and Rotterdam. Most of the historic towns of Belgium and The Netherlands are located in this lowland zone.

The interior of The Netherlands has a slightly more varied topography. It is a gentle landscape of undulating heathland and woodland – quite different from the flat, intensively cultivated landscape of the coastal lowlands.

Two of The Netherlands' three National Parks are located in this zone. The Veluwe (in the south) is particularly popular.

3 The Ardennes. These mountains are located in southern Belgium and Luxembourg. They rise to 450–600 m and consist of attractively wooded, rounded mountains with a variety of rivers and lakes. Their climate is on the raw side (*see* Fig 2.1 on page 17), with persistently cloudy weather, over 850 mm of rainfall a year and up to 120 frost days per annum.

The character of tourism in The Netherlands

The domestic market

In 1985 5.1 million Dutch people took their main summer holiday at home. The length of these holidays averaged 14 days, and the vast majority were self-catering (*see* Fig 15.3).

There are many campsites, particularly in the west of The Netherlands. Another form of self-catering holidays has recently become popular. The firm, Center Parcs, operate high quality self-catering complexes with a range of all weather/all year round sports and leisure facilities. They had seven sites in The Netherlands which attracted 1.5 million visitors in 1986, and an additional two

	(%)
(a) *Serviced accommodation*	
Hotels/guest houses	7
(b) *Self-catering*	92
made up of:	
chalets	33
Tents	15
caravans/trailer tents	32
boats	6
apartments	2
youth hostels	4
(c) *Other*	1

Fig 15.3 Domestic summer holidays (three nights or more) in The Netherlands (1985)

sites in Belgium. Their sites consist of 120–160 hectares of woodland and water features. Self-catering bungalows, with high quality facilities and a range of indoor entertainments (e.g. TV and video) are set in the woodland, grouped around a central complex. This is dominated by a large indoor fun pool (with an artificial sub-tropical climate), shopping, dining and additional sports facilities. These may include tennis, squash, bowling alleys, windsurfing, canoeing and cycling. The company has also opened similar ventures in West Germany, France and the UK (in Sherwood Forest).

In contrast to most European domestic markets, the Dutch tend to prefer inland locations. The two coastal provinces (of N and S Holland that include most of the sand dune belt) receive only 15.3 per cent of all campsite nights. Gelderland (which includes the Veluwe) takes 20.7 per cent of campsite nights while the interior south has a third and the rest of The Netherlands' interior a quarter.

The explanation of this unusual distribution is twofold:

1 the coastal districts are very crowded: they accommodate half the country's population at densities of 634 people per km^2. Dutch holiday-makers like to escape to less urbanised environments for their holidays; and
2 the population living near the coast use it for daily and weekend recreation and therefore seek less familiar landscapes and activities for their domestic holidays.

Dutch outbound travel

In 1986 it was estimated that about 5.5 million Dutch took holidays abroad, and again, seaside destinations were not the most popular. In spite of its high relative costs, West Germany attracted 13 per cent of Dutch travellers, but France was the most popular individual destination, where the Central Massif and the French Alps were the most popular. Austria and Switzerland accounted for an additional 17 per cent of Dutch foreign holidays. The contrast in landscape and the opportunity for winter sports activity would appear to be major factors accounting for these Dutch travel patterns. The remaining coastal Mediterranean countries take only 27 per cent of Dutch visits abroad.

Foreign holidays by the Dutch tend to be quite long (17 days' average stay), mostly in self-catering accommodation (58 per cent of all holiday-makers) and most travel by car (56 per cent).

Foreign tourism to The Netherlands

The small size of The Netherlands encourages day visits rather than staying visitors. In 1985 it was estimated that 21 million foreigners made cross-border shopping trips into The Netherlands while an additional 13 million visitors made day leisure excursions across the frontier. The pattern of foreign staying holidays also reflect the small size of the country. Overseas visitors stay only 2.8 days (average in 1985) and come mainly for business trips or city breaks. Business tourism accounts for half the hotel nights in The Netherlands, and is concentrated in the heavily populated regions of North and South Holland and Utrecht (i.e. primarily in Amsterdam, The Hague and Rotterdam, Europe's main port).

Foreign holidays, on the other hand, are focused on Amsterdam. The city is built around an extensive canal system and has many 17th century buildings. It is a cosmopolitan city with sophisticated night life, and used to be known as Europe's 'sex capital'. Amsterdam's Schiphol airport is a major European communications centre: it is Europe's fifth largest airport, with 12 million passengers, 66 per cent of whom travel to other parts of Europe. The Netherlands is also traversed by important Northern European road routes, while Rotterdam is Europe's biggest port. It is, therefore, not surprising that an estimated five million direct transit tourists pass through the country each year.

	% arrivals at registered accommodation
West Germany	35
UK	14.1
USA	8.9
France	6.9
Belgium	5.7
Total number = 4.8 million	

Fig 15.4 Origin of staying visitors to The Netherlands (1986)

Tourism in Belgium

The Belgian domestic market

After fluctuating around 19–21 million in the 1970s and early 1980s, it was estimated that the domestic market in Belgium dropped to 17.7 million visitor nights in 1986. Sixty-four per cent of these were in coastal locations, such as the traditional resorts of Ostend, Knokke and Blankenberg and were strongly peaked in July and August (*see* Fig 15.2). Belgium has a short coastline in relation to its size, so that most of its population does not have the routine daily contact with the sea and waterways as do the Dutch. The lure of the sea coast thus appears to be much greater for the Belgians. However, the Belgians share the Dutch preference for self-catering accommodation: in the summer of 1985, 28 per cent of domestic coastal visitor nights were in campsites and 50 per cent in other forms of self-catering facilities, such as flats, villas, or apartments. After the coast, the next most popular domestic destination was the Ardennes mountains, with six per cent of all summer domestic tourist nights.

Foreign visitors to Belgium

In 1988, Belgium received 2.7 million tourists. Foreign visitors to registered accommodation generated 10.06 million nights, mainly from adjacent countries – Fig 15.5 indicates their origin.

	% nights
Netherlands	35.7
West Germany	15.5
UK	10.7
France	9.7
USA	7.3
Italy	2.7
Spain	1.9

Fig 15.5 Foreign visitor nights at Belgian registered tourist accommodation (1987)

Belgium's attractions do not draw people from far afield (apart from Americans who include Belgium on their European tour). The average length of stay is short (under two days) but the visitor population is made up of several types of tourist:

1 Businesspeople and bureaucrats, who stay very short periods in the more expensive hotels in Brussels, Belgium's Capital, which is the head-quarters of the EC, NATO and of many multi-national companies.

2 City break visitors to Brussels and the 'heritage towns' of lowland Belgium. There are at least nine towns with extensive and well-preserved medieval quarters, with Antwerp, Bruges and Ghent being the most popular. These three towns took 85 per cent of the urban visitor nights outside Brussels.

Bruges is an unspoilt medieval city (*see* Chapter 5) built around a network of canals. Its narrow winding streets, picturesque old gabled buildings and hump-backed bridges give it a special character, sometimes likened to Venice. It contains many medieval buildings, for example the Belfry and Cloth Hall dating from 1248, the Town Hall from 1376 and many 12th and 13th century churches. The city also has several museums including the Groeninge museum which houses many fine works of art.

Ghent has also retained its medieval centre. The Castle was built in 1180 but Ghent Belfry and Cloth Hall date from 1300 and 1452 respectively. St Bravos Cathedral, built in the 15th century, houses many fine works of art of the period. The city is also famed for its flower show and flower pageants. Antwerp's main square dates from the 16th century; its huge gothic cathedral is outstanding among its many fine churches and chapels.

Brussels, Belgium's capital, also retains some medieval buildings but the main central square (Grand Place) is the main focus of the city. It was rebuilt in 1696, and it flanked by the gothic-style Town Hall, the Maison du Roi, and the Guild Houses.

The medieval cities form the main attractions for visitors from the USA, Italy, Spain and Switzerland, while the West Germans and British share their interest equally between the coast and the historic towns.

3 Holidaymakers who stay longer, mainly in self-catering accommodation and on the coast. Twenty-nine per cent of foreign visitor nights were to coastal locations, which were particularly attractive to the French, West Germans and British visitors. The Dutch once again favoured inland destinations: 65 per cent of Dutch visitors to Belgium went to the countryside, particularly the Ardennes.

4 Day excursionists, who visit Belgium for shopping or day leisure trips. In 1985 it was estimated that Belgium received 15 million cross-border day visitors.

5 Transit tourists. Like The Netherlands, Belgium is strategically located on the European route network. Routes between the Paris basin and North Germany pass through Belgian territory, while ports, such as Ostend, Zeebrugge, receive ferry traffic from the UK. It is estimated that seven million direct transit visitors passed through the country in 1985.

Outbound tourism from Belgium

France was the main destination for Belgian visitors with just over three million arrivals in 1985. Mediterranean destinations (Spain, Italy and Yugoslavia) were next in popularity (2.1 million arrivals) while the Alps came third (with 644 000). There are thus striking similarities between the pattern of foreign travel of the Dutch and Belgians (although it has been noted that the Belgian market is smaller). Very few Dutch and Belgians stay in each other's countries, perhaps due to their mutual lack of outstanding physical tourist resources, their small size and the ease of day-tripping between them.

Luxembourg

The total number of tourists to Luxembourg is small on European terms, (only 760 000 staying visitors in 1988 and an estimated two million day visitors) but they are crucial to the economy of this tiny country. Tourism is Luxembourg's third most important industry, and the country relies very heavily on Belgium and The Netherlands, who together generate 72.6 per cent of all foreign visitor nights in Luxembourg. Much of the tourism is business-orientated (Luxembourg City is the headquarters of the EC bank and many other foreign banks) but some tourists visit Luxembourg's share of the Ardennes mountains.

The total population of Luxembourg is about 366 000. It generates about one quarter of a million tourist trips abroad each year, most to neighbouring countries.

Germany

Germany has been divided since the end of the Second World War. West Germany (or, officially, the Federal Republic of Germany) became a

Western-style democracy. Its economy and currency has become one of the strongest in the world, while makes it an expensive country for foreigners to visit but gives its residents high spending power abroad. With an affluent population of over 61 million, it is a major tourist generating country.

East Germany (or the German Democratic Republic) was absorbed into the communist bloc and its economic performance fell far behind that of West Germany. Travel between East and West Germany was gradually restricted until the building of the Berlin Wall in 1961 brought it finally to a complete halt. East German tourists were, therefore limited to destinations within the communist bloc. It was not until the era of 'glasnost' and 'perestroika' in the USSR and the collapse of communism in 1989 that the borders were reopened, and the process of reunification began.

Full reunification was completed in October 1990, followed by a period of economic and political readjustment. The long-term economic consequences remain to be seen, although it is anticipated by some that the success of the West German economy will spread to the east, which is bound to increase travel by East Germans. On the other hand, the period of readjustment might temporarily slow down West Germany's economic progress, with a corresponding lull in the growth of outbound travel. This could have great impact on the destination regions that rely very heavily on the West German market. What is certain is that travel patterns will change with the new political geography of Germany and Eastern Europe. However, the tourist resources stay the same and the tourist attractions of Germany as a whole will be considered together, although tourist statistics refer to West Germany only.

Germany's physical resources

Germany can be divided into five main physical regions (*see* Fig 15.6):
1 the coast;
2 a section of the North European plain;
3 the central uplands, including the Harz mountains in the north and the Black Forest in the south;
4 the Bavarian Alps; and
5 The Rhine Valley, including the Rhine Gorge.

Fig 15.6 Regions and tourist resources of Germany

The coast

Germany has a short coastline in relation to its size. The North Sea coast is fringed with low sand dunes and gently sloping mud flats. The climate is cool, with a summer average of 15–17° C, and humid. On the island of Sylt the dunes are much bigger and the beaches more sandy, and in spite of the climate, a popular seaside resort has grow up which caters mainly for the domestic market. The coastline is broken by three estuaries which provide opportunities for sailing. The port of Hamburg is sited on the Elbe estuary. The Baltic coast is a more attractive and varied, though subdued, coastline, consisting of bays, inlets, sand bars and spits, low cliffs and drowned moraines (which give a fretted and broken coastline such as on Rügen island). The self-catering holiday centres of the Baltic coast put it among the top six most popular holiday regions of West Germany.

The resorts of Poel Island (offshore of Wismar) and Rostock are also crowded and popular seaside resorts for the East German domestic market. Kiel is a major ferry port which links Germany with the Scandinavian countries across the Baltic sea.

The North European plain

The landscape here is one of subdued relief, with rolling sandy heaths (e.g. Lüneburg) on the higher land and lakes in the hollows. The lakes become more frequent towards the east. The picturesque town of Schwerin is located on one of these lakes. The region attracts few holiday-makers, however, as the lowlands of the Nordrhein-Westphalia region are heavily industrialised (for example in the Ruhr region) and are the focus of business tourism only.

The central uplands

These varied broken uplands are most heavily used for tourism on their northern section (close to the heavily populated industrial regions of Germany) and on their southernmost edge.

The northern block includes the attractive scenery of the Sauerland, Teutoburger forest and the Harz mountains. All are popular domestic tourist destinations. The Sauerland borders the industrial area; it rises to just over 900 m and is a mixture of forests rivers and lakes, with many caves. The Teutoburger hills are much lower, consisting of parallel forested scarps running into the north German plain. Again, their accessibility from industrial Germany explains their popularity, rather than any exceptional quality of their scenery. The isolated block of the Harz mountains rises to over 1250 m and has heavy winter snowfall which warrants the development of winter sports resorts. The northern edge of the Harz is steep with rocky cliffs, but the mountain tops are rounded with subdued relief. In places this high moorland is cut by deep forested valleys. The Thuringian Forest to the south of the Harz is a long, steep-sided ridge, also eaten into by deeply incised valleys. It has an even colder winter climate, with considerable winter snowfall. The ridge continues eastward into the highly dissected forest plateau of the Erzgebirge, which is bounded by a precipitous scarp on its SE side. This northern section of the central uplands is bounded by the Rhine Gorge to the west, and the Elbe Gorge to the east (on the Czech-German frontier). The Elbe gorge is located in a region known as 'Saxon Switzerland'. The Elbe has eroded the sandstone rock into craggy landscapes that are almost desert and canyon like, and has cut a dramatic deep cliffed gorge (200 m deep) through this landscape.

The southern half of Germany's central uplands includes two main tourist regions: the Black Forest and the Bavarian Forest (*see* Fig 15.6). The Black Forest is the second most important tourist area for both the foreign and domestic markets, taking 16 per cent of all tourist bednights in 1986. It is a highly dissected plateau rising to 1635 m in the south, bounded by steep slopes to its south and west. The landscape is a mixture of dramatic, deep valleys, forest, open moorland and mountain pastures. There are many holiday resorts with a variety of self-catering and family accommodation. Baden-Baden is a well established spa town, whose reputation was based on hot mineralised springs. There are many other spa towns in the area, while Triberg and the lakeside resort at Titisee are also tourist centres. Freiburg is a quaint university town with a gothic cathedral dating from the twelfth century. Tübingen lies to the west of the Black Forest and is an outstanding example of a well preserved medieval town. The Bavarian Forest is a similar landscape area, though perhaps more heavily wooded and not attaining the heights of the Black Forest. This region is also famous for the Wagner Festival held at Bayreuth, and for the unspoilt medieval towns such as Regensburg.

The Bavarian uplands and plateaux lie between the Black Forest and the Bavarian Forest. This region also has many historic and cultural centres set in attractive landscapes, including Rothenberg an unspoilt medieval town encircled by its original city walls and Augsburg which has buildings dating from the ninth to the 18th centuries. Munich is the capital of Bavaria and is a major cultural centre, but is also famous for its beers celebrated at the Oktoberfest, and also for the Fasching carnival.

Germany is famed for ancient towns that have been bypassed by modern development, and attractive examples can be found throughout the central uplands in southern Germany, for example Heidelberg.

The Bavarian Alps

The far south of Germany just reaches the first ranges of the Alps, and the German-Austrian border runs along the crest of the Calcareous Alps. The Zugspitz is the highest peak in Germany at 2968 m, and winter sports resorts, such as Garmisch and Partenkirchen are located nearby. Oberammergau, location of the Passion Play that is held once every ten years, is also sited in this area (*see* Fig 15.6). Bavaria as a whole (i.e. the Alps and the Uplands) is the most popular tourist region in Germany for both domestic and overseas visitors, with 29 per cent of all tourist bednights in 1986.

The Rhine Valley

The Rhine flows north from the Alps along a wide, flat-floored north-south trench from Basel to Frankfurt. The Black Forest rises to the east while the Vosges mountains flank the river on the French side of the valley. Between Frankfurt and Bonn, the valley becomes much narrower where the river has cut a steep-sided gorge through the surrounding uplands. The most dramatic landscape is between Koblenz and Bingen (*see* Fig 15.6). South-facing slopes are terraced for vineyards and the ruins of medieval castles are perched on crags above the river. River cruises along the Rhine have been popular for many years.

Boppard and Rudesheim are the most popular resorts that form the focal point of many Rhine cruises. They are located in the most dramatic gorge section of the Rhine. Some cruises also visit Cochem on the Moselle. These resorts are characterised by steep narrow streets sloping down to riverside promenades, and by many lively wine taverns.

As well as being an important tourist resource, the Rhine Valley is a very important route carrying tourist traffic from the industrial areas of the Ruhr south to the Alps and beyond.

Up to 1990, inbound tourism has been concentrated on the Rhineland, the Black Forest and Bavarian Alps. Changes in the regional distribution of tourism following reunification will take time to become established. The short-term effect has been an increase in domestic day excursions across the old border in both directions. In 1990 there was a chronic shortage of international standard hotel accommodation in former East German territory, and staying tourism (apart from VFR travel) cannot increase until the new tourist infrastructure is provided. Meanwhile a transitional phase is expected, characterised by day-trips to the east from hotels based in former West German border towns (such as Lübeck, Coburg and Kassel).

Tourism in Germany

(N.B. pre-1990 statistics relate to West Germany only). It is estimated that foreign and domestic tourists generated a minimum of 218 million tourist nights in registered tourist accommodation in Germany in 1986. The domestic market accounted for 83 per cent (190 million) of these, but it is not growing fast – it grew from 11.2 million holidays in 1985 to only 12.6 million in 1988). This is because each year more Germans travel abroad (20.9 million in 1985 to 27.2 million in 1988). Germans have always preferred to stay in hotels, boarding houses or inns but recently self-catering accommodation has become a little more popular, with much of this new capacity being located in Bavaria.

	Bednights in registered accommodation (%)	Purpose of visit %			
		Holidays	VFR	Business	Transit
Netherlands	19.4	–	–	–	
USA	14.7	37	20	20	
UK	8.8	31	25	37	
France	4.8	29	25	46	
Denmark	4.6	47	13	4	32
Switzerland	4.5	41	28	31	
Italy	4.3	–	–	–	
Sweden	4.0	36	17	6	34
Belgium	3.6	54	25	9	12
Australia	3.4	–	–	–	
Japan	3.4	40	14	36	

Fig 15.7 Foreign visitors to West Germany (1987)

Figure 15.7 shows that in 1987, West Germany attracts a large number of visitors from a wide range of countries for many different purposes, but that the average length of stay was estimated as only four nights. A fairly low proportion came for holidays, reflecting the high cost of travel to a country with a strong currency and high standard of living. A surprisingly high proportion visit friends and relatives (particularly from USA and UK, perhaps partly associated with the stationing of NATO Troops in West Germany). A high proportion of visitors from UK, France, Switzerland and Japan were on business trips: many international trade fairs and conferences take place in Germany, for example, at Hannover, Hamburg, Düsseldorf, Cologne, Stuttgart and Munich, and it is estimated that the business travel market is expanding faster than the holiday trade. About a third of the visitors from Scandinavia were in transit, on their way south.

However, many transit visitors do not stay overnight in the country. Figure 15.8 gives an estimate of the breakdown of border arrivals in 1985. The huge number of transit travellers underlines Germany's strategic location on routes to France, the Alps and the Mediterranean. The number of day-trippers (particularly shoppers) from Eastern Europe (e.g. East Germany and Poland) rose very rapidly in 1989.

Outbound tourism from West Germany

Outbound tourism from West Germany has grown steadily through the worst of the recession. However, the proportion of West Germans taking holidays and the proportion of these holidays taken abroad is increasing (see Fig 15.9). Also an increasing proportion of holidays are package trips and more are by plane to more distant destinations.

	Estimated number of visits (million)
Tourist arrivals	28
Excursionists (i.e. day visits on leisure or shopping trips)	100
Direct transit travellers (i.e. passing through without stopping)	70

Fig 15.8 Estimated border arrivals of foreign tourists to West Germany 1985

	1970	1975	1980	1985	1988
% population taking a holiday	42	56	58	57	65
% taking holidays abroad	53	54	60	66	68
% taking holidays by car	61	61	59	60	59
% taking holidays by plane	8	12	16	18	20
% taking package tours	17	18	26	34	38

Fig 15.9 Growth of tourism in West Germany

West Germans are the world's biggest spenders on travel and tourism, accounting for about 16 per cent of total travel expenditure worldwide in 1985. The tourist industries of many European countries rely very heavily on the West German outbound market.

The Mediterranean has been the most popular destination for West Germans for many years (accounting for at least 44 per cent of their foreign holiday visits in 1988). Italy is the most easily accessible Mediterranean destination that West Germans can reach by road. Spain is, however, rapidly increasing in popularity, and in 1988, was nearly as popular a destination as Italy. The Alps (Austria and Switzerland) account for 17.7 per cent of West German foreign holiday trips and Scandinavia 5.9 per cent (*see* Fig 15.10).

| | Holiday visits | | | |
	1982 (million)	1985 (million)	1988 (million)	1988 (%)
Italy	3.6	3.9	4.6	17
Spain	3.2	3.5	4.3	16
Austria	3.3	3.2	3.8	14
France	1.6	1.7	2.6	9.5
Yugoslavia	1.2	1.8	1.8	6.6
Greece	0.6	0.9	1.2	4.4
Switzerland	0.6	0.8	1.0	3.7
Turkey	–	–	0.8	2.9
Netherlands	0.7	0.6	0.8	2.9
Denmark	0.7	0.7	1.0	3.7
Scandinavia	0.2	0.5	0.6	2.2
UK	0.3	0.4	0.7	2.6
Outside Europe	1.4	1.5	3.0	11.0

Fig 15.10 German outbound tourism

Long-haul destinations have become far more popular: most are to the United States, but numbers fluctuate according to the relative strengths of the dollar and Deutschmark. The Far East is the second most important destination region, with a high proportion of business travellers to countries such as Japan and Singapore. However, Thailand attracted nearly 100 000 German visitors in 1985, most of whom were holiday tourists. Other popular long-haul holiday destinations include Sri Lanka, the Maldives and Kenya.

It is evident, therefore, that any change in the economic conditions in West Germany that might influence West German travel patterns would have far-reaching consequences for the tourist industries and economies of many countries of the world.

Conclusion

Just as the divide between East and West Germany has been removed, so the political divide between the countries of Central and Eastern Europe has also been lifted. The two regions should no longer be considered in isolation. The physical units of Benelux and Germany extend eastwards and they share many ethnic and historic characteristics with Eastern Europe. Up to 1990 the two regions operated as two separate tourist areas. The Eastern European countries had well established domestic tourist markets but very limited international tourism except some travel between them (particularly to the better coast and climates to the south of the then communist bloc).

Benelux and Germany were integrated into the tourist flows of Western Europe with strong coastward and southerly tourist flows to other European and Mediterranean countries. The possibility of east-west travel may create new patterns of tourism to be superimposed on these predominantly north-south tourist flows. It is likely that the relative economic performance (rather than the political affiliations) of the countries of Central and Eastern Europe may play the more significant role in shaping these new travel patterns. The new patterns of domestic travel evolving within the boundaries of the now united Germany may be mirrored in changing patterns of international tourism.

QUESTIONS AND DISCUSSION POINTS

1 What effect has the reunification of Germany had on patterns of German tourism?
2 How does the physical nature of the Netherlands appear to influence the pattern of Dutch domestic and outbound tourism?
3 Belgium has been described as being located at the 'crossroads of Europe'. In what ways does its inbound tourism reflect this strategic location in Europe?

ASSIGNMENTS

1 You are a travel journalist. Write a short article for the travel column of a Sunday newspaper on the range of special interest holidays in the Benelux countries.

2 You work for the British Tourist Authority. The Authority is planning a survey of German visitors to Britain to find out the appeal of Britain to the Germans, the characteristics of their visits and expenditure, and their satisfaction with their visit to Britain. The survey results will be used: (a) in a marketing drive in Germany; and (b) to help design policies to increase British attractions to the Germans. Write a briefing paper for the head of the research team on the nature of the German outbound market at present and design a draft questionnaire for the survey and suggest when and where the interviews might be carried out.

CHAPTER 16

Eastern Europe and the USSR

LEARNING OBJECTIVES

After reading this chapter you should be able to:

- assess the tourist potential of the climatic, landscape, historical and cultural resources of the Eastern European countries and the Soviet Union.
- be aware of the profound political and economic changes taking place in Eastern Europe and the Soviet Union and their implications for the development of domestic, inbound and outbound tourism in each country.

Introduction

Eastern Europe is an easterly extension of the non-Mediterranean core of Europe, and it is made up of the territories of Poland, Czechoslovakia, Hungary, Bulgaria and Romania.

Physically they are made up of:

1 An easterly extension of the Northern European plain. (running into north Poland and the Baltic States).

2 An easterly extension of the Northern European uplands.

3 The Carpathian mountains (which extend into Czechoslovakia and Romania from the easterly end of the Alps).

4 The Plains of the Danube. The Danube flows from the Alps, southeastwards to the Black Sea. Its lower valley is cut into two sections (by the southern tongue of the Carpathians). The first part of the valley consists of the wide open, rolling plains of Hungary, while the other is located in southern Romania.

5 The Balkan mountains of Bulgaria. These two fingers of uplands run east-west from the Yugoslavian mountains towards the Black Sea.

The countries of this region were part of the 'communist bloc'. The series of revolutions in 1989 and 1990 removed their communist regimes and they began the difficult political and economic transition from centrally planned to market economies. Before 1990 they had formed the political buffer between Western Europe and the USSR. The Soviet Union's vast territory stretches almost halfway round the world from the Baltic Sea to the Pacific (through virtually 170° of longitude). It consists of 15 republics, of which the Republic of Russia itself is by far the largest. Up to 1990 the USSR and the Eastern European countries had significant domestic tourism (the communist regime's providing for workers holidays) and some international travel was allowed between them (and to other communist countries of the world) though information about their tourist industries was not always easily accessible. New patterns of tourism may develop as these countries go through the difficult period of political and economic restructuring. The following chapter, therefore, concentrates on the tourist potential of their physical, cultural and historic resources.

Poland

Poland has the largest population of all the Eastern European countries at 37.9 million. It is one of the most heavily industrialised, but its industrial technology is outdated and its infrastructure is poor. The manufacturing and mining industries provide 28.4 per cent of Poland's jobs, but unemployment is expected to increase as the economy is modernised. The Poles have a low income per head – estimated at 2070 US dollars per head in 1988 – so in spite of a large population who have had limited opportunities for international travel for many years, Poland is unlikely to be a major international tourist generating country until it has overcome its economic problems. Day-trips out of Poland, and business tourism from the West may thrive during this period of restructuring but Poland's own tourist resources are likely to have to continue to cater for the substantial domestic market, and may attract some cultural tourism from Western European countries.

Poland's tourist regions

The Baltic sea coast

The Baltic sea is one of the world's enclosed sea environments (*see* Chapter 3) and has a very low tidal range, and rarely experiences large storm waves. The 524 km of the Polish coast is, therefore, one of marine deposition, and is characterised by the accumulation of sand dunes, spits and narrow sand bars all along the coast. These cut off lagoons on their landward side. Locally the waters are heavily polluted, e.g. at Gdansk, but elsewhere the broad sandy beaches are heavily used for domestic tourists, particularly at the beach resorts of Swinoujscie (for Stettin), Kolobrzeg, Ustka, Leba, Hel and Sopot (the local resort for Gdansk) (*see* Fig 16.1). Although it meets domestic needs, the region has climatic limitations and is unlikely to attract large numbers of international visitors: the July average temperature is only 17.7° C, at Swinoujscie, and the summer months of June, July and August are the wettest, although the annual total is fairly low at 627 mm and decreases eastwards. However, its proximity to the Scandinavian market may encourage more visitors from Norway and Sweden, particularly as there are good summer ferry connections into Gdansk and Swinoujscie.

Gdansk has rebuilt its historic centre but is better known now as the birthplace of Solidarity. It is also a major port, business and shipbuilding centre.

The northern plains of Poland

Poland's share of the North European plain is studded with shallow lakes, which formed in the hollows between glacial moraines deposited in the last ice age. Poland has more lakes than any other European country (except Finland). The well-wooded Mazurian lake district is the best known region, with picturesque landscapes of lakes nestling between the steep-sided but low hills. The area is used for camping, walking, and boating activities. The plains south of the lake zones are featureless and open with few trees. Warsaw, Poland's capital since 1596, is sited on the southern edge of these plains. Its historic centre is a World Heritage site (*see* Chapter 4) and has been rebuilt and completely restored after being severely damaged in World War II.

The hills and mountains of southern Poland

The plains rise gradually southwest to the tilted block of the Sudeten hills, which are dominated by Krkonose. The mountains are used by large numbers of Polish day-trippers from the nearby Silesian industrial region.

SE Poland and the Carpathians

Again, the plains rise gradually south until they reach the ridge of the Beskid Mountains near the Polish-Czechoslovakian border. The main ranges of the Carpathian mountains lie beyond the Beskids. The highest group is the Tatra mountains (in the 217 km^2 national park); they are glaciated granite and limestone mountains with dramatic alpine landscapes; and prolonged winter snow cover. Zakopane is a busy all year round resort catering for walkers and climbers in summer and skiers in the winter season (December to March). The historic city of Krakow is 100 km north of the Tatras. It has been a university town since 1364 and flourished in medieval times as it was sited on the crossing points of important trade routes. It has the largest medieval square in Europe and has many churches, museums and art galleries; the town escaped destruction in the Second World War and is listed by UNESCO among the top 12 art cities of the world. Nearby are cultural attractions of a different kind; for example the Wieliczka Saltmines, which have been worked for 5500 years, are 13 km east of Krakow (*see* Fig 16.1).

The sombre site of Oswiecim (Auschwitz) lies 54 km to the west of Krakow. The Auschwitz and Birkenau concentration camps are now museums and memorials. The Ojcow National Park is 22 km north of Krakow, it has a landscape of forested valleys, cliffs and caves. Czestochowa is a little further north again, where the Jasna Gora monastery is a place of Christian pilgrimage for the Poles. All the sites are busy with visitors, from all over Poland, but particularly from the nearby industrial regions. Krakow, the saltmines and Auschwitz are World Heritage sites, and the combination of resources in the Krakow region may well also appeal to the Western European tourist market.

The Bieszczady Mountains National Park is located in the far southeast corner of Poland. This, too, is a World Heritage site: like all Polish National Parks, it is subject to policies of environmental protection, but it is still used for summer hiking and winter cross-country skiing.

Czechoslovakia

Czechoslovakia has the biggest and best organised tourist industry of the Eastern European countries. It has a good network of hotels and campsites throughout the country and attracted about six million foreign staying visitors and over 15 million day visitors in 1988, although 93 per cent came from Eastern Europe. Czechoslovakia is also a heavily industrialised state, whose industry has been based on the burning of low quality coal in large quantities which has caused widespread environmental pollution. Czechoslovakia's extensive forests have thus been badly affected by acid rain. Nevertheless, it is among the most affluent of the Eastern European countries, and has a relatively low national foreign debt. It is perhaps better placed to weather the difficulties of economic restructuring, and with a population of 15.5 million, has the potential to generate significant outbound tourism, particularly as it is a mountainous landlocked country lacking any major resources for water-based tourism. Czechoslovakia consists of two upland masses – the Bohemian Massif to the West, and Slovakia to the east – divided by a central corridor of lower land (the Odra-Moravia corridor).

The Bohemian Massif

Czechoslovakia's capital, Prague, lies at the centre of the region, in a bowl, the rim of which is formed by a series of mountain ridges (*see* Fig 16.1). The Polish-Czechoslovakian border follows the crestline of the Krkonose (or Giant) mountains. These have rounded tops and are cut by forested valleys and receive heavy snowfall in winter. Harrachov is an old established ski centre. This and other resorts are promoted for both winter and summer tourism.

The German-Czech border follows first the Krusne Hory (Ore) mountains and then the ridge of the Bohemian forest (the Sumava mountains). All the forests of this western half of Czechoslovakia have been particularly badly affected by acid rain. Prague is a major European art centre with a wealth of buildings of architec-

Fig 16.1 Poland, Czechoslovakia and Hungary

tural and historic interest, including an area of medieval castles along the hilltops above the river Moldau. There is also a major art and music festival held in Prague in Spring.

Apart from Prague, most of the other tourist attractions lie around the edge of the region, just inside the mountain rim. There are smaller unspoilt medieval towns at Cheb, Ceske Budejovice and Cesky Krumlov. In the west there are a series of spa towns: Karlovy Vary (Carlsbad) is a Victorian-style spa town, based on 12 hot mineral springs, and Marianske Lazne which also expanded into the 19th century, has 140 mineral springs. The industrial city of Plzen is nearby, and is famous as the home of the pilsner beer brewery.

The summer tourist season runs from May to October. The hottest month (July) reaches a temperature of 19° C in Prague, but June, July and August are the wettest months of the year. The winters are cold and dry, and average January temperatures fall to minus 21° C at Karlovy Vary and Ceske Budejovice. Snowfall is light except in the mountain regions.

The Odra-Moravia corridor

This is a region of open rolling countryside, which carries important N-S routes which link the industrial region of Poland to Austria and Hungary. It is also one of Czechoslovakia's more important industrial zones.

Slovakia

The Tatra mountains form the core of this region (see Fig 16.1). The triangular peaks rise to 2655 m and are massive and craggy. The lower slopes are densely forested, while alpine vegetation survives above 1800 m. The 50 000 km² Tatra National Park provides a refuge for chamois, wildcats, lynxes, bears and wolves. The highest peaks hold permanent snow, and snow lies for about seven months above 750 m. Precipitation is highest in summer, but the clear dry winter weather allows annual sunshine totals to reach 2000 hours. Resorts such as Stary Smokovec and Tatranska Lomnica function as both winter and summer resorts, while Strbske Pleso and Novy Smokovec are also promoted as health resorts.

Ridges from the High Tatras run southwest, while the low Tatras lie due south. These mountains' tops tend to be more rounded and less scenically dramatic, except where limestone outcrops, to produce the splintered and craggy skylines characteristic of the Calcareous Alps, and caverns with stalactites and stalagmites below ground. In addition to the natural attraction of the region, there are unspoilt medieval towns such as Levoca and Bardejov.

Hungary

Hungary has a population of 10.7 million and is one of the less affluent of the former communist countries. In 1988 its income per head was estimated to be 2010 US dollars per head. The country has large foreign debts and although the country has embarked on a programme to modernise its economy and attract inward investment, increased unemployment appears inevitable. The country already has a well developed tourist industry (the second biggest in East Europe after Czechoslovakia) even though Hungary has no coastline and no outstanding landscape resources. In 1988 it received 10.5 million staying visitors, and eight million day visitors. Nearly 30 per cent of its visitors were from Western Europe.

Tourist resources

Most of Hungary is in one physical unit: the oval expanse of the flat Pannonian plains. Its climate is typically continental; dry cold winters and warm summers with thundery outbreaks of heavy rain. Being lower and further south, the summers are a little warmer (generally reaching 21–22° C in July) than the more northerly countries of Eastern Europe.

Hungary can be split into two tourist regions: the north and the south.

Northern Hungary

This part includes most of Hungary's hill land. A ridge of uplands runs SW-NE parallel to Hungary's northern frontier. They reach just over 1000 m in the Matra-Bukk range, NE of Budapest. Limestone outcrops near the Czech border and there is a 22 km long complex of impressive scenic caves at Aggtalek. Vines are cultivated on the southern slopes of the hills and Eger, a historic city full of Baroque palaces and churches, is at the centre of the 'Bulls Blood' red wine district.

The Danube cuts a sinuous course through this range of hills north of Budapest. This 'Danube Bend' region is scenically attractive and historically important. The hills overlooking the Danube's course were old strategic sites, controlling routes north towards Vienna. Many medieval castles and palaces were built on the heights above the river, for example at the historic Esztergom and Visegrad, and the castle area of Budapest itself. The capital is made up of two original settlements – Buda is the older medieval part while Pest is the commercial centre. Budapest has been called the Paris of Eastern Europe: it is a lively, cultured city with opera, theatres and plenty of nightlife. Short cruises are available from Budapest and river boats link the capital with the towns upstream.

The Bakony Hills run southwestwards from Budapest. Lake Balaton is located at the southern foot of the range. The lake is 77 km long and is the biggest freshwater lake in Europe and is landlocked Hungary's most important tourist resource. The lake has sandy beaches and is quite shallow, with an average depth of three metres. It is warm enough in the summer season (June to mid-September) for bathing and sailing and a series of resorts have grown up, for example at Siofok, Balatonfured and Tihany. There are campsites, hotels, holiday cottages and workers' hostels around the lake.

Southern Hungary

The rest of Hungary consists of rolling cultivated lowlands and to the east the vast level grasslands of the 'Puszta' where nomadic herdsmen raise cattle and sheep. Pecs is a large historical city in the south, while Hortobagy with its fairs and horseshows is the centre of the livestock region.

Romania

The 1989 revolution in Romania was more turbulent, and in spite of the execution of the dictator Ceausescu, the break with communism and the pre-revolutionary regime appears less clear-cut than in the other Eastern European countries. The economic difficulties are greater and the process of economic, political and social readjustment may be painful for the 23 million residents.

The country has a range of coastal and inland resources to meet domestic needs, and it may be some time before Romania generates outbound tourists in any numbers.

Before the revolution, international tourist arrivals were few, just 3.5 million staying visitors and under one million day visitors. This was partly due to the political situation, although Romania was one of the few communist bloc countries to promote sun-sea-sand package tours for the Western European market along the Black Sea coast.

The country is only a little smaller than the United Kingdom, and its centre is an upland plateau. The U-shaped Carpathian mountain chain stands out above the tablelands, and continues north across the border through the Ukraine and into Czechoslovakia. The uplands are framed by flat plains on its other three sides. The country's tourist resources are scattered throughout these regions (see Fig 16.2).

The Carpathians and uplands of Transylvania

The forested northern Carpathians are relatively inaccessible but the monasteries in the Bukovina region are fortified and their churches are extensively painted with 16th century frescos, for example at Sucevita, Moldovita and Voronet. The central plateau of Transylvania is also a remote and unspoilt rural area and as yet has little tourist infrastructure. There are perfectly preserved medieval towns such as Sighisoara at its centre.

The higher mountains, e.g. the Bucegi and Fagaras which rise over 2500 m in the southern Carpathians have been better developed for hiking and winter sports and are extensively used by the domestic and East European markets. Sinaia and Busteni are the main winter sports centres for the Bucegi mountains and the cable cars link with marked trails for summer hiking. Brasov (which has a medieval centre) is another popular tourist destination. The Fagaras moun-

Fig 16.2 Romania and Bulgaria

tains are even more popular for hiking, but the summers are cool and the mountain climate can be wet. The best months for hiking are August and September, while snow cover for winter sports lasts from November to April. Risnov and Bran Castles (both dating from the 14th century) are situated in the foothills of these mountains. Bran is promoted as Dracula's castle but the much less accessible ruined castle, Poienari Citadel, further west is thought to be the real fortress of Vlad Tepes on whom the Dracula legend may be based.

The far western tip of the Carpathians almost meets the Yugoslavian mountains. The Danube, which marks the Romania-Yugoslavia border, has cut a deep gorge as it flows between the two mountain blocks. Between Orsova and Turnu Severin the narrow gorge is known as the Iron Gates; however, the river has been dammed for a hydro-electricity scheme, and there is now a lake where the river used to thunder through.

The Plains

1 The western plains are a continuation of the Hungarian plains. Timisoara is the gateway to Romania for overland routes from Western Europe (via the Danube valley from West Germany, Austria and Budapest in Hungary). The region has few tourist attractions.

2 The Wallachian Plains. The lower Danube valley is a landscape of gently undulating open farmed countryside. It has a fairly dry climate (Bucharest, Romania's capital, has 579 mm per annum). The capital has interesting churches and parts of the old town of Bucharest remain but many historic buildings have been demolished during city centre redevelopment in the Ceausescu era. However, there is some evidence of conservation: 297 rural buildings have been assembled as an outdoor village museum in one of the city's parks. The Danube delta is a wetland area of considerable wildlife interest. Two hundred and fifty species of birds inhabit the marshy areas, while tourist boats take visitors along the main channel of the delta system.

3 The Moldavian plains form a gently sloping plateau to the east of the Carpathians. It is basically an agricultural area with extensive vineyards and some orchards, but there are few tourist features.

The Black Sea coast

The Black Sea is an entirely enclosed tideless sea, where summer temperatures rise to averages of 21 to 23° C. South of the Danube delta, the coast is gently sloping with soft, white, sandy beaches. The old established resort of Mamaia caters specially for Western European package holiday visitors. The string of resorts south of Constanta (Saturn, Venus, Aurora, Jupiter, Neptune and Olimp) were designed to cater for East European workers and in the 1980s were frequented by large numbers of East Germans and Czechs as well as Romanians. They have a

range of accommodation from hotels to campsites. Eforie Nord is also a spa where black mud from nearby Lake Techirghiol is used for curative mud baths.

Bulgaria

Bulgaria has a relatively small, but economically important, foreign tourist trade. It receives fewer staying visitors than Romania but a relatively high proportion come from the West, bringing much needed foreign exchange. Tourism is one of the more efficient sectors of the economy. Bulgaria, however, has the same economic problems as the rest of Eastern Europe, with an over-reliance on outdated heavy industry and a shortage of consumer goods. Few Bulgarians were allowed to travel abroad before 1989, and economic forces may constrain their ability to use their new freedom of international movement, though living standards began to improve in the late 1980s. Bulgaria's own varied tourist resources may continue to meet most domestic needs as well as changing international demand. The country has a wide range of historic, landscape and coastal resources, located in two main tourist regions – the mountains and the Black Sea coast (*see* Fig 16.2).

The mountains

The Balkan mountains (the Stara Planina)

This round-topped, forested ridge rises to over 2300 m and is over 600 km long. It runs from east to west across the northern half of Bulgaria. The northern flanks of the ridge are gently sloping but the southern face is steep, dropping sharply to the 'Valley of the Roses', where 70 per cent of the world's rose oil is produced. The roses bloom between late May and early June. There are many historic settlements in the region, for example Veliko Tarnovo, Bulgaria's capital between 1186–1393, the monasteries dating from 1600 at Trojan, and an open air museum of Bulgarian history at the village of Koprivstica.

Sofia, the modern capital, lies on a plateau between the Stara Planina and the mountains of Southern Bulgaria (the Rhodopi massif). The city is strategically located on the crossing of routes connecting the Adriatic with the Black Sea, and Turkey with central and northern Europe (via Belgrade and Hungary). Indeed, a high proportion of Bulgaria's 3.2 million day visitor arrivals are Turks travelling by road across Bulgaria to work in Western Europe. Sofia is a cultural and historic city, but local heavy industry makes it one of the most polluted parts of Bulgaria.

The Rhodopi massif

Most of this plateau lies over 2000 m, but the highest peaks reach 3000 m. In places the landscape is similar to the Alps, with bare rocky peaks rising above heavily forested slopes. The edges of the massif are deeply incised by steep, wooded valleys. Snow may lie all year round on the higher north-facing slopes, and there is plentiful winter snow cover for the development of ski resorts, notably at Vitosa (to meet Sofia's local needs), Borovec (an upmarket resort) and Pamporovo (designed for package tourists).

The summers are cool but the Rila mountains are extensively used by East Germans for summer hiking. There are also many historic monasteries in these mountains, such as Rila and Batchkovo, where Bulgarian Christianity survived during Turkish colonisation of the country between the 14th and 19th centuries.

The Black Sea coast

Bulgaria has a mostly sandy coastline of about 370 km with some very large sandy beaches. The summer climate is warm (reaching 22.8° C in July at Burgas) but rainfall peaks in June and December though totals are quite low (500–600 mm per annum). Although Burgas is roughly on the same latitude as Dubrovnik, its more continental location means that the winters are cold (January averages 2.0° C at Burgas and 1.7° C at Varna), which rules out the possibility of any winter coastal tourism. The summer season runs from June to September and the resorts are busy, although not as crowded as Romania's 60 km or so of sandy Black Sea coast. The main concentrations of hotels are at the resorts of Zlatni Pjasaci (known as 'Golden Sands'), Drouzbha, and Slantchev Briag ('Sunny Beach') where British and West German package tourists are accommodated. Varna and Nessebur are historic towns that also function as resorts. Other resorts provide a range of bungalow, private room and campsite accommodation extensively used by Czechs, Poles, East Germans and Bulgarians. Sixty per cent of all Bulgaria's tourist accommodation is on the coast.

The Union of Soviet Socialist Republics

The USSR is a vast area of 22.4 million km^2 and spans a considerable range of climatic zones from the arctic conditions and tundra of the north to the extremes of the continental interior. Its landscapes and cultural resources are equally as varied. The USSR has a population of 286.7 million made up of many ethnic groups and nationalities, including Russians, Ukrainians, Uzbecks, White Russians and the Turkish peoples of central Asia. Up to 1990 these were organised into 15 republics, by far the biggest of which is the Russian Soviet Federative Socialist Republic (known as the Russian Federation), covering 76 per cent of the area of USSR, and containing Moscow, Leningrad, Rostov and the River Volga. Figure 16.3 shows the full list of the republics (*see also* Fig 16.4).

Estonia Latvia Lithuania	On the Baltic coast
Byelorussia Ukraine Moldavia	On the eastern European flank of USSR
Georgia Armenia Azerbaijan	Transcaucasia (the area bordering Turkey and Iran, between the Black and Caspian Seas)
Russia (the RSFSR) –	the vast central area of USSR
Turkmenia Tajikistan Uzbeckistan Kirghizistan Kazakhstan	Central Asian republics

Fig 16.3 Republics of the USSR

By 1990, the policy of 'glasnost' (openness) and the 'perestroika' (restructuring) of the economy, society and structure of USSR has led to the ending of communist power in almost all of Eastern Europe, and the uncovering of national-

Fig 16.4 Republics of the USSR

Key
USSR Republics

1 Estonia	7 Georgia
2 Latvia	8 Armenia
3 Lithuania	9 Azerbaijan
4 Byelorussia	10 Turkmenia
5 Ukraine	11 Tajikistan
6 Moldavia	12 Uzbeckistan
	13 Kirghizistan
	14 Kazakhstan
	15 Russian Federation

ism, ethnic rivalries and dissatisfaction with the pace of change in the USSR itself. This has resulted in ethnic conflict in some republics, for example in Azerbaijan, and attempts by others, such as the Baltic States, to gain complete independence. The Soviet Union has an uncertain future and the 1990s will inevitably see a long period of political readjustment and, perhaps, instability which may deter tourism.

Up to 1989, international tourism to Russia has been centrally controlled and special facilities, e.g. hotels, special shops, have been provided for the exclusive use of incoming visitors in selected destinations. By 1989, however, 147 centres had these facilities and were open to foreigners. Special facilities have to be provided for foreign tourists because the domestic market relies mainly on dachas (weekend wooden summer houses in the countryside near the cities), 'Sanatoria' and camping for its holiday accommodation, none of which can be easily adapted for use by international visitors.

Communications are generally poor, particularly the roads, as only six per cent of the

Fig 16.5 Tourist resources of western USSR

or whether separate facilities in specific locations will continue to be set aside for foreign travellers. If the latter course is taken, then the choice of location of these investments will continue to regulate the spatial patterns of international tourism in USSR.

Up to 1989 there were five main destination areas:

1 Moscow and the River Volga (in Russia);
2 Leningrad (in Russia);
3 Kiev and Odessa (in the Ukraine);
4 the Black Sea resorts (mostly in Russia); and
5 the eastern Black Sea and the Caucuses (Georgia, Armenia and Azerbaijan).

These are all located in the most accessible westerly part of USSR, and only represent a fraction of the possible attractions of the region. Even the most westerly parts of the Soviet Union, e.g. Kiev and Odessa (*see* Fig 16.6) have a continental climate, with very cold winters and warm to hot summers but with a summer peak of rainfall. The climate will always be a constraint and the inbound tourist season is inevitably going to be quite short. The climate becomes more extreme nearer the centre of USSR, so Moscow's winters are even colder and minimum temperatures may drop to minus 16° C, though the summers are almost as warm as Kiev's.

If the changes in the Soviet economy eventually yield more widespread affluence for its population and outbound tourism to world destinations is generated, then this climatic pattern would suggest a latent demand for winter sun holidays.

It is clear that the USSR is going through a period of profound change and new patterns of

population own cars. Most of the domestic resort areas are tied to public transport routes.

Although the USSR has a large domestic tourist market, the infrastructure is thus not suitable for international visitors. It remains to be seen whether the domestic market will eventually demand more Western-style tourism,

	Kiev (central Ukraine)		Odessa (northern Black Sea)		Moscow (Western Russia)	
	Av. Temp °C	Rainfall mm	Av. Temp °C	Rainfall mm	Av. Temp °C	Rainfall mm
Jan	− 6.0	28	− 4.0	23	−11.0	28
Feb	− 4.9	20	− 2.0	18	− 9.3	23
Mar	− 0.5	38	1.6	28	− 4.4	30
Apr	7.0	43	9.0	28	3.3	38
May	14.0	43	15.0	33	11.5	48
June	18.0	61	20.0	58	16.5	51
July	19.2	76	23.0	53	19.0	71
Aug	18.1	61	21.4	30	17.0	74
Sept	14.0	43	16.5	35	11.0	56
Oct	8.0	43	11.0	28	4.4	35
Nov	1.0	38	5.0	40	− 2.2	41
Dec	− 4.4	38	− 0.5	33	− 8.2	38

Fig 16.6 Climates of western USSR

tourism will no doubt emerge. Political and climatic factors will have significant influences on the way in which these patterns evolve.

Conclusion

The tourist resources of the countries of Eastern Europe and the Soviet Union are very varied. The region covers many different cultural and climatic zones. They present great opportunities for cultural, landscape and special interest holidays. But (like Central Europe) they have very little coastline. Countries such as Belgium, Holland and Germany have access to a limited section of the North Sea Coast, while Germany and Poland and the Baltic Republics have short stretches of Baltic Sea coasts: neither coasts are climatically suited to coastal tourism. Bulgaria and Romania have short sections of coastline bordering the Black Sea which is further south and, therefore, warmer than the Baltic or North Seas but not as favourable as the Mediterranean. It would not be surprising if the Eastern European countries and the adjacent Soviet republics generated high demand for sun, sea and sand destinations with a Mediterranean quality climate. The Benelux countries and West Germany certainly do (*see* Chapter 15), but political and economic conditions in the ex-communist countries of Eastern Europe have not allowed such demand to be expressed in the past. The political constraints are now essentially removed: given political stability and improving economies these countries (who have a combined population of well over 100 million) could begin to increase pressure on their nearest or most accessible Mediterranean destinations, e.g. the northern Adriatic (via Vienna and Zagreb) or the northern Aegean through Belgrade to Salonica (via the Moravia-Vardar corridor). The initial factors limiting such developments are now economic rather than political.

Up to 1990, international tourism to both Central and Eastern European countries has been based on their landscape and cultural resources. However, mass international holiday destinations are confined to the Alps. The Carpathians in Eastern Europe are much lower than the Alps (rising to 2655 m) but their interior continental location gives them prolonged snow cover, though it would be surprising if they developed a tourist industry on the scale of that of the Alps. It is more likely that the first wave of international tourists to flow into Eastern Europe will be business and city break/cultural tourists particularly from the nearby affluent Central European countries. These changes will depend primarily on the speed with which the tourist infrastructure can be extended and improved to meet the needs of international tourists, and on the priority each government gives tourism amid the many profound economic problems that they face in the 1990s.

QUESTIONS AND DISCUSSION POINTS

1 Discuss the economic and political consequences of the 1989 upheavals in Eastern Europe. How have they affected the development of tourism in these countries?
2 What further economic and political changes must take place before Eastern Europe generates international tourists on the same scale as that of the core of Western Europe?
3 Which destinations in Eastern Europe might have most appeal to the Western European market and why?

ASSIGNMENTS

1 You work for the government of one of the Eastern European countries (specify which one). You have been sent to an international conference in Britain on 'New Opportunities for Tourism in Europe'. Your government has been given 15 minutes of the conference programme time for you to make a brief presentation to the delegates on the attractions and opportunities for tourism in your country. You have also been allocated some exhibition space in the foyer of the conference hall. Prepare notes for your presentation and write the information packs for the exhibition.

2 You work for 'Meddy-Sun', the tour company specialising in sun, sea and sand holidays for the mass market in the Mediterranean. The company is concerned about the growth of possible competition from the development of the Black Sea coast. Write a briefing report to your chief executive, comparing and contrasting the nature of the sea, coast and climate of the Black Sea and the packages offered there, with those of Spain, Portugal, Yugoslavia and Greece (where the company currently operates). Update your chief executive on political and economic developments in the Black Sea region and make recommendations as to whether or not the company should respond to the competition or not.

CHAPTER 17

United Kingdom and Ireland

LEARNING OBJECTIVES

After reading this chapter you should be able to:
- assess the tourist potential of the climatic, landscape, historical and cultural resources of the United Kingdom and Ireland
- distinguish the regional distribution of these geographical resources and their development and use for tourism
- demonstrate a knowledge of the main tourist resorts and tourist centres
- understand the role of the United Kingdom and Ireland in the general pattern of European tourism
- be aware of the dynamics of domestic demand and outbound tourism and the implications for established domestic tourist resorts and destinations.

Introduction: United Kingdom

The United Kingdom comprises England, Scotland, Wales, Northern Ireland, plus the Channel Isles and the Isle of Man. This area is the geographical base on which international tourism statistics are collected. On the other hand, domestic tourism statistics relate only to Great Britain (defined as just England, Scotland and Wales). Great Britain has a long established domestic market that has developed over more than a hundred years (*see* Chapter 1).

The basic geographical pattern of the infra-structure for domestic tourism, e.g. seafronts, piers, hotels, road and rail communications, was established by the 1960s. Most holiday facilities were concentrated in the south of England (along the south coast, and into the southwest peninsula) where the best combinations of temperature and sunshine are to be found. The coastal holiday developments in other regions were clustered near the densely populated industrial regions of the north, serving both their holiday and day-trip needs, e.g. Blackpool for the northwest, the north Wales coast for Merseyside and Birmingham, and Scarborough for the northeast.

This pattern of development once again reflects the characteristic pattern of national southward tourist flows (to the south and southwest) and regional coastward flows to the nearest accessible seaside (*see* Chapters 7 and 8). Since the growth of mass tourism overseas, there has been a shift in the nature of domestic tourism. In spite of the economic problems of the 1970s and 1980s, an increasing number of British people have holidayed abroad, to take advantage of the hotter, sunnier and more reliable climates of, first the Mediterranean, and now increasingly other destinations further afield. The old British seaside resorts have been unable to compete with the climate, cost and often more modern accommodation and better service offered by overseas destinations. The number of traditional family summer holidays of one or two weeks taken in Britain has fallen, leaving the British resorts to cater for those who do not wish to or are unable to holiday abroad. However, the nature of domestic tourist demand changed dramatically in the 1970s and 1980s with new demands for more varied types of holidays, self-catering holidays, shorter additional holidays and business tourism. At the same time, higher standards of accommodation, service and environmental quality are expected. While overseas destinations can develop rapidly to meet new needs, the domestic scene has been slower to adapt: the older holiday regions have a strong interest in maintaining old patterns of holidaymaking as they have so much (in terms of jobs and capital) invested in the existing infrastructure. Massive investment is needed to modify, update and add to facilities in order to compensate for their climatic disadvantage, and not all resorts have the prospects of a sufficient volume of trade to justify this new investment. The existing undeveloped coast is jealously guarded from new development by conservation policies, so coastal sites for modern developments are extremely limited. On the other hand, new tourist developments have been encouraged where they can meet other social and environmental needs, for example in the rejuvenation of inner city areas, in supporting the economy of ailing agricultural regions or in redundant docklands.

The domestic tourist industry has thus been going through a painful period of response and adaptation to the new demands generated by the changing structure of the domestic market. The response has been incremental – encouraged by the Government but led by the initiatives of individual companies. Although optimistic forecasts are made, it remains to be seen whether domestic short breaks and business tourism will grow enough to sustain the domestic market. Increasing affluence and improved accessibility to the Continent in the 1990s may accelerate the growth of overseas travel by the British.

International tourism to Britain is on a comparatively small scale (in terms of trips made) though of almost the same monetary value (in terms of expenditure) as the domestic market. It is far more geographically confined: overseas tourists are attracted by the historic and cultural resources of the country. They congregate in the urban areas of London, Stratford, Oxford and Cambridge and a handful of other historic towns, while international business tourism is also confined to the conurbations. Very few overseas visitors go to Britain's coast or countryside.

The changing structure of the UK domestic market

Population growth and structure

The population of the UK was 56.8 million in 1986. Government population projections anticipate modest growth to 59 million by the year 2000, and to stabilise around 59 to 60 million for the following 25 years.

Changes in the pattern of holidaymaking

Prospects for the growth of the tourist industry, therefore, depend on changes in both the population structure and changes in holidaymaking habits (i.e. the population taking more or longer holidays) rather than simply on population growth. For example, in 1985, 15.1 per cent of the population was 65 years or older (the highest proportion of elderly people of all EC countries), and with increasing life expectancy, the number of elderly is expected to grow, and if economic conditions allow their incomes to remain high, they may provide a new market of relatively affluent and leisured people who may wish to travel more than their predecessors did. Similarly the 45–59 year group will grow; a group with loosening family ties and plenty of disposable income, who are clearly potential overseas visitors. But this may be balanced by the projected decline in 20–24 year olds, who have always been keen foreign holiday takers. An increase in the 25–34 year old group, whose time and expenditure preoccupations are with family building, may lead to more emphasis on self-catering budget domestic holidays.

Evolution of patterns of holidaymaking

Holiday taking has grown substantially in the post-war period (*see* Fig 17.1). In 1973 it was estimated that British residents made 144 million tourist trips (including both domestic and foreign visits). The oil crisis of the mid-1970s and the recession of the 1980s retarded the growth of holiday taking, and it is only since the mid-1980s that the total number of trips has consistently exceeded the volume of 1973. However, the balance between domestic and foreign trips has shown a more consistent pattern of change.

Foreign holiday taking has steadily grown from five million trips in the 1960s (with only a

minor check in the 1970s) to 27 million in 1987, while the domestic market has fluctuated mainly in the range of 123 to 132 million trips since 1980.

The domestic market

The total size of the domestic market regained its pre-oil crisis level in 1987. However, the total number of domestic holiday nights has decreased over this period, from 530 million in 1978 to 495 million in 1987, so the total size of the domestic market has shrunk a little. This is due to a structural change in the type of holiday taken. The traditional main (one or two week) family holiday in a British seaside resort has declined dramatically by 14 per cent between 1977 and 1987, and has shifted from serviced to self-catering. There has been a small increase in second holidays of four or more nights and in short break holidays (of one to three nights), but this growth has not been enough to offset the decline in traditional holidays (*see* Fig 17.2). Business tourism has however shown stronger growth, e.g. from 17 million to 20 million trips between 1978 and 1980 when domestic tourism as a whole was at its least buoyant.

Year	In Britain		Abroad	
	Million trips	**Expenditure at 1987 prices (£ m)**	**Million trips**	**Expenditure at 1987 prices (£ m)**
1970			8.0	
1971			9.4	
1972			10.6	
1973	132		11.7	
1974	114		10.7	
1975	117	2150	11.9	917
1976	121		11.5	
1977	121		11.5	
1978	119		13.4	
1979	118		15.4	
1980	130	4550	17.5	2738
1981	126		19.0	
1982	123		21.0	
1983	131		21.0	
1984	140		22.0	
1985	126	6325	22.0	4871
1986	128		25.0	
1987	132	6775	27.0	7255

Fig 17.1 All tourism by British residents (for all purposes) (1970–87)

	Million trips		
	1976	**1980**	**1986**
Main holidays 4+ nights	27	24	19
Additional holidays 4+ nights	11	13	13
Short holidays 1–3 nights	30	32	32
Total trips	68	69	54

Fig 17.2 Volume of British domestic holidays (1976–86)

Location of holiday	Short breaks %	All holidays %
Seaside	42	37
Small town	14	14
Large town	14	11
London	9	5
Countryside	18	27
Not specified	5	5

Fig 17.3 Destination of tourist nights in Britain in 1987

These changes in the structure of the market have had significant consequences in terms of accommodation used and led to a shift in the spatial location of tourism. The main holidays have used serviced accommodation less and less, leading to a conversion of hotels to other uses, e.g. flats, old people's homes. Some of the spare capacity in seaside hotels has been promoted for, and taken up by, the conference trade (business tourism) on weekdays, and by the short break market at weekends. But short break holidays on the whole use the same type of accommodation as the overall domestic market (e.g. only 17 per cent and 18 per cent respectively using hotels) though spatially short breaks are more likely to be taken by the seaside and in towns and less likely to be rurally based than main holidays (*see* Fig 17.3). Business tourism is more likely to use hotels and be located either in the seaside resorts for conferences, or in the major conurbations. Business and short break tourism are less peaked in demand than main holiday taking.

The economic impact of these different types of holiday are very different. Business tourists are the highest spenders while short breaks bring in least money (*see* Fig 17.4).

Day-tripping

Day-trips are not strictly included in the definition of tourism, but day-trippers visit the same range of attractions and compete with holidaymakers for road space at weekends and holiday times. There is evidence that levels of day-tripping hold up better than holidaymaking in periods of economic difficulty: when times get hard, people cut down or cut out their holidays but still visit the more local attractions on day-trips. Day-trippers spend significantly less on their visits than do tourists but can create significant management problems at tourist attractions. Day-tripping is much more responsive to changes in the weather than is tourism and in good weather outdoor attractions may be very busy but get negligible attendances in the rain. The overall level of day-tripping is difficult to measure accurately and estimates of the total volume vary. However, the 3327 tourist attractions that record accurate admission figures (which do not distinguish between tourists and day-trippers) counted 233 million visits in 1987.

	% of expenditure	(GB domestic tourism) 1986
Holidays	50	5.5% short breaks (1–3 nights) 7.0% other short holidays 37.0% long holidays (4+ nights)
Holidays VFR	9	
VFR solely	8	
Business/conferences	30	
Other	3	
Total expenditure	100 = £7150 m.	

Fig 17.4 Expenditure on domestic tourism

Overseas visitors to the UK

The number of overseas visitors to Britain grew steadily in the 1970s (in spite of the oil crisis) to a peak in 1977–9 at about 12.5 m. Numbers fell away in the worst of the economic recession in the early 1980s to a low of 11.4 million in 1981, since when the numbers of visits has gradually climbed again to 15.6 m visits in 1987. The expenditure has also steadily climbed (from £2797 m in 1979 to £6260 m in 1987) in spite of the average length of stay of overseas visitors having fallen. In the 1980s, holidays made up around 43 per cent of all visits, business trips 21 per cent and holiday/VFR 18–21 per cent but as in the domestic market, the business travel contributes more than its proportional share of income (24 per cent of income in 1987 but only 21 per cent of trips).

Nearly half of Britain's overseas visitors came from EC countries in 1987, of whom 40 per cent came on holiday and 26 per cent on business trips (*see* Fig 17.5). The North American market has always been important, though Britain became less reliant on this market in the 1980s (*see* Fig 17.6). Overseas tourism to UK is basically business tourism, VFR and cultural tourism, so it is spatially highly concentrated on towns, and particularly concentrated on London, with 49 per cent of visits, 45 per cent of nights and 63 per cent of expenditure (*see* Fig 17.7).

1988	Trips (million)	Nights (million)	Expenditure (million £)
London	9.4	72.1	3576
SE England	1.8	16.4	404
E Anglia	0.8	8.4	180
Thames and Chiltern	1.3	12.0	315
S England	1.0	6.6	161
West Country	1.2	10.7	250
Heart of England	1.0	8.4	203
E Midlands	0.5	4.5	89
North West	0.9	8.6	198
Yorkshire and Humberside	0.8	6.4	149
Cumbria	0.2	0.9	25
Northumbria	0.3	3.0	99

Fig 17.7 Regional distribution of overseas visitors to England

The spatial distribution of tourism in Great Britain

Domestic holidays are strongly concentrated in England (*see* Fig 17.8). In 1988 76 per cent of domestic holidays of four nights or more were taken in England, 11 per cent in Wales and 12 per cent in Scotland: when short breaks are included the concentration in the South is even more marked.

Visitors from	1973 %	1987 %
North America	25.6	21.4
EC	46.3	49.2
Rest of Europe	10.9	9.7
Rest of World	15.8	18.1
Total no.	8.2 million	15.6 million

Fig 17.5 Overseas visits to Great Britain

Visitors from	1973 %	1987 %
USA	31	18
W Germany	10	10
France	9	13
Ireland	6	6
Netherlands	5	5
Belgium/Luxembourg	3	3
Australia	3	4
Italy	–	4

Fig 17.6 Leading generators of foreign visitors to GB

	Million trips	Million nights	Expenditure (£ million)
England	61.0	285	3925
Scotland	5.8	34	719
Wales	7.0	40	460

Fig 17.8 Holiday tourism in Britain by the British 1988 (all holidays of one night or more)

This distribution reflects the two main factors of climate and population distribution. The westerly uplands of Scotland and Wales have a wealth of landscape and coastal resources but a wetter cloudier, cool and unreliable climate. Second, the British population is concentrated in the

South East and (in spite of the relatively short distances between regions) most holidays are taken close to home.

The attractions and patterns of tourism will be described for each region in turn.

The distribution of tourism in England

There are 12 tourist regions in England (*see* Fig 17.9). Holiday tourism is strongly concentrated in the south: the three southern regions (S, SE and SW) account for nearly 40 per cent of all British holidays (*see* Fig 17.10), and have the warmest, driest and sunniest weather in Britain (*see* Figs 17.11 and 17.12). Only eight per cent of all holidays are taken in the two northernmost regions (Cumbria and Northumbria). These parts of England have cooler, wetter and cloudier weather and are also a long way north of the major concentrations of population (i.e. the main tourist generating areas). Very few holidays are taken in the land-locked regions of the Heart of England and Thames and Chiltern.

It has been noted that overseas tourism shows a totally different spatial pattern (*see* Fig 17.13)

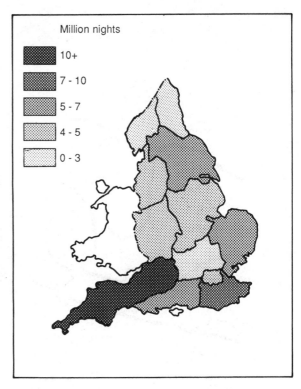

Fig 17.10 Regional pattern of domestic holiday trips

Fig 17.9 Britain's tourist regions

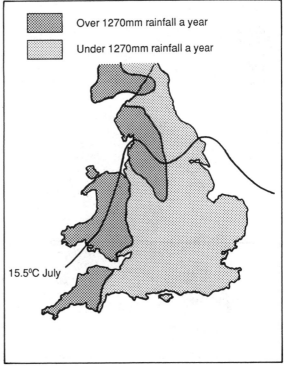

Fig 17.11 Rainfall in England and Wales

Fig 17.12 August sunshine in England and Wales

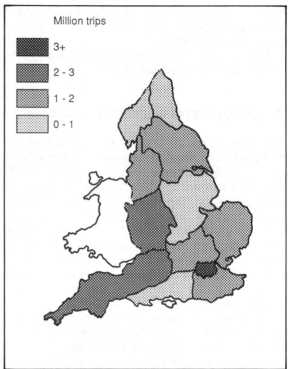

Fig 17.14 Regional pattern of business tourism

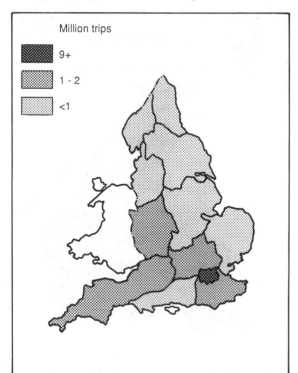

Fig 17.13 Regional pattern of overseas tourism

with the emphasis on London and the South East, the inland regions of Thames and Chiltern (the location of Windsor and Oxford) and Heart of England (the location of Stratford-upon-Avon). However, the West Country does receive almost as many overseas visits as the Heart of England region.

Domestic business tourism shows a pattern halfway between these two extremes: London, Heart of England (site of the National Exhibition Centre in Birmingham) and the West Country (where conference facilities are located in many resorts) are the leading regions (*see* Fig 17.14). When all forms of tourism are amalgamated (including all domestic and foreign) and expressed in terms of nights spent in each region, London emerges as the leading destination (*see* Figs 17.15 and 17.16).

London is important as a location for overseas visits, for business tourism (domestic and international) and to a lesser extent for domestic holidays and short breaks. The West Country and the South East are the next most important regions: they have a good mix of holiday,

Rank Order	Region	Million tourist nights
1	London	103.0
2	West Country	92.7
3	South East	55.4
4	East Anglia	48.4
5	South	45.6
	North West	45.6
7	Yorkshire and Humberside	38.4
8	Heart of England	36.4
9	Thames and Chiltern	34.0
10	East Midlands	31.5
11	Northumbria	19.0
12	Cumbria	13.9

Fig 17.15 All British and overseas tourism to England (1988)

business and overseas tourism, but with domestic holidays being the most significant. Tourism is reasonably evenly spread amongst the other regions though the two most northerly regions (Cumbria and Northumbria) are the least visited and are consistently ranked lowest for all forms of tourism.

Thus, England appears to conform to the general pattern of tourist movement (the

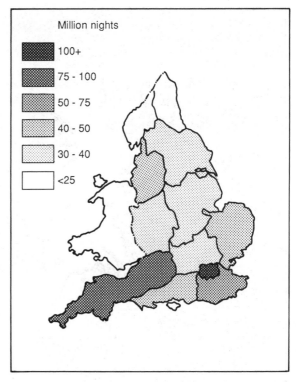

Million nights

- 100+
- 75 - 100
- 50 - 75
- 40 - 50
- 30 - 40
- <25

Fig 17.16 All tourism

	Destination regions										
	Northumbria	Cumbria	Yorkshire and Humberside	NW	Heart of England	East Midlands	Thames and Chiltern	London	SE	S	West Country
	%	%	%	%	%	%	%	%	%	%	%
Origin region											
Scotland	7	9	3	7	2	2	2	4	1	1	1
North	36	15	12	8	2	4	2	4	2	2	2
Yorkshire and Humberside	11	10	32	11	6	14	5	5	3	3	4
North West	10	31	10	27	8	7	7	9	6	4	5
East Midlands	4	4	6	6	5	29	6	5	4	9	6
West Midlands	5	5	6	8	25	9	5	8	5	6	12
East Anglia	1	2	4	2	2	4	7	3	4	3	2
South East	19	20	22	22	33	24	54	47	66	56	38
South West	4	2	5	7	13	5	9	11	8	13	25
Wales	3	2	2	3	6	3	2	5	2	3	4
	100	100	100	100	100	100	100	100	100	100	100
Total number of nights spent in each tourist region by British holidaymakers	16 million	13 million	32 m	37 m	28 m	27 m	22 m	31 m	39 m	39 m	82 m

Fig 17.17 Regional patterns of domestic tourism

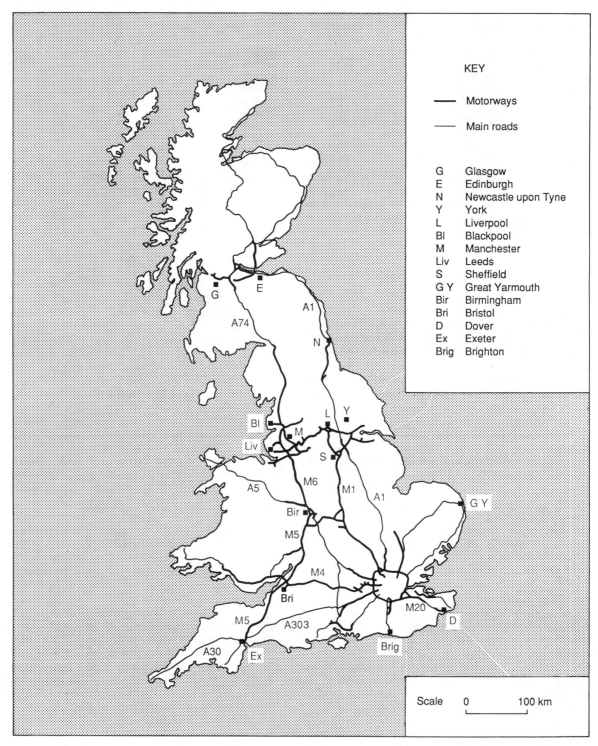

Fig 17.18 Main road routes in UK

predominant flows being southward and coastward). However, a surprisingly high proportion of the British tourists stay within their own regions, or go to adjacent regions: travel distances are relatively short. Figure 17.17 shows the relationship between the regions that people visit and the regions in which those visitors live (i.e. each column shows the proportion of visitors to a given region that live in other regions). About a third of the visitors to the northern tourist regions live in that region; around a quarter of the visitors in the Midlands tourist regions live in the Midlands, while the South East is the dominant tourist generating region for the southern tourist regions.

Seventy per cent of Britain's population lives in the NW-SE band stretching from the South East, through the Midlands to the Merseyside and Manchester conurbations. The dominant radial communications patterns facilitate the southward flow of tourists (*see* Fig 17.18)

towards London and the South East. It was not until the M5 was built and later extended to Exeter that travel from Manchester and Birmingham to the West Country was eased. This motorway, and the more recently constructed East-West links are the only significant elements of the network cutting across the radial pattern.

The regional road networks are also extremely radial, centred on the regional conurbations (e.g. Manchester, Birmingham, Bristol).

Regional patterns of tourism in England

London

1 Concentration of tourism in West and West Central (WC) London. In 1988 over 20 million tourists (British and overseas) and an estimated 40 million day trippers visited London. All but business travellers come for the historic buildings,

Fig 17.19 Main attractions of London

cultural and traditional events, the shops, restaurants, nightclubs and other entertainment. The vast majority of these attractions are located in the West of Central London (the 'West End') (*see* Figs 17.19 and 17.20) causing considerable congestion in the peak summer months. Although 68 per cent of British visitors stay with friends and relatives there is considerable pressure on hotel accommodation. British staying visitors are reasonably well spread through the year (the peak holiday months balanced by the growing short break market in spring and autumn) but the numbers are swelled in the summer by day-trippers and overseas visitors (*see* Fig 17.21), to a peak in July and August. During these months the most acute congestion can be expected in the middle of the day (12.30–3 pm). The congestion and conflicts between the needs of local communities and tourists have led some boroughs (such as Westminster) to limit new hotel developments. There is a growing shortage of hotel accommodation in London, made worse by Britain's housing policy in the second half of the 1980s when the budget hotels and bed and breakfast accommodation were used to house London's homeless (in 1988 11 000 spaces were thus taken up) and other budget accommodation has tended to trade up to more profitable four-star grade facilities.

	Million visits
Central London and West End	
British Museum	3.83
Westminster Abbey	3.25
National Gallery	3.22
Madam Tussauds	2.70
Science Museum	2.43
Tate Gallery	1.58
Natural History Museum	1.36
London Zoo	1.32
(Plus Buckingham Palace, main shopping streets etc. that do not record attendances)	
West London	
Kew Gardens	1.18
Hampton Court	0.53
City of London, Docks & Greenwich	
Tower of London	2.18
Tower Bridge	0.53
St Paul's Cathedral	2.5 (est)
National Maritime Museum	0.7
Cutty Sark	0.4

Fig 17.20 Attendances at leading London tourist attractions 1988

	By British residents %	By overseas residents %
Trips started in:		
January – March	25	18
April – June	23	26
July – September	20	34
October – December	31	22
	100	100

Fig 17.21 Seasonality of London's tourism (all staying visitors)

The focus of international tourism in the west of London is reinforced by the location of Heathrow on the western fringe. There is also a shortage of hotel accommodation close to the airport. Heathrow is the major international gateway into both Britain and Europe.

It is estimated that tourism generates nearly 200 000 jobs in London, and contributes £4700 m to London's economy. In order to meet the growing demand for tourism in London, and to sustain its economic benefits, there is an urgent need to resolve some of the environmental problems it causes, perhaps by spreading tourism more widely through Central London. Since the Greater London Council (London's strategic planning authority) was abolished in 1986, the London boroughs are responsible for promoting and controlling new developments, and they act primarily in the interests of their own residents. The London Tourist Board (which lacks any powers to enforce the implementation of its policies) has, however, taken the initiative to coordinate the policies of the boroughs and produced the Tourism Strategy for London in 1987. This provides the framework within which measures could be taken to spread tourism pressure and benefits more widely. However, the lack of an overall strategic planning authority and the current reliance on market forces may still lead to the over-concentration of tourism development in Central London.

2 Tourism in East Central London. There is a secondary concentration of tourist activity to the east of Central London. The City of London (the location of the stock market and the Bank of England) is the centre of business tourism, and St Paul's, the Tower of London, and Tower Bridge attract vast numbers of holidaymakers and day-trippers (*see* Fig 17.20). The slightly less popular attractions at Greenwich lie even further to the east (in LB Greenwich), and the old London Docks lie in the centre of this cluster of attractions. The city centre docks in many of Britain's city ports have become outdated, and port activity has either declined or has relocated on new greenfield coastal port sites, e.g. Tilbury for London, Avonmouth for Bristol, where larger modern container dock facilities can be provided. The derelict city centre docks have been the site of active redevelopment in many cities and London is no exception. The London Dockland Developent Corporation is the body responsible for rejuvenating an area of 20 km^2 (and over 88 km of waterfront) in London. Much of the redevelopment is for upmarket housing and commercial land uses but significant tourist developments have also occurred. Firstly, the docks have been linked to the City business area by the Docklands Light Railway, and the new London City Airport (built on the former quay between the Royal Albert and King George V docks at North Woolwich) links European destinations within a 600 km radius (principally Amsterdam, Brussels and Paris) of the City of London.

This improved transport infrastructure will, no doubt, encourage business tourism to this part of London, and new hotel developments in the docks are envisaged. There are also many opportunities to attract holiday tourists and day-trippers to this part of London through the conservation of historic buildings, and the development of the water sports potential and the other leisure opportunities of the docks. On the other hand, local communities would prefer to see the land developed for low cost housing to meet the needs of adjacent deprived inner city residents; and these developments remain the focus of local controversy.

The West Country

The southwest peninsula is Britain's second ranking tourist region after London (*see* Fig 17.15) in terms of tourist nights spent. It is essentially a rural region whose main resources are its mild climate, its inland countryside attractions, its sandy beaches and undeveloped coast.

Its main tourist function is as a holiday region (69 per cent of its British visitors and 57 per cent of its overseas tourists come on holiday, while under 23 per cent visit friends and relatives and only 12 per cent come on business trips). Tourism is highly peaked: 42 per cent of the region's British visitor and 47 per cent of its overseas visitors come between July and September, when there is great congestion in the resorts and on the main access routes (the M5 and A30). The region has only one large resort – Torbay. Elsewhere the tourist accommodation is spread between the smaller resorts (such as Sidmouth, Dawlish, Teignmouth, Newquay, Minehead and Burnham-on-Sea) quaint old fishing villages, such as Clovelly and Polperro and more modern developments, such as caravan sites and new holiday villages. The south coast of the peninsula is a mixture of cliffs, sandy beaches and estuaries which provide good conditions for sailing. The north coast is more rugged, with rocky cliffs interspersed with small sandy coves and bays. Much of the coast is undeveloped. A large proportion is covered by the Heritage Coast designation (*see* Fig 4.13 on page 49) where landscape conservation policies take priority over tourist development and car access is strictly limited. Pedestrian access is encouraged and a long-distance footpath follows the whole length of the coast.

Inland, the rolling countryside provides an attractive backdrop to the many unspoilt historic villages, such as Lacock in Wiltshire, Selworthy in Somerset, towns, such as Dunster in Somerset, and the Roman and Georgian town of Bath in Avon, and historic monuments, for example Stonehenge in Wiltshire, Buckfast Abbey on the southeastern flanks of Dartmoor, and Wells Cathedral on the edge of the Mendips. The region's National Parks provide the biggest areas of open countryside: Dartmoor is characterised by large expanses of bleak, open moorland punctuated by dramatic rocky tors. Exmoor has a softer landscape: the moorland is limited to the crests of the hills which are cut by deep wooded valleys. Bodmin Moor, the Quantocks and the Mendip Hills provide smaller areas of open countryside. All these landscapes provide opportunities for walking, pony trekking, farm tourism and other rural activity holidays.

The past and present industries of the region have also been exploited for tourism, e.g. 19th century mineral workings have been restored at Morwellham Quay on the Tamar north of Plymouth, and several cider works throughout Devon and Somerset are open to visitors. In addition there is a range of man-made attractions, such as miniature railways, model villages, complexes such as Somerwest World at Minehead, the Tropicana Pleasure beach at Weston and the English Riviera Conference Centre at Torbay. Only a handful of these attractions receive more than half a million visitors a year, but the region is characterised by a huge variety of small attractions providing the tourist with a lot of choice. Most are located within easy reach of the coast where the tourist accommodation is concentrated. Because this adds to the pressures and congestion along the coast, many of the local authorities attempt to limit and restrain new tourist development in the coastal zone, while encouraging it in the remoter inland rural areas. At the same time the English Tourist Board and the local authorities are trying to promote the region and further diversify its tourist product (e.g. into conference and business tourism in the larger resorts). This is because the region relies so heavily on holiday tourism. The West Country has felt both the impact of the recession and the full effects of the shift from serviced accommodation to the rented and self-catering sectors in the late 1970s and early 1980s. For example, Torquay experienced a 22 per cent decline in tourist nights between 1977 and 1984. At the same time there was an 11.2 per cent decline in the use of serviced accommodation in Cornwall. The region is characterised by many small hotels (83 per cent had under ten bedrooms in 1988). These small businesses were hit particularly hard and there was a strong trend towards conversion either to elderly persons' homes or self-catering units.

The south coast (the South and South East tourist regions)

The coast of the south of England is different in character from that of the Southwest. Southern England is essentially a lowland region with few cliffs, except where the chalk hills meet the coast at Dover, Beachy Head and in the Isle of Wight, and the limestone produces cliffs on the Purbeck coast of Dorset. The coast consists of a series of sandy and shingly beaches from Sheppey to Selsey, most of which were developed in the 19th century as traditional seaside resorts or more recently for commuter or retirement settlements.

The coast of the Solent (the channel between the Isle of Wight and the mainland) is less developed as it consists of a series of muddy marshes and estuaries, totally unsuited to beach tourism but the harbours are ideal for sailing and other boating activities. The countryside is not dramatic, although the North and South Downs, the heathlands of the Weald, and the woodland and heaths of the New Forest are very attractive and are heavily used by both tourists and day-trippers. Apart from the coast, the leading destinations of the region are Canterbury Cathedral and Thorpe Park (both with over one million visitors in 1988). The former is of great historic and architectural interest, while Thorpe Park is a modern theme park, developed from reclaimed gravel pits. It is very easily accessible, being close to the M25 on the southwest outskirts of London. Kent, Surrey and Sussex are very easily accessible from London and all the resorts and facilities here cater as much for day-trippers and commuters from London as for staying visitors. In spite of this, the traditional resorts have still experienced mixed fortunes. The larger resorts that have enough visitors to attract and justify new investment have diversified. Brighton has a 5000 seat conference centre and marina, while Deal and Eastbourne have new all-weather leisure facilities. Some of these resorts experienced an upturn in business in 1988 but the smaller resorts continue to decline.

A high proportion of the tourist traffic in the South East is transit traffic to and from the continent. The shortest and most heavily used ferry routes are from Dover and Folkestone to the ports of northern France and Belgium, but there are also ferries from Sheerness to Flushing (in Holland) and from Newhaven to Dieppe. Only four per cent of all the visitors travelling through Kent actually stay in the county: most traffic flows directly between the Channel ports and London (via the A2/M2 and A20/M20 routes). The completion of the Channel Tunnel will make cross-Channel day-tripping more attractive, and there have already been collaborative marketing exercises promoted by Kent County Council and Nord Regional Council in France to encourage transfrontier tourism. However, it is anticipated that the region will still be ignored by most longer stay international tourists using the fixed link, who will continue to pass through rather than stay in Kent.

Air travellers show the same pattern of behaviour. London's second international airport, Gatwick, is located in Surrey. It handled 19.4 million passengers in 1987 (22 per cent of

UK total air passengers) but most of these tourists head straight for London on arrival.

Transit traffic via Southampton is on a very much smaller scale. Hampshire and East Dorset rely much more on holiday tourism, although some centres in this part of the region have also attempted to expand and diversify into conference, short break and heritage tourism. Bournemouth, for example, has a 4000 seater conference centre, and Portsmouth is marketing its naval history and maritime connections. Nelson's flagship *Victory*, *HMS Warrior* (dating from 1860) and the recently recovered *Mary Rose* (Henry VIII's flagship) each attract over 300 000 visitors a year, and a new marina with its associated water-based leisure and conference facilities opened between 1986 and 1988.

East Anglia

This region, too, is mainly a lowland area with a low and gentle coastline. Most of the Essex coast is muddy and the estuaries form ideal locations for sailing rather than seaside tourism and there are a series of yachting centres on the Crouch, Blackwater and Stour estuaries. Harwich, at the mouth of the Stour is the main ferry port for Germany and Scandinavia. The good transport links with London mean that the resorts on the Essex coast (Southend, Clacton, Frinton and Walton) cater mainly for day-trippers. The coast becomes much sandier further north. Great Yarmouth has a huge sandy beach and is the biggest resort in East Anglia, with 2¼ million visitors to its pleasure beach in 1988. Inland from Great Yarmouth lie the waterways of the Norfolk Broads which are popular for boating holidays and all forms of water sports. The shallow inland waters are safe for even the most inexperienced yachtsmen. The management of the wildlife in the increasingly polluted wetland environment of the Broads has caused concern for many years. The pollution comes from sewage effluent and agricultural run off rather than from the impact of tourism. The Broads are now funded and managed in a way similar to the ten National Parks of England and Wales, though it is not a National Park by name (*see* Fig 4.13 on page 49). The total number of boats and their distribution is regulated in the interests of wildlife in order to minimise the impact of tourism on the Sites of Special Scientific Interest and National Nature Reserves.

The Midlands and North of England

Coastal resorts become relatively less important towards the north of England with a few notable exceptions. Blackpool is one of the most successful resorts in Britain in spite of its northerly location and its badly polluted coastal waters. It relies heavily on day-trippers from the adjacent conurbations. The Pleasure Beach at Blackpool is estimated to attract 6½ million visitors a year, but the resort has a wide variety of other indoor facilities (The Tower, the Sandcastle Centre and Louis Tussaud's Waxworks) and outdoor attractions (e.g. the Zoo and the Lights). The lights come on in the autumn and extend the season by many weeks. On the east coast, Scarborough (a spa town of the 18th century) is the main seaside centre. It undertook substantial investment in the late 1970s and early 1980s to update its facilities and expand its conference accommodation.

The countryside of northern England is more mountainous and dramatic than the lowlands of the South and Southwest, and extensive areas of the uplands are designated as National Parks (*see* Fig 4.13). The North York Moors and Yorkshire Dales National Parks cater extensively for day-tripping and rural farm-based and activity holidays. The Peak District is the most heavily used of all the National Parks (with a lot of camping and caravanning) though permanent accommodation is strictly limited within the Park boundaries. Cumbria (whose main resource is the Lake District National Park) relies much more heavily on staying holidaymakers who are more likely to use hotels. The Northumbria National Park (the site of Hadrian's Wall) is the least visited of all the National Parks. It is the cultural and historic resources of these regions that lure visitors (particularly the overseas visitors) northwards. Cultural associations have made Stratford-upon-Avon (with Shakespeare) and Oxford (with the University) and to a lesser extent Grasmere (with Wordsworth) and Haworth (with the Brontës) such well known tourist destinations. Many overseas visitors also visit the historic cities of York and Chester. In 1988 York Minster (an 11th century Gothic cathedral) received 2.1 million, and the Yorvik Viking Centre 860 000 visitors.

The West Midlands and the conurbations of Yorkshire and Lancashire were the centres of the industrial revolution and saw the early growth of iron, steel, pottery, wool and cotton manufacturing. This industrial heritage is also being developed as the focus of urban tourism aimed at the short break market. The Ironbridge Gorge Museum (in Telford, Shropshire) was one of the first to conserve and promote industrial archaeology in 1971. Sites along the River Severn have since been restored and opened to the public, and the 42-acre open air museum at Blists Hill has been expanded. In 1988, the complex attracted over 400 000 visitors. The Black Country Museum in Dudley (Worcestershire) is a similar though more recent development, while the open air museum at Beamish (Newcastle upon Tyne) attract 467 000 visitors. Bradford was among the first of the northern cities to develop an integrated package of attractions (including industrial archaeology, Asian cuisine, the Brontës, and the sites of popular TV serials) to generate tourism to what was thought of as an unlikely destination.

The other major northern cities have followed suit. Manchester has adapted derelict sites to new tourist uses: the GMex Centre, completed in 1986 is an exhibition and events arena developed from a converted train shed of the old Central Station. The Castlefield site in Manchester (designated in 1982 as Britain's first Urban Heritage Park) is a complex of new museums of science and industry, air and space, transport and electricity all converted from redundant buildings and linked to other attractions such as the Granada studios (where the TV set of *Coronation Street* is located) and remains of a Roman fort. Liverpool has also adapted its redundant dockland for new uses: the Albert Dock complex (consisting of shopping, catering and maritime museum facilities surrounding the dredged and cleaned dock basin) is estimated to attract 3½ million visitors a year.

Birmingham has capitalised on its central location and good road and air links to develop the National Exhibition Centre which now accounts for 30 per cent of UK exhibition space. The Midlands are also the location of Britain's most popular theme park (Alton Towers) and Britains first 'Center Parcs'. (*see* Chapter 15).

Scotland and Wales

These two regions typify upland Britain. They are areas of mountain landscapes of moorland and forest with sparse populations and dramatic undeveloped coastlines. However, their north-westerly location leads to an unfavourable climate for tourism (cooler, cloudier and wetter than south and east Britain). They are more remote from the population centres of England. Only South Wales is easily accessible (via the M4) from London. Scotland is linked to the main road network by good trunk roads (e.g. A74 Carlisle-Glasgow and A696/A68 east coast route from Newcastle upon Tyne to Edinburgh) but access beyond Edinburgh and Glasgow into the Highlands is more difficult.

Scotland

The total volume of tourism in Scotland was 73 million bednights (1987). The majority of the holiday trips were generated by Scots (53 per cent) and 45 per cent from England. Foreign travellers accounted for 15 million bednights. Tourism is highly seasonal and concentrated during the better weather of July, August and September. Trips lengths are quite short (averaging under five nights). Main holidays are strongly concentrated in the Highlands but business VFR and international tourism is more focused on the cities and population concentrations of the Central Lowlands. The Borders and Southern Uplands receive little tourism.

1 The Central Lowlands. This region consists of the Valleys of the Clyde, Forth and Tay, and is the most urban and industrialised region of Scotland, although most of the heavy industries are in decline. Edinburgh is a beautiful city and is the cultural and social centre of Scotland. Its dramatically sited 14th century castle is a major attraction, with the Royal Mile which links the Castle to the Palace of Holyrood House. The latter is mainly 17th century but is associated with Mary Queen of Scots who was executed in 1587. The city also has a substantial and well-preserved Georgian area. The annual Arts Festival (The Edinburgh Festival) attracts many visitors from the South, but international visitors to Scotland also concentrate here. The Castle, The Royal Botanic Gardens and The Royal Scottish Museum (all located in Edinburgh) were among Scotland's leading attractions in 1988.

Glasgow, as European City of Culture in 1990 rivals Edinburgh as a centre of tourism, and the

Burrell Collection was Scotland's leading attraction (with over one million visitors) in the late 1980s. Glasgow's art galleries and museums also attracted large numbers of tourist and the city is also the home of Scottish opera, theatre and orchestras.

There are many other urban attractions in the region. St Andrews has an attractive coastal location and is famous for its golf, University, Castle and Cathedral, while Glamis and Scone also have historical connections. The Magnum Leisure Centre at Irvine is a major attraction in the west of the region with over a million visitors in 1987. The industrial archeology of the region has been less exploited than in England. New Lanark is a 200-year old cotton spinning village near Glasgow that has been restored and provided with tourist facilities. It is one of the most important industrial archeological sites in the UK and has been nominated as a World Heritage Site. Yet it received only 80 000 visitors in 1985. Whisky distilleries, such as Glenfiddich, which appear more associated with the image of Scotland, attracted twice as many visitors.

The countryside bordering the Central Lowlands is heavily used for tourism and day-tripping, particularly Loch Lomond and The Trossachs, The Queen Elizabeth and Argyll Forest Parks in the Grampians to the north of Glasgow.

2 The Highlands. The most outstanding, remote and unspoilt mountain and coastal scenery is located in the north and west of Scotland. It is an ancient landscape of rounded and worn down mountains which contrast strongly to the jagged peaks and precipitous slopes of the geologically younger mountain regions of the world such as the Alps, Rockies or Himalayas. The region is basically a dissected plateau which slopes down towards lower land on the east coast. The highest mountains are mostly on the western edge and lie in the path of rain-bearing winds from the southwest. These western mountains, therefore, have heavy rain (the core of the Highlands receive over 2500 mm and is the wettest part of the British Isles), but is relatively mild. The heaviest snowfall occurs in the Cairngorms (in the colder centre of Northern Scotland). The range forms the highest land in the United Kingdom. They were estimated to receive around 200 000 visitors in the summer season of 1987. The scenery and remoteness are the most important qualities valued by walkers in the area. In winter the upper slopes keep enough

snow to support a ski industry centred on Aviemore, but the high cost and unreliable climate make it a relatively unattractive destination for southerners compared to Alpine packages. The Cairngorms appear to cater for more local demand.

The West Coast is rocky and deeply indented. The inlets (known as sea lochs) have a landscape reminiscent of fjords (though not on the dramatic scale of the Norwegian coast). There are many islands along the west coast; Skye is the most developed for tourism, although Mull, Jura, Islay and Arran are also popular. Many locations in the Highlands are also associated with Scotland's romantic history and folklore, for example Glencoe, Skye and Loch Ness.

The country is sparsely populated and the main industry for many of the small villages on the West Coast is now tourism. Inverness is the main urban centre and gateway to the Highlands.

The offshore islands (the Outer Hebrides, Orkney and Shetland) are accessible by air and sea but are less frequently visited. The east coast of Northern Scotland is drier and sunnier than the west but still averages less than five hours sunshine per day in August, and July temperatures average between 13 and 14° C. This effectively rules out beach tourism on any significant scale in Northern Scotland. Landscape and activity holidays (hill walking, skiing, fishing, golf and climbing) are climatically more appropriate.

3 The southern uplands. These uplands, like the Highlands consist of the denuded remains of an ancient range of mountains; the landscapes consist of rounded hills and moorlands, forests and rolling agricultural landscapes in the lower areas. They serve the local leisure needs of the population of Scotland's Central Lowlands, but are largely bypassed by tourists from the south on their way to Glasgow, Edinburgh or the Highlands.

Wales

The more southerly location of Wales makes beach tourism possible. The coast receives only a little more rain than southwest England but the mountains inland generate orographic rainfall and totals increase rapidly inland to average over 1525 mm pa in the higher areas. The coastline averages 5.5–6.0 hours' sunshine a day in August compared to 6–7 hours in southwest England) and the best beaches average between 14.5 and 16.5° C in July.

The Principality is much more accessible to the English market; its landscape, coast and historic resources are more heavily used by English visitors. The best beaches are located in the Gower peninsula (South Wales), the Pembrokeshire National Park (in the southwest of Wales), in the Isle of Anglesey and the Lleyn Peninsula in the northwest, and along the north Wales coast. The latter is close to the Merseyside conurbation and has a string of traditional resorts, e.g. Rhyll, Llandudno and Colwyn Bay. The Rhyll Suncentre is the leading attraction.

Much of the coast of Central Wales is cliffed and the beaches are inaccessible around Aberystwyth and Barmouth, which were both developed to cater for visitors from the Midlands conurbations. There are good surf beaches in the southwest-facing coves in South and West Wales. The undeveloped estuaries around the coast of Wales are ideal for boating activities and there is great pressure to develop them for marinas.

Wales has a wealth of historic resources, notably the medieval castles, such as Caernarfon, Conway, Chepstow, Pembroke, Harlech and Beaumaris. Heritage attractions based on Welsh industry and crafts have also been successfully promoted (such as the Llechwedd slate caverns in Snowdonia, and the Big Pit mining museum in South Wales). As in other parts of the UK, redundant docks in Swansea and Cardiff have been redeveloped for tourism and watersports. The landscapes of Wales are sparsely populated and unspoilt. Southwest Wales is subdued (the land is basically a dissected plateau) and more intensively cultivated than much of the rest of Wales. Even so, many holdings are small and of marginal profitability. Many farms and cottages are sold at relatively low prices and become second homes for the English, much to the annoyance of many of the local people.

The problem of rural depopulation and the replacement of locals by temporary residents is more acute in the more accessible but agricultural harsher environments of the Central Uplands, and particularly Snowdonia. These landscapes are scenically more attractive than southwest Wales and are much closer to the conurbations of the Midlands and Northwest England. Central Wales is mountainous with stretches of forest, remote rounded grassy uplands and deep valleys. The Elan Valley has been flooded and the reservoir lake adds interest but its fluctuating water level sometimes mars the landscape. Apart from the second-home owners, this part of Wales is generally bypassed by visitors who prefer the coast or the more dramatic landscapes of the Snowdonia National Park in North Wales. Gwynedd is Wales's major tourist region and has by far the greatest concentration of hotel bedspaces.

The Snowdonia region has an ideal combination of outstanding landscape, good beaches nearby, historical attractions (ranging from Harlech Castle to Criccieth (Lloyd George's birthplace) and from the Ffestiniog Railway to water-powered wool mills, weaving Welsh tapestry) and opportunities for activity holidays (e.g. pony trekking and climbing). For the less active, Snowdon's summit is accessible by the mountain railway.

The third National Park in Wales is the Brecon Beacons (adjacent to the heavily populated region of South Wales). Its inland location and less dramatic landscapes of rounded grassy mountains make it a less popular destination than Snowdonia. However, it is particularly noted for its activity holidays which include pony trekking, hill walking, lake sailing, canoeing and pot holing in the caves of the limestone region on the southern edge of the Park. The Park is also used for day visiting from the South Wales towns, and new opportunities for countryside recreation (e.g. Aberdare and Afan Argoed Country Parks) have been created in the reclaimed industrial valleys of South Wales between the towns and the Brecon Beacons.

The remainder of the UK

1 The Province of Northern Ireland has great tourist potential. It has miles of undeveloped coast and countryside, though it shares an unfavourably wet and cloudy climate with northern England. Political unrest and terrorist activity have effectively inhibited tourist developments since 1970.

2 The Isle of Man (located in the Irish Sea at a similar latitude) also has attractive landscape and coastal resources but its relative inaccessibility constrains tourist development.

3 The Channel Islands are located off the French coast, due south of west Dorset and consequently have a slight climatic advantage over most of the English coast. Between May and August maximum temperatures reach 20° C and sunshine averages eight or nine hours a day. The islands are accessible by both air and ferry. Development in the islands is strictly controlled and they offer quiet undeveloped coasts and an old-fashioned and relaxing pace of life. No cars are allowed on the smaller islands of Herm and Sark, and there is a maximum speed limit of 30 mph on Alderney.

Overseas trips from the UK (1988)		
	Summer season (million trips)	**Winter season (million trips)**
Visiting friends and relatives	1.95	1.24
Holidays	14.47	6.05
Business trips	1.73	1.94
Other (inc. shopping educational, sporting etc.)	0.54	0.43
Total	**18.69 m**	**9.66 m**

Fig 17.22 UK outbound tourism

UK outbound tourism

Travel abroad from the UK has grown rapidly since 1970, and the majority of the trips (82 per cent in 1988) were for holidays (*see* Fig 17.22). Although Britain has a wealth of attractive beaches and varied countryside, the weather is so unreliable that the British people prefer to travel abroad to a coast where sunshine is guaranteed. Visits abroad by the British substantially outnumber overseas trips to Britain; this pattern was also set in the 1970s and has been maintained into the 1990s.

Holidays taken by the British abroad are likely to be twice as long as domestic visits, and expenditure per trip is proportionally even higher: the average cost of a holiday of over four nights in Britain was £109 in 1987, while a comparable foreign holiday cost £425 including the cost of travel. However, cheap fares and a stronger pound has made foreign holidays relatively cheap in the late 1980s. A strong pound encourages the shift from domestic to overseas tourism, while also making Britain a less attractive destination for foreign visitors.

Summer holidays overseas tend to be spread over a relatively long season in order to avoid the worst congestion at airports and at continental resorts. Threequarters of these holidaymakers travel by air and 64 per cent of the trips are package tours. Hotels are the most favoured form of accommodation (often the larger modern hotels in the resorts). Spain, France and Greece are the most popular summer destinations (*see* Fig 17.23).

Beach holidays are the most important, with the majority of visitors to Spain, Greece, Portugal, Yugoslavia, Tunisia (and since 1987 Turkey) taking two-week coastal resort holidays. During the 1980s Spain has maintained its share of sun-

Destination	'000 trips	*Destination of British foreign holidays* Million nights	% travel by air	% inclusive tours	Expenditure per night (£) excluding fares
Spain	4 393	57.9	92	70	19.1
France	2 419	27.4	16	45	18.7
Greece	1 606	21.4	99	84	20.1
Irish Republic	749	6.2	21	0	17.9
Italy	713	9.8	77	62	21.3
Portugal	604	8.4	98	66	20.9
Yugoslavia	588	7.2	–	–	–
West Germany	476	5.5	46	28	20.0
Total (inc other destinations)	15 058	214.1			

Fig 17.23 UK summer holidays abroad (1987)

Destination	000 trips	% inclusive tours	Main holiday type
Spain (inc Canary Is)	1 945	71	Winter sun
Portugal (inc Madeira)	265	69	Winter sun
Greece	208	82	Winter sun
Austria	330	85	Winter sports
Switzerland	145	55	Winter sports
France	945	50	Winter sports/city breaks
Italy	221	73	Winter sports/city breaks
Irish Republic	410	0	Visiting friends/relatives
West Germany	258	22	Visiting friends/relatives and city breaks
Total (including other destinations)	6 858		

Fig 17.24 Winter season holidays abroad (1987/8)

sea-sand holidays (at about 45 per cent of all beach holidays) but Greece and Yugoslavia have rapidly become more popular, with an increase of 21 per cent and 24 per cent per annum respectively in their numbers of British visitors from 1983 to 1987. Beach tourism, particularly in the form of inclusive tours, is growing rapidly and the promotion of new destinations such as Turkey is helping to meet this demand. Italy, being slightly more expensive, has shown a decline of 0.7 per cent in the number of British visitors, and is losing its market share in the face of this new competition. The numbers of British travelling to France has remained little changed during the 1980s, but it provides a much wider range of holidays from shopping trips, camping or caravan touring, rural farmhouse/gites holidays as well as beach tourism, which appeal to the more mobile and independent British holiday-maker. Visits to the Irish Republic and to West Germany are predominantly visits to friends and relatives.

Winter holidays show a greater diversity of types of holiday and of destination. It is estimated that about 40 per cent of winter trips were to winter sun destinations, 15 per cent for winter sports, 15 per cent for city breaks and 18 per cent visiting friends and relatives.

Long-haul travel

A substantial proportion (43 per cent) of long-haul trips made by the British are to North America. The numbers fluctuate from year to year depending on the relative strengths of the dollar and the pound. In 1987/88 there were 1.12 million trips, 729 000 (64 per cent) of which were summer season visits. A high proportion of these summer visits were for beach holidays: Miami is now a more important gateway into the USA than New York for British summer visitors. Winter visitors also seek winter sun holidays, but around a third of all trips to North America are to visit friends and relatives. Visits average around 23–25 days (much longer than European trips) and only about 18 per cent use inclusive tours. Long-haul travel to other parts of the world is much more evenly spread throughout the year (with over 700 000 trips in both the summer and winter seasons). As high a proportion as 37 per cent of the trips are to friends and relatives, for example in Australia, New Zealand, India and the Caribbean. However, 33 per cent of these long-haul trips are inclusive tours: a great variety of packages are now available, ranging from wildlife safaris in East Africa, trips down the Nile to see the Egyptian temples and tombs, cultural trips to Bali, Himalayan treks, and winter sun holidays to exotic destinations such as The Gambia, Thailand and the Caribbean. Most of these trips are high cost holidays, often over £2000 (1988 prices).

Republic of Ireland

Ireland is the remaining outlying region of northwest Europe. It is relatively isolated from the tourist resources and tourist markets of mainland Europe. Its extreme westerly Atlantic location puts it at an immediate climatic disadvantage when competing for international tourists. The winters are mild but the summer weather is cool and is as variable as England, but

	Av temp °C	Rainfall mm
Jan	6.6	139
Feb	6.6	132
Mar	7.1	114
Apr	9.0	94
May	11.0	81
June	14.0	81
July	15.0	96
Aug	15.0	122
Sept	14.0	104
Oct	11.0	142
Nov	9.0	139
Dec	8.0	167

Fig 17.25 Valentia's climate

it is always wetter (*see* Fig 17.25). Valentia is located in the extreme southwest of Ireland. Its climate is far from ideal but is typical of the southwest which is Ireland's leading tourist region (*see* Fig 17.26). However, the mild, moist climate does allow plant growth virtually all year round, making the landscapes particularly green.

The most attractive and popular scenic re-sources are in the west. The coast here is very indented with many bays and drowned valleys, for example in the Cork and Kerry region, and numerous offshore islands (e.g. Galway and Connemara). Ireland's mountains are also located in groups around the coast, e.g. the Twelve Pins in Connemara, the mountains of Kerry, and Wicklow just south of Dublin. Many of these landscapes are quite unspoilt and not very intensively used for tourism. The centre of Ireland is an expanse of rather featureless flat or rolling landscapes, and is the least popular tourist region of Ireland (*see* Fig 17.26).

	% of tourist revenue
Southwest	21.8 – includes Cork and Kerry
Dublin	18.8 – major cultural centre
West	13.0 – includes Connemara
Southeast	11.8 the Wicklows and Dublin's
East	10.2 hinterland
Northwest	9.6
Mid-West	8.4
Midlands	6.5 – the featureless interior

Fig 17.26 Spatial distribution of tourism in Ireland (1986)

The total volume of tourism to Ireland hovered around 2.5 million in the 1980s but reached 2.66

million in 1987. Its main market is the UK. Seventy per cent of its visitors came from England, Scotland, Wales plus Northern Ireland, but few (less than 30 per cent) visited Ireland for their main holiday. Most (57 per cent) were visiting friends and relatives and 23 per cent came on business. Many Irish have emigrated over the years in response to Ireland's economic problems and lack of jobs, and it is these people, or their descendents who make up the bulk of Ireland's visitors. The spatial distribution of this type of tourism will depend more on the residence of the friends and relatives than the natural resources of the country, although many VFR trips are combined with holiday trips.

The Irish also emigrated to the USA in search of work, so the USA is the next most important source of Ireland's tourists. Nearly 400 000 visitors from America spent time in Ireland in 1987: about 10 per cent of these were Irish natives, another 15 per cent had Irish parents and 51 per cent had some ethnic link to Ireland. The American tourists were the highest spending visitors to Ireland, and Ireland has been vigorously marketed in the USA. In spite of the political differences between the Republic of Ireland and Northern Ireland the tourist boards of the two parts of Ireland have combined to market a joint Irish package to the Americans.

The 'troubles' in Northern Ireland began in 1969 and resulted in a drastic reduction of tourism from the UK to the Republic of Ireland, from which it has only recently started to recover. Nevertheless, there is a large volume of day-tripping from Northern Ireland to the Republic: in 1986 this was estimated to be 7.4 million.

QUESTIONS AND DISCUSSION POINTS

1 Describe the trends in British domestic and outbound tourism. Do you expect these trends to continue?
2 What explanations can be put forward to explain the fact that a very high proportion of England's domestic tourists take holidays in the region where they live?
3 What geographical disadvantages does Britain experience when trying to attract European tourists? To what extent can good marketing overcome these disadvantages?

ASSIGNMENTS

1 (*a*) You are the tourism officer employed by the County Council of one of the English counties (you may specify which one). The districts in the county and the county itself have made financial contributions to a fund earmarked for a programme to jointly market the tourist attractions of the county. The steering group has asked you to prepare and present a paper at their first meeting. It should identify the character of the country and its constituent districts and suggest a theme around which its attractions should be marketed. Be prepared to explain the reasons for your proposal at the meeting.

(*b*) *Several months later*. The steering group has decided on the theme, the target market/s, and the main media to be used (leaflets plus adverts and articles in the local/regional press). Again you have been asked to do some research and prepare a paper for the next meeting. Your brief this time is to investigate where the county's current tourists come from, and to suggest where the promotional material should be distributed (i.e. countrywide or targeting particular regions of the country, or indeed overseas). Again, you are expected to make a brief presentation to the meeting, explaining the reasons for your recommendations.

2 You work for a new UK-based tour company 'Culture Vultures' specialising in tours for inbound tourists to Britain's historic and cultural centres. The company acknowledges that it must include the most popular destinations in Britain but it is company policy to introduce some less well known, less crowded and less commercialised destinations in its tours where possible. Your chief executive has asked you to draw up itineraries suitable in length and choice of attractions for:
(*a*) Visitors from the USA;
(*b*) Japanese parties; and
(*c*) The German market.

3 You are responsible for organising the international conference on 'New Opportunities for Tourism in Europe'. You expect several hundred delegates to attend; you cannot miss the chance to demonstrate the best of the new developments in tourism in Britain to this international audience. You can do this by your choice of conference venue (to demonstrate the accessibility, convenience and suitability of Britain as a conference venue), and by organising two half-day trips from the venue to examples of new British attractions or tourist initiatives that represent the best of the new opportunities for tourism in Britain. These trips are part of the conference programme.

Select a suitable conference venue, demonstrating its accessibility and the quality of its conference facilities and accommodation. Construct the itineraries for the two half-day trips, making sure they fulfil the above requirements and also give the delegates an enjoyable experience.

Northwest Europe: Scandinavia

LEARNING OBJECTIVES

After reading this chapter you should be able to:

- assess the tourist potential of the climatic, landscape, historical and cultural resources of Scandinavia
- distinguish the regional distribution of these geographical resources and their development and use for tourism
- demonstrate a knowledge of the main tourist resorts and tourist centres
- understand the role of Scandinavia in the general pattern of European tourism
- be aware of the constraints imposed on the development of tourism in Scandinavia by its climate and latitude
- be aware of the political and economic organisation of Scandinavian countries and the consequences for tourism within and between Scandinavian countries.

Introduction

The region consists of the countries of Norway, Sweden, Finland, Denmark and Iceland, a wide region of some variation but with a strong common cultural identity.

Scandinavia lies well to the northwest of the industrial and urban core of Europe; Copenhagen (Scandinavia's most southerly capital) lies at approximately the same latitude as Edinburgh, and one third of Scandinavian territory is north of the Arctic Circle. The influence of this northerly latitude on climate and tourism is profound. The region has long, harsh, dark winters with 19½ hours of total darkness in December in Lappland. The summers are brief and cool, although they enjoy prolonged daylight (18½ hours in Stockholm in June).

The popular perceptions of the landscapes of Scandinavia are dominated by the images of dramatic fjords in Norway, the ice caps and volcanoes of Iceland, the lakes and forests of Finland and the quieter, agricultural landscapes of Denmark. These perceptions are partly based on fact but in reality there is a greater variety of landscape types in the region.

In spite of having dramatic and varied coasts and landscapes, which are sparsely populated and largely unspoilt, Scandinavia has few international tourists from outside its own boundaries, for which the unfavourable climate and short season are two explanations.

These environmental influences are reinforced by economic factors; Scandinavians enjoy a very high standard of living and thus show high propensities for travel (*see* Fig 18.1). But the countries are seen by other Europeans as expensive destinations when compared to the sunny and relatively cheap Mediterranean. On the other hand, Scandinavians show a strong tendency to travel to the resorts of Greece and Spain, particularly for winter sun holidays, as well as frequent travel between their respective countries.

Cultural unity

Scandinavia lay outside the influence of the ancient world of the Mediterranean: it was never incorporated into the Roman world; and it was remote from the main cultural centres of medieval Europe (*see* Chapter 5). Its cultural roots and cultural unity stem from the development of the Viking culture 800 AD–1100 AD, which spread from the Baltic region throughout Finland, Sweden, Norway and Denmark. Their seafaring, piratical and trading way of life led them to colonise the Faroe Islands between 820–900 AD, Iceland and Greenland (877 AD) and, around 1000 AD, reached North America. The core regions of Viking settlement, where most of the historic relics are situated, were the Helsinki coast of Finland, Stockholm and its hinterland, the islands and east coast of Denmark and pockets of colonisation round the Norwegian coast, for example Oslo, Bergen and Trondheim.

From Viking times to the 19th century, the political development of the region has been characterised by the development and expansion of power, stagnation and decline of various parts of Scandinavia – for example, Denmark was dominant in the 13–14th centuries, and Sweden from 1400 to 1800.

Due to its isolation and inaccessibility, the region was largely bypassed by the industrial revolution and the internal development of the Scandinavian countries have not been greatly influenced from outside. Nordic co-operation stems from 1856, though this did not become expressed in legal terms until 1962 (the Helsinki Agreement) whereby many of the laws of the countries have been harmonised. Citizens of Nordic countries do not need work permits and customs regulations are co-ordinated. Passports are not routinely checked which means that travel for Scandinavians between Scandinavian countries is very easy and the area is basically one whole domestic tourism unit.

Travel for Scandinavians between their countries is also made physically easier by co-operation in the planning, provision and management of the transport infrastructure. For example, the airlines of Denmark, Norway and Sweden were merged in 1951 to form the Scandinavian Airlines System (SAS). In the Öresund region (the channel between Copenhagen and Sweden) transport and urban planning is co-ordinated to provide good links and ease travel between Denmark and Sweden. There are four ferry routes across the sound which carry high volumes of passenger traffic (e.g. 21 million ferry passengers in 1982).

Scandinavia as a tourist generating area

The region has a relatively small population – 22.8 million in 1988 (*see* Fig 18.1) but the Scandinavian countries are among the most affluent in the world.

They appear to owe their affluence to a healthy mining and manufacturing sector and the willingness of the workforce to retrain and acquire the new skills needed for a modern economy, although the economy was hit hard by the recession in 1981 and 1982.

The population as a whole has a high level of holiday entitlement (five weeks plus) and holiday making, but much use is made of rural and coastal second homes, located in the sparsely populated countryside not far from the cities. Thus, self-catering family holidays form the bulk of domestic tourism. The total volume of domestic

	1988 GDP per head US dollars	1988 population (millions)	1984 % owning a second home in own country	Holiday departure rate – 1980–86 (4 nights +)
Norway	13 890	4.2	55%	72–77%
Sweden	11 890	8.4	45%	71–93%
Denmark	11 240	5.1	29%	64 %
Finland	10 870	4.9	–	43 %
Iceland	10 720	0.2		

Fig 18.1 Levels of affluence and tourist generation in Scandinavia

tourism is shown in Fig 18.2.

Outdoor activities are particularly popular with the Scandinavians, for example over 70 per cent of Swedes take part in one or more active pursuits, such as swimming, boating, climbing, fishing and sledging, and 68 per cent go ski touring. Business travel is growing, particularly since 1982.

	Domestic nights in hotels and registered supplementary accommodation (million)
Sweden	25.83
Norway	11.36
Denmark	11.60
Finland	8.85

Fig 18.2 Domestic tourism – Scandinavia (1987)

Because of the ease of travel for nationals within Scandinavia, comprehensive data on tourism between Scandinavian countries does not exist. However, Fig 18.3 would suggest that at least one third to one half of the foreign arrivals are travellers from within Scandinavia, and the

governments of Norway, Sweden, Denmark and Finland have encouraged their tourist boards to promote 'stay at home' Scandinavian holiday-making. The cultural affinity between the countries reinforces the tendency to travel within Scandinavia and the harmonisation of laws and the co-operation between the countries makes it easy.

Physical and climatic resources of Scandinavia

Physically, the region consists of a series of countries grouped round the enclosed Baltic Sea, plus two groups of North Atlantic islands (Iceland and the Faroes) which have climates and cultures in common with Baltic Scandinavia.

Baltic Scandinavia

Physically and climatically, the region can be split into three district sub-divisions.

1 The western fjord coast and Scandinavian mountains – a ridge that forms the backbone of

From	% foreign nights to Denmark/Finland hotels only	Iceland arrivals at frontiers (%)	Norway nights hotels only (%)	Sweden nights registered accommodation (%)
Denmark	–	12.5	16.3	9.1
Finland	2.4	2.4	2.7	8.5
Norway	15.5	7.8	–	34.3
Sweden	22.7	12.1	14.0	
% total nights arrivals	40.6	34.8	33.0	51.9

Fig 18.3 Travel between Scandinavian countries 1987

the Norwegian–Swedish peninsula;
2 The lower lands surrounding the Baltic; and
3 Denmark.

The Scandinavian mountains and fjord coast

The highest part of the mountain chain hugs the west coast, with the two highest groups of peaks lying at opposite ends of the chain. In the far north, the mountains rise to just over 2100 m, while the middle section round Trondheim Fjord is a little lower. The highest peaks (2481 m) are found in the Jotunfjell mountains at the southern end of the chain.

During the last glaciation the thickest part of the Scandinavian ice cap was centred on these mountains. The immense erosive power of the ice gouged out deep steep-sided valleys as the ice cap spread and flowed outwards under the force of its own weight.

Peaks with typical alpine landscape of rocky ridges, sharp peaks and crests stand out above the valleys, creating a dramatic landscape with very high relative relief (up to 1500 m).

The lower sections of the glaciated valley systems were flooded by the sea after the ice cap melted creating the classic fjord coastal landscape, fringed by a whole series of offshore skerries and islands. The narrowest and longest fjords are to be found on the coast of the southern half of the mountain chain. In the north they are a little wider, though they still create magnificent landscapes. The lower slopes of the mountains are clad in coniferous forests, with pockets of fertile farmland. The climate of the higher peaks and of the northern mountains is too cold for trees, which give way to open arctic and tundra vegetation.

Climatically the region is wet, windy, cloudy and short of sunshine, but the coast is not so cold in winter as the rest of Scandinavia. The mountains lie across the path of the prevailing westerly winds which bring comparatively mild moist Atlantic air onto the west coast (*see* Fig 18.4). This air rises over the mountains producing a great deal of turbulence, cloud and orographic precipitation (up to 2057 mm per annum in Bergen, and even 4000 mm in the northern snowfields) much of which falls as snow on the mountains in winter. The coast, however, is normally kept ice-free in winter due to the north atlantic drift (*see* Fig 18.5). The region receives the heaviest rainfall of the whole of Scandinavia.

Fig 18.4 **July temperatures in Scandinavia**

Fig 18.5 **January temperatures in Scandinavia**

The summer is also cool and cloudy, with average temperatures below 15° C in July.

Unfortunately, this region which has such superb coastal and landscaped qualities lacks a climate suitable for mass tourism.

The lower lands surrounding the Baltic: the continental interior

The eastern flanks of the mountains drop away gradually to the lowlands fringing the Baltic. The mountains are cut by straighter glaciated NW-SE valleys, often with lakes in them, draining into the Baltic, or into the North Sea in southern Norway.

In sharp contrast to the mountains, the lowlands are characterised by very low relative relief (generally under 100 m); and due to the scouring action of the spreading ice sheets, they no longer have any clearly defined valleys. Water, therefore, cannot escape to the sea and floods the shallow depressions in the land surface to form the intricate and extensive lake systems, so characteristic of the Finnish lake district and of southern Sweden.

A band of distinctive 'fissure valley landscape' runs diagonally across southern Finland and southern Sweden. Here, the land surface is cut by a network of narrow steep-sided valleys and hollows, frequently lake – filled, interspersed with plateau-like blocks of often bare ice scoured rock.

At the coast, this landscape creates a very beautiful series of islands, for example in South-west Finland, Åland and Stockholm, the latter stretch being much used by Stockholmers for summer holidays. On the west coast of Sweden there are greater accumulations of sand between the rocky stretches and this is again popular for domestic tourism and is known as Sweden's 'Golden Coast', (see Fig 18.6).

In spite of its northerly latitude, the summer climate of this part of Scandinavia is favourable for coastal tourism. It is both much drier and warmer than the west-facing fjord coast of Norway. As the westerly air flow passes over the mountain crest, the turbulence dies down, the winds drop and the now relatively dry air subsides into the Baltic region and the cloud melts away. Thus, on the east side of the Scandinavian mountains the rainfall totals are low and decrease from south to north (e.g. Gothenberg and Oslo in the south have 711 mm

and 584 mm rainfall per annum respectively, while the north end of the Midnight Sun Coast (on the Gulf of Bothnia) has only about 317 mm). Although there is a summer (July/August) maximum, this falls in short, thundery outbursts that interrupt the generally sunny weather.

The combination of low cloud cover and high latitude (with long hours of daylight) give high annual sunshine totals (over 2100 hours a year) and average summer temperatures climb to 18° C in Southeast Finland in July and daily maxima may reach 25–30° C – near the temperatures reached in the Mediterranean. However, the summer season is short and winters are intensely cold; the Baltic and Gulf of Bothnia freeze over in winter.

Denmark

Denmark's landscape and coast are very different to those of the rest of Scandinavia. The gently undulating landscape is subdued; more than half the country is below 30 m, and around 70 per cent of the countryside consists of man-made agricultural landscapes. The coast is a more significant leisure resource, and the country has 7300 km of beaches. The west coast is fringed by a continuous 320 km stretch of sand dunes, which enclose lagoons on their landward side. The strong offshore currents sometimes make seabathing dangerous here and the coast is not extensively developed for tourism. The Baltic coast (on the east) and the islands provide a mixture of open bays, deep inlets and good beaches, providing ideal conditions for sailing and other water sports. The most developed section of the coast (the Danish 'riviera') lies between Copenhagen and Helsingor.

Spatial distribution of tourism in Scandinavia

Norway

Oslo and its hinterland is the focus of Norway's domestic and international tourism. Oslo is the capital, and is the cultural and artistic centre of the country. It is, for example, the location of folk, maritime and whaling museums, and Viking remains and burial mounds are found locally. The hinterland of Oslo is also significant for domestic tourism. Nearly 30 per cent of

Fig 18.6 Main tourist regions of Scandinavia

Norway's domestic hotel nights (1984) were spent in the series of forested valleys which run from the flanks of the Dovrefjell, Jotunheim and Hardanger Plateau down to the Oslo fjord (Norway's Eastern Valleys, *see* Fig 18.6). The valleys are thus easily accessible from Oslo and provide for a wide variety of scenic and activity holidays. Winter and summer skiing activities are enjoyed at the resorts in the upper reaches of the valleys, e.g. at Tynset in the upper Glomma valley, and summer activities such as walking, riding and all water sports in the middle and lower sections of the valleys, e.g. at Kongsvinger, Elverum and Rena in the lower Glomma valley.

The other tourist regions are centred around Bergen in the Western Fjords, where nearly 10 per cent are domestic hotel nights; the Telemark coast where bathing beaches are interspersed with rocky coasts and harbours (seven per cent domestic hotel nights); and the Trondheim region (five per cent nights) (*see* Fig 18.6)

Sweden

In Sweden, tourist activity is more widely spread. Stockholm and its hinterland is, of course, the main centre for both domestic and international tourists. In addition to the city night life, the region includes the archipelago of over 2000 islands just offshore, many of which are accessible by boat, and provide opportunities for scenic and water sports tourism. The Stockholm and Uppsala area receives nearly 17 per cent of domestic tourist nights (hotels and supplementary forms of accommodation). The next most popular region is the Golden Coast (*see* Fig 18.6) which includes a 400 km stretch of sandy coast with excellent beaches mixed with a variety of other coastal landscapes. It accounts for over 14 per cent of domestic tourism. The other three main tourist regions of Sweden – the Swedish lakes, the Glass Country (the centre of Swedish glass-making) and the Midnight Coast – are about equal in popularity with the domestic market, each taking about 10 per cent of the domestic trade.

Finland

Finland shows the same differences between international and domestic tourism as the other Scandinavian countries. International arrivals are strongly concentrated on the capital, Helsinki, (46.6 per cent arrivals in 1984) at the expense of the rest of the country, whereas Helsinki accounted for only 18 per cent of domestic tourism. A third of domestic tourists makes for the inland lakeside venues throughout the Finnish lake district; international visitors tend to reach only the lakes just inland of Helsinki. A further 15 per cent of domestic overnight stays are in the northern territories, i.e. Lappland and the Finnish Midnight Sun Coast, whereas only 9 per cent of international visitors venture so far north.

Tourism in all three countries is very strongly seasonal (*see* Fig 18.7).

Overseas visitors.	% Bednights 1984		
	Finland	**Norway**	**Sweden**
April	5.1	3.8	2.6
May	8.4	6.1	3.8
June	13.7	15.4	11.6
July	17.1	21.0	39.7
August	16.0	17.9	22.5
September	8.6	7.6	4.9
October	6.5	3.8	3.5

Fig 18.7 Seasonality of Scandinavia's tourism

Domestic tourism is also peaked in the summer season June–August but not so strongly, for example 30.8 per cent Swedish domestic tourism is in July and 12.6 per cent in August. This inevitably leads to low overall occupancy rates, ranging from a low of 35.7 per cent for Swedish hotels in 1984 to a high of 53.2 per cent for Finland. A range of types of accommodation is available, from hotels, farmhouses, self-catering chalet villages and forest cabins, to well equipped camp sites.

About 60 per cent of travel in Scandinavia is by Scandinavians, and 40 per cent comes from outside the region. Non-Scandinavians rely mainly on the hotels, and the majority of these tourists come from the adjacent north European countries, but surprisingly large numbers come from North America. However, there was extensive immigration from Scandinavia to USA in the 19th century, and these cultural ties are still strong.

| From | Foreign tourist bednights ('000) to | | | |
	Denmark (hotels) 1987	Finland (hotels) 1984	Norway (hotels) 1987	Sweden (registered accommodation) 1987
West Germany	943	278	505	1194
UK	304	108	346	301
Netherlands	100	44	120	375
France	76	59	119	146
North America	444	185	457	395
Switzerland	–	80		76
Italy	88	45		108
USSR	–	246		–
Other Scandinavian	1896	762	733	3680
Total	4480	2113	3865	7089

Fig 18.8 International tourism in Scandinavian

Outbound travel by Scandinavians in contrast is not primarily to the adjacent North European countries. If Scandinavians travel outside their own region they make for the sun. Spain and Greece account for over 60 per cent of all the inclusive tours by charter aircraft in 1985.

| Destination | % travellers in 1985 from | | |
	Finland	Norway	Sweden
Spain	41.9	50.5	41
Greece	24.3	20.1	19
Cyprus		4.8	7
UK		7.3	6
Italy	8.16	2.6	4
France		2.6	4

Fig 18.9 Scandinavian outbound tourism

A substantial proportion of the flights to Spanish territory are to the winter sun resorts in the Canary Islands. Thirty per cent of all the Norwegian tour passengers and 26 per cent of Finnish package tourists are bound for the Canaries, providing an escape from the gloom of the Scandinavian winter.

Tourism in Denmark

Denmark's unexceptional physical resources do not make it a significant tourist destination on European terms. Nevertheless, the volume of its incoming tourism is on a par with that of Sweden or Finland. The majority of its visitors (36 per cent of bednights) are by Scandinavians, but it relies heavily on the West German market for 28 per cent of bednights. Its extensive coastline and its common border with Germany make it an attractive destination of German coastal tourists, and West Germans account for 60 per cent of all camping bednights in Denmark. For other nationalities, it is the cultural and historical heritage of the country that is the main attraction. It has many attractive villages and castles, and as it still has a constitutional monarchy, there are palaces and pageantry associated with the royal family. There are also several Viking museums, e.g. at Helsingor and Copenhagen. Copenhagen is the main focus of international tourism. Apart from its historic attractions, the city is famous for its breweries and for the Tivoli Gardens (a major and old established amusement and theme park).

Iceland

Although Iceland is culturally part of Scandinavia and it shares a northerly latitude (just south of the Arctic Circle), it is physically nearer Greenland. Its isolation and character make it a very specialist destination, with only very few international visitors (only 128 800 in 1988).

The island stands astride the central ridge running down the length of the Atlantic Ocean, marking the zone where the ocean floor is splitting and spreading, as the continents of

Europe and North America drift further apart. As the earth's crust split, molten rock escaped from the seabed which built up to form Iceland. As this process is still active, there are intermittent volcanic events on the island which have created a landscape of mountains, lava fields, geothermal springs, geysers and bubbling mud holes.

The older volcanic landforms have been modified by glaciation, and the mountains are blanketed with snow in winter. The coast has a fjord-type landscape, particularly in the northwest. Much of the island is uninhabited, with the majority of the 250 000 population concentrated in the capital, Reykjavik, or other small coastal settlements. Much of the island is untouched wilderness. Its particular appeal is its unpolluted environment, its landscape, geology and wildlife. Its tourist season, in common with Norway, Sweden and Finland, is short, perhaps even shorter than countries with culturally based tourism, as access to the mountains is often by unsealed roads which are often unpassable until well into the summer months. Accommodation in the remoter parts is basic (simple farmhouses, youth hostels or huts), although there are first class hotels in Reykjavik.

In 1988 47 per cent of Iceland's visitors came from other Scandinavian countries, 27 per cent from USA, 12 per cent from West Germany and 8 per cent from the UK.

QUESTIONS AND DISCUSSION POINTS

1 'The attractions of Norway and Sweden appeal to such a specialised market that these countries will never attract very large numbers of non-Scandinavian visitors'. Discuss whether you think this is a true or a false statement.
2 In 1985 it was estimated that Denmark received roughly 15 million day excursionists, 5 million direct transit travellers and only 5 million staying visitors. To what extent does Denmark's size and geographical location explain this pattern of inbound tourism?
3 List the most popular foreign holiday destinations of the Scandinavian market. Offer explanations for this pattern of outbound tourism from Scandinavia.

ASSIGNMENTS

1 A newly set up tour company called 'Scandal' specialises in tours for the UK market in Scandinavia. Currently they offer tours to the main urban centres (Copenhagen, Oslo and Stockholm). They have commissioned you as a consultant to write a short report outlining the geographical potential of the rest of Norway, Sweden and Denmark for tourism, the types of holidays that might take advantage of this potential, the seasons of the year in which such holidays might best be offered, and the potential market. Make recommendations as to how the company could develop a range of new tours to complement its city tours.

2 You work for a cruise company that is considering a plan to develop cruises in the Baltic. You have been asked to assess the geographical opportunities and constraints on such developments. Write a preliminary report:

(a) describing the climate of the Baltic and indicating the months during which cruises would be most attractive. Note any other constraints that might limit the operation of such cruises;

(b) listing the places of interest that could feature on the itineraries and the nature of their special interest;

(c) identifying the markets to whom such cruises might appeal; and

(d) recommending whether or not you think the company should go ahead with more detailed investigations and aim to develop such cruises.

Africa and the Middle East

This section seeks to answer the following questions.

1 What is the volume, character and spatial pattern of tourist activity in the continent of Africa and the Middle East?

2 What is the role of the region in the general pattern of world tourism?

3 What and where are the region's tourist resources?

4 What are the long-term economic and political problems that inhibit the expansion of tourism in the region?

The whole of the region lies in the economic periphery of the world, and is characterised by generally low levels of tourism (poorly developed or non-existant domestic markets, and very limited in- and outbound international tourism). The region is beset with political and economic problems: many of its countries are politically unstable, and consequently the region has many recent or ongoing civil wars. There are also longstanding international disputes between certain countries in the region. Nevertheless, the region has outstanding tourist resources that are promoted for international tourism where local political circumstances allow.

The region falls into two zones, divided by the natural barrier of the Saharan and Arabian deserts. The northern part, described in Chapter 19, consists of the mainly Islamic countries of the Middle East and the countries bordering the east and south Mediterranean (from Syria to Morocco). Functionally, however, this part of Africa and the Middle East belongs to the European tourist region.

The other half of the continent, described in Chapter 20, lies south of the Sahara desert and is known as Subsaharan Africa. It extends roughly from latitude 15° N to the Cape of Good Hope; and also includes the islands off the African coast (in the western half of the Indian Ocean). In terms of its world tourist function, the region is truly peripheral.

CHAPTER 19

North Africa and the Middle East

LEARNING OBJECTIVES

After reading this chapter you should be able to

- assess the tourist potential of the climatic, coastal, landscape, historical and cultural resources of North Africa and the Middle East.
- distinguish between the regional distribution of these geographical resources and their development and use for tourism
- demonstrate a knowledge of the main tourist resorts and tourist centres
- understand the role of the region in the general pattern of world and European tourism
- outline the political, religious and economic constraints on tourist development in the region.

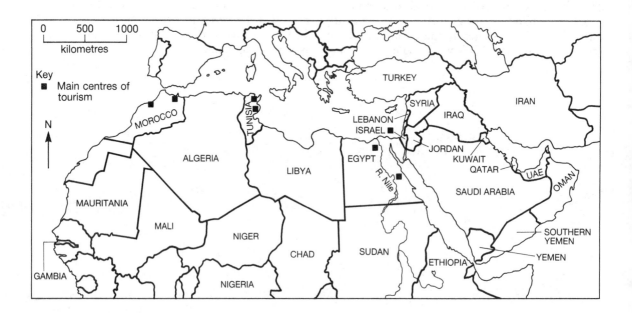

Introduction

The region covered in this chapter consists of the part of Africa that lies north of the Sahara desert and the Middle East. Figure 19.1 shows that, with only two exceptions (Israel and Lebanon), the vast majority of the populations of each country are Moslems. The region forms the heart of the Islamic world, although Fig 19.1 also indicates that the majority of the world's population of Moslems live outside the region, in the countries of Turkey, USSR, Pakistan, India, Bangladesh, Indonesia and Nigeria.

The predominant religion imposes some constraints on the development of Western-style tourism (*see* Chapter 4), but not in all the countries of North Africa and the Middle East. Western-style tourism in the region is on a small scale as yet, and is currently located in some of the countries making up the eastern and southern shores of the Mediterranean Sea (i.e. from Syria to Morocco). These countries possess coastal, climatic and cultural resources that have the potential to attract Western tourists. They lie in the sphere of influence of the European tourist market and may be considered as functionally

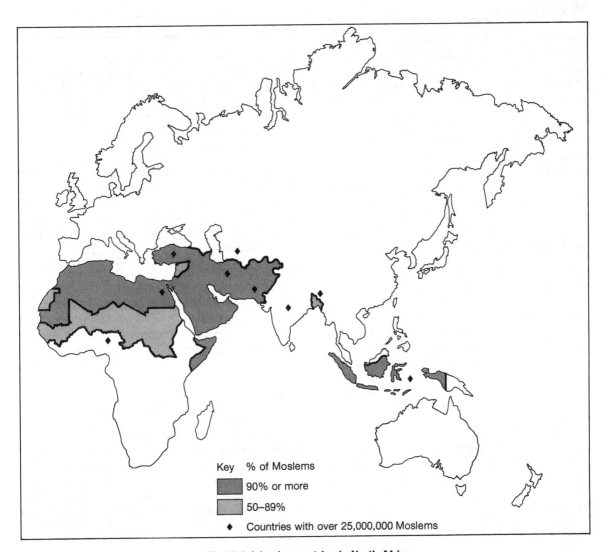

Key   % of Moslems

▨ 90% or more

▦ 50–89%

◆ Countries with over 25,000,000 Moslems

Fig 19.1 Islamic countries in North Africa

part of the European tourist system (*see* Chapter 6). In 1988 they received 8.9 million tourists.

On the other hand, tourism is hardly developed at all in the remainder of the Middle East (i.e. in Iran, Iraq, Saudi Arabia, Jordan, Yemen (north and south), Oman and the Gulf states). The total number of tourists to the region as a whole was estimated at only 6.9 million in 1988. The Gulf War will disrupt the pattern of tourism and further inhibit its development in the region as a whole for a considerable period.

Tourism in the countries bordering the Mediterranean

As well as their Mediterranean coastal resources, these countries, Syria, Lebanon, Israel, Egypt, Libya, Tunisia, Algeria and Morocco, have climates ranging from Mediterranean through semi-arid to desert conditions (*see* Fig 8.2 on p 91). They also have a wealth of cultural and historic resources (*see* Chapter 5).

It is more the political situation that deters visitors from venturing to the region in any large numbers or investors from developing it extensively. Syria, for example, has little interest in Western-style tourism, although Latakia is a coastal resort catering for Arab visitors. Lebanon has been suffering from a violent civil war, and the longstanding hostility between Israel and the Arab states has still to be resolved. Political problems within Israel have also reduced the country's attraction to Western visitors. Egypt, having played a mediating role in Middle East politics and having made peace with Israel, is better placed to take advantage of Western tourism, but to date, has directed tourism development inland or towards the Gulf of Aquaba and the Red Sea, rather than to its Mediterranean coast. Libya, being an Islamic fundamentalist state, does not welcome Western tourism.

Tunisia, Algeria and Morocco are physically closer to the European market and are politically a little more orientated towards Europe, and beach resorts have been promoted in Tunisia and Morocco. In practice, however, Western-style tourism has been limited to a relatively few locations in the region where and when political circumstances allow: in Tunisia, Morocco, Egypt and Israel.

In the latter two countries, it is mainly their cultural and historical features that draw international visitors to this inherently politically unstable region. Beach visits may be an added extra on tour itineraries but are not usually the primary purpose of the holiday though Israel marketed sun, sea and sand holidays in the 1980s which attracted less than 300 000 visitors in 1987 – mainly from Scandinavia (but also some from West Germany, Switzerland and the Netherlands). Thus, Egypt and Israel are not strong competitors with other Mediterranean countries for the mass beach tourist market.

Israel

Israel's cultural attractions are unique. The 'Holy Land' sites are of equal historical and religious significance to Jews and Christians alike, while Jerusalem itself is also of major religious importance to Moslems. Jerusalem is clearly the main tourist destination while Galilee (including Nazareth) and Bethlehem (the latter in the Israeli-occupied West Bank) are also much visited (*see* Fig 19.2). It is estimated that around 20 per cent of non-Jewish visitors come on a pilgrimage or specifically for religious purposes, while touring and sightseeing (including Holy Land Tours) are the main interest of 30 per cent of all visitors.

Israel, however, has many other sites of religious and historical interest which are sometimes included on tours, for example Acre (the site of a major crusader stronghold), Jericho and the Dead Sea.

Tel Aviv, Israel's capital, is located on the Mediterranean coast and is the other major destination of the country. It has the twin attractions of both modern cultural facilities and fine sandy beaches. Natanya is another important Mediterranean beach resort that is a little more popular with the domestic market than with international visitors. The Red Sea resort of Elat in the far south of the country is much more frequently used by Israeli holidaymakers.

Since 1980 Israel has attracted just over one million foreign visitors a year but its international tourism is greatly affected by political events and is influenced by media-generated perceptions of the scale of political unrest. The American market (which makes up around a quarter of

Fig 19.2 The Middle East

Israel's foreign visitors) are particularly sensitive. Visitor numbers drop when violent events occur but tend to recover in time. Israel's international tourist industry will always be subject to these fluctuations until long-term political stability is established in the region. On the other hand, Israel has a substantial VFR component to its incoming foreign tourism (39 per cent of Jewish visitors and 22 per cent of all visitors). Israel has attracted Jewish immigrants from many parts of the world which generates a significant flow of people wishing to visit their friends and relatives now resident in Israel. These visitors may be less responsive to the political events.

Egypt

Egypt's tourism is focused around the monuments, tombs, temples and settlements of the Pharaohs. These outstanding archaeological remains are located inland, along the Nile Valley from Cairo to above the Aswan Dam. Western-style coastal tourism (with its emphasis on sunbathing, bars and lively entertainment) does not fit easily into an Islamic culture though the Egyptians themselves do visit the seaside and there are crowded public beaches near Cairo. Western tourism is accepted at the most popular tourist cities but coastal bathing is not yet a major element of Egypt's tourist industry. However, the Government has set up plans in the late 1980s to diversify its tourism product into sun, sea and sand (and conference) tourism. Like Israel, Egypt has access to the Red Sea as well as to the Mediterranean and most of the coastal tourist initiatives are located in Sinai or along the Red Sea coast further south. Here Hurghada is the main resort where there is good snorkelling. The fish are particular abundant on the coral offshore. In 1990 seven tourist villages were under construction on the Red Sea for Western visitors.

In addition to the cultural constraints on tourism, the climate imposes some limits. The region has a hot desert (rather than a Mediterranean) climate and average temperatures reach 27° C in Cairo but 32° C inland, e.g. at Aswan. From June to August, daily maximum temperatures rise far higher, which Western tourists tend to find stressful, in spite of the low relative humidities. The peak seasons for Western tourism are spring and autumn (March to April and October). However, visitors from other Arab countries (i.e. 37 per cent of Egypt's total) are not deterred by the very high temperatures in mid-Summer and most arrive in June, July and August. Such visitors sometimes find these high temperatures a little lower than those experienced in their own country, where summer averages may rise to 35° C.

Most cultural tours include Cairo for the Giza sphynx and the Pyramids, the museum with Tutankamun's treasure, and Memphis. The other most important archaeological sites on the tourist itineraries, such as the Valley of the Kings and the Karnak Temples, are within reach of Luxor and Aswan on the mid-Nile. Tourists generally transfer from Cairo by air (or rail in winter), often picking up 4–6 day cruises which ply between Luxor and Aswan. By 1986 there were 82 cruise ships in operation with new ships being added to the Nile fleet each year.

Egypt draws its tourists from all over the world: the USA, Sudan, Saudi Arabia, France, West Germany, UK, Italy and Japan are the most important visitor generating countries. Since making peace with Israel in 1979, Egypt has been one of the more politically stable Middle Eastern countries and its total tourism has grown steadily in the 1990s. However, the 1985 Achille Lauro hijack and bombing of Libya in 1986 led to a sharp (temporary) decrease in visitors from USA. This was more than compensated for by the growth in numbers from other sources, and the total number of all tourists continued to climb. In 1987 Egypt received 1.8 million non-Arab visitors. Up to 1990 Egypt has not suffered the fluctuations experienced by Israel, but the 1990 Gulf crisis is estimated to have had a more significant effect (with the October 1990 peak down by about a half) and the long-term future of Egypt's tourism is also dependent on the resolution of the region's political problems.

The North African coast

The Mahgreb, consisting of the countries of Tunisia, Algeria and Morocco, is the only significant centre of tourist development in the south of the Mediterranean. Even so, tourism is small scale: the three countries together account for less than four per cent of the total Mediterranean tourist trade. They are closer to the centres of population in Western Europe but their development for tourism perhaps relates more to their political past: all were formerly French colonies.

They, therefore, have cultural links with potential Western markets; European languages are spoken, and although the people of the Mahgreb are Moslems, Western visitors are more welcome. The countries also have a good basic infrastructure that was established in colonial times. The good road systems in Morocco for example are a valuable foundation for the development of tourism. However, the three countries have very different styles of tourist development. Tunisia specialises in mass beach tourism, Morocco on a varied product for prestige tourism, and Algeria is only recently becoming involved, and tourism here is still on a very small scale.

The Mahgreb

The Atlas mountains run SW-NE roughly parallel to the North African coast from Tangiers to Tunis (*see* Fig 19.3). They average 1–2000 metres, though the peaks rise to 4000 m. In the High Atlas in Morocco, land over 2500 m has snow for four to five months in the winter. The ranges that back the coast are lower but are rugged, with deep gorges, scarped rocky coasts, and steep hillsides. Southern Tunisia is a different physical world, it consists of the level lands of the edge of the Sahara Desert with rock and sand dune deserts, low lying salt lakes and scattered fertile oases, and which have a true hot desert climate. Here summer maxima climb to 40° C and the diurnal temperature range can be as high as 15° C. Once again, the Mediterranean climate is limited to the narrow coastal strip of the mountains, and Tunis has a monthly average of 26° C from June to September.

Fig 19.3 Countries of the Mahgreb

Tunisia

Ninety per cent of Tunisia's tourism is coastal. The accommodation is concentrated in purpose-built holiday villages outside and separate from the major urban centres. The coast consists of three zones:

1 The north coast from the Algerian border to Cap Bon. The coast west of Bizerta is known as the Coral Coast. Coral grows underwater (though not in reef formation) and divers collect it for commercial use. The coast is slightly cooler and moister than Tunisia's desert coast and it has good beaches and coves between rocky outcrops, but it is relatively underdeveloped for tourism, though plans exist to add an airport and 10 000 hotel bedspaces at Tabarka.

Tunis itself caters for both foreign business as well as excursion tourism, and there are attractive beach resorts nearby. East of Tunis the coast is green with citrus groves, olive trees and vineyards. This whole section of coast had 17 per cent of Tunisia's bed spaces (mostly concentrated in Tunis) but only 9.6 per cent of bednights in 1986.

2 The west coast (The Sahel). This runs south from Cap Bon to Sfax and is the most intensively developed for beach tourism. There are three clusters of resorts around Hammamet Sousse and Sfax. The beaches are big, wide and sandy, while inland the countryside is a patchwork of olive groves, grainfields and sheep grazing. In 1986, the region had 64 per cent of Tunisia's bed spaces, but took 69 per cent of bednights. The stretch of coast between Monastir and Sfax was expanding its accommodation stock most rapidly of all Tunisia's tourist areas in the 1980s.

3 The Gulf of Gabes. The coasts of the Tunisian Sahara are flat, sandy and dry. Average summer temperatures in Djerba reach 28° C in August, and sea temperatures rise to over 25° C, while in winter the average air temperature is 11° C in January. The island of Djerba has big, sandy beaches with only few rocky patches. Most of the hotels are low-rise and are located on the island's east coast where there is a 20 km stretch of sandy beach. The climate allows year round tourism, although the high season runs from April to October. Winter tourism is being actively promoted and there is growth in off-season visits by West Germans, British and Scandinavians.

Here, as along the whole of Tunisia's coast, there are plentiful opportunities for water sports, such as fishing, scuba diving, sailing and water skiing. The mainland coast is dry, though Zarzis and Gabes are coastal oases and the resorts are surrounded by palm trees, and an almost tropical environment. The region as a whole has 16 per cent of Tunisia's bed spaces and 18 per cent of tourist nights in 1986.

4 The interior. Although the coast is Tunisia's main resource, there are many historic and cultural attractions. The pre-Roman civilisation at Carthage, the Roman amphitheatre at El Djem and the Moslem city of Kairouan, founded in 671 AD are all destinations of day-trips from the resorts. Day excursions also penetrate into the deserts and inland oases in the south, though there are only a handful of hotels located away from the coast.

Visitors to Tunisia

Tunisia relies heavily on the European mass market. In 1987, 83 per cent of the 1.8 million visitors came from Europe. Nearly 79 per cent arrived by air, and half of these came by charter flights via Monastir airport which was purpose-built for the charter market. France ruled Tunisia as a colony from 1881 to 1956, and not surprisingly the majority of Tunisia's visitors came from France, although the West German market is almost as important (and, since 1985 more important in terms of visitor nights in registered accommodation). Over one quarter of a million Algerians crossed the border into Tunisia in 1987, while Britain remains the third most important market when tourist numbers and nights spent are taken into account.

The number of Algerians and Libyans visiting Tunisia has fluctuated in the 1980s due to:

(a) changing travel restrictions place on Algerians by their own Government. Algerians visit for shopping trips and to visit friends and relatives; and

(b) the evolving diplomatic relations between Tunisia and Libya (the border was closed for a period between 1983 and 1987) but since the border was reopened, Libyans have also visited Tunisia for shopping trips and to visit friends and relatives (in 1988 the total number of tourists had increased to 3.4 million). Visits from other Middle Eastern Arab countries have declined since 1983.

Algeria

Algeria was also a French colony, and was frequented by wealthy French and British tourists in the late 19th century. However, the country has not encouraged modern tourism, although it has similar resources of climate, coast and culture to Tunisia. Until recently, Algeria has had little economic incentive to promote tourism, as 95 per cent of its foreign income comes from the export of oil and gas. However, in the 1980s the economy faltered as the price of oil and gas gradually fell, and unemployment rose. The Algerian Government began to consider tourism as a means to solve these economic problems. In 1987/8 the Government took a more positive approach including measures to attract private investment alongside or in partnership with the Government, and undertook more serious marketing, for example by producing promotional literature in languages other than French. It remains to be seen whether these initiatives will be sustained by the Algerian Government and will attract investors, and indeed whether the Western European market will be prepared to come to Algeria. In 1987, tourism was still on a small scale, with only 48 000 bed spaces and just threequarters of a million visitors. Most of these were from France, and included mainly business tourism with few holidaymakers. In the past, Algeria's attempts to promote beach tourism have been rather half-hearted and have led to small, isolated developments well away from the urban areas. These create resorts of limited appeal which are difficult for the tour operators to promote.

Morocco

Morocco has 3000 km of coast, though much is west of the Straits of Gibraltar and faces the Atlantic rather than the Mediterranean. The Atlantic coast is the better developed for tourism and competes with the Mediterranean resorts though it is also a significant site for winter tourism.

	Number
Mediterranean coast	17 320
Atlantic coast – Centre	12 194
– South	28 863
Interior	10 002

Figure 19.4 Distribution of bed spaces in Morocco (1985)

The country's resources are varied, ranging from long, sandy beaches (at Agadir), desert and mountain landscapes, ski resorts in the High Atlas, and a wealth of historic cities. During the 1970s and 1980s, the Government encouraged upmarket tourism, although later it tried to encourage family-orientated mass tourism. The total volume of Morocco's tourism appears to relate to the price differences between Spain and Morocco.

Morocco's regional resources

1 The Mediterranean coast. The coastline is a mixture of creeks, bays, cliffs and sheltered beaches, with good opportunities for swimming and water sports. It is essentially undeveloped, apart from the relatively new resorts of Al Hoceima M'Diq and Restinga-Smir (all summer-only resorts). Nador and Saidia are longer established (see Fig 19.3). Attempts have been made to market these as competitive seaside resorts but in fact they have declined in popularity in the mid-1980s. The cosmopolitan city of Tangiers (which has both Mediterranean and Atlantic beaches) lies opposite to Gibraltar and is the gateway for car and passenger ferry arrivals from Spain. It also has an international airport.

2 The Atlantic Coast. The northern parts are rocky but have some good beaches, while the biggest sandy beaches are towards the south. Agadir has a superb eight km beach; it is a modern luxury resort, rebuilt as a holiday city after the old city was destroyed by a major earthquake in 1960. It has a range of accommodation from luxury high-rise hotels to self-catering, and golf, horse riding and tennis facilities in addition to water sports. South of Agadir (on the Sahara desert coast) there are long stretches of undeveloped white sandy beaches. The coast is on the same latitude as the

Canary Islands (which are only 45 minutes away by air) and the Moroccan coast is similarly suited to winter tourism.

3 The interior. Morocco is the oldest Moslem kingdom in the world, and was independent until it became a French protectorate in 1912. The cities of Fez, Meknes and Marrakesh are sited on the western flanks of the Atlas and have all been the country's capital in the past (Rabat, on the coast, is the modern capital). The ancient city of Fez was founded in 808 AD, while Marrakesh has medieval alleyways and a wealth of ancient monuments, palaces and tombs, and Meknes was laid out in the 17th century. All form the focus of cultural tourism. Skiing has been developed in the mountains above Meknes, and at Oukaimeded which is only a half hour's drive from Marrakesh. The desert landscapes of the south have yet to be extensively developed for tourism, although the sand and rock deserts, oases and the dramatic gorges of the Dades and Todra have great potential.

Visitors to Morocco

In 1988, the country welcomed 2.8 million visitors. Excluding Moroccans who are resident abroad and who return to Morocco for holidays, the biggest share (26.8 per cent) come from France, reflecting Morocco's colonial past. Nearly 20 per cent come across the Straits of Gibraltar from Spain, while the UK and West Germany each contribute around 11 per cent. The American market dropped away in the 1980s (from 100 000 in 1985 to just 38 000 in 1986) following the Achille Lauro hijack. On the other hand, better political relationships between Morocco and Algeria have allowed Algerians to visit Morocco in growing numbers for shopping trips.

The Middle East

In spite of the high per capita incomes of Middle Eastern oil-exporting counties, they are included in the economic periphery of the world (*see* Fig 1.2 on p 6). Their capacity to generate outbound tourism is considerable but the potential of the region as a tourist destination is extremely limited, and, physically, the climate is a major constraint. The Arabian peninsula is a true desert with temperatures as high as the Sahara. Its vast and gently sloping plateau is a gravel surface with patches of sand dunes. Iraq's territory covers the valleys of the Tigris and Euphrates, and its climate is dry (under 300 mm of rain per year) with extreme temperatures averaging 34° C in the summer, while the January average drops to 10° C. Iran's mountainous territory has a little more rain (up to 500 mm pa) but the altitude makes winters even colder. The natural environment is thus inhospitable. The countries have many historic and cultural resources, however (*see* Chapter 5) but none of the factors that might encourage Western inbound travel can operate in this part of the world – in fact, circumstances combine to reduce the likelihood of Western-style tourism.

First, the political circumstances of the region deters tourism, and the Iran-Iraq war of the 1980s and the more recent Gulf War have effectively put a stop to tourism development here. Second, the prevailing Islamic way of life does not find Western tourism acceptable, and there are increasing trends towards Islamic fundamentalism. Sharjah had begun to encourage stopover tourism in the early 1980s but local opposition (triggered off by concerns over the erosion of Islamic culture and traditions) led to Sharjah banning the sale of alcohol: this effectively stopped its inbound tourism. Third, the oil-rich countries of the region have no economic incentive to develop tourism for Western visitors, and Western travel to the Middle East (where it does exist) is essentially business tourism: Saudi Arabia does not even issue visas for pleasure travellers.

Thus, it is clear that the region is truly on the periphery of the Western world's tourism. However, the region is the focus of international travel for other groups of the world's population. Saudi Arabia is an important destination for Moslem pilgrims visiting Mecca. These travellers come from countries with large Moslem populations, notably Nigeria, Indonesia, Egypt, Yemen, Iran and Pakistan. It was estimated in the mid 1980s, for example, that about 2.5 million pilgrims arrived in Mecca each year, including 1.5 million from foreign countries.

Conclusion

North Africa and the Middle East have much to offer the tourist. Many of the region's countries have a very varied resource base, and could meet the needs of a wide range of tourist markets: they are located in the economic periphery but immediately next to the expanding European tourist region (*see* Chapter 7). However, cultural attitudes and political events have controlled the spread of European tourism into the region in the past. Any major political change in the Middle East will have profound economic and political consequences for most of these countries, due to their strategic location, and their political affiliations. This will no doubt continue to be the case until long-term political stability is established in the Middle Eastern region.

QUESTIONS AND DISCUSSION POINTS

1 In what ways do you think Western tourists should modify their behaviour in Islamic countries in order to avoid offending the local population?
2 To what extent do you agree with the proposition that Israel will always have a significant inbound tourist industry, irrespective of the political circumstances she finds herself in?
3 Locate, name and date the main historic resources of the region. Are all of them currently developed for tourism? If not, why not?

ASSIGNMENTS

1 You work for 'Meddy-Sun', a tour company that specialises in sun, sea and sand holidays in the Mediterranean for the North European mass market. The company's business in Spain and Yugoslavia has declined and your chief executive is considering sites in the south and east Mediterranean for new tours to compensate for the poor performance of the existing range of tours to the north Mediterranean coast. He has asked you to prepare a report briefly reviewing the opportunities for the development of tours to the south and east Mediterranean coast from Syria to Morocco. He has specially asked you to:

(*a*) compare the suitability of the coasts and climates of each country;

(*b*) assess the risk factor – that is the political situation and each government's attitude to the promotion of Western tourism; and

(*c*) the accessibility of each country.

In your conclusion, list (in order of preference) three possible sites for new tours.

2 You work in the research department of a major world tour operator. You have been given a continuing brief to periodically update the chief executive on the current political situation in the Middle East and to advise him of the implications of the situation for the operations of the company. Write your annual review of the Middle East, outlining the current political situation, and drawing attention to any implications of recent developments there for the company's current or future operations.

CHAPTER 20

Subsaharan Africa

LEARNING OBJECTIVES

After reading this chapter, you should be able to

- assess the tourist potential of the climatic, landscape, wildlife and cultural resources of Subsaharan Africa
- outline the regional distribution of these geographical resources and their development and use for tourism
- understand the role of the region in the general pattern of world tourism
- outline the political and economic constraints on tourist development in the region.

Introduction

Subsaharan Africa includes all of Africa except the countries on the coast of the Mediterranean sea, and the heart of the Sahara desert itself (*see* Fig 20.1). Thus, Subsaharan Africa extends from latitude 15° N to the Cape of Good Hope at 35° S. The region is part of the world's economic periphery (*see* Chapter 1) and is similarly peripheral in terms of its world tourist function; it receives 1.4 per cent of the world's total international tourist arrivals (*see* Chapter 7). In 1988, 5.4 million tourists visited the region (*see* Fig 20.2). Its countries are mainly in the first phase of the development of tourism, i.e. they have yet to develop any significant domestic market, although a tiny but affluent elite may indulge in international travel (*see* Chapter 1). There are, therefore, few countries able to generate tourists within the region itself.

The region consists of three major physical units: the west coast; the major area of plateaux and uplands; and the offshore islands.

West Africa		Eastern Africa	
Benin	45	Burundi	99
Burkina Faso	55	Comoros	8
Gambia	74	Djibouti	27
Ghana	114	Ethiopia	62
Ivory Coast	178	Kenya	677
Mali	51	Madagascar	34
Niger	33	Malawi	99
Nigeria	341	Mauritius	240
Senegal	256	Réunion	55
Sierra Leone	75	Rwanda	36
Togo	104	Seychelles	77
		Somalia	40
Middle Africa		Sudan	37
Central Africa Rep	5	Tanzania	188
Cameroon	142	Uganda	40
Chad	21	Zambia	108
Congo	39	Zimbabwe	449
Gabon	20		
Tome	1	**South Africa**	
Zaire	39	Botswana	384
		Lesotho	110
		South Africa	805
		Swaziland	254

TOTAL 5.422 million

Fig 20.2 Tourist arrivals Subsaharan Africa 1988 (*000*)

Fig 20.1 Subsaharan Africa

1 The west coast (from The Gambia to Congo) which is mostly coastal lowlands and river basins. There are good beaches in Gambia, Ivory Coast, Togo and Ghana. The climate makes an abrupt transition from tropical on the edge of the Sahara (e.g. Banjul in the Gambia, *see* Fig 2.8, p 22) to true equatorial in Ghana. The tropical climates (with a clear dry season) have some European winter sun tourism, but most of the 1.26 million arrivals (1988) are generated within West Africa or are business tourists: only ten per cent of the top hotel arrivals are pleasure travellers.

2 The plateau lands and uplands. The rest of Africa is basically physically a tilted plateau with its highest areas in the east (over 2000 m in places), while it drops to about half that elevation in the west. In some areas the plateaux are deeply dissected.

Climatically the plateaux can be divided into three sections:

(*a*) the more mountainous arid 'Horn of Africa' (Consisting of war-torn Ethiopia and Somalia), which received only 102 000 visitors in 1988.

(*b*) The Kalahari Desert on the southwest coast (Namibia and Botswana). The semi-arid lands of Botswana are within South Africa's tourist hinterland and the region had over 400 000 arrivals in 1988.

(*c*) The remainder of East and South Africa. The high plateaux are very extensive, but in East Africa they are cut by series of N-S rift valleys, in which large lakes have formed. The valleys are bordered by old volcanic mountains, e.g. Kilimanjaro creating an area of outstanding landscape. The region has a tropical climate (i.e. alternating dry and wet seasons), with two wet periods close to the Equator (October and April/May) merging into a more clearly defined dry period (June-August) and wet season to the south of the Equator. The altitude modifies the temperatures and January average temperatures vary between 19 and 22° C (depending on altitude and latitude) while in July they may fall to between 10 and 15° C. This is the climate that sustains the open tropical savanna grasslands and mixed forest and grass which can yield rich farmland, but when undisturbed supports the great herds of herbivores (zebra, wildebeeste, antelope, elephant and giraffe etc.) and their predators, that form the focus of wildlife tourism throughout the region (*see* Chapter 4). East Africa (Kenya, Uganda, Tanzania, Zimbabwe, Mozambique, Malawi and Zambia) received about 1.56 million visitors in 1988 but most tourism is concentrated in Kenya and Zimbabwe (*see* Fig 20.2).

South Africa, with its more advanced economy, is the only significant tourist generator of the region yet it also attracts inbound tourism. South Africa plus its neighbours, Lesotho and Swaziland attracted about 1.4 million visitors.

3 The islands off the east coast of Africa (in the Indian Ocean). These include Madagascar, Réunion, the Seychelles and Mauritius. These islands cater for a total of around 400 000 upmarket international visitors seeking tropical island destinations

Characteristics of tourism in Subsaharan Africa

Much of the region has a range of outstanding tourist resources (climate, landscape, wildlife and coastal). However, the political and economic environment has inhibited their development. Most countries of Subsaharan Africa have very low per capita GNP ranging from the poorest such as Ethiopia, Burkina Faso, Guinea Bissau, Malawi, Mali and Zaire, all with under 200 US dollars per head in 1988, through to the richest three, Congo, Gabon and South Africa, with over 1000 US dollars per head.

Most of these countries rely on exports of a limited range of primary products to the developed world: for example Zambia exports copper: Nigeria exports palm oil; Kenya, tea and coffee; and Ivory Coast, coffee. These economies are crippled when world prices of these products fall and fuel prices rise; most countries have huge foreign debts and foreign exchange is needed to service the debts. Income from tourism would be a welcome source of foreign currency but their very poverty means that the infrastructure required for Western-style tourism is not available or cannot be maintained where it is provided: roads and communications are poor and there are few top quality hotels, with few experienced or qualified people able to manage the tourist businesses.

If the tourist infrastructure is provided by overseas investments the country risks losing the economic benefits: in the Gambia, for example, the airlines, hotels and tour operators are owned by foreign interests and the profits are taken out of the country. These difficulties generate an ambivalent attitude to tourism in some African governments, and may also raise doubts in the minds of potential Western tourists as to the morality of such development.

Other factors also inhibit the development of a tourist infrastructure. Many of the Subsaharan countries are politically unstable: wars and disputes siphon off scarce resources and rapid changes of regime disrupt attempts to plan tourist development. The region has experienced conflicts resulting from the process of decolonisation (with wars of independence waged against former colonial powers as occurred in Zimbabwe, Angola and Mozambique). The other sources of conflict in the region are inter-ethnic disputes, often a result of ethnically inappropriate boundaries between countries. Political units established in colonial times disregarded the spatial pattern of ethnic territories, and border disputes between countries and civil wars generated by ethnic rivalries within them have been the result. There is almost a built-in element of political instability in the region, and since the 1960s there have been more than 20 major wars and 40 successful coups.

The region thus has a poor image overseas. The perceived dangers of political unrest, the extreme poverty and poor quality of the tourist infrastructure, combined with the danger of AIDS and other tropical diseases make it difficult for African countries to attract large numbers of tourists, and tourism is limited mainly to special interest travellers to pockets of relative stability in the continent.

The Gambia is one such pocket of stability in West Africa. It is a tiny country of only 4361 square miles, consisting of not much more than a strip of land along the banks and around the mouth of the River Gambia itself. Nevertheless, it has been successfully promoted as a winter sun destination for the north European market.

Eastern Africa

Kenya

Kenya has been another of the more politically stable countries, although even here there was a coup attempt in 1983, and has been most successful in developing wildlife and beach tourism. These two types of tourism have slightly different seasonal rhythms. The dry seasons (January and July–September) are the best for wildlife viewing as the drought draws the animals to the water holes where the tourist lodges are built. The short rains in October/November do not deter visitors as this is the period when the animals gather in vast numbers in the Masai Mara for their annual migration. It is the period of the 'long rain' between March and May that is the 'low' season for wildlife tourism because the animals disperse from the waterholes (as other water sources become available), the unsealed roads make the safari drives difficult and the savanna grass grows tall and hides the animals. The low season for the beach resorts is longer as they are primarily winter sun attractions for the Northern Hemisphere market. Their peak occupancy rates are achieved between November and February. Only ten per cent of Kenya's bed capacity is in the wildlife parks but they have a much higher occupancy rate but with short average stays. Thirty-seven per cent of the bed capacity is on the coast, and accounted for 44 per cent of the bednights in 1985. The main beach centres are Mombasa, Diani Beach and Malindi (where coral reefs grow offshore), while the Lake Nakuru, Tsavo, Amboseli, Aberdare, particularly the Masai Mara National Parks, are among the most popular wildlife areas, where the 'big five' (lion, leopard, elephant, buffalo and rhino) can be seen. Most visitors come from Europe, particularly West Germany and UK, and from the USA. Kenya's Nairobi airport is the main international gateway to East Africa.

Tanzania has perhaps even more spectacular game (particularly on the Serengeti and in the Ngorongoro crater) but Tanzania's economy suffered particularly badly in the 1980s and tourism was deliberately not given a high priority. Tourist accommodation was poorly maintained and transport has been limited due to fuel shortages. Uganda's tourist industry was destroyed and the National Parks decimated during the Amin era (visitor numbers fell from 85 000 in 1971 to 12 700 in 1983) and tourism has hardly recovered, although facilities were being restored and tourism encouraged in the late 1980s. Zimbabwe on the other hand has shown a stronger expansion since its independence in 1980, though most of its visitors came from South Africa or Zambia (accounting for over 70 per cent of its tourists). Only about a quarter of its visitors come from Europe or America. In addition to its wildlife it has the attractions of the Victoria Falls, the historical monument of Great Zimbabwe (the archaeological remains of a once thriving, black civilisation) and many opportunities for sport and activity holidays.

South Africa

South Africa and its hinterland form a distinct tourist subregion. Its political policy of apartheid has led to its international isolation, though holiday visitors from Europe increased sharply in 1987/8 in response to the beginnings of internal change within South Africa. The country has a good tourism infrastructure and a well established white domestic market while the black population's growing middle class is beginning to participate more widely in domestic tourism too. The Kruger National Park (near the Mozambique border) is probably Africa's most intensively used wildlife park with half a million visitors (and over 1 million bed nights) in 1988, but South Africa has many other parks and game reserves. The country also has many good beaches while Cape Town and Durban are the main urban tourist centres. Just over half of South Africa's inbound tourists come from other African States (including 23 per cent from Zimbabwe), while UK visitors dominate the overseas arrivals.

The future of tourism in South Africa is inextricably bound up with the process of political change in the country. A peaceful transition to majority rule may allow domestic and international tourism to blossom, while internal political instability will inhibit the country's development.

Islands off southeastern Africa

Madagascar is the largest of the islands off the east coast of Africa but it is least developed for tourism, has few hotels and caters for special interest (including wildlife) holidays. Réunion, Mauritius and the Seychelles are the main island destinations. These are mostly mountainous, jungle-covered islands, but are fringed by unspoilt beaches and coral reefs. They are relatively expensive winter sun destinations for the European market, and tourist development is closely controlled in order to maintain its quality. Their high season is roughly November to January, but they do have a secondary peak in August when the climate is drier but cooler. The French make up nearly one third of the tourists travelling to Mauritius (up to 1810 it was a French possession) while the UK is the main market for the Seychelles. The latter group of islands is also noted for its wildlife. Its isolation has led to the evolution of many species of very rare plants and birds unique to the Seychelles, or even species limited to one island within the Seychelles group.

Conclusion

Subsaharan Africa thus has a wealth of climatic, coastal and wildlife resources suitable for tourism, but its peripheral location, its poor economic circumstances and general conditions of political instability all inhibit its development for tourism and limit international tourism to but a few dispersed locations within the continent.

QUESTIONS AND DISCUSSION POINTS

1 Can the expansion of international tourism in the poorer economies of Africa help develop those economies; or can tourism only be successfully promoted once the economy has been improved by other means?

2 Where are the main concentrations of international tourism in Subsaharan Africa? Do these locations share any characteristics (e.g. the nature of their resources, their economic or political conditions) in common?

3 Where are the current conflict zones in Subsaharan Africa? To what extent might these regions have tourist potential if they were politically stable?

ASSIGNMENTS AND EXERCISES

1 You work for a tour operator that specialises in worldwide wildlife holidays, but their only African destination at present is Kenya. You have been asked to prepare a report identifying other suitable destinations in Subsaharan Africa. Select at least three other possible locations where new tours might be promoted; identify their wildlife interest and indicate the market to which they might appeal.

2 A small company specialising in adventure holidays is considering developing an 'Africa: coast to coast' safari. Is it possible to construct a coast to coast route across Subsaharan Africa (either east to west, or north to south) that (a) avoids countries that are currently experiencing war or civil unrest; and (b) that includes some of the major sights of Africa? What would be the risks of undertaking such a business venture?

The Americas

Introduction

This section of the book seeks to answer the following questions.

1 What and where are the main tourist attractions in the Americas?
2 Where are the main tourist generation regions located in relation to the tourist destinations? What is the pattern of flow of tourists between them?
3 To what extent do the patterns of tourism in the Americas parallel that of Europe and its adjacent regions?
4 What is the role of the Americas in the general pattern of world tourism?

The main tourist resources of North America (i.e. USA and Canada) are described in Chapter 21. These countries belong to the world's economic core (*see* Chapter 1) and their affluent mobile populations are concentrated in the eastern half of North America, particularly in the north east between the Great Lakes and the Eastern Seaboard.

The predominant flow of tourists is southwards to the better climates of Southern California, Texas and Florida within the USA, but also to Mexico and the Caribbean. These latter destinations, along with the rest of Central and South America are discussed in Chapter 22.

Most of Central and South America belongs to the world's economic periphery, and they are also peripheral in terms of their tourist function (*see* Chapter 7).

Many similarities exist between the pattern of tourism in the Americas and that of Europe and Africa: the most densely populated regions lie to the north, while Florida, Mexico and the Caribbean possess tourist resources that mirror those of the Mediterranean; the two regions fulfil a very similar tourist function in relation to the generation regions to their north. Likewise, Africa and South America, are regions with similar economic and political problems, and both are peripheral in terms of their tourist function, attracting very few international tourist arrivals.

CHAPTER 21

North America

LEARNING OBJECTIVES

After reading this chapter you should be able to

- assess the tourist potential of the climatic, landscape, historical and cultural resources of Canada, and the USA
- distinguish between the regional distribution of these geographical resources and their development and use for tourism
- demonstrate a knowledge of the main tourist resorts and tourist centres
- understand the role of each country in the general pattern of North American tourism
- assess the similarities and differences between patterns of tourism in North America and Europe.

Introduction

The continent is part of the world's economic 'core' (see Chapter 1) and is a huge, unbroken landmass of 21.5 million sq km stretching from beyond the Arctic circle in the north to the region of the Tropic of Cancer in the south. Its climates range from polar to subtropical (see Fig 21.1), the best tourist climates being the Mediterranean type (on the west coast) and subtropical (to the south).

This region possesses an immense range of natural landscapes – deserts, mountains, lakes, plains and wetlands, but has a short coastline in relation to its size (see Fig 21.2).

The continent's territory is divided between only two countries: Canada and USA. Its population (of c 271 million) is heavily concentrated in a pocket between the Great Lakes and the east coast. This is the highly urbanised and affluent economic core of the continent. But this region has a humid continental climate: long, hot, uncomfortably humid summers and intensely cold winters. Although the region meets some of its own tourist needs, this combination of factors generates a strong southerly flow of tourists down the east side of the continent to the subtropical coasts of Florida, Mexico and the Caribbean (see Fig 21.2). The island states of the Caribbean and Mexico itself are more economically backward than USA and Canada, making them attractive destinations on account of the relatively low costs of living, but are at present low generators of tourists themselves (see Chapter 22). This general pattern of climate, economic development and tourist movement very closely parallels that of Europe. However, there are four significant differences between the characteristics of European and North American tourism.

1 The first difference relates to **spatial patterns of tourism**. North American tourist flows are not entirely N-S. In North America, there is a secondary population concentration on the Pacific Coast of the USA in the Mediterranean climatic zone which is cut off from the rest of USA by the Rockies. It is a very affluent region (California's 28 million population produces more than the whole UK economy). Its population generates very high levels of tourism within the region but it also attracts some visitors from the continent's economic core, generating a secondary significant westerly flow of tourists across the Rockies to the Pacific coast (*see* Fig 21.2) in addition to the southerly flow from Pacific Canada. The continent's most dramatic landscape features, e.g. the deserts and Rocky Mountains, are also located in the west. Twenty-six of the USA's 41 National Parks and 84.8 per cent of its public outdoor recreation land are located in its mountain and Pacific regions. This distribution of resources also generates a significant, though much smaller, westward drift of tourists to the inland deserts and mountains.

2 The other differences between the general patterns of European and North American tourism relate more to the **nature of tourism** rather than its spatial distribution.

The southerly flow of tourists down the east side of North America, although primarily a summer phenomenon, is a little less sharply seasonal than that of Europe. The climatic differences between North American tourist generating and destination regions are more extreme in winter than in most of Europe (i.e. the winters around New York and Toronto are colder while Miami and the Caribbean are warmer than the corresponding regions of Europe). This leads to stronger climatic 'push' and 'pull' factors which generate a much stronger winter sun holiday trade in North America, making destinations around the Gulf of Mexico (particularly Florida) virtually all year round

Fig 21.1 Climatic regions of North America

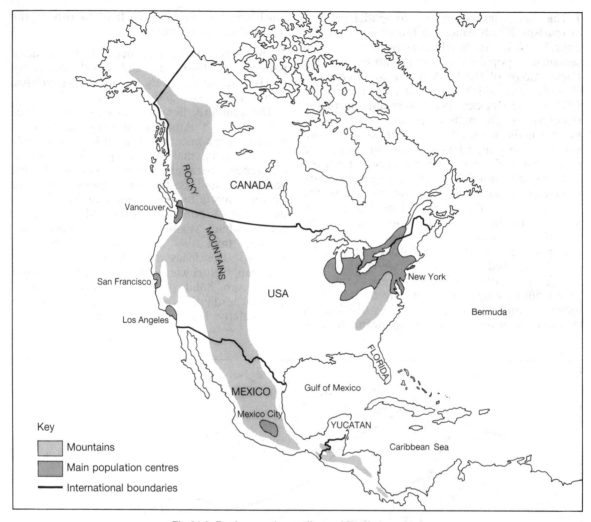

Fig 21.2 Regions and coastlines of North America

destinations (*see* Chapter 2). In Europe most of the Mediterranean destinations are just not quite warm enough to sustain such high levels of winter sun trade: European winter sun seekers have to travel further afield to destinations outside Europe (such as the Canary Islands and the Gambia).

3 North American tourism differs most strikingly from European tourism in that it lacks historic resources and cultural variety. The native (Red Indian) population of the continent was nomadic and left few permanent features to mark their development, although Central America's ancient urban civilisations have left many historic

sites. White colonisation of the continent dates from as late as the 17th century, and settlement only gradually spread westwards from what is now North America's economic core. Much of the continent with the exception of Mexico shares a common language and culture. Therefore, in contrast to most European cities, urban tourism in North America is based on the cities, climates, their modern culture and their manmade entertainment facilities, rather than their history, architecture or cultural variety. The relative lack of historic resources, and the strong cultural ties that still link it to the Europe generate a substantial transatlantic flow of North

American tourists to Europe. The modern cultural links between the two continents reinforces this trend.

4 The final difference between European and North American tourism is perhaps more apparent than real though it does have important consequences. The two main tourist generating countries (USA and Canada) are both huge and, apart from their lack of historic towns, possess a great variety of tourist resources; they can each meet most of their needs for travel and tourism within their own borders. Therefore, most of the tourist movements within the continent are registered as domestic rather than as international trips. This contrasts sharply with the high level of international tourism in Europe (*see* Chapter 1). However, this does have important implications for the nature of tourism in Canada and USA. Political constraints on tourist travel in North America hardly exist. There is a unity of travel infrastructure within each country which facilitates

long distance travel: in 1988 the average domestic round trip in USA was over 1500 km, and the population generated 840 million vacation trips of over 160 km. Although it may not be reflected as international tourism statistics, the volume of travel and tourism in North America is huge, and is strongly concentrated in three regions: the Pacific Coast, the subtropical south and in the economic core of the Atlantic Seaboard (*see* Fig 21.3). When tourism is measured in terms of receipts, Texas also appears as a significant tourist region.

The United States of America

The economic core

Many parts of the USA have significant levels of tourism (*see* Fig 21.3) but tourist activity is strongly focused on three regions: Florida;

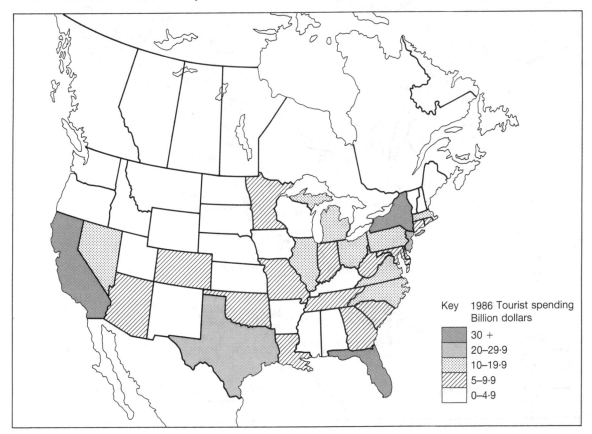

Fig 21.3 USA tourist spending (1986)

California and its region; and the states of the northeast of the USA that form the country's economic core.

The northeast of the USA

Roughly 40 per cent of the population of the USA live in this region which is made up of the states of New York, Pennsylvania and Virginia, plus the smaller states of Maine, New Hampshire, Vermont, Massachussetts, Connecticut, Rhode Island, New Jersey, Delaware, Maryland and West Virginia. The population is concentrated on the coast in the great string of cities centred on New York (*see* Fig 21.4).

The industrial and heavily urbanised hinterland of New York extends inland as far as Chicago.

This part of America is not only the major tourist generating region of the continent but is also the main domestic tourist destination region. Measured in terms of domestic tourist spending on trips over 40 km from home, this core area of USA received 37.6 per cent of all domestic tourism in 1986. Of this regional total, two thirds of the tourist activity was focused on the three states around New York (New York State itself, plus New Jersey and Pennsylvania).

The popularity of the region as a tourist destination is due in part to the variety of its tourist resources. Its climate, though not ideal to live and work in, provides conditions for both summer coastal tourism and winter sports activity. Average summer (July/August) temperatures rise to 21 to 22° C on the coast and over 23° C inland, but there is a general peak in rainfall

Fig 21.4 Tourist resources of northeastern USA

over these same months (223 mm at Newhaven) and humidity is uncomfortably high for city life, though bearable on the beach. In winter, temperatures are generally below freezing from December to February with heavy snowfall, allowing winter sports to take place on the mountains inland. These rural areas also provide opportunities for hiking, camping, canoeing, hang-gliding and other outdoor sports in summer.

Although North America is short of historic resources, the best of them are in this region. The Pilgrim Fathers landed on these shores in 1620 and there are a few 17th century buildings remaining and some 18th century streets in the older cities. Finally, the region is a thriving centre of modern culture and business, epitomised by New York itself.

The coast

The sandy coast from Cape Hatteras to Cape Cod is fringed by sand bars or dunes for much of its length. Dangerous offshore currents inhibit its development for tourism round Cape Hatteras itself which is left as a wildlife refuge. Between Norfolk and Long Island there are safe, sandy beaches and a string of resorts, such as Virginia Beach, Ocean City, Wildwood and Atlantic City.

Atlantic City is one of the older resorts, and had suffered a decline in the face of competition from Florida and California, until casino gambling was legalised in 1977. By 1987 it was USA's fourth most popular city, with an estimated 31.8 million visitors and a gaming revenue of 2.73 billion dollars. Most of the casino arrivals came by road for day visits from a 160 km radius, and the resort (like many declining north European seaside resorts) is attempting to diversify into the conference trade and is also upgrading its airport to increase its catchment and attraction for staying visitors (both business visitors and casino arrivals). The sandy Atlantic beaches of Long Island and the access roads to them are very congested with day visitors from New York at the weekend, although some parts are exclusive haunts of the wealthy.

The coast north of Long Island becomes more indented and varied with opportunities for sailing (e.g. Newport, Rhode Island, and Martha's Vineyard) but again, many of the New York elite own second homes here in exclusive and expensive developments, with many private beaches. These are mixed between the more popular resorts. The coast of Maine is much more rocky and less intensively developed towards the north, although the Acadia National Park (on Mount Desert Island) is very crowded in July and August. Although it is small, it is the second most popular National Park in USA and receives about four million visitors a year.

Bermuda is another coastal destination for the residents of this part of the USA. This group of islands is located 960 km east of Cape Hatteras in the Atlantic Ocean. Bermuda is roughly at the same latitude as Madeira and has a similar subtropical climate, although quite windy in winter. It is, therefore, mainly a summer destination (with a peak season between May and August). The English character of the islands (they are a British Dependency) and quiet setting appeal to the USA market, and 95 per cent of their half million visitors come from the USA.

Historic and cultural resources

Many of the USA's historic sites are in the coastal zone, where the first settlements and ports grew up (e.g. Boston) where early industry was established and where many important events of both the War of Independence and Civil War took place, (e.g. at Valley Forge and Gettysburg near Philadelphia). Annapolis is a beautiful colonial town on the coast near Washington DC, while Williamsburg in Virginia is another restored colonial town. Many of the big cities are major modern cultural centres. Philadelphia is an important business centre, although it has recently declined as a conference venue due to competition from Baltimore, New York and Washington. Washington DC is the federal capital and attracts tourists to the White House and its important galleries and museums. It has broad avenues, classical-style buildings and is cleaner and greener than most American cities. In 1988 it attracted 19.6 m visitors (6.2 million of whom stayed in hotels and motels while 4.8 m were day-trippers; the rest visited friends or relatives). 1.62 million visitors were foreign arrivals and tourism is vital to the city's economy as visitor spending contributed 2.5 billion dollars in 1987 and only the Federal Government supplies the city with more jobs. It is a more important tourist destination than New York in terms of visitor numbers but not in terms of visitor spending. In 1987 New York City received an estimated 17.8 million visitors but they spent about 16.5 billion dollars on its theatre, cinema, museums, jazz clubs and other entertainments, and conference facilities. New York is still a major gateway for foreign visitors to USA, and it took about a 14 per cent share of the country's foreign visitor expenditure.

Rural resources

The coast is backed by a series of uplands. The interior of Maine is remote, forested and studded with lakes and rivers that are good for white water rafting. Nearer the urban area, the White Mountains (rising to 2000 m) in New Hampshire are much more heavily used, for hiking in summer, for Fall Foliage Tours in the autumn (the state is 90 per cent forested) and skiing in winter. New Hampshire attracted 10 million visitors in 1987, 65 per cent of whom came in summer and autumn. The Green Mountains in Vermont are lower (up to nearly 1500 m) but are still well visited for both autumn colours (which are best at the end of September) and skiing (e.g. at Stowe). The Catskill Mountains in upstate New York have lost much of their traditional markets to newer attractions; the Adirondacks have good quality winter sport facilities (for example Lake Placid hosted the Winter Olympics in 1980), while the Hudson Valley and the Finger Lakes have attractive landscapes and extensive vineyards (*see* Fig 21.4). The most dramatic scenic attraction is, of course, the Niagara Falls. The Canadian side offers the better view and is more commercialised. The city of Niagara Falls on the US side attracted ten million visitors in 1987. The first ridges of the Appalachians rise in New Jersey and run SW, parallel to the coast; the Shenandoah National Park is only 128 km from Washington DC but remains a wilderness area. The Appalachians increase in height towards the south where the Great Smokey Mountains National Park is located. This is the most popular and heavily used of all the USA's National Parks and attracted 11 million visitors in 1987.

Florida

Florida is the size of England and Wales together. It is a low lying region (its highest point is only 115 m above sea level), with a subtropical climate and all year round tourism (*see* Figs 2.15 and 2.16 on p 26). Winter and spring are the high seasons. The summers are wetter and more humid with a risk of hurricanes in August/September. It has a gentle sandy coastline and its flat interior is a mixture of cattle ranches, lakes, orange groves and swamps.

Florida's tourist industry began in about the 1870s when it was a winter holiday area. Many wealthy Americans have second (winter) homes here, but since the mid 1920s many more retired to the state, and its population is growing at three times the rate of the USA as a whole. The region now has a huge tourist industry; in 1987 it received 34 million out-of-state visitors. An almost equal number arrived by car as by air (*see* Fig 2.16). Its tourist receipts (from in and out of state visitors) reached 40.2 billion dollars, providing 1.28 million jobs, (23 per cent of the state's jobs). Apart from its climate, Florida's

Fig 21.5 Florida's tourist resources

tourist resources are threefold: the beaches, man-made attractions and natural features (*see* Fig 21.5).

The coast

Much of the coast is fringed by offshore sand bars which are linked to the mainland by causeways crossing the enclosed lagoons, for example at Miami Beach and Fort Lauderdale which has 400 km of lagoons, rivers and canals on its landward side. The water is shallow and warms up quickly; it may reach at 30° C maximum temperature between June and September. On the Atlantic Coast there is a more or less continuous string of resorts from Miami Beach to Daytona Beach, all are busy but some have a particular character. Miami Beach is lined with multistorey hotels and is also a retirement centre. It is struggling to maintain its position as a leading resort but is diversifying into conference business and is becoming more popular with North European package tours. The wealthy elite moved north and many have property in Palm Beach, while the flat, hard sands of Daytona Beach are popular with holidaymakers from the New York region and students during the spring break. The beaches between Daytona and the state border are relatively quieter, though more heavily used by carborne visitors. On the Gulf Coast (the west coast) of the peninsula there are some of the state's best white, sandy beaches, e.g. between Fort Myers and St Petersburg (*see* Fig 21.5). The latter resort is also a major retirement centre.

Natural features

The far southern part of the peninsula is less developed. The Everglades National Park is a subtropical wetland, with abundant wildlife but is under threat from pollution and falling water levels. Winter is the best time to visit when it is drier and there are fewer mosquitoes. The tip of the peninsula is fringed by living coral reefs which form the basis for the marine Biscayne National Park. The Florida Keys are a chain of coral islands curving away from the peninsula but linked by a road, and the coral region provides good snorkelling.

The man-made attractions

Vast amounts of capital have been invested in man-made entertainments to augment Florida's natural attractions. The biggest attraction is Walt Disney World, 24 km south of Orlando. It is a huge complex of three theme parks (Magic Kingdom, The Epcot Centre, and Disney MGM Studios Theme Park) plus two water parks (River Country and Typhoon Lagoon) an entertainment complex, hotels and conference centre. The Epcot Centre (The Experimental Prototype Community of Tomorrow) alone cost one billion dollars. The whole complex covers 11 200 hectares and is estimated to attract 26 million visitors a year. There are many other smaller sports facilities and attractions, e.g. dolphinaria but the other major feature is the Space Centre at Cape Canaveral. The central part of Florida (where these attractions are located) is equally popular with air and car visitors.

Visitors to Florida

Visitors arrive in Florida by car and air in roughly equal numbers, although air arrivals are in the majority in winter (January-March), while car arrivals are slightly more numerous throughout the summer (*see* Fig 2.16 on page 26). The peninsula has a good road system and is linked to the interstate highway system. The car arrivals are more likely to stay in the north of Florida, which is the most accessible part by road, while the air arrivals frequent the areas round the airports, although many do hire cars on arrival. Thus, air arrivals heavily outnumber car arrivals on the Gulf Coast around Tampa airport, and particularly on the Gold Coast in the far south between Miami and West Palm Beach airports. However, these balance out and the total number of visitors in each region is fairly even; only the 'Space Coast' is relatively less popular (*see* Fig 21.5). Air and car arrivals show similar patterns of use of accommodation: most use hotels but about a third visit friends and relatives. Other forms of accommodation are hardly used. Florida has a huge and expanding stock of hotels but due to the non-seasonal nature of tourism, they have high occupancy rates (72.9 per cent in 1987). However, in spite of the heavy use of hotel accommodation, package tours are not popular with the domestic market (in the mid 1980s only 12 per cent of air arrivals were booked on a tour). The visitors know the region well as between 80 and 90 per cent have been before, and many have retired friends or relations living in Florida.

Transit tourists form a much smaller, though important, element of Florida's visitors. Miami is the main port of embarkation for Caribbean cruises and over a million passengers join their cruise ships here each year.

California

The state is the USA's leading tourist region, both in terms of number of trips and tourist expenditure (i.e. when domestic and international visitors are taken together). It is a long (1600 km) narrow (average 400 km wide) area of land. Some 91 per cent of its 28 million population live in cities, most of which are located on the coast, and 80 per cent of the population lives within 64 km of the sea. Much of the tourist trade depends on domestic day and weekend trips to the coast but it is still one of America's most important international tourist destinations. The state has a Mediterranean climate (*see* Chapter 2) and a varied coastline of sandy beaches, surf and cliffs, but it also has a wide range of inland resources (man-made, scenic and climatic), again all within easy travelling distance from the coastal conurbations. The physical regions of California run roughly N-S parallel to the coast and are:

1 **the coast**
2 **the coastal ranges** – rolling hills between 610–1220 m high
3 **the Central Valley**, a wide, flat-floored, intensively cultivated region
4 **the Sierra Nevada range** of the Rocky Mountains, which rise to 5000 m.

These landforms have been moulded by movements along fault lines in past geological times. Central Valley, Death Valley and Coachella Valley have not been eroded by rivers but have all been created by blocks of land dropping between rising mountain masses. Indeed, parts of Death Valley and Coachella Valley have dropped well below sea level. These processes have created spectacular landscapes of huge relative relief: the lowest point of Death Valley (−84 m) rises to the highest point in the main part of America (Mount Whitney at 4418 m) within 112 km. Although these landforms were

created millions of years ago, intermittent movement still occurs along these fault lines, triggering off earthquakes and volcanic activity. San Francisco is sited on one of the major faults (the San Andreas Fault) and experienced a devastating earthquake in 1906. Its modern buildings are designed to withstand earth tremors and relatively little damage was done by the fairly severe earthquake that hit Santa Cruz (90 miles south of San Francisco) in October 1989. Mount Lassen, in its own National Park, is the most recently active volcanic peak in California (with eruptions between 1900 and 1921) but now it produces only sulphurous steam. In neighbouring Washington State, Mount St Helens (in the same mountain chain and related to the same fault line) erupted dramatically in 1980, and more sporadically since then. The Sierra Nevada mountains in California (which are the southern continuation of these mountains) currently have no active peaks.

The climate and tourist development

The state enjoys a Mediterranean climate on the coast but it is much modified by the presence of the mountains inland, and by other factors on the coast (*see* Fig 21.6).

The coast

The climate becomes hotter and drier towards the south of California.

1 The north coast
The coastal temperatures are depressed by the cold south-flowing California current (*see* Fig 21.7), which cools warm coastal air to produce frequent fog banks along the coast, particularly in the San Francisco region (Point Reyes, for example, has 1860 hours of fog a year), but the 'fog belt' extends from Monterey north into Oregon. North of San Francisco the fog, cool offshore waters, heavy surf, and increasing rainfall make the beaches unattractive for swimming and much of the coast is undeveloped, though rugged and very beautiful. Landscape and wildlife are the main attractions and camping and hiking the main activities.

In the far north however, the Redwood National Park is a significant attraction, where giant redwood trees thrive in the moist coastal

		July Average temp °C	Jan Average temp °C	Annual Total rainfall mm
North Coast	(Eureka)	13.3	8.0	925
Central Coast	(San Francisco)	15.0	10.0	500
South Coast	(San Diego)	21.0	13.0	233

Fig 21.6 Climate of the California coast

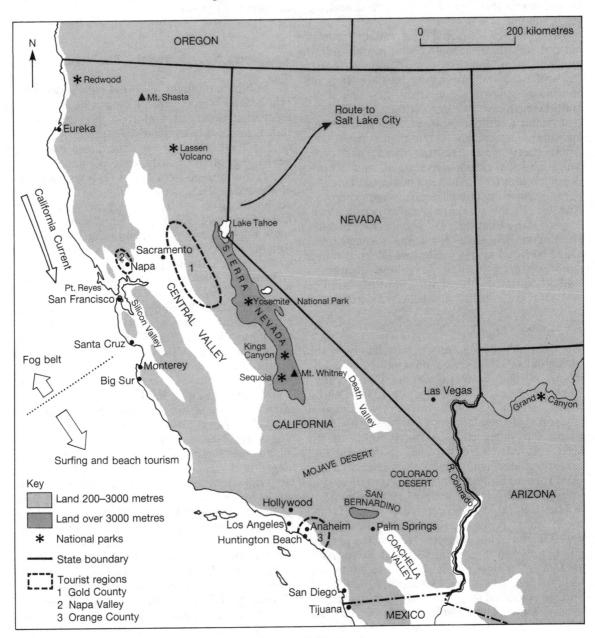

Fig 21.7 California

conditions and grow to 121 m tall and 6.6 m in diameter.

2 Central and southern coasts

Surfing and beach tourism starts in the Santa Cruz/Monterey area and intensifies southwards, and the beach resorts are often set among outstanding coastal scenery. The main developments, however, are between Los Angeles and San Diego, where the climate is the hottest and the sea is warmer.

San Francisco attracted 12.8 million visitors but Los Angeles is the main centre of California's tourism and is the USA's most popular tourist city with 49.3 million visitors in 1987. It is an enormous, sprawling, suburban city linked by multi-lane freeways. Its attractions include Hollywood (with its tours of film studios and nightlife), Disneyland, seven theme parks and Knotts Berry Farm (another theme park with white knuckle rides). Disneyland and Knotts Berry are located at Anaheim in Orange Country but the area is functionally part of sprawling Los Angeles. Pacific coastlines receive ocean 'swell' waves (*see* Chapter 3) and Los Angeles' Huntington Beach is styled as the 'surfing capital of the world'. Further south, San Diego is also a major resort, attracting 32 million visitors in 1987. Tourism on the south California coast is very large scale, urban and beach-orientated.

The Central Valley

The Central Valley lies on the rain shadow of the coastal hills. California's main wine region is just inland of San Francisco in the Napa Valley where wine-tasting tours operate. The Central Valley proper is a flat, intensively cultivated landscape of irrigated crops. Its western slopes, where the valley rises to the foothills of the Sierra Nevada, were the site of the mid-19th century gold mining region that generated the 'gold rush' to California. The area is marketed to tourists as the 'Gold Country' (*see* Chapter 5).

The Central Valley gets drier towards the south where it rises to merge into the Mojave desert inland of Los Angeles. The San Bernardino mountains (which are high enough to provide enough snow for winter sports) separate the Mojave desert from the Coachella Valley. Palm Springs is located at the foot of this range where lowest winter temperatures reach 30° C. This desert resort is fashionable and expensive with many swimming pools and golf courses but many attractions close in the hottest summer months.

Death Valley is further inland and is in the complete rain shadow of the much higher Rockies (Sierra Nevada). It is also a no-go area in summer as it is even hotter: maximum temperatures can reach 53° C and averages 47° C in July. The coolest period is November to March and the best tourist season is spring when wild flowers are briefly in bloom.

The Sierra Nevada and the Rockies

These high mountains lie in the path of westerly rain-bearing winds. Precipitation is heavy and as most of it occurs in winter, at this altitude the rain turns into heavy snowfall (up to 1000 mm) on the west-facing slopes. The more northerly peaks, e.g. Mount Shasta, have permanent snow that generates glaciers. Lake Tahoe (which is easily accessible as it lies near the E-W route across the Rockies from San Francisco to Salt Lake City) is a major attraction. It has 6 m of snow but is also a very sunny location, and is a thriving ski resort in winter and a busy summer water sports and hiking centre.

Three of USA's oldest established National Parks, Yosemite, Sequoia and Kings Canyon attract substantial numbers of visitors. Yosemite has spectacular landscapes with sheer rock faces dropping 1000 m to a forested valley and is visited by three million people each year. Parts of the Park get very congested in July and August but the remoter parts remain quieter. Two other major Rocky Mountain tourist attractions lie across the State border but are accessible from Los Angeles. These are Las Vegas (in Nevada State) and a little further inland the Grand Canyon (in Arizona). Las Vegas is the commercial and neon-lit gambling city, full of casino hotels and entertainment. It attracted 16.2 million visitors in 1987, and they spent 8.6 billion dollars in the city. The Grand Canyon is further up the Colorado valley where the river has cut a spectacular 1500 m deep gorge in the flat plains of the Arizona desert. It is also a popular National Park, with 3.5 million visitors. Another short cross-border attraction is, of course, Tijuana, only a 15-minute journey into Mexico from San Diego. In 1987 42 million Americans crossed the border here, and 19 million spent time in the city.

Many of the other states in the USA have important tourist attractions; for example, Texas has Gulf Coast beaches, the Houston Space Centre, theme parks, etc.; there are abundant outdoor recreational opportunities in the mountain states of Colorado, Utah, Wyoming, Idaho and Montana, while adventure cruises sail up the west coast to Alaska. However, the three main regions – California, Florida and the northeast of the USA – possess the greatest concentrations of tourist resources and attract by far the largest numbers of tourists.

Visitors to and from the USA

International visitors to the USA

A total of 30.6 million foreign visitors swelled the number of tourists in the USA in 1989. These visitors can be divided into two groups:

1 from neighbouring countries (i.e. Mexico and Canada). These made up 50 per cent of the total. Most Canadians were lured south to Florida, but New York and California were also important destinations. However, most Canadian and Mexican tourists to USA arrived by overland routes (66 per cent of Canadians arrived by car). Overland Mexican arrivals tended to stay within the 40 km US border zone; only just one million penetrated further into the interior of the USA.
2 from overseas – literally. Of these overseas and intercontinental travellers, 44 per cent came from Europe (and of these the biggest share came from UK with a total of 1.2 million); 27 per cent came from Asia mostly from USA's biggest overseas market, Japan. Many of the three million Japanese holidaymakers to US territory stayed in the Pacific Island of Hawaii or Guam. Japanese visitors to the US mainland tended to come in groups, often combining business trips with sightseeing. On average overseas tourists visited two states during their trips (*see* Fig 21.8).

Twenty per cent of all overseas visitors entered USA via Los Angeles or San Francisco. California, which faces the Pacific, has significant Asian immigrant communities and is also the major entry point for Asian visitors. It is also the country's major location of new high-tech industries that the Japanese are likely to visit (e.g. computers in Silicon Valley in San Francisco).

	% of all overseas tourists
1 California	37.1
2 New York	28.3
3 Florida	19.0
4 Hawaii	14.0
5 Washington DC	10.0

Fig 21.8 Most popular destinations for overseas tourists to the USA (1987)

New York remains the primary point of entry (with 29 per cent of all overseas visitors first arriving there) and it is the major gateway for European visitors, though increasing numbers fly straight into Florida now that Orlando airport has increased the number of direct flights from abroad. Miami also received 11 per cent of all overseas arrivals direct.

Outbound tourists from the USA

For a country of 245 million people, the USA generates the very low number of only roughly 30 million citizens travelling abroad, and the vast majority of these stayed in Canada (13.3 million) or Mexico (2.66 million staying visitors who arrived by air). However, huge numbers of Americans made day-trips across these borders – an estimated 23 million made a trip to to Canada and over 50 million to Mexico in 1985. Forty-four per cent (6.4 million) of the staying overseas travellers made for Europe, with the UK and Germany the most popular destinations. Another 18 per cent stayed in the Far East while 24 per cent (3.8 million) holidayed in the Caribbean.

It is clear that the statistics relating to international movement in and out of USA need to be interpreted with some care in order to get a clear picture of the real volume and direction of tourist flows. It must be remembered that the total of 30 million American overseas travellers may exclude visitors to the American Caribbean islands of Puerto Rico and the US Virgin Islands and the Pacific Island of Hawaii, the 50th state of the USA. American tourists to these islands are included in domestic tourist statistics.

Canada

Canada is another huge country and has a similar geographical pattern of physical regions and a similar distribution of population as the USA, but it has a very much smaller population (of only 26 million in 1988). Vast areas of Canada are sparsely populated and there are extensive tracts of untouched wilderness (*see* Fig 4.6 on p 43), with outstanding scenic attractions, and much undeveloped coast. However, its more northerly latitude means that the summer season is relatively short: in Vancouver (on the west coast) average temperatures reach over 16° C for only two months (July and August) and in St John's (on the east coast of Newfoundland) for August alone. Beach tourism thus has only limited development, and Canadians are drawn south to the better climates of the coastal resort areas of USA or the winter sun resorts in Mexico and the Caribbean. Toronto, located in the heart of the most densely populated region of Canada has longer summers with temperatures over 15° C from June to September.

In general terms, Canada's pattern of domestic tourist movement is broadly similar to that of the USA, with major concentration on destinations in the most densely populated eastern provinces of Ontario and Quebec, and a secondary focus on the Pacific Coast (in British Columbia and Alberta) in the west. Canadian outbound tourism to USA is also strongly concentrated in the far east and west, particularly in the states just across the USA border (for example, to the states of New York, Maine and Michigan in the east, and to Washington in the west). The longer haul travellers on the eastern seaboard travel south to Florida or the Caribbean, while those in the west are drawn to California or Mexico (*see* Fig 21.9). Canadians made about 11 million visits to USA in 1985.

Eastern Canada: Ontario and Quebec

Ontario being the most southerly part of Canada has the warmest summers of the country: Toronto has four months averaging over 15° C and maximum temperatures can reach 26° C. It is the economic heart of the country with one third of the country's population, and half its industrial resources. Ottawa (the capital) and Toronto are the main urban centres. Ottawa has a thriving cultural life with Canada's main museums and the National Arts Centre (a complex of theatres, concert halls and art gallery). Toronto is a more cosmopolitan city with good shopping, entertainment, cultural attractions and pleasant parks. The outstanding natural attraction in Ontario is the Niagara Falls, though there are two small National Parks (Georgian Bay Islands and Point Pelee) nearby in the south of the province.

Quebec is the French-speaking province with its own special cultural heritage and character. Montreal is the main urban centre and retains some of its historic past in the cobbled streets and old buildings of Vieux Montreal. The modern city and port that has enveloped the old centre is lively and cosmopolitan. Outside the urban areas the Laurentian mountains (a region of lakes, forests and mountains) are popular for camping, hiking and water sports in summer and skiing in winter. The Gaspé peninsula offers wildlife, forests and dramatic coastal landscapes (particularly at Percé).

Western Canada: British Colombia and Alberta

British Columbia has Canada's best scenic, coastal and climatic resources. Its coastline is

	West coast		East coast	
Domestic (value in million Canadian dollars 1984)	British Columbia Alberta	971 855	Ontario Ouebec New York Michigan	1973 1006 2025 881
International (Number of trips by Canadians 1985) (000 trips)	Washington	1358	Maine Vermont	660 601
	California Mexico	660 203	Florida Bermuda and Caribbean	1459 514

Fig 21.9 Regional pattern of Canadian tourism

spectacular, with fjords, islands and some good sandy beaches backed by mountains rising to 4000 m. The far southwest of the province has a climate well suited to tourism with sunny, warm summers but mild winters. Vancouver is the main city, in a beautiful coastal setting. Vancouver Island is a focus of tourism with good coastal resorts, mountain landscapes and excellent fishing. There are several National Parks inland in the Rockies, (such as Glacier National Park).

In Alberta, the Banff National Park is located in the higher ranges of the Rockies but on the drier eastern flanks. Its climate, dramatic mountain landscapes and hot mineral springs have led to the development of summer health and winter skiing tourism.

International tourism to Canada

International tourism to Canada is also concentrated in the east (Quebec and Ontario with about 10 million visits in 1986) and the west (British Columbia, 4 million). Eighty-two per cent of Canada's total in bound tourism (of 15.5 million in 1988) came across the border from the USA. The UK and France (reflecting VFR tourism), West Germany and Japan account for the bulk of the rest (with 3.4, 1.5, 1.7 and 2.1 per cent of arrivals respectively in 1988).

The vast majority of Canadian outbound tourism is to USA; most visits (both staying and day-tripping) are to the northern states. But around 40 per cent of Canadian outbound travel is to sun (winter and summer) destinations in the southern USA, Mexico or the Caribbean. In 1988 just over one million trips were made to Northern Europe (mostly to UK), and around 38 per cent of these were VFR trips.

QUESTIONS AND DISCUSSION POINTS

1 What makes Florida such a successful all year round tourist destination?
2 Why is tourism in California concentrated so strongly in the south of the state?

3 To what extent is it true to say that Florida is the 'Spain' of North America?

ASSIGNMENTS

1 You work in a travel agency in London. A British couple, Mr and Mrs Smith are planning a visit to their aunt and uncle, Mr and Mrs Robson who live in Toronto, in the autumn. The Robsons are celebrating their silver wedding in November and the Smiths wish to arrange a one-week winter sun holiday for them (a 'second honeymoon') as a silver wedding present. The Smiths do not know much about North America or its region and have asked you to suggest some likely destinations that might suit their aunt and uncle (who are in their late 50s but like a bit of fun and enjoy sightseeing). Select at least two possible destinations and outline their main attractions, showing how they might appeal to Mr and Mrs Robson.

The Smiths will be visiting Toronto for three weeks but would like to spend another week or 10 days in Canada and the USA before they return to England. They want to see as much as possible but do not want to spend too much of their time travelling between destinations. They do not have to return via Toronto. Suggest an itinerary for them.

2 A young couple have won a two-week holiday in Florida in a prize draw, and they are very excited at the prospect of visiting the USA, but they are not sure that Florida is for them. They have the opportunity of taking the cash value of the prize and are thinking of doing that and spending the money on a holiday in another part of the USA. They are in their 20s and are active, outdoor people with a keen interest in wildlife and the environment, although they do like beach and watersports if the beach is not too crowded. They are very undecided as to what to do and have come to your travel agency to find out more about Florida and other destinations in the USA that might suit them better, before they choose to take the prize holiday or the money. Advise them on the attractions of Florida that they might enjoy and the aspects of it that they might dislike, and suggest other possible destinations in the USA that they might find more appealing. Would the cash value of the prize cover all the cost of these alternative destinations?

CHAPTER 22

Central America, the Caribbean and South America

LEARNING OBJECTIVES

After reading this chapter, you should be able to

- assess the tourist potential of the climatic, landscape, historical and cultural resources of the Caribbean, Central and South America
- distinguish the regional distribution of these geographical resources and their development and use for tourism
- demonstrate a knowledge of the main tourist resorts and tourist centres
- understand the role of each region in the general pattern of world tourism
- assess the similarities and differences between the Caribbean and the Mediterranean as major world tourist destinations.

Introduction

Central America consists of the narrow strip of land that links the continents of North and South America. Mexico is the largest country of Central America and also its main tourist destination. The rest of Central America is split into seven small – and sometimes politically unstable – states, all of which (Belize, Costa Rica, El Salvador, Guatemala, Honduras, Nicaragua and Panama) have negligible tourist industries.

The southern coast of the United States and the coast of Central America form the northern and western boundary of an enclosed sea. The northern part of the sea is called the Gulf of Mexico and the southern half is the Caribbean Sea. The Florida peninsula, plus the arc of the Caribbean islands mark the sea's eastern limit, while the South American coast completes the enclosure. As the whole region lies between the latitudes 10° N and 30° N, its climate is tropical,

and many parts of the coast and islands are developed for beach tourism for the North American market. It is clear that this enclosed sea fulfills a similar tourist function (in relation to the industrial areas of North America) as the Mediterranean does for Northern Europe. In terms of the world's functional tourist regions (*see* Chapter 7), Mexico and the Caribbean are as much part of the North American tourist system as the Mediterranean is part of Europe. On the other hand, the struggling economies of Mexico and the Caribbean states put them unequivocally in the world's economic periphery (*see* Chapter 1) and they generate few tourists themselves. However, as a tourist destination, they are far from peripheral: if Florida and the Gulf coast of the USA are included, the region attracted well in excess of 70 million staying tourists in the mid-1980s, making it the leading destination for the North American market.

The other seven small Central American states

and the whole of the huge continent of South America, in contrast, received no more than nine million tourists between them. This part of the Americas is truly peripheral in both economic and tourist terms. This chapter will, therefore, describe the tourism of Mexico and the Caribbean in some detail while the final part of the chapter deals briefly with the rest of Central and the whole of South America.

Mexico

Introduction

Mexico is a mountainous country: over half is above 1000 m. The structure of the Rocky Mountains continues south to form the spine of Mexico, but here the mountains are known as the Sierra Madre. They rise southwards to culminate in a series of volcanic peaks (of up to 6000 m) that surround the high level plateau where Mexico City is located, at about 2300 m. The only extensive lowlands fringe the Gulf of Mexico and they widen out to form the bulk of the Yucatan peninsula. Mexico has a substantial population of 82 million which is heavily concentrated on the high plateau around Mexico City. The city's population is still growing very rapidly, and in 1989 was approaching 20 million.

However, Mexico has major economic problems, with an enormous foreign debt and a GNP per head of only 2080 US dollars. Hence, her large population generates relatively little domestic or international tourism, but Mexico has a wealth of tourist resources and the country functions mainly as a tourist destination for the United States.

Cultural resources

Mexico has a long history of Indian urban cultures that have left thousands of archaeological sites including temples, pyramids and palaces. The Mayans, Toltecs and Aztecs are but three of the six civilisations that existed at different times before Spanish colonisation (*see* Chapter 5). Three centuries of colonial rule (up to Mexico's independence in 1821) has added the Spanish dimension to language, culture and architecture. The fusion of Indian and Spanish architecture

produced the 'Mexican colonial' style. A few towns that grew up in the colonial period and that still have many unspoilt buildings in this style are preserved as national monuments, where new building is forbidden. Taxco and San Miguel de Allende are two such towns, while cities where colonial and Indian remains occur together include Cholula, while Oaxaca has a more Indian emphasis. The Teotihuacan pyramids (56 km north of Mexico City) is one of the most important and most visited Aztec/pre-Aztec sites and dates from 400–800 AD. All these cities form part of a group of historic sites located on the high plateau within reach of Mexico City, where the climate is dry, sunny and pleasant (*see* Fig 22.1).

A second group of Mayan and Toltec sites (also with temples and pyramids) is to be found in the humid tropical lowlands of the Yucatan, e.g. at Palenque, Uxmal and Chichen Itza. Mexican culture, ancient and modern is one of the country's important tourist resources, and tourists crossing the US-Mexico border experience a very abrupt change in culture.

Climatic and coastal resources

In contrast to the ancient Indian sites, the purpose-built seaside resorts are modern and American in style. These resorts are concentrated in the Yucatan (on the Gulf coast) but some are also scattered all along Mexico's Pacific coast. The climate of the northern part of the Pacific coast is very hot (up to 37° C) and dry all year round; in fact it is a continuation of the desert of southern California. Sea breezes moderate the temperatures, and allow all year round tourism. Loreto and Cabo San Lucas (on the Baja California peninsula) are two fairly small modern resorts, while the resort of La Paz is based on an older settlement. All these resorts are accessible by road from California. Further south along the Pacific Coast, the climate is much wetter, until, South of the Tropic of Cancer, it becomes humid (75–80 per cent RH) with a pronounced wet season and temperatures that hover around 28° C all year. Acapulco, for example, has very heavy rain between June and September (over 250 mm each month) but December to April is a period of drought. It has a typical west margin tropical climate (*see* Chapter 2). Acapulco, and

Fig 22.1 Mexico's tourist resources

the other coastal resorts in this climate zone, function as winter sun resorts for the US market in the same way as the Gambia does for Europe. Acapulco's beach is lined with high rise hotels and with 16 700 hotel rooms (in 1988) it is Mexico's biggest coastal resort. All the other traditional resorts (including Vallarta and Mazatlan in the tropical zone) together provide another 24 300 hotel rooms (*see* Fig 22.1).

Two major purpose-built coastal complexes are sited on the tropical Pacific coast. Ixtapa/Zihuatanejo has a 25 km beach backed by high-rise hotels providing nearly 4000 hotel rooms. A potentially much bigger development (that could expand to 27 000 rooms) is the Bay of Huatulco project, covering a 35 km stretch of coastline. Its first phase (providing 1400 hotel rooms) was officially opened in 1988, and land is allocated for an airport and many other facilities in the next phases. These planned resorts together attracted 1.6 million visitors in 1987.

On the north coast of Mexico (the Gulf Coast) there are fewer resorts. Some of the coast is industrialised with offshore oil fields. There is, however, a cluster of purpose-built modern resorts on the tip of the Yucatan peninsula where the waters are clear and unpolluted, with good coral and excellent snorkelling, e.g. at Isla Mujeres, Cozumel and Cancun. Cancun was the first to be opened in the late 1970s, and has 10 000 hotel rooms with another 15 000 in the pipeline for the early 1990s. In 1987 it attracted over a million visitors, but suffered severe damage in September 1988 when the peninsula was struck by Hurricane Gilbert. Most of the resort was repaired in time for the 1989 season but all Caribbean resorts run the risk of being hit by a hurricane in the late summer.

Patterns of tourist use

Mexico is very heavily dependent on the US market, which provides 84 per cent of its visitors. About four per cent come from Canada, and another few per cent from Europe. Accurate visitor statistics are, however, not available. In 1988 Mexico reported 5.7 million staying visitors while in the USA it was estimated that 13.5 million of its citizens made stops of at least one night in Mexico. Others estimate at least 50 million – but possibly up to 75 million – day visitors cross the border from USA each year.

Whatever the real figures, these estimates do give an impression of the spatial distribution and scale of Mexico's tourism. In terms of the type and volume of tourism, Mexico can be divided into two zones:

1 The border zone (about 160 km into Mexico from US border). This area is heavily used by car-borne day trippers who cross into Mexico via the 12 main points of entry (*see* Fig 22.1). Mexican border towns tend to be highly commercialised, with souvenirs, gambling, prostitution and hustle, while officials on the US side of the border are vigilant for illegal Mexican immigrants. Tijuana is characteristic of this style of development. Towns a little further from the border are still busy and commercialised but retain a little more of their original Mexican character.

2 The interior and tropical coast. Here, tourism is geared more to the needs of staying visitors (who fly in) and the coastal resorts are clustered round their airports. Tourist rely on air transport because Mexico's highways vary in quality. Those focusing on Mexico City are good, and the highway running down Baja California peninsula is paved but narrow with few services, but elsewhere many roads are unsealed, and night-time driving is dangerous. Nevertheless 40 per cent of US visitors to the interior of Mexico arrive by car (mainly to Mexico City and its region), but the majority fly into the country. The pattern of air routes was reorganised in the late 1980s with the lifting of restrictions on charters and the liquidation of Mexico's domestic airline (Aero-Mexico). Mexico City remains the main international airport but there are over 25 smaller international airports which take flights direct from USA cities to the resorts (e.g. Miami-Cancun). New patterns of visitor movement will evolve as the air routes become stabilised once more.

Tourism is extremely important to Mexico's economy. It is now the second major source of foreign revenues and the biggest source of employment in the country. Its reliance on the US market is a problem and paradoxically US citizens are low spending visitors (spending only 290 US dollars per head on average). This is because so many visit only for a day. Canadians and Europeans spend much more (on average 710 and 1150 dollars per head respectively in 1987) and Mexico is trying to attract more long-haul visitors for whom it is a relatively attractive destination. In the late 1980s, the weak peso made it 30 to 40 per cent cheaper than many competing destinations and it has a similar range of cultural, historic, coastal and climatic resources to destinations such as Thailand.

The Caribbean

Introduction

The Caribbean islands are strung along a 4000 km arc which sweeps eastwards from Florida to the Venezuelan coast. The islands surround the fairly shallow enclosed Caribbean Sea. The water is warm (24–29° C) clear and free of pollution, so that coral reefs fringe some of the islands, for example off the north coast of Jamaica and West of Andros in the Bahamas). The tropical climate is dominated by the easterly trade winds that blow at 5–20 knots from the mid-Atlantic towards Mexico. Temperatures are generally over 25° C but relative humidity is usually over 70 per cent, although conditions are made comfortable for tourism by the trade winds themselves and by daily land and sea breezes. Rainfall does occur all year round but the winter is generally drier (some islands do have a clear, dry winter season). The winds drop and relative humidity increases in the wet summer months, and the later summer may be disrupted by hurricanes which, over the course of 7–10 days, track from east to west across the Caribbean, before they peter out when they hit the coast of the Gulf of Mexico. Only the islands close to the South American coast are exempt from this danger.

Average annual frequency (% of total hurricanes)	
January	1
February	1
March	1
April	1
May	2
June	4
July	16
August	25
September	25
October	15
November	6
December	3

Fig 22.2 Frequency of Caribbean hurricanes

The most catastrophic hurricanes appear to occur at the end of the wet season (in September), when wind speeds may exceed 170 mph, and the storms bring intense rain and high seas: any island lying in their path may experience very great damage, although there is usually a reasonable warning of their approach. Not surprisingly, the tourist high season in the Caribbean is in winter (40 per cent of the region's bednights are between January and April) but there is a secondary summer (July/August) peak in spite of the weather. May/June and September/October are the low months. The main attraction of the islands is their combination of climate and coastal resources: beach tourism dominates but most of the islands also offer a wide range of others water-based activities, such as fishing, snorkelling, diving, sailing and cruising. The region relies very heavily on the North American market – 60 per cent of its 9.7 million staying visitors came from the USA in 1988.

Regional variations

The distribution of visitors is not evenly spread throughout the region. There are variations between the islands in terms of:

1 their **physical character and relief**;
2 their **climate** (which is related to their relief);
3 their **colonial background**, political affiliations and economic organisation; and
4 their **accessibility** (which is related to their political backgrounds as well as their physical location).

Thus, these factors combine to make some islands very significant centres of tourism (with over a million arrivals) while others receive barely 10 000 visitors each year.

Variations in the physical character of the islands

There are three types of island (*see* Fig 22.4).

1 Very flat low lying limestone islands, made of accumulations of coral debris or limestone sand. These occur on the outer side of the arc of islands, and include the Bahamas, Turks and Caicos, Anguilla, Barbuda, Antigua, the eastern half of Guadeloupe, Barbados, and Aruba, Curaçao and Bonaire in the south. Parts of Cuba

	Tourist arrivals 1988	Cruise arrivals 1987/8
Northern Caribbean		
The Bahamas	1 475 000	1 136 000
Turks and Caicos	47 000	
Cuba	298 000	
Jamaica	649 000	291 000
Cayman Islands	219 000	325 000
Haiti	133 000	
Dominican Republic	1 116 000	
Puerto Rico	2 077 000	723 000
US Virgin Islands	599 000	950 000
British Virgin Islands	176 000	
Eastern Caribbean		
Leeward Islands and Windward Islands		
(The Lesser Antilles)		
Anguilla	26 000	
St Maarten	480 000	389 000
Saba	25 000	
St Eustatius	18 000	
St Kitts–Nevis	70 000	31 000
Antigua and Barbuda	187 000	
Montserrat	18 000	
Guadeloupe	159 000	65 000
Dominica	32 000	12 000
Martinique	209 000	297 000
St Lucia	125 000	83 000
St Vincent and Grenadines	64 000	66 000
Barbados	451 900	229 000
Grenada	62 000	127 000
Southern Caribbean		
Trinidad and Tobago	188 000	
Bonaire	34 000	
Curaçao	155 000	107 000
Aruba	278 000	

Fig 22.3 The Caribbean Islands: tourist arrivals 1987–8

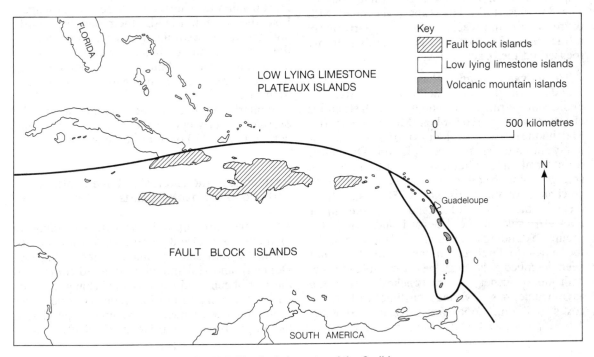

Fig 22.4 Physical character of the Caribbean

are also very low lying plains. These islands generally have the best sandy beaches, with the exception of Curaçao where at least two artificial beaches have been built. These islands also have the climatic advantage of having little rain (generally under 1200 mm per annum) with a very clear winter drought (*see* Fig 22.5).

	Annual rainfall (mm)
North Bahamas (Nassau)	1185
South Bahamas (Turks Is)	750
Central Caribbean (Anguilla)	762
(Antigua)	1251
South Caribbean (Bonaire)	512

Fig 22.5 Rainfall in the flat limestone islands of the Caribbean.

The climate does bring other problems. All these islands suffer a shortage of water particularly when local populations are swelled by influxes of tourists. Nassau supplements its limited local supply with both desalinated seawater and water shipped in from the bigger Bahamian islands. The flat, desert-like landscapes, vegetated with thorn scrub and cactus, are not particularly attractive, and tourism in these islands is firmly focused on the beach and water sports.

2 The volcanic islands. These are mountainous islands with dramatic landscapes created by extinct or dormant volcanoes. The last major eruption was in 1902 when Mount Pelée (on Martinique) destroyed the town of St Pierre, but many mountains, for example on Dominica, Montserrat and Guadeloupe, still have hot springs, sulphur craters and active geysers. The volcanic mountains rise to 1500 m and have created the string of islands on the inner (western) side of the Leeward and Windward groups, extending from the tiny island of Saba in the north to Grenada in the south. Saba has been described as having a 'near vertical landscape, with lots of scenery but no beaches'. The group as a whole has a varied coastline with cliffs, coves and some good sandy beaches. St Kitts-Nevis, St Vincent and Montserrat have some beaches made of black volcanic sand, although Montserrat is one of the islands with rather few beaches, while St Martin has at least 32 white, sandy beaches. Heavy surf sometimes makes the windward sides of the islands less attractive, e.g. on the rocky east coasts of St Vincent and the Grenadines. These windward sides of the islands are also much wetter. The high mountains lie across the path of rain-bearing winds and generate very intense orographic rainfall, which increases with altitude, for example from 2000 mm at sea level to over 4500 mm on the mountain slopes. The rain comes in short, violent downpours but with clear sunshine in between. The west (leeward) sides of the islands are generally much drier as they sit in the rain shadows of the mountains. Most of the resorts and settlements are in such sheltered locations. The vegetation of these islands is much lusher than the flat, limestone islands, with tropical jungle in the wettest parts.

3 Non-volcanic mountainous islands. The Central Caribbean islands (Southern Cuba, Jamaica, Hispaniola, Puerto Rico and the Virgin Islands) are made of uplifted, flat blocks of rocks. They consist mainly of fairly high plateaux with mountain ridges running east-west which rise to over 3000 m in the Dominican Republic. In places the plateaux are deeply incised with narrow valleys, giving rise to attractive landscapes. Like the volcanic islands, their rainfall is fairly high but varies according to aspect. For example, the windward side of Jamaica receives 3328 mm per annum (at Port Antonio) while Kingston (in the lee of the hills] receives 870 mm (*see* Fig 2.6 on p 21).

Similarly on Puerto Rico, Humaçao on the exposed easterly end of the island gets 2121 mm per annum while Ponce has only 909 mm.

Variations in the islands' political, cultural and economic backgrounds

The islands are culturally varied, depending on their past colonial and present political affiliations. From the 16th century Spain, France, England, Denmark and Holland all established colonies in the Caribbean, and some islands changed hands during the competition for trade. America later acquired some islands, for example, it purchased the Virgin Islands from Denmark in 1917 and in the 20th century many of the British Islands became independent. Each island's language, architectural style, and political organisation is a result of its colonial background. The Cuban revolution of 1959 turned this island into a socialist state and cut it off from western trade and from American tourism. Up to 1989, Americans, though not forbidden to travel to Cuba, were not allowed to spend US dollars there.

Fig 22.6 indicates the variety of cultural and political organisation in the Caribbean.

The remaining islands are mainly English-speaking British colonies or independent islands. The economies of most of the islands (except Trinidad) are highly dependent on tourism, and their governments are generally keen to promote tourism. Hence there is some competition between them to attract visitors. However, in many islands, the currency is closely linked to the US dollar and there is relatively little difference in price between them. Levels of use depend more on accessibility. The major exceptions are firstly Haiti and the Dominican Republic – both very poor countries with weak currencies that make them the cheapest Caribbean destinations and thus attractive to US market, but their poverty and political instability has tended to inhibit potential US visitors and constrain the growth of their tourist industry. Nevertheless 71 per cent of the 911 000 visitors to the Dominican Republic are from the USA.

The second exception are the colonial islands who have European currencies, which make them relatively more expensive for the North American market. Language differences may create another barrier and these islands tend to have relatively fewer visitors from USA. On the other hand, Europeans visiting the Caribbean will be more likely to visit their own colonies.

Distribution of tourism in the Caribbean

The general pattern of accessibility has led to a strong concentration of tourism in the northern half of the Caribbean (*see* Fig 22.7). Not only are the northern islands nearer to the North American markets but, apart from Cuba, all the other factors combine to make them the most attractive and accessible. Air routes reflect the political affiliations of islands, and these are also crucial in moulding the flow of tourists into the region.

The Bahamas are closest to Florida market, and Miami is one of the region's most important links into the international air travel system but some of the more distant islands also have direct air links to other markets. Puerto Rico has flights from New York and other eastern seaboard

Island	Political status	Official language	Currency
Bahamas	Independent	English	*
Cuba	Independent (socialist)	Spanish	Cuban peso
Jamaica	Independent	English	Jamaican dollar
Barbados	Independent	English	Barbados dollar
Trinidad	Independent	English	Trinidad/Tobago dollar
Haiti	Independent	French	Gourde
Dominican Republic	Independent	Spanish	Dominican peso
Puerto Rico	Commonwealth of USA (not an American state but Puerto Ricans are USA citizens)	Spanish	*
US Virgin Islands	Unincorporated US territory	English	*
UK Virgin Islands	British Colony	English	*
St Martin ⎱	One island, half French	French	French franc
St Maarten ⎰	half Dutch	Dutch	*
Guadeloupe ⎱	Both overseas	French	French franc
Martinique ⎰	departments of France	French	French franc
Curaçao	Netherlands' territory	Dutch	Guilder
Bonaire	Netherlands' territory	Dutch	Guilder
Aruba	Dutch in transition to independence	Dutch	Guilder

*(denotes US dollar is legal tender)

Fig 22.6 Cultural and political background of selected Caribbean Islands

Fig 22.7 Caribbean islands

airports, where the vast majority of its visitors come from. Puerto Rico is the main hub for the eastern Caribbean, but St Maarten also has direct flights from several US and European cities, while Guadeloupe and Martinique have direct connections to France (where more than half their visitors live) and Antigua and Barbados receive direct flights from UK.

These more accessible islands are the focus of tourism in the southern half of the Caribbean and also act as distributors for the smaller islands in the Windward and Leeward groups. Aruba, Curaçao and Bonaire are isolated from these groups of islands and have fairly low visitor numbers. Most of Aruba's tourists come from USA but substantial numbers of Venezuelans visit Curaçao by ferry from the South American mainland.

Cruise traffic in the Caribbean

The south of the Caribbean is also isolated from the main centres of cruise activity (Miami and Puerto Rico) which are all located in the north of the region. There are three types of cruises:

1 short one to four day cruises from Miami to the Bahamas, and from Puerto Rico to the US Virgin Islands.
2 one-week cruises from Miami to the northern Caribbean and Yucatan, and from San Juan (in Puerto Rico) to the south.
3 two-week cruises from Florida to the whole of the Caribbean. These are declining in popularity and the southernmost islands have lost substantial numbers of cruise arrivals.

The remainder of Central America and South America

This region includes the seven small countries of Central America, Guatemala, Belize, Honduras, El Salvador, Costa Rica, Nicaragua and Panama (*see* Fig 22.7), and all the countries of the continent of South America (*see* Fig 22.8). The countries are a little more affluent than the other regions of the world's economic periphery and generate much more intra-regional tourism than Africa or South Asia. In 1988 its poorest country, Bolivia, had a per capita GNP of 470 US dollars while 12 of the 19 countries had GNPs of over

1000 US dollars per head. On the other hand nearly all the countries of Latin America have experienced very rapid inflation in the 1980s and have enormous foreign debts.

These Latin American countries also have a reputation of political instability: some countries still have military dictatorships while others are returning to democracy, but the region's long-standing reputation for violence (e.g. associated with cocaine trafficking in Colombia, and terrorism in Peru) is hard to overcome. Indeed, most of Latin American countries have been involved in some civil, border or general war since 1973. North American media coverage of these events is very important because the region is very dependent on the USA for its inter-regional visitors. About threequarters of a million North Americans travelled to South America in 1987.

Attractions and resources of South America

The continent is made up of three physical units (*see* Fig 22.8):

1 The Andes which run the whole length of the west coast of South America. The mountain chain splits and runs through Central America to merge into the Rockies.
2 Two major river basins (the Amazon and the River Paraguay) which drain into the Atlantic on the east coast.
3 A large area of plateaux and uplands separating the two river basins.

The natural resources of the continent include the mountain scenery of the Andes, the tropical rainforest environment of the Amazon, spectacular waterfalls where the major rivers descend from the plateaux into the lowlands and good beaches on the coasts of Venezuela, Brazil and Argentina. But it is the culture of the Andes, the ruins of the Inca cities (particularly in Peru) and the Spanish colonial architecture of many of the Andean cities that make South America unique.

Most of Peru's tourism is concentrated on one route which focuses on its Inca and Spanish colonial heritage. This starts from the capital and gateway (Lima) and takes visitors into the Andes to Cuzco, a well-preserved Inca/Spanish city that receives over 100 000 tourists a year (*see* Fig 22.8). Machu Picchu is accessible from Cuzco

Fig 22.8 Latin America's resources

Key

- Land over 2000 metres
- Plateaux
- Rainforest
- * Waterfalls
- —— International border

and it is the most famous of the ruins of the Inca cities. It has a spectacular setting on a precipitous ridge in the mountains. Access to the ruins is by bus and train, but the Peruvian transport system is at capacity.

There are many other attractions in Peru such as Arequipa (the best preserved colonial city in Peru), the Colca Canyon (the world's deepest canyon and a focus for adventure tourism) and the Amazon. But the inadequacy of the communications system and a prolonged air dispute with the USA, the poor quality and shortage of hotels and the political situation are major factors that have limited the growth of tourism to around 300 000 throughout the late 1980s. However, the quality of its cultural and historic resources are attractive to the European and North American markets which supplied more than half its tourists in 1986.

Venezuela is also heavily dependent on the US and European markets, accounting for around two-thirds of its visitors. The main attractions are firstly the beaches near Caracas and Margarita island, and secondly the Canaima National Park in the jungle of the Orinoco highlands where the Angel Falls are located (this is the world's highest waterfall which drops 1005 m).

Colombia, Argentina, Brazil and Uruguay are the main Latin American destinations in terms of tourist numbers (with 0.8, 2.1, 1.7 and 0.8 million arrivals respectively in 1988). Argentina and Brazil have better developed tourist infrastructures which cater for the well-developed domestic markets as well as international visitors. Brazil for example has an effective internal transport system and good air access which allows widely spaced attractions to be included in a single tour.

Salvador and Sao Paulo have outstanding beaches, while Rio is famed not only for its Copacabana and Ipenema beaches but also its shopping and night life. Inland attractions include the modern architecture of the capital, Brasilia, and the natural attractions of the Iguassu waterfalls and the Amazon jungle.

Brazil draws most of its tourists from neighbouring South American countries: 44 per cent of its visitors come from Argentina and Uruguay. Argentina and Colombia have similar catchments: for example Chile, Brazil and Uruguay provided most of Argentina's tourists. These countries thus form their own isolated tourist system, receiving few tourists from outside South America. The sheer distance of these destinations from the main Northern Hemisphere tourist generating zones inhibits inter-regional travel to these countries. This reinforces the region's other disadvantages of poverty, poor tourist infrastructure and political instability. Although special interest long-haul international tourism is growing on a world scale, this region may not be the first to benefit.

QUESTIONS AND DISCUSSION POINTS

1 With reference to Fig 22.3 on p 267, rank the top ten Caribbean destinations (in terms of tourist *plus* cruise arrivals). In which part of the Caribbean are the five most popular islands? What explanations can you put forward for this pattern of tourist use?
2 Discuss the relative significance of location, accessibility and colonial history in determining the volume and nationality of tourist arrivals to the Caribbean islands.
3 What geographical factors combine to make Mexico the leading international destination for American tourists?

ASSIGNMENTS

1 An American professor of history living in New York State has just completed a book on the ancient cultures of Mexico, Central America and the Andes. She wishes to go on a quick tour of the most important historic sites in order to take photographs which will illustrate the book. Construct an itinerary for her.

What is the shortest time in which she could complete the trip? Is she likely to encounter any climatic problems that might interfere with her photography, and if so, when?

2 You work for a cruise company based in Puerto Rico. Your existing 7 and 14-day cruises are declining in popularity. Your chief executive has asked you to review the cruise routes and draft three new itineraries (7 or 14 days in length focused around particular Caribbean themes). He has asked you to include one itinerary illustrating the theme of 'cultural variety in the Caribbean', and a second to demonstrate the wealth and variety of natural landscapes and environments to be found in the Caribbean.

Prepare a report, outlining and explaining these two itineraries. Include a third itinerary illustrating another theme of your own choice.

Asia and the Pacific Region

This section of the book seeks to answer the following questions:

1 What characteristics make the Pacific region (as defined by WTO, *see* Chapter 7) the third most important region of the world?
2 What and where are the main tourist generating countries (actual and potential) in the region?
3 What and where are the major tourist destinations, and what are the patterns of tourist travel around the region?
4 How does South Asia relate to the Pacific region in terms of its tourist development and tourist flows?

Introduction: the Pacific

The Pacific is a vast region extending through all the world's climatic zones (from arctic to equatorial). Its centre is empty ocean but almost 65 per cent of the world's population live in the countries bordering the Pacific (i.e. on the 'Pacific Rim'). With a total of about 30 million tourist arrivals, it is the world's third most important tourist region, after Europe and North America (*see* Chapters 1 and 7) and its tourism is growing faster than any other region of the world. The countries of the Pacific Rim are culturally varied and at different stages of economic development and contrasting affluence: some belong to the world's economic core and some to the periphery (*see* Fig 1.2 on p 6). Therefore, their ability and inclination to generate tourists differs as widely.

The affluent Westernised countries (USA, Australia, New Zealand) in practice generate relatively low numbers of international tourists in the region (less than 10 million altogether). The poor South American and war-torn Southeast

Asian countries, such as Vietnam, Kampuchea and Laos, play virtually no part at all in tourism in the region. In between, lie the developing Asian countries, e.g. South Korea and Taiwan, and the ex colonies, such as Singapore and Malaysia, which generate modest but growing numbers of tourists, while the population giants, Japan and China, have only relatively recently decided to end their isolation from the rest of the world. Since 1964 when Japan eased constraints on travel to and from her shores, outbound tourism has grown very rapidly to over eight million in 1987, and Japan is already the leading tourist generator in the region. This eight million represents only a small proportion of Japan's 122 million population. The potential exists, therefore, for further great increases in outbound tourism if the taste for foreign travel spreads throughout the Japanese population, and the rapid growth of Japanese outbound tourism is one of the factors fuelling the growth of tourism in the region as a whole. Hawaii is the major destination of the region. It is politically part of the USA, although it lies in the geographical centre of the Pacific region. Around six million tourists flocked to Hawaii's beaches in 1988, but the islands rely heavily on a handful of countries (specifically USA and Japan) for their visitors.

Thailand, on the other hand, attracts less than half that total but draws tourists from many Pacific nations as well as long-haul travellers from Europe. It has a much more varied resource base with beach, cultural and landscape attractions. Singapore and Hong Kong have less varied resources but their ex colonial status is reflected in the high numbers of Europeans visiting them. Several other developing countries in the West Pacific also attract two to three million visitors but have more localised catchments (e.g. Japan and Malaysia).

The vast size of the Pacific means that relatively few travellers cross its whole expanse (with those that do being mostly Americans and Japanese) though the romantic image of the Pacific does lure tourists from the rim into the more accessible of the mid-ocean archipelagoes. Most of the tourist movements in the region are N-S journeys along the Pacific coast of Asia, mainly between a series of fairly small countries scattered along the western edge of the region. A small number of tourists leak out of the region towards Europe (but well over one million Europeans arrive in the Pacific in exchange). A very few travel westward from the Pacific to South Asia or vice versa. South Asia looks towards Europe and North America for its tourists and is not really functionally part of the Pacific tourist system.

The Pacific region consists of three cultural and economic subdivisions, each of which has its own style of tourism.

1 Australasia (Australia and New Zealand). Australia and New Zealand are Western countries with strong domestic markets and international tourism that was limited to the nearest Pacific islands but is now rapidly extending to the rest of the Pacific region.

2 The Pacific islands, and Asian archipelagoes (the Pacific groups, Indonesia and Philippines). These are peopled by Asians or Polynesians; some are developed for Western-style beach tourism.

3 Mainland Asia and related islands. (The eastern cultures of the Asian 'Pacific Rim' (i.e. East and Southeast Asia)). This part of the region is characterised by rapidly growing travel between its own countries, and also by the development of cultural and beach tourism for the Western market.

South Asia

This region has its own distinct pattern of tourism that has more in common with the 'peripheral' continents of Subsaharan Africa and South America.

Chapter 23 will describe tourism in Australasia, while Chapter 24 deals with the rest of the Pacific and Asia.

CHAPTER 23

Australia and New Zealand

LEARNING OBJECTIVES

After reading this chapter you should be able to

- assess the tourist potential of the climatic, landscape, historical and cultural resources of the region
- distinguish the regional distribution of these geographical resources and their development and use for tourism
- demonstrate a knowledge of the main tourist resorts and tourist centres
- understand the role of Australia and New Zealand in the general pattern of tourism in the Pacific region
- assess the attractions of Australia and New Zealand as long-haul destinations for the UK market.

Introduction

The two countries are physically very different from each other and are over 1900 km apart, but have similar colonial backgrounds and (in terms of the size of the Pacific region) they are near neighbours. Their physical resources complement each other, each providing what the other lacks.

This combination of factors has resulted in their tourist industries being very dependent on each other, and thus they form a distinct sub-region of the Pacific. But as economies of the other Pacific countries have developed, Australia's tourism in particular has become more integrated with that of the region as a whole, and it is becoming less and less appropriate to consider them in isolation from the rest of the Pacific region.

Political, economic and tourist links between Australasia and the rest of the Pacific have been strengthening: in the 1980s the number of Japanese (and other Asian) visitors travelling to Australia has dramatically increased. The Japanese are choosing to invest heavily in Australia's tourist infrastructure (particularly in northeast Australia), while Australians are travelling more widely in the Pacific.

Australia's physical characteristics

Australia is a huge continent (only a little smaller than the USA). The journey across Australia from north to south (e.g. Adelaide to Darwin) is 2623 km by air, and east-west (e.g. Sydney to Perth) is 3278 km. The population is small, only 16.2 million in 1988, and 86 per cent live in the urban areas which are concentrated on the east coast. Vast areas of the interior are very sparsely populated, the roads carry little traffic and there are extensive tracts of wilderness (*see* Chapter 4).

Fig 23.1 The main tourist resources of Australia and New Zealand

The main climatic, physical and tourist regions of the continent are as follows (*see* Fig 23.1):

1 the tropical north;
2 the subtropical east coast, and the Great Dividing Range;
3 the Mediterranean southwest; and
4 the desert and semi-desert of the centre.

The tropical north

The north coast has a wet tropical climate (*see* Fig 2.7 on p 22) with a clear, dry season between May and October. Darwin is the only settlement of any size in Australia's north (the 'Top End'), and it has an international airport. Kakadu National Park is the main attraction here: it is a World Heritage Site on account of its landscape, aboriginal rock art and its wetland wildlife (water buffalo, crocodiles and many species of water birds). Accommodation in the Park is strictly controlled and access to the Park is by coach, car, four-wheel-drive and by boat. Adventure and activity holidays are popular.

The east coast

This can be divided into three tourist regions:

1 The north (Rockhampton to Cape York). Here the main attractions are the coastal rainforests, the Great Barrier Reef and the tropical climate (similar to Darwin). Its main tourist season is the dry, sunny Southern Hemisphere winter (Cairns' driest months are July to October). The Great Barrier Reef is an immense series of offshore coral reefs, cays and islands: it provides the best scuba diving, snorkelling and big game fishing area of the world, and the reef is closest to the shore in the Cairns-Port Douglas region. Day-trips (e.g. in big high-speed catamarans) operate from here and other coastal towns, while longer trips and diving expeditions are also available. In 1988 the world's first 'floating hotel' (a boat permanently moored on the reef) was anchored off Townsville. It is estimated that the half million visitors to the reef in 1986 generated 2.2 million visitor days' use of the reef. The tourist pressure on this vulnerable ecosystem is managed by the Great Barrier Reef Marine Park, who zone it for different levels of use (some areas being reserved for 'look, don't take' tourism where destructive activities such as reef walking, collecting and fishing are not allowed). The accommodation ranges from exclusive island resorts (e.g. Lizard Island, Bedarra Island) to modern international hotels in the major resorts (as at Cairns) through to backpackers' accommodation. The coast is backed by the Atherton Tablelands which are the northern part of the

Great Dividing Range. There are several National Parks in the tropical rainforest (e.g. Bellenden Ker and Cape Tribulation), and the swift flowing rivers are ideal for white water rafting.

Long stretches of coast are completely undeveloped where they are designated as National Parks. Tourism here is essentially a dry season business. The intense rains and danger of poisonous jellyfish in the inshore waters in the Southern Hemisphere summer (December-March) limits the main tourist season to the months of May-October. Hence, during these months the north Queensland coast functions as a 'winter' resort for the population of Sydney and Melbourne but as a 'summer' destination for travellers from the Northern Hemisphere. It attracts relatively few overseas visitors but the upgrading of Cairns airport is encouraging direct flights from Japan, the USA and Europe, and Cairns is in fact a slightly shorter flying time from Tokyo than is Hawaii.

2 Brisbane region. Thus Brisbane is at the centre of the major holiday area for the population of southeast Australia. Although this part of the Queensland coast is visited all year round, it is primarily a winter sun destination. The high temperatures, humidity and rainfall in December-February makes it a little less attractive in this season (*see* Fig 23.2).

The central stretch of coast is most intensively developed for beach tourism particularly along the Gold Coast (to the south of Brisbane) and the Sunshine Coast (to its north). The Gold Coast is a 40 km stretch of unbroken sandy beach and the development is typified by Surfers Paradise, where the beach is backed by high-rise hotels and apartment blocks, with a range of attractions such as casinos, seaworld, and theme parks in the vicinity.

The Gold Coast is served by Coolangatta Airport 27 km south of Brisbane, while the Sunshine Coast, to the north of Brisbane, is

	Summer season			Winter season			
	Dec	**Jan**	**Feb**	**June**	**July**	**Aug**	**Sept**
Av max temp °C	29.1	29.4	28.9	20.8	20.3	21.8	24.0
Av min temp °C	16.6	26.6	20.4	10.7	9.3	10.1	12.7
Rainfall (mm)	127	152	165	76	51	51	51

Fig 23.2 Brisbane winter and summer climate

more accessible via Brisbane Airport. The Sunshine Coast is a little less intensively developed. Noosa, for example, is a quieter resort with smaller hotels, and is adjacent to a National Park. The resorts cater for all water sports, including surfing. Japanese interest is also increasing in this region, as it is along the whole of the Queensland coast. By 1988, the Japanese had bought up 70 per cent of land earmarked for development along Queensland's Gold Coast, and 800 million dollars had been invested in Queensland tourism projects. By 1987 only about 215 000 Japanese visited Australia but Japanese arrivals to Queensland are growing at twice the rate of Japanese travel to Hawaii.

3 Sydney-Melbourne region. This is where most of Australia's population is concentrated. The climate here has wetter winters and drier summers (*see* Fig 2.14 on p 26) and thus complements Brisbane's climate. Most summer coastal activities can take place here, and the local beaches cater for day-trips throughout the year and for summer tourism. There is good surfing though some beaches are dangerous due to offshore currents. The cities, however, are the main focus of tourism, particularly for international VFR tourists. Sydney is situated on the banks of a long branching inlet, spanned by the Harbour Bridge, so provides a beautiful setting for Australia's leading city of 3.5 million people. Ferry transport in the city forms an attractive alternative to the crowded roads. The architects of the Opera House also took advantage of the dramatic waterside site between the Bridge and the Botanic Gardens to create the now world-famous building.

Melbourne is Australia's second largest city, with a population of 3.0 million, and it has good restaurants, gardens and plenty of opportunity for land-based sports. The nearby coastline is cliffed, rugged and dramatic, and its landscape and wildlife (e.g. pelicans, seals and penguins) are particular attractions.

The Great Dividing Range is Australia's major mountain chain that hugs the east coast from Cairns to Melbourne. It reaches its highest point in the Snowy Mountains between Sydney and Melbourne and although the highest point, Mt Kosciusko, is only 2230 m, it is high enough for heavy winter snow. Ski resorts such as the village of Thredbo in the Kosciusko National Park provide for winter sports holidays. There are many other National Parks scattered along the length of the range, providing landscape, wilderness and activity holidays that can be combined with beach tourism based on the coastal settlements (for example, Lamington National Park near Brisbane and the Blue Mountains west of Sydney).

Australia's capital, Canberra, is also sited on a plateau high in the Great Dividing Range. This modern and spacious city is laid out round an attractive artificial lake and is surrounded by mountain ridges.

4 Tasmania. The island of Tasmania is Australia's southernmost territory; its climate is cooler than the rest of Australia, with maximum temperatures reaching 21° C in summer and 11° C in winter. Rainfall is spread evenly throughout the year and is heaviest in the southwest of the island. Its farmed landscapes are more 'English' than much of Australia, though it also has tracts of untouched upland and wilderness, with dramatic waterfalls, gorges, mountains and lakes. The island's capital, Hobart, is small with only 180 000 people, and also has a beautiful harbour setting. The island, however, is not a major tourist area.

The Mediterranean southwest of Australia

The west coast also spans a wide range of climatic zones but it is sheltered from rainbearing winds and is generally drier than the east coast, with long stretches of desert. The best tourist climate is in the small pocket of Mediterranean type climate around Perth. Average summer temperatures rise above 21° C (December-March) and rainfall is very low. In winter the rainfall increases and temperatures drop to 13° C. This is also the only population concentration on the west coast, but is very remote from the rest of Australia.

Its climate is not a powerful enough magnet to draw tourists the long distances from the Sydney and Melbourne beaches in summer, while Perth's winter climate cannot compete with the east coast winter sun resorts in Queensland. Southwest Australia is thus one of the few areas of the world with a Mediterranean climate that is not a major tourist region, in spite of its spectacular unspoilt beaches, excellent yachting facilities, desert landscapes, abundant spring wild flowers and inland historic mining towns.

The arid centre (the 'Red Centre')

Most of Australia's interior is hot desert, or arid zone land, with under 225 mm rainfall a year. There is little surface water, though underground sources can be tapped at the natural springs and waterholes or by artesian wells, so water shortage is not an overriding constraint on tourist development.

The landscape is dominated by open plains of very low relative relief and indeterminate internal drainage. Intermittently flowing seasonal rivers flow westward off the Great Dividing Range into salt lakes (e.g. Lake Eyre) in vast internal basins. Trees line these watercourses while elsewhere the desert is covered in tough tussocky grass or scrub. Further west, the desert is drier and is a mixture of stony plains, sand dunes and claypans. The landscape is red and dusty due to iron oxide deposits which coat the rock surface. The plains are interrupted in the geographical centre of Australia by a series of mountain ranges (e.g. the Macdonnell, Musgrave and Petermann Ranges). More isolated outcrops (remnants of very ancient mountains) are located in the basins between these ranges. Ayers Rock and Mt Olga in the Uluru National Park are the best known of these dramatic isolated rocks. Ayers Rock rises 370 m from the flat plain; it is the major tourist attraction and is accessible from the nearby Yulara resort, a well-designed tourist centre which provide accommodation ranging from international standard hotels to open air camping. It has its own airstrip but most visitors come by air to Alice Springs and then transfer (by air or coach) to Yulara. The climate (*see* Fig 2.10 on p 23) is hot but does not inhibit tourism if visitors are careful.

Patterns of tourism in Australia

Domestic tourism

Eighty per cent of tourism demand (in terms of tourist nights) is generated by the domestic market, which has grown steadily in the 1980s by two to three per cent pa. This represents a real increase in trip taking as the population has been growing at only 1.5 per cent over the same period. In the 1988/89 season Australian residents took 46 million trips from home. Most were summer (Dec/Jan) holidays on the beaches of the southeast, or winter holidays to the Queensland coast, with smaller numbers of ski trips to the Snowy Mountains or visits to the Red Centre. Only 8.5 per cent of domestic holiday trips involve air travel, a surprisingly low figure for such a huge continent but it reaffirms the fact that the population can meet most of its tourist needs relatively locally, particularly in the southeast of the country. Most travel is by road. Car travel is easy on the rural roads which are empty by European standards. Good intercity, long-distance coach services are also available between the cities of the southeast and to the Brisbane coast. The further flung resort areas – i.e. Darwin, Alice Springs, Cairns and Tasmania – rely much more heavily on air transport, and tourism in these locations was very badly hit by the prolonged domestic pilots' strike in 1989/90.

Inbound tourism

International tourists to Australia use the internal airlines far more extensively than do domestic tourists: 45 per cent of foreign visitors fly within Australia and over half visit more than one state: on average UK, Japanese and Americans visited 2.2 to 2.4 states. Even so, international tourism is heavily concentrated in the more populated southeast, particularly in New South Wales (and in Sydney). This pattern of tourism partly reflects the high VFR element (over a quarter of all foreign visitors stay with friends or relatives while this figure rises to 29 per cent of New Zealanders and 52 per cent of all UK tourists to Australia).

State	% of all domestic arrivals	% of all foreign arrivals
New South Wales	36.0	38.5
Australian Capital Territory (i.e. Canberra)	1.6	6.1
Victoria	23.3	18.7
Queensland	18.4	18.9
South Australia	7.6	7.8
West Australia	7.3	7.2
Tasmania	3.3	1.1
Northern Territory	1.2	3.1

Fig 23.3 Spatial distribution of international and domestic tourism in Australia (1984) 1994

Australia is essentially a winter destination for the Northern Hemisphere: 32 per cent of overseas visitors come between October and December, with UK visitors particularly concentrating on November and December with a secondary peak in March. Climate, plus the family nature of the Christmas festivities, would appear to account for this pattern.

Australia is a long-haul destination for all markets and inbound tourism was badly hit by the world recession of the 1980s. After a period of rapid growth in the late 1970s tourist numbers stagnated between 1980–85. The following three years were marked by exceptionally rapid growth of inbound tourism triggered off by world economic recovery which coincided with several hallmark events in Australia, i.e. the 1986 Americas Cup Yacht Race near Perth and the bicentennial celebrations and Brisbane's Expo, both in 1988. International tourism had more than doubled from 800 000 in 1979 to reach the two million mark in 1988.

The composition of Australia's international tourism has changed significantly over the same period. In 1979 Australia's tourism was very highly dependent on the New Zealand market which provided 34 per cent of its inbound tourists. Since then the numbers of tourists from other Pacific Rim countries has dramatically increased; for example Japanese tourists increased from 41 636 in 1979 to 352 000 in 1988, visitors from USA from 97 000 – 320 000 and the number of tourists from other Asian countries also tripled.

Tourists from Asia now account for 33 per cent of Australia's inbound tourism, North America another 18 per cent and New Zealand now only 24 per cent. This does not represent any decline in the popularity of Australia as a destination for New Zealanders. In fact the reverse is true. Australia is increasing its market share of the New Zealand outbound trade, and the numbers of New Zealanders visiting Australia has doubled through the 1980s. Rather, it represents the faster growth rates of tourism from the rest of the Pacific and the increasing integration of Australia – both politically and in its acceptance of Asian immigrants – with the rest of the Pacific region.

UK tourism to Australia has increased but at a much slower rate (from 114 000 to 260 000 between 1979 and 1988) and in the late 1980s accounted for only 11 per cent of Australia's foreign visitors.

Outbound tourism

In 1987 only 1.6 million Australians travelled abroad. Its outbound tourism shares many characteristics with that of the USA: its own huge territory can meet most of its travel needs, while adjacent countries (in this case New Zealand) take the bulk of outbound travellers and significant numbers visit Europe, to visit friends and relations and for cultural tourism. However parallel with the changes in Australia's inbound tourism, Australians are travelling more widely to the Asian Pacific rim (e.g. Bali, Hong Kong, Thailand and Malaysia), rather than just to the nearest Pacific islands, such as Fiji and New Caledonia.

Destination	% Outbound tourists		
	1974	1984	1987
Asia	19.2	30.0	33.7
Oceania	35.1	29.8	25.7
Americas	8.1	12.3	13.3
Europe	32.6	26.5	25.2
Africa	0.9	1.2	1.3

Fig 23.4 Australian outbound tourism 1974–1987

New Zealand's tourist regions

This country consists of two islands (totalling about 267 000 km^2) of varied climate and landscape with the latter being its main tourist resource.

New Zealand's isolation and emphasis on landscape tourism result in a small (though economically important) tourist industry with about 850 000 visitors in the 1987/1988 season. The country has a population of only 3.3 million (in 1988), of whom 75 per cent live in North Island, and who generated 666 000 outbound trips in 1988. New Zealand's tourism is highly dependent on Australia, which is both the leading destination for New Zealand's outbound travellers but is also the main source of New Zealand's tourist arrivals. Like Australia, however, the country is gradually becoming more integrated to the Pacific region.

North Island

1 Auckland peninsula. This is the largest area of lowland, the most densely populated and has the mildest climate of the whole of New Zealand. Auckland, like Sydney, has an east margin warm temperate climate. In the summer period (December-March) temperatures range between 14° C and 23° C, while the winter is cooler (7–14° C), with some rain all year round but a winter maximum with a total of 1650 mm pa. On average, Auckland is a few degrees cooler than Sydney but with about the same amount of rainfall. North Island averages about 2000 hours sunshine a year. The climate is pleasant and allows beach tourism in summer, but given its greater isolation from its markets it cannot compete with the other beach tourist destinations of the Pacific region. The landscapes of the Auckland peninsula are green and fertile and quite English in character, although there are also areas of vineyards. Auckland and The Bay of Islands are the main tourist attractions, and Auckland is one of the major international gateways.

2 The centre of North Island. The region has several volcanic mountains and still shows signs of volcanic activity and tourists can see geysers, hot springs and boiling mud pools at Rotorua, the centre of the thermal region. The nearby lakes of Rotorua and Taupo are also centres for watersports. New Zealand's native population, the Maoris, are of Polynesian origin and there is a Maori Village and Arts and Crafts Centre at Rotorua which attracts many visitors. Rotorua's varied attractions make it the country's leading destination with 60 per cent of all holiday visitors.

The volcanic peak of Mt Ruapehu lies at the heart of North Island and the popular Tongariro National Park lies further south.

South Island

The Southern Alps dominate the Island, forming its spine. The mountains reach 3760 m and divide the wild, wet and rugged West Coast (which receives up to 4000 mm rainfall per annum) from the sunnier and drier east. The climate is significantly cooler than North Island. In winter the mountains receive heavy snowfall and have excellent skiing conditions which attract many Australian tourists. The landscapes are spectacular, with glaciers such as the Fox and Franz Joseph glaciers and fjords, e.g. Milford Sound, on the southwest coast. The Tasman glacier provides all year round skiing. The Island has seven National Parks with many opportunities for outdoor activities, such as climbing, walking, canoe safaris, jet boating and white water rafting. Although much of the Island is rugged and mountainous, the road system is good, with little traffic; the attractions are accessible and distances between them fairly short. Independent car touring (and camper vanning) is the main travel mode, although bus/coach touring is also important. Queenstown (on Lake Wakatipu) is an old goldmining town but is within easy reach of the main scenic attractions of South Island, and it is the leading South Island tourist centre.

Inbound and outbound tourism

Most Australians visiting New Zealand come for holidays, although there is also a strong VFR and business element. More than half the visitors from UK come to visit friends and relatives. The growing Japanese and American elements of the inbound tourist market are dominated by holidaymakers.

Tourism by New Zealanders is becoming more outward looking. The outbound market grew rapidly in the late 1980s while domestic tourism was declining. Domestic nights and trips dropped in 1985, 1986 and 1987. North Islanders appear to be substituting trips to South Island by international travel to Australia and other more distant destinations, such as the USA and the UK. However, other Pacific destinations, e.g. Singapore, Japan and Hong Kong, are becoming increasingly popular. As with Australia, New Zealand is becoming more integrated into the Pacific region.

QUESTIONS AND DISCUSSION POINTS

1 New Zealand has always depended heavily on the Australian market for her international tourists. Is the relationship between Australia and New Zealand changing and, if so, how and why?
2 Why do you think the Perth region of Australia is relatively little developed for tourism (domestic or international), in spite of its favourable Mediterranean-type climate?

ASSIGNMENTS

1 Three young friends have saved up to go to Australia together next year. They are all interested in wildlife, adventure and wilderness holidays and they wish to see as many of Australia's different natural environments as possible and to try as many different activities as possible.

Their list of places they want to visit include Kosciusko National Park (the Snowy Mountains), Uluru (the Red Centre), Cape Tribulation (rainforest), the Great Barrier Reef, and Kakadu (for the wetlands). They can only take a month off work and they have to co-ordinate their leave. They have come to your travel agency for advice before they tell their employers when they want their holiday next year.

Is there any one month in the year when it would be suitable to visit all the National Parks on their list? If not, in which month would they be able to visit most of the Parks in comfort (and which ones would they have to leave out)? Advise them on the weather, road conditions and activities they could do at that time of year in each part. Also, suggest a route to and through Australia that would minimise internal travel distances.

CHAPTER 24

Asia and the Pacific Islands

LEARNING OBJECTIVES

After reading this chapter you should be able to

- assess the tourist potential of the climatic, landscape, historical and cultural resources of the region
- distinguish between the regional distribution of these geographical resources, and their development and use for tourism
- demonstrate a knowledge of the main tourist resorts and tourist centres
- understand the role of East and Southeast Asia, and the Pacific Islands in the general pattern of tourism of the Pacific region
- identify the contrasting pattern of tourism in the Indian Subcontinent (South Asia)
- assess the attractions of Asian and Pacific long-haul destinations for the UK market.

Introduction

Asia and the Pacific contain some of the world's most densely populated countries. China, with a population of 1062 million in 1988, and India, with 800 million, are the population giants of the regions, followed by Indonesia (175 million), Japan (122 million), Bangladesh (107 million) and Pakistan (104 million). With the exception of Japan, all these countries have very low GNP and are in the first phase of tourist development (*see* Chapter 1).

Japan

Japan is a far more affluent country (*see* Chapter 1) and is the only significant tourist generator out of all these countries. In fact it rivals the USA as the major tourist generator of the region; and is thus a major influence on tourism in the region, but overseas travel in Japan is still very much minority activity among its population. Social pressures and the strong sense of duty to the company still make work very important, and much leisure time in Japan is spent with colleagues rather than with the family. Although officially Japanese employees are entitled to two or three weeks' paid leave, it is often not taken up. In the mid-1980s, the Japanese, on average, took only about eight days' holiday per year, and working men feel unable to take more than a few days' holiday at a time. A break of four consecutive days is still considered a long holiday, and in 1987 53 per cent of the Japanese travelling abroad spent only one to five days away. The one exception is the Japanese honeymoon when a longer holiday of an average of 7.9 days, and overseas travel is then accepted. Ninety-three per cent of the 700 000 couples getting married each year take their honeymoon overseas. The Japanese Government is trying to encourage

KEY

1	Philippines	8	Tuvalu	15	Samoa
2	Marianas	9	Marquesas	16	Tonga
3	Hawaiian Islands	10	Galapagos	17	Cook Islands
4	Caroline Islands	11	Solomon Islands	18	Society Islands
5	Marshall Islands	12	Vanuatu	19	Tuamotu
6	Kiribati	13	New Caledonia	20	Tubuai Islands
7	Phoenix Islands	14	Fiji		

more people to take time off and to travel. It is trying to make a five (rather than a six) day working week the norm, encouraging summer holiday taking and it aims to increase Japanese overseas trips to ten million a year by 1992.

The growth of Japanese outbound tourism has been very rapid, doubling from 4.2 million in 1983 to 8.4 million in 1988, and already reaching over 9 million by 1989. This is beginning to erode the social pressures that make the Japanese feel guilty about taking time off. Attitudes to leisure are beginning to change, particularly among the younger generation. The desire to travel does apparently exist: a survey in 1987 indicated that 46 per cent of the Japanese would like to travel 'if given the chance'. Once cultural norms change to allow the Japanese a more

leisure-orientated lifestyle in which holidays are more freely taken, the whole pattern of regional and world tourism could change a great deal. Japanese society puts an emphasis on formality, conformity and politeness, and individuals travelling abroad may be apprehensive about language difficulties, about 'doing the wrong thing' and causing embarassment. The Japanese, therefore, have a strong cultural preference for group travel and in the mid-1980s, 50–80 per cent of travellers to long-haul destinations (i.e. to unfamiliar cultures) went on package tours. The corresponding proportions were much lower to destinations such as Taiwan (32 per cent) and South Korea (14 per cent) where Japanese is spoken and there are stronger similarities in culture.

Fig 24.1 China and Japan

The main overseas destination for the Japanese tourist is the United States of America (with about one and a half million visiting Hawaii, and roughly the same number crossing the whole expanse of the Pacific to the North American mainland in 1988). Taiwan, Hong Kong and South Korea are the main local Pacific destinations, with each attracting roughly one million Japanese, while China, Singapore and Guam each received about half a million. However, Japanese tourism is growing fastest to New Zealand, Australia, China and Canada. The bulk of Japanese outbound travel is thus within the Pacific region, but substantial numbers of Japanese do also visit Europe.

Japan has much less regional significance as a tourist destination. Although Japan received over two million visitors in 1986, the strength of the yen in the late 1980s made it a relatively expensive destination, particularly for Asian visitors (who make up nearly half of Japan's inbound tourists). At a time when most of the other politically stable Pacific destinations have been rapidly increasing their tourist arrivals, Japan has been losing its visitors. Nearly half of Japan's tourists come from USA and Taiwan. On average, 51 per cent of Japan's inbound travellers come as tourists, and the pleasure market is increasing. Significant proportions of Asian visitors come to see friends and relatives, while business tourism is more important for many European visitors. Cultural and historical attractions are the focus of tourism in Japan, for example, the old Imperial cities of Kyoto, Nara, Kamakura and the architectural heritage of Takayama and Kanazawa and the urban centres of Osaka and Tokyo. Other attractions include skiing resorts, a Tokyo Disneyland and the landscape of the Fuji Hakone National Park.

China

China has a vastly larger population than Japan

but its economic and political circumstances have inhibited the development of its tourist industry until very recently. In contrast to Japan, its major role has been as a tourist destination. Around 12 million ethnic Chinese visit the country from the adjacent territories of Hong Kong, Macao and Taiwan.

In 1978, China, after years of isolation from the rest of the world, adopted an 'open door' policy. This encompassed both the modernisation of China's economy as well as its opening up to western travellers. One of the main incentives for China to promote tourism after 1978 appears to have been the country's need for foreign currency. In spite of teething troubles resulting from the lack of tourist infrastructure and experience, the number of non-Chinese visitors grew very rapidly in the 1980s to 1.8 million in 1988. These were essentially cultural and special interest tourists. The historical resources of the country are immense (*see* Chapter 5). The ancient capitals, such as Xian, site of the tombs and terracotta army, Beijing and Hangzhou, go back 3000 years and attract appreciable numbers of foreign visitors.

Luoyan is another major historical centre that has yet to be developed on the same scale. Contemporary cultural events are also a major attraction, such as lantern and kite festivals, in addition to Chinese cuisine, herbal and traditional medicine, arts and handicrafts. China also has spectacular landscapes, e.g. Yangtse gorges, the strange round humps and rock formations of the limestone mountains of Guilin, and the Huangshan mountains. China also has some beautiful undeveloped beaches. The development of tourism in China is constrained by three factors:

1 **Climate**:
2 **Infrastructure**; and
3 **Politics**.

Although China spans several climatic zones, the climates of the interior are affected by continental influences, with very cold winters and equally extreme (hot) summers; for example the average temperature in Beijing is minus 4° C in January and 26° C in July. Spring and autumn are the best times, though spring can be wet in the south and on the east coast.

The infrastructure is in the process of development. In the late 1980s transport was still generally poor, with a poor road system and few airports that can handle 747s or 737s. By the end of 1988, the whole country had 220 200 hotel rooms.

The political attitude of the Chinese is, of course, the major factor. The modernisation programme for the economy (with a move away from a centrally planned economy towards a market economy) brought rapid growth in the GNP (up 11 per cent in the year 1987/8) but also 30 per cent inflation. The 'open door' policy and greater contacts with the West brought demands from China's students for greater democracy. In 1989 the regime reacted violently to quell these demands, and Western tourists (particularly Australasian and American) responded by staying away, and tour operators withdrew. The Chinese are, however, keen to see tourists return and the UK and European market began to recover, although it inevitably takes time for confidence to return. Travel by the Japanese and other Asians to China was not so drastically affected. The way in which China approaches and solves its domestic economic and political problems will no doubt be reflected in the extent to which foreign tourism is encouraged or constrained. The internal economic and political reforms were also beginning to generate a domestic tourist market. The extent to which China becomes an international tourist generator and destination entirely depends on its political evolution. With such immensely varied resources and such a huge population it could radically alter the patterns of tourism in the Pacific region.

The remainder of Southeast Asia

The other main centres of tourism in the Pacific region are located along the edge of the Pacific in a string along the coast of Southeast Asia: they are the small territories of South Korea, Hong Kong, Taiwan, Macao, Malaysia and Singapore, plus the larger country of Thailand. South Korea and Taiwan have a variety of resources, such as spectacular scenery, beautiful beaches and distinctive cultures, but they function mainly as holiday destinations for the Japanese market.

In the mid-1980s, between 45 and 55 per cent of their visitors came from Japan, about 16 per cent from North America and the bulk of the rest were holidaymakers from other Asian countries. Thirty to 50 per cent of the Western visitors were business tourists.

Hong Kong and Singapore

Hong Kong and Singapore are both tiny island territories with limited tourist resources, but have significant inbound tourism (5.5 and 3.8 million respectively in 1988). They both have colonial links with Britain and are major world, as well as regional, commercial and industrial centres. This is reflected in the fact that 45–50 per cent of their visitors are non-Asian and high proportions are business tourists – up to 40 per cent in Singapore and 22 per cent in Hong Kong. They both have large international airports and many of the non-Asian holidaymakers are likely to be international travellers making stopover visits. The average length of stay in Singapore was 3.5 days in 1985, and over 85 per cent of arrivals came by air. Both countries are in competition with Thailand for this stopover trade, as Bangkok airport is another of the region's main hub airports. Hong Kong is due to be returned to China in 1997 and its future, both as a commercial and tourist centre, will depend on China's policies and the response of Hong Kong to them.

Malaysia

Malaysia has a wealth of unspoilt beaches, cultural and wildlife resources, but as yet depends very heavily on its neighbours (Singapore and Thailand) for the vast majority (about 75 per cent) of its 3.3 million visitors. Japan is its next most important market.

Thailand

Thailand has a similar variety of resources but has been more active in developing and promoting its beach resorts and received 4.2 million visitors in 1988. Some of Thailand's beaches face the sheltered Gulf of Siam (on the enclosed South China Sea) while others face the Indian Ocean.

The resorts do not experience the big surf of the beaches open to the Pacific (*see* Chapter 3). The climate is hot and is similar to the Indian monsoon regime with three clear seasons – a 'cooler' dry season from the end of October to February (when temperatures may drop to 26° C); a very hot dry season between March and May, when Bangkok's average temperature reaches 35° C; and the wet season from June to October. Phuket has 1270 mm of rain in the space of these five wet months. For Europeans, Thailand is very much a winter sun destination, and North American visitors favour October to December, but for intra-regional visitors, July and August are secondary peak months. This adds up to a remarkably even spread of visitor numbers through the year, making the country as a whole a non-seasonal destination.

The biggest beach resort is Pattaya, about two and a half hours by road south of Bangkok (*see* Fig 24.5). It is a lively, modern resort with some big hotels, sports facilities, all beach activities (from waterskiing to coral diving) and lively nightlife with discos, cabarets and bars. Thailand is notorious for its sex tourism and prostitution, although Bangkok is the main location of these activities. The other beach resorts in Thailand are quieter, ranging from Hua Hin and nearby Cha Am, to the islands of Ko Samui and Phuket on either side of the Malay peninsula. Both Ko Samui and Phuket have their own airports, and are accessible from Bangkok (one hour's flying time) but Phuket is rather more intensively developed. The island has a mixture of sandy beaches, rugged headlands and lagoons.

The beach resorts of Thailand are complemented by inland attractions. The Buddhist temples, Grand Palace, cultural attractions such as Thai dancing, and the cheap shopping make Bangkok an attractive stopover and holiday centre, though the city is very polluted and congested. The far north of Thailand, particularly the Chiang Mai region is being promoted for its landscape, culture and historic ruins.

Thailand thus has a great variety of tourist resources and is an independent kingdom that has been politically stable for a long time – an unusual feature in a fairly turbulent region. These advantages have resulted in its successful promotion as a tourist destination and, as shown in Fig 24.2, it attracts visitors from a much wider range of countries than most Pacific destinations.

	% arrivals	
North America		
USA	6.7	8.3
Canada etc	1.6	
Europe		
UK	5.2	
W Germany	4.2	
France	3.7	22.5
Other European	9.4	
Pacific		
Malaysia	21.9	
Japan	9.7	
Singapore	6.8	50.7
Taiwan	5.5	
Hongkong	3.7	
Australia	3.1	
Other		
(Middle East, South Asia, rest		
of Pacific)	18.5	
	100 %	

Total number of arrivals = 3.483 million

Fig 24.2 International tourist arrivals to Thailand (1987)

Island destinations in the Pacific

The Pacific is huge and empty, but there are groups of islands scattered over it. The Hawaiian group is very isolated, located virtually in the centre of the Pacific, almost midway between Japan and the USA, but in spite of this, it is the major destination of the whole Pacific region, with about six million visitors in 1988.

Hawaii

Hawaii is one of the states of the USA, but it is a long way from the American mainland (San Francisco is 3840 km and five to six hours' flying time to the east). It is even more remote from the western edge of the ocean. (Tokyo is 6160 km to the west.) However, deregulation of the American airlines has led to intense competition and airfares to Hawaii are relatively cheap, making it a popular tropical destination for both US and Japanese markets. The state of Hawaii consists of five main islands (*see* Fig 24.3). Hawaii is the name of the biggest island but it is relatively little used by tourists; the state capital, Honolulu, and most of the tourist activity is centred on the island of Oahu, where the main

Fig 24.3 The Hawaiian islands

international airport is situated. The island group is made up of the exposed tips of undersea volcanic mountains, which rise nearly 4500 m above sea level. Most of the volcanoes are dormant but Mauna Loa (on Hawaii Island) is still active and forms the centre piece of the Hawaii Volcanoes National Park.

The climate is subtropical with relatively little seasonal variation (*see* Chapter 2) and tourism also shows little seasonality. There is a slight but not very marked peak in June, July and August. The Hawaiian islands are in the same climatic situation as the volcanic islands of the east Caribbean: they sit in the path of the trade winds that blow from east to west. Like the Caribbean islands the Hawaiian group have wet, humid climates with very heavy rainfall on their eastern sides (which catch the torrential orographic rain), while the western ends of the islands are dry, sheltered and sunny. Honolulu (*see* Fig 2.9 on p 23 for climatic statistics) is in a sheltered site and has only 607 mm a year. The exposed eastern slopes of mount Waialeale on Kauai have an average of 12 344 mm pa, and is among the wettest places on earth. With this amount of rainfall the mountain slopes are eroded into steep ridges and ravines clothed with lush tropical vegetation. These landscapes are in sharp contrast to the volcanic features and produce a varied and dramatic backdrop to the tourist beaches. Much of the coast, however, is cliffed and rugged. Waikiki beach is quite small and very crowded, backed by high rise hotels and condominiums. Less developed beaches with good surf lie on the north side of the island, while there are also ample opportunities for scuba diving and snorkelling on the coral reefs. Oahu has 58 per cent of all Hawaii's accommodation (in 1985), while the island of Maui has 21 per cent of the accommodation stock, and some bigger swimming beaches. Hawaii also offers cultural attractions.

The islands' population is a blend of various ethnic groups (including Japanese, Chinese, Philippino, Afro-Caribbean, Puerto Rican) plus the native Hawaiians. It is a multicultural destination though museums, hula and Tahitian dance shows and Luau pig roast feasts demonstrate Polynesian culture.

The majority (63 per cent) of tourists come from USA mainland and a high proportion of these from California and other west coast states, and the average stay is 11 days. Twenty per cent of Hawaii's visitors come from Japan and, although they spend more per head, they stay only five days on average. Canada, Australia and Europe contribute roughly another four per cent each. The Americans tend to be repeat visitors, and they show an increasing inclination to explore the less developed islands after their first visit. Direct flights from US mainland to Maui, for example, have encouraged this trend, and a quarter of the visitors to Hawaii now bypass Oahu altogether. Further expansion of Hawaii's tourist industry is likely to be focused on the spreading of tourism more widely throughout the islands. Hawaii is America's most popular tropical destination; it has an appealingly different local culture but the advantages of a common language, currency and basic legal framework as USA. Above all it has political stability. A weak dollar only serves to reinforce all these advantages.

The other Pacific Islands

There are three other main groupings of islands in the Pacific Ocean:

1 Micronesia – the islands clustered off the Southeast Asian coast (between Japan and New Guinea) which cater mainly for the Japanese, receiving a total of 851 000 tourists in 1988.

2 Melanesia – the strings of islands in the expanse of ocean to the north of New Zealand and northeast of Australia, whose visitors come mainly from Australasia. In 1988 they received 339 000 visitors.

3 Polynesia – groups of islands widely scattered over the centre of the South Pacific Ocean. This is the least visited island region, with only 275 000 tourists in 1988.

The islands vary in character from flat barrier reef islands or coral atolls, to mountainous volcanic islands, e.g. the Marianas and Tahiti (where the mountains rise over 2000 m). Many of the volcanic islands also have offshore coral reefs enclosing calm lagoons that are ideal for beach and swimming activities, while more exposed beaches have good surf. The islands essentially have the same physical and climatic attractions as Hawaii.

The climate of Rarotonga (in the Cook Islands) is shown in Fig 2.9 on p 23. Apart from those immediately on the Equator, the Pacific islands are subject to occasional tropical storms (cyclones) which, like the hurricanes of the Caribbean, can devastate their tourist infrastructure. Vanuatu was struck by a cyclone in 1987 which resulted in a sharp decrease in tourist activity, and Guam suffered in 1980.

The islands are grouped into archipelagos, each consisting of hundreds of islands scattered over thousands of square kilometres of ocean; for example the Cook islands (in Polynesia) are spread over an area of ocean the size of Western Europe. Distances between archipelagos, islands and their tourist markets are vast and they are generally much less accessible than Hawaii. Tourism on the islands entirely depends on air links and on the routes the airlines choose to take. The levels of investment needed to create an international airport, hotels and tourist infrastructure simultaneously is normally not available, so tourism is limited to a few islands where circumstances have favoured such developments specifically Guam, the North Marianas, Tahiti and Fiji. Guam is a self-governing territory of USA, and the US military base provided the necessary infrastructure of airport, airline and hotels. The Japanese have also invested in hotels and the island caters mainly for the Japanese honeymoon market. The island is also being marketed in Australia in competition with Hawaii as a tropical island destination. Tahiti has benefited from investment from France to build up its tourist industry and offers a similar (but less crowded and commercialised) product to Hawaii, through it is one of the most expensive Pacific Island destinations. Fiji has experienced a significant decline in

Island	% arrivals			
	From USA	*From Australia and New Zealand*	*From Europe*	*From Japan*
(a) Micronesia				
Guam	6.5	0.1	3.1	85.3
North Marianas	18.2	0.1	0.5	78.1
(b) Melanesia				
Fiji	33.6	42.9	12.2	–
Vanuatu	5.0	55.5	4.6	2.4
(c) Polynesia				
French Polynesia (Tahiti)	52.8	9.0	29.0	–
Cook Islands	16.2	62.0	16.5	–

Fig 24.4 Catchments of Pacific Islands (1988)

tourism since the 1987 coups (a result of conflicts between the indigenous Polynesians and ethnic Indian populations of the island), while riots in New Caledonia in 1985 and in Vanuatu in 1988 have also deterred visitors.

The pattern of travel to the islands is very sectoral. Guam and the North Marianas depend almost entirely on visitors from countries to their north (78 per cent coming from Japan). Melanesia depends more on the adjacent Australasian market who provide around half the tourists to Papua/New Guinea, the Solomon Islands and Vanuatu.

Polynesia draws a wider mix of visitors (*see* Fig 24.4), although Fiji, New Caledonia and Vanuatu have lost popularity among Australians and New Zealanders after the local political disturbances. The Australasian market has transferred to other island destinations, such as Bali in Indonesia, the Cook Islands (particularly Rarotonga), Norfolk Island and the more distant but rapidly developing Asian mainland resorts, for example in Thailand.

The island states of Indonesia and the Philippines

These archipelagos are much closer to the Asian mainland, and form the barrier which effectively encloses the South China Sea, separating it from the Pacific Ocean proper. They are both very extensive groups of islands: Indonesia consists of 13 600 islands, while the Philippines has over 7000 islands. They are all fairly large jungle-covered mountainous islands, some with active

or recently extinct volcanoes. The densely populated Indonesian islands lie along the Equator and have uncomfortably hot and humid climates. The country is predominantly Islamic (*see* Fig 19.1 on p 233), but this does not inhibit tourist development. However, it is the mainly Hindu island of Bali that is most extensively developed for tourism (cultural tourism focused on its temples, processions, dances, gamelan music and festivals, plus beach and stopover tourism). Indonesia attracted 1.6 million visitors in 1988, mainly from Australia and Europe.

The Philippines received almost the same volume of tourism but caters more for the US and Japanese markets. The islands have been notorious for sex tourism and lively nightlife, but have recently tried to change their image by promoting sports, such as golf, and beach tourism. However, the political events of the 1980s and the continuing undercurrent of political instability that has constrained the growth of tourism here.

Conclusion – the Pacific Region

The region is one of geographical contrasts; of very affluent and of very poor countries; of very different Western and Eastern cultures; of countries with wide appeal, drawing international travellers many thousands of kilometres across the huge region, and countries that depend more heavily upon the developing tourism of their neighbours. It does, however, have a functional unity in that most of its tourism is generated within its own region, and tourism throughout the region is very buoyant.

South Asia: the Indian Subcontinent

This region, although structurally part of Asia and adjacent to the focus of tourism in the Pacific region (*see* Fig 24.5), is functionally quite separate from the Pacific region. It shows all the economic, political and tourist characteristics of the economic periphery (*see* Chapters 1 and 7).

Like Subsaharan Africa, all the countries of the region are very poor: in 1988 their GNP per head ranged from 150 US dollars in Bangladesh to 380 in Pakistan, although India and Pakistan have a growing middle class and a growing domestic tourist market.

Again, in common with Africa, and indeed Latin America, it is the local political circum-stances that determine the extent to which international tourism is developed.

Burma has been ruled by a military regime which has kept this Buddhist country effectively closed to tourists. The regime was defeated in democratic elections, but in 1990 had still refused to give up power.

Sri Lanka had a growing beach tourist industry until intercommunal strife broked out, and it too was effectively closed for tourism by 1990. Pakistan, too, has had a turbulent political history, encompassing both military dictatorship and democratically elected governments, while India has been the most stable democracy of the region, although it has its own local internal ethnic and intercommunal problems. The main

Fig 24.5 The Indian Subcontinent and surrounding region

region of long-term political instability has been the Pakistan/Indian border region of Kashmir and the Punjab, where international border disputes and the Sikh Separatist movement have caused intermittent problems. However, the intercommunal friction that led to the partition of India and Pakistan is never far below the surface. These problems have constrained the growth of tourism to a very low level indeed, in spite of the region having a wealth of scenic and cultural resources.

The region consists of four physical subdivisions, each of which has a very distinctly different type of landscape, and different tourist resources and tourist potential.

1 The Himalayas which form an arc of mountainous territory extending from Afghanistan and the West of Pakistan in the west, through North India, Tibet and the mountain kingdoms of Nepal, Sikkim and Bhutan, to the ridges which curve south through Burma. The mountains are geologically young and produce the same dramatic scenery of parallel ridges, jagged, eroded peaks, with deeply cut steep-sided river valleys. The terrain makes the land remote and inaccessible. The Himalayan chain is the highest and most extensive mountain range of the world.
2 The valleys of the Indus and Ganges. These two rivers and their tributaries drain from the Himalayas and they flow across immense, flat and fertile plains stretching in a virtually unbroken arc from Karachi to Calcutta. Their lower reaches are subject to flooding, and Bangladesh (whose territory is mainly the delta and lower flood plains of the Ganges and Brahmaputra) is subject to repeated flooding from both the sea and river.
3 The Deccan plateau of South India. The much dissected plateau is highest along India's west coast and slopes gently downwards towards the north and east.
4 The islands. The biggest island, Sir Lanka, lies off the east coast of India; and the Maldives, is a group of much smaller islands which offer sun, sea and sand tourism with coral reefs for diving and snorkelling in a tropical climate.

Tourist resources and the development of tourism

West of the Thar Desert the region has a 'three

season' climate. The winter (November to February) is the coolest season and is most suited to tourism. Temperatures begin to rise through March to peak in May, when the average daily maximum is 40° C in Delhi and Jaipur, and 41° C in Agra. In south India it is even hotter. Although this hot season is dry, it is too hot for most sightseeing activities in the plains and in peninsular India, though it is cooler in the mountains. The 'monsoon' breaks in June and lasts until October. This rainfall is variable in its amount but torrential in nature. The high land on the west coast of peninsular India is in the path of the rainbearing winds and receives particularly heavy rain (Goa has 752 mm in the month of June alone). Similarly the west-facing coast of the Bay of Bengal (Assam and Burma) has exceedingly heavy rain at this time of year. Rainfall decreases inland but June still marks the abrupt change from hot, dry to hot, wet conditions.

Delhi and Agra have their rainfall peaks in July with a monthly total of 177 mm and 228 mm respectively. Most cultural tours of India operate from October to March, while the mountain regions are best in April and September/October.

The cultural resources of the region are rich and varied, ranging from ancient archaeological sites in Pakistan, to magnificent Hindu and Mughal buildings in India; the modern Moslem, Hindu and Buddhist cultures and ways of life also provide a great variety of experiences for the tourist. Although the countries are very densely populated and there is great pressure on the land, there are pockets of wildlife interest where national parks and reserves provide opportunities for wildlife tourism.

India is the only significant tourist destination in the region, yet only attracted 1.6 million visitors in 1988, but its policy is to promote and diversify its tourism. Beach tourism is developed in the Goa region but cultural tourism is the mainstay of India's tourist industry. It is focused on the Mughal cities, palaces, forts and tombs of the plains of north India (e.g. the 'Golden Triangle' of the Red Fort at Delhi, Fatehpur Sikri and the Taj Mahal at Agra and the palaces at Jaipur).

However, there are many other regions of India with great tourist appeal such as the Rajput palaces and castles, the crafts and folk music of the desert region of Rajasthan, the frescos and temples of the Ajanta and Ellora caves at Aurangabad (inland of Bombay) and the Hindu architecture and carvings at Mahabalipuram and Karchipuram in South India near Madras. Wildlife and scenic and activity holidays are combined in the Himalayas, with Kashmir the main destination when political circumstances allow. Nepal, Sikkim and Bhutan are being opened up to tourists, and tours, treks and camping in Nepal are increasingly popular for the more active and adventurous tourist. Nepal attracted just over one quarter of a million visitors in 1988. The high altitudes of some of these destinations make them inappropriate for the less fit.

A large proportion of visitors (48 per cent in the mid-1980s) to India and the Himalayan kingdoms come from Europe and North America (particularly USA, UK, West Germany and France). It is significant that South Asia draws tourists from a much wider range of European countries than does Subsaharan Africa.

Pakistan's tourism is also focused on the mountains in the north, although the archaeological sites of the Indus valley also have great potential. Only a quarter of Pakistan's visitors come from Europe, and just six per cent from USA while half come from India (particularly VFR tourism). Pakistan's inbound tourism has fluctuated between 400 000 and 450 000 in the late 1980s.

The Maldive Islands, off the southwest coast of peninsular India attract even fewer tourists (156 000 in 1988), but they represent an upmarket long-haul tropical island destination, mainly catering for the European market. The islands are low-lying coral atolls, and tourist development is limited to certain islands in the group and is segregated from the local population in order to minimise its cultural and environmental impact. The islands function as a winter sun destination (December to March). They compete with the other Indian Ocean islands, such as Mauritius and the Seychelles (*see* Chapter 20) rather than with the Pacific Islands.

QUESTIONS AND DISCUSSION POINTS

1 Why do you think tourism in the Pacific region is growing so much faster than in the other tourist regions of the world?
2 The Pacific islands each have their own distinct tourist catchment areas: describe and explain them.
3 How do you explain Thailand's success as a long-haul destination for the European and North American markets?

ASSIGNMENTS

1 You work for a tour company 'Faraway Holidays' that specialises in long-haul special interest holidays for the UK market. Your company wants to develop new three-week tours to East and Southeast Asia, specialising in the history and culture of the region. You have been asked to construct an outline itinerary for the three-week tour which is to include at least three contrasting cultures, starting and ending at international airports. Outline the main historical and cultural features to be visited, and indicate some of the difficulties the company may have to face if they decide to go ahead and develop the tour.

2 You work for a tour company that specialises in tours to India, Pakistan and Nepal. Tours to the 'Golden Triangle' (Delhi, Agra and Jaipur) are successful but customers are expressing an increasing interest in visiting other parts of India and seeing other aspects of the region's culture and environment.

Can you meet this need by providing short optional additions to the 'Golden Triangle' tours – and, if so, for how long, and to which destinations – or are there other parts of India that could be developed for separate tours (if so, where, when and to what attractions)? Are there any parts of the Indian Subcontinent that should be avoided for any reason?

Write a report to your chief executive identifying the opportunities for expanding and diversifying your tours to the Indian Subcontinent.

Conclusion: The Dynamics of Change

PART 8

Three of the regions described in this book – Europe, North America and the Pacific – account for most of the tourist activity of the world. They show well-established patterns of tourist development, trends that evolve slowly following a fairly predictable course during each successive decade. Their relative political and economic stability has enabled this to occur.

There are many other countries of the economic periphery that have the climatic and natural resources to make them highly attractive tourist destinations; few have yet reached the stage of economic development to make them potential international tourist generators. Although there may be economic incentives for encouraging inbound tourism from affluent countries (i.e. the need for foreign currency), there is much debate about the undesirable impact (social and environmental) that such tourist developments may have in very poor countries. Furthermore, many of these countries are not politically stable, and few tourists will risk travelling to a country of uncertain political stability or where the enforcement of law and order is doubtful. There are a few islands of political stability where tourist industries of some size have been established, but patterns of tourism here are perhaps more prone to sudden changes. Events such as natural disasters, political unrest or changes in transport services may stop tourism virtually overnight. Thus tourism is an activity open to sudden decreases in volume, particularly in politically unstable areas.

Tourism tends to increase in response to political change or new opportunities rather more slowly, over a period of several years as markets re-adjust to new circumstances. 1989 and 1990 have so far marked a period of great change in world politics, firstly the revolutions in the countries of the communist bloc, and secondly in the Islamic world of the Middle East, which together could lead to significant expansion of tourism in some parts of the world, but also to sharp declines in other areas.

At the beginning of the 1990s, the USSR and the ex-communist countries of Eastern Europe are evolving new political and economic structures and their people face a period of difficulty and great re-adjustment. The removal of communism is resulting in the expression of many deep-seated ethnic rivalries and intercommunal conflicts that have long historical roots. In Yugoslavia, for example, after conflicts between ethnic Albanians and other Yugoslavians, there is growing tension between Serbs and Croats. A very different Yugoslavia may emerge if, indeed, the country survives as a political entity. The consequences for Dalmatian coastal tourism are unpredictable. The reunification of Germany and the political evolution of USSR may also have profound effects on the pattern of tourism in Western and Eastern Europe. The decline of communism may have opened up a whole range of new tourist possibilities but it has also uncovered many political problems and a period of political instability and readjustment is bound to follow.

At the time of writing (August 1990) the Middle East is in a deepening political crisis triggered off by Iraq's entry into Kuwait. The Middle East has been a region of periodic conflict since the Second World War, with fundamental and continuing sources of political conflict. Problems in the region not only have an immediate effect on travel to and from its constituent countries, but the threat of world terrorism or the disruption of oil supplies to the rest of the world inevitably have major economic consequences for international travel. Chapter 1 has described the impact of the oil crisis of 1974 on the world's economy and on world tourist activity in the 1970s and 1980s and this could be repeated on a greater or lesser scale.

Tourism is one of the world's economic activities that is particularly sensitive to political and economic events and the patterns of tourism described in this book could change fairly suddenly.

However, the natural, cultural and climatic resources remain essentially unchanged by such events. The early chapters of this book have suggested ways in which travel patterns evolve, and highlighted the factors and processes that appear to influence tourist flows and later chapters have illustrated patterns of tourism in various regions of the world. These factors will continue to exert an influence and will play a part in both modifying existing flows and in moulding new patterns of tourism in changing political contexts in the world in future.

It is hoped, therefore, that this book has not simply described world tourism as it was in the late 1980s, but has enhanced the readers' ability to interpret and understand these new patterns of tourism as they evolve.

ASSIGNMENTS

1 You are a tourism consultant with special expertise on world cruising. Your client, a Greek shipping magnate, has spare capacity in his shipyards and is considering building a new seagoing cruise ship. He wishes to be briefed on the main cruise destinations in the world, and the main world cruise markets before he decides whether to build the ship.

Your brief is to:
   (a) Provide a brief comparative assessment of the major world cruise destinations, their size, location, geographical character and attractions.
   (b) Provide a brief comparative assessment of the main world markets for cruising, their character, size and geographical location.
   (c) Provide an outline of the existing level of competition and the potential for new cruise developments.
   (d) Make a reasoned recommendation of which cruise market and destination the new cruise ship should be designed for.
   (e) Provide a detailed account of the chosen market and particularly the travel links between market and cruise destination.
   (f) Provide a full account of the geographical attractions of the cruise destination area, and the choice of ports of call.
   (g) Make a reasoned recommendation of which location in the destination region should be chosen as the port of embarkation. Suggest at least two different itineraries, starting from this embarkation point. The length of the itinerary and the nature of the cruise should be appropriate for the chosen market.

You should present your work in report format.

2 A young couple living in the UK have been left some money by an eccentric aunt who has directed that it should be spent on a year's round-the-world trip. They wish to visit:
   (a) the historic sites of Greece, Egypt, China, and India and the Andes mountains;
   (b) the wildlife of East Africa, the Amazon rainforest and the Great Barrier Reef;
   (c) the landscapes of the Himalayas, the Rockies and Alaska;
   (d) the attractions of Disneyland and New York; and
   (e) two different tropical islands.

They would like to stay at least one month in each of India, China and Australia and two in the United States. Are there any locations on their list that you (as a travel agent) would advise them to avoid due to political problems?

Arrange an itinerary for them: the itinerary should minimise time spent travelling between destinations; it should indicate the starting date and time of year that they will arrive in each destination. Is it possible to arrange an itinerary that allows them to enjoy ideal climatic conditions in each and every destination? Are there any destinations that they might have to leave out on climatic grounds?

3 You are the editor of a journal for the UK travel trade. Write a brief editorial article reviewing the current political and economic circumstances of the world, and assessing the general prospects for world tourism in the coming year.

Index